James Robinson Newhall

History of Lynn, Essex County, Massachusetts

Volume II - 1864 - 1893

James Robinson Newhall

History of Lynn, Essex County, Massachusetts
Volume II - 1864 - 1893

ISBN/EAN: 9783337033330

Printed in Europe, USA, Canada, Australia, Japan

Cover: Foto ©ninafisch / pixelio.de

More available books at **www.hansebooks.com**

ALONZO LEWIS — At age of 37. ALONZO LEWIS — At age of 63.
Poet and Historian.

CHARLES F. LUMMUS — At age of 32. JAMES R. NEWHALL — At age of 38.
First Lynn Printer.

[See page viii.]

(a 7)

ST. MARGARET'S CHURCH, KING'S LYNN, ENGLAND.

[*See page vii.*] ST. STEPHEN'S CHURCH, LYNN, MASS.

(*a* 5)

CITY HALL, LYNN, MASS.

[See page vii.]   TOWN HALL, KING'S LYNN, ENGLAND.   (a 3)

1. Now Sea st.   2. Timothy Alley.   3. Wm. Richards.   4. Viall's slaughter-house.   5. F. S. & H. Newhall's morocco factory.   6. Winthrop Newhall's tannery.   7. Water trough.   8. Benj. Alley.   9 and 10. Solomon Alley.   11. Richard Pratt.   12. Pelatiah Purinton.   13. John Alley, jr.

14. Now Summer st.   15. James Alley.   16. Simeon Breed.   17. Dr. Lummus.   18. Capt. Jos. Mudge.   19. Jerusha Williams.   20 and 21. Stephen Smith.   22. Gamaliel W. Oliver.   23. J. B. Ingalls.   24. Rev. Enoch Mudge.   25. Methodist meeting-house.   [See page vii.]   (a 1)

MARKET STREET, LYNN, IN 1820.   (South-west Side.)

HISTORY

OF

L Y N N ,

ESSEX COUNTY, MASSACHUSETTS:

INCLUDING

LYNNFIELD, SAUGUS, SWAMPSCOTT, AND NAHANT.

VOLUME II.

1864-1893.

BY

James R. Newhall.

PUBLISHED BY
ISRAEL AUGUSTUS NEWHALL and HOWARD MUDGE NEWHALL.

LYNN, MASS.:
THE NICHOLS PRESS — THOS. P. NICHOLS.
1897.

NOTE.

THE volume of the HISTORY OF LYNN, by Alonzo Lewis and James R. Newhall, known as the 1865 Edition, embodies our history from the first settlement, in 1629, to 1864. . . Another volume, by the last-named writer, bringing the history down to 1883, was published. . . The main body of the volume now in hand is this last-named work — with a Supplement continuing the Annals on to 1890 — thus furnishing what is believed to be a complete HISTORY OF LYNN from its first settlement, in 1629 to 1890 — *two hundred and sixty-one years.*

INDEXES. — On page 295 commences a full Index of the preceding pages. On page 310 is the Index to the Pictorial Addenda. And at the close of the Supplement is the Index to that department.

LYNN, 1890. J. R. N.

THE present book, Volume II, HISTORY OF LYNN, is the same work described in the note above, with the addition of Annals to January 1, 1893, notes having been left by the author, prepared to that date before his decease.

This volume is published, as left by its author, and in the same form as the 1890 book, bringing the HISTORY to 1893, a period of *two hundred and sixty-four years.* His preface is left intact, and if the reader will substitute 1892 for 1882 on page iii, it will serve for this book.

The Supplement begins on page 329, continuing the Annals from page 96. Its Index is on page 379.

LYNN, 1897. I. A. N. and H. M. N.

ERRATA.

On page 57. line 8, *read* 20.000,000 *instead of* 2.000,000.
On page 107, line 12, *read* Thos. Hudson *instead of* Godson.
On page 132, line 7, *read* eight *instead of* one.
On page 134, last line. *read* July *instead of* June.
On page 162. line 8, *read* January *instead of* March.

PREFACE.

It may properly be remarked that the volume now in the reader's hand, is intended in one sense to be complete in itself; that is, to embody a general view of our history, from the beginning of the settlement to the present time. Yet, so far as its record is in the form of annals, it is supplementary to the 1865 edition of the History of Lynn; and the reader as he proceeds will find many references to that work. This course was adopted for the purpose of economising in the matter of space, by avoiding repetition, and at the same time apprising the reader where further information upon a given topic might be found. For the same general purpose, also, occasional reference is made to the "Centennial Memorial." And the writer is, on the whole, prepared to claim, with some confidence, that this volume, in connection with that of 1865, embodies a full and reliable history of the place from the first settlement, in 1629 down to 1882, with as few repetitions, reviews, or recapitulations as would be consistent with an intelligent and comprehensive view.

There has been no waste space to be provided for; and some things have been omitted with hesitancy, where the press of matter upon the writer's attention allowed him only the privilege of choice; a privilege that he has always exercised in a manner that seemed most desirable for the reader.

There is, in a work of this kind, far more danger of omission than redundancy. And it is almost certain that the reader will think of some topic which it appears to him has not been set forth with desirable fullness. But before concluding that there is an omission, accidental or intentional, it would be well to consider whether the matter is of general interest or of interest only to himself and perhaps a few others, or to any limited or particular class.

While it has not been thought expedient, when speaking of persons, to extenuate in a degree to give false coloring to character, nothing has been set down in malice. The endeavor has been to give an honest and fair account of whoever and whatever has come under notice.

With the reception of his former imperfect works by those whose opinions are of value, the writer has had abundant reason to be pleased ; and all courteous and well-intended suggestions have been gratefully received and duly considered. Whether his escape from criticism is attributable to excellence or insignificance is a question about which he need not trouble himself. The unfledged critic, as every writer knows, often fancies that he has demolished an author when he has only amused him. And it is well for both writer and reviewer to bear in mind that no author can be written down by any pen but his own — nor written up, as to that matter.

That the book is entirely free from error, is beyond the bound of expectation, though much care has been taken to have all the statements correct. It would be extreme arrogance to claim for it what perhaps no other printed book ever yet possessed — perfect accuracy. A word is said, on page 253, touching the duties and perplexities of authorship. And on page 251 an account is given of the different editions of the History of Lynn. The present volume corresponds in the size of page and general style with that of 1865, and both are stereotyped.

CONTENTS

(v)

VI. CONCLUSION : beginning on page 285 :
In this Section appear compendious remarks of a somewhat
desultory character, but pertinent and in accord with the
general purpose of the volume.

VII. THE INDEX : occupying the closing pages of the volume :
This contains all the personal names in the book, arranged
alphabetically with the subjects.

VIII. PICTORIAL ADDENDA : page 311.

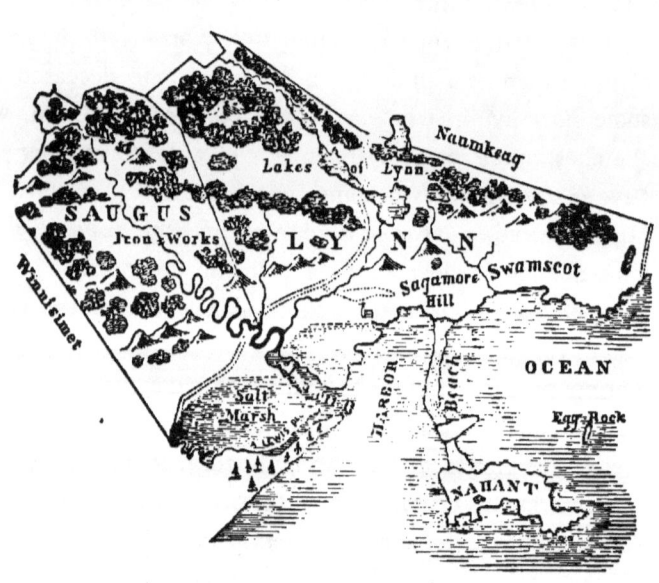

TERRITORIAL DIAGRAM OF ANCIENT LYNN.

ILLUSTRATIONS.

PRECEDING the title-page are four pages of Illustrations, to wit:

1. Market street, Lynn, (south-west side,) as it appeared in 1820.

2. Town Hall, King's Lynn, England, and City Hall, Lynn, Mass.

3. St. Margaret's Church, King's Lynn, England, and St. Stephen's, Church, Lynn, Mass.

4. Two Portraits of Alonzo Lewis, one of Charles F. Lummus, and one of James R. Newhall.

Respecting each of these a word or two may properly be said:

The View in Market Street gives, in two sections, the entire south-westerly side, as it was sixty years ago. This drawing, and several others in the present volume, were made by the skillful young draughtsman, William T. Oliver, of course from details furnished by older persons. In his grandfather's shop — indicated by 22 — William Lloyd Garrison worked at shoemaking. The writer well remembers the street as it was at that period, and can confidently attest to the remarkable fidelity of the picture.

The Town Hall, and St. Margaret's Church, of Lynn, England, were carefully drawn, by Mr. Oliver, from photographs kindly sent to the writer by Solicitor J. J. Coulton. The Hall is ancient; but the precise date of its erection seems doubtful. The style, in the main parts at least, will be recognized as early English; though additions have evidently been made, without a very careful eye to architectural unity. The front is composed of alternate squares of flint and freestone, the former beautifully squared and fitted. *St. Margaret's* was built about the year 1100, and hence is now near eight hundred years old. It was built by the first Bishop of Norwich, who also built the Cathedral at Norwich and Church of St. Nicholas at Yarmouth, to expiate his simony. It was from the wall of this ancient temple that the stone which with its friendly inscription rests in the vestibule of our St. Stephen's, was taken. See page 86; also page 76. Pictures of our own *City Hall*, and *St. Stephen's Church*

(vii)

accompany these, but it is unnecessary to go into details here, concerning them, and the reader is referred to pages 93 and 259.

The Portraits to some extent speak for themselves. The beardless one of Mr. Lewis represents him at the age of 37, and is copied from one of Pendleton's lithographs, executed in 1831. Mr. L. himself considered it a good likeness; and as he showed it to the writer on the eve of the publication of his volume of poems, in which it appeared, and elicited the innocent remark that it certainly did the subject no injustice in the matter of personal appearance, he rather sharply intimated that the critic's own discernment was not above criticism. The bearded one, which represents him at the age of 63, will be recognized by many who well remember him, as very accurate. The likeness of Mr. Lummus represents him at the age of 32. It is from a painting by Wheeler, who for some time made his home in Lynn — a good artist, but in some respects an erratic character. Mr. L. thought it a good likeness; and so thought his friends. The remaining one of the four is from a daguerreotype taken at the age of 38. These Portraits as they appear all on one page, seem a little crowded, to be sure; but then, in former years, the individuals not unfrequently stood "shoulder to shoulder" in their labors, though it will not be claimed that the air was invariably serene when the three met to make melody in the old Mirror office, fifty years ago.

The other Illustrations, being generally accompanied by explanations, seem to need nothing beyond mere enumeration here.

Autographs. A large number of fac-similes of interesting autographs appear in our volume, any one of which may be readily found by referring to the index, under the head "Autographs."

HISTORY OF LYNN.

INTRODUCTION.

It has been a favorite custom with some New England historical writers to claim that our coast was not only discovered but temporarily occupied, here and there, by the Northmen, or Vickings, not far from the year 1000. Mr. Bancroft, however, rather treats the idea as fanciful; and his opinion is certainly sufficient to justify grave doubts. But without occupying space to review the grounds on which of late much earnest disputation has been indulged in, we will quote from Mr. Lewis a passage that most concerns ourselves, and append to it a remark or two which discoveries made since he wrote seem to require:

The Scandinavian manuscripts inform us that in the year 986, Eric the Red, an Icelandic prince, emigrated to Greenland. In his company was Bardson, whose son Biarne was then on a voyage to Norway. On his return, going in search of his father, he was driven far to sea, and discovered an unknown country. In the year 1000, Leif, a son of Eric, pursued the discovery of the new country, and sailed along the coast as far as Rhode Island, where he made a settlement; and because he found grapes there, he called it Vineland. In 1002, Thorwald, his brother, went to Vineland, where he remained two years.

It is very reasonable to suppose that these voyagers, in sailing along the coast, discovered Lynn, and it is even probable that they landed at Nahant. In 1004, we are informed that Thorwald, leaving Vineland, or Rhode Island, "sailed eastward, and then northward, past a remarkable headland, enclosing a bay, and which was opposite to another headland. They called it Kialarnes, or Keel-cape," from its resemblance to the keel of a ship. There is no doubt that this was Cape Cod. And as they had no map, and could not see Cape Ann, it is probable that the other headland was the Gurnet. "From thence, they sailed along the eastern coast of the land to a promontory which there projected — probably Nahant — and which was every

(9)

where covered with wood. Here Thorwald went ashore, with all his companions
He was so pleased with the place, that he exclaimed: 'Here it is beautiful! and
here I should like to fix my dwelling!' Afterwards, when they were prepared to go
on board, they observed on the sandy beach, within the promontory, three hillocks.
They repaired thither, and found three canoes, and under each three Skrellings—
(Indians.) They came to blows with them. and killed eight of them, but the ninth
escaped in his canoe. Afterwards a countless multitude of them came out from the
interior of the bay against them. They endeavored to protect themselves by raising
battle-screens on the ship's side. The Skrellings continued shooting at them for a
while and then retired. Thorwald had been wounded by an arrow under the arm.
When he found that the wound was mortal, he said, 'I now advise you to prepare
for your departure as soon as possible; but me ye shall bring to the promontory
where I thought it good to dwell. It may be that it was a prophetic word which
fell from my mouth, about my abiding there for a season. There ye shall bury me;
and plant a cross at my head and also at my feet, and call the place Krossanes—
[the Cape of the Cross]—in all time coming.' He died, and they did as he had
ordered ; afterwards they returned." *Antiquitates Americanæ. xxx.*

The question has arisen whether Krossanes was Nahant or Gurnet Point. There
is nothing remarkable about the latter place, and though so long a time has passed,
no person has thought it desirable to dwell there, but it is used as a sheep pasture.
It is far otherwise with Nahant, which answers to the description well. An early
writer says that it was "well wooded with oaks, pines, and cedars;" and it has a
"sandy beach within the promontory." Thousands also, on visiting it, have borne
witness to the appropriateness of Thorwald's exclamation—"Here it is beautiful!
and here I should like to fix my dwelling!"

This is pleasant reading, and it would be desirable to sustain
the conclusions, or suppositions, if in honesty it could be done.
It would be highly gratifying to our gentle neighbors of the
peninsula to be assured that they have in keeping the dust of the
distinguished Vicking chief, who was not only famous himself,
but the head of a line which has given the world some of its
most brilliant lights — among others the renowned sculptor Thorwald. And the blissful faith, romantic and doubtful as it is,
may, possibly, after all, be well founded, though if it should prove
otherwise, the favored region has an abundance of other blessings
to fall back upon. The authority on which the conclusions embodied in the above extract appear to rest, is a famous Danish
work, published at Copenhagen, in 1837. It is a very learned
work, but by an author who seems to have occasionally permitted
his enthusiasm to get the better of his judgment ; for it is now
generally conceded by the more keensighted class of antiquaries,
that it advances theories that cannot be sustained.

That the Vickings did visit lands far to the south of Greenland,
is quite certain ; but whether they came within Massachusetts

bay, Vineyard sound, or the Narragansett waters, is doubted. The Vicking lodgment that received the name Vineland, is, in the foregoing extract, unhesitatingly placed in Rhode Island ; but it should be remarked that intelligent authorities have given it a very different location. Some have placed it as far north as Nova Scotia, or even Labrador, in which latter country dwelt the Esquimaux, who, according to Hartwig, were called Skrellen·· gers, or screamers — not simply Indians, as the quotation has it. The evidence of the old mill at Newport, and the hieroglyphic rock at Dighton, has been ruled out ; and with it has gone much of the authority that attached to the great work which so unwarily adopted them as monuments of Vicking genius and handiwork. The mill was undoubtedly erected by an early settler, for the worthy purpose of grinding his neighbors' grists ; and the hieroglyphic adornments were most probably the work of some Indian, proud of his artistic acquirements or an aspirant for historic fame. It has been supposed that the Indians had no mode of writing, no way of expressing an idea by visible characters ; but recent examinations and discoveries have proved that the fact is otherwise. And by the way, speaking of the Newport mill and the Dighton rock inscription, it seems remarkable that no one appears to have observed that the two so differ in mechanical expression, if the term is allowable, that it is hardly possible they could have been the work of the same people.

At all events, if these roving Northmen were here at the early period claimed it is evident that they did not brave the ocean terrors for any legitimate purposes of discovery, or with any tangible convictions touching the existence of unknown lands. They were adventurous freebooters, brave, reckless, barbarous ; bent on making themselves possessors of whatever they coveted, by force, fraud, or any other means suggested by their brutish genius. And so they pursued their savage career, occasionally driven from their contemplated course by the violence of the elements, but never from their purpose of rapine and murder by the gentler instincts of humanity. But yet it becomes us to be a little chary of our denunciations of these people, for they were our own forefathers. From their loins sprang the brave Saxons who have been so lauded as a race, and whose blood we so love to claim flows in our own veins.

A lively imagination will often make surprising discoveries, trace unexpected analogies, and form captivating theories, where we of the duller sort discern nothing unusual. And who that has reflected on the diversity of human minds has not felt almost hopelessly bewildered. There is as much difference among minds as among faces ; and would that there might be invented a mirror in which to trace our mental features as we do our physical, in the looking-glass. There is little difficulty in recognising leading characteristics. We know the mathematical mind by its preciseness ; the poetical by its ready discernment and love of the beautiful ; the semi-preternatural by its delight in things striking and marvellous. Now, in our friend Lewis's mind were combined, in a somewhat peculiar manner, the two latter qualities indicated. He had poetical conception and a love of the marvellous ; and under their prompting, stimulated by the fascinations of historic imagery, without doubt wrote the foregoing paragraphs.

It is quite interesting to observe with what avidity intelligent as well as untrained minds will accept any thing that tallies with their peculiar bent ; and quite as interesting to observe how the same minds will reject the most reasonable conclusions that do not accord with their ideal prepossessions. Then there are some who will believe any thing that requires the most feverish credulity to grasp, and others who will believe nothing that demands but a small degree of faith. We often treat with scorn and derision those much better and abler than ourselves simply because we are incapable of comprehending their ideas, if ideas they have. As to that, however, most of us have ideas enough, such as they are, but fail to systematise and express them, when they happen to be of value, in a way to give force or even to be understood. Education helps to do something here. But then our gifts are various ; and with many the gift of slothfulness is so overwhelming that with the best of tools little work is done. It was not intended, however, to indulge in a sentimental strain, but rather, in a homely way, and as correlative to what has been said, to remark that it is really astonishing to observe how even accomplished scientists may be deceived and led to erroneous conclusions by baseless suggestions, adroitly made, in matters which they might be supposed constantly to hold in full survey.

In the writer's own experience there once occurred an incident so aptly illustrative of the point, that he would fain narrate it in this connection though he must do so with diffidence and morti-fication — diffidence lest he should be charged with vanity, and mortification at having been the apparent cause of disturbance in many worthy minds : When a young man, he one day hap-pened in the printing office of a friend, who saluted him with a " Come, write us something for tomorrow's paper." The reply was, " If you will hand me a stick and rule and show me to a case — [a request that all printers will understand] — I will set you up something without writing." The proposition was com-plied with, and a piece of perhaps half a column in length imme-diately set up and left without any further care. It purported to detail some wonderful changes going on among the heavenly bodies ; was simply in a sportive vein and expected to be so understood. Some of the statements were so glaringly inconsis-tent with established facts that it was astonishing to observe the manner in which it was received by even wary savants. It was copied throughout the country, and referred to in pulpit discourses ; and a New York paper — the Commercial Adver-tiser, if we were rightly informed — stated that it was trans-lated into various languages and published all over Europe. The editor of the paper among other letters received one from Professor Olmstead of Yale College urgently requesting informa-tion respecting its origin, and adding that he had been seriously annoyed by the numerous letters he had received asking for explanations which he could not give, notwithstanding he had twice given notice through the New Haven papers that he knew nothing about it. It was subsequently announced that at the National Observatory, in Washington, it had been declared a romance. The affair finally died away, much to the relief of the innocent author. Yet there were some amusing things about it. , One of the most scholarly men in town, remarked, on reading it, that he had for several nights observed that Venus presented the remarkable appearance spoken of. The ease with which even intelligent minds may be led astray, as illustrated by this incident, is instructive. However, it is claimed that every thing has its use ; and without the vein of credulity and habit of super-ficial observation the quack philosopher, the counterfeit philanthropist, and the patent medicine maker would not flourish as they do.

Taking a step further down in the history of the territory we occupy, we come to the Indians. A great deal of virtuous sentiment has been expended, we will not say wasted, upon them. That there were here and there noble spirits need not be questioned ; for the Creator never left a people in so forlorn a condition that there were not some among them in whose breasts faint glimmerings at least of his own divine light remained. But the great body of the red men were of an extremely low order — cruel and implacable — with little conception of a higher life, or of human progress ; ambitious only of triumph over enemies, of dexterity in physical torture, and the extension of tribal authority. Yet they were as susceptible as any other people to the redeeming influences of the faith their invaders held. What they soon would have become had the settlers pursued a more kind and pacific, yea, honest course, must ever remain among the undetermined questions with which human history abounds. But as it was, they began rapidly to dwindle away ; for big guns and catechisms cannot alone save a people ; especially where new, alluring, and destructive vices press forward in their company.

There were, indeed, but few Indians in and about Lynn at the time the settlers came, and not half a score who were above the common level. Montowampate, who lived on Sagamore Hill, was a chief who stood much on his dignity. He was married during the year in which the first settlers came, being then twenty years of age. The marriage was celebrated with much barbaric pomp. But a while after, the wife went on a visit to the home of her maidenhood, and when the time for her return came a difficulty arose between the husband and his father-in-law on a point of etiquette, that seemed to threaten serious consequences, to the young couple especially. Matters, however, were finally adjusted and the dusky bride returned to her allegiance. The great question of woman's rights was to some extent involved ; and duty, dignity, and love, seemed to hold as fitful sway in those untutored hearts as in hearts trained to more refined worldliness. Then there was Poquanum, or Black Will, who appears to have been shrewd, venturesome, and unscrupulous ; and by his sale of Nahant to farmer Dexter, for a suit of clothes, left the town a legacy, in the shape of legal involutions which they would gladly have buried with him.

But the pages of our 1865 volume contain so much of all that is known of the red men who pursued the game in our woods and the fish in our waters, that it would be almost impertinent to enlarge here. Before taking another step along in our history, however, let us say a word or two respecting Indian land titles, which seem to have been of a rambling, uncertain character. The settlers were generally willing to pay for what they occupied ; that is, pay something ; perhaps a hatchet or a hammer for forty acres ; and the pretended owners were seldom averse to selling ; indeed they were much too willing, for they would sell a tract over and over again as long as a purchaser could be found. Some of the chiefs claimed a right in the nature of eminent domain ; a right that seems usually to have been undisputed. The lands, however, were of little direct value to the Indians, for they were not an agricultural nor a pastoral people. The question of titles was long one of difficulty and dispute. By the spirit of the Charter it was plain enough that the settler could hold by occupation, subject to the native ownership. But perplexity in determining who the right owner was, often arose, for chiefships were so interwoven that nothing appeared clear. Governor Andros assumed that the signature of an Indian was of no more value than the scratch of a bear's claw — and he did what he could to make it so. But it is quite evident that the settlers held otherwise, or were at least anxious to guard against a contingency which they feared might arise.

It was with this feeling, no doubt, that the people of Lynn, in 1686 — more than fifty years after the plantation was established — procured from the heirs of the deceased chief Wenepoykin, a release to them of all claim to the lands here, those heirs affirming in their deed that their ancestor was the true and sole owner of "ye land that ye towns of Lynn and Reading aforesaid stand upon, and notwithstanding ye possession of ye English, dwelling in those townships of Lynn and Reading aforesaid." These heirs, it would appear, claimed under the sovereignty of their ancestor, and did not admit that they had been legally dispossessed. The purchasing settlers probably did not much care what they did claim, as the consideration was trifling, and they had no fear of the appearance of others, at that late period, with further claims. And the Indians must have seen of how little value the territory could in the future be to them. Yet to Lynn, this release might prove of the greatest value, in view of the position a new administration. might assume. The following are fac-similes of the Indian signatures to the deed.

David Kunkshamooshaw and Abigail his wife.

Cicely *alias* Su George

Mary Ponham *alias* Quonopohit.
[James Quonopohit, Mary's husband, was a fair
    penman, and signed his name in full.]

INDIAN SIGNATURES TO THE DEED OF LYNN.

Here we must bid adieu to our red brethren, ardently hoping that the remaining few of their forlorn and abused race may yet receive what is their just due, be sanctified and redeemed, and finally in the blissful land of reconciliation joyfully meet their arrogant supplanters, they too sanctified and redeemed by the same regerating love.

—

Having thus in a necessarily brief and hence somewhat unsatisfactory manner, spoken of the Northmen and the Indians, we come to greet the European settlers — our own forefathers. And here our "Introduction" may properly end, as in the following pages, together with the volume which has gone before, many of the old worthies and their successors of every period down to the present, are summoned in to tell their own stories and illustrate their own times.

ANNALS.

[NOTE. These Annals are continued on from the History of Lynn, published in 1865, in which they begin with the year 1629, the date of the commencement of the settlement.]

1865.

MONDAY, April 3d, was a time of great rejoicing in Lynn, the news of the fall of Richmond, the head quarters of the revolted States, being then received. Bells were rung, cannon fired, flags raised, and bonfires kindled. Many buildings were beautifully illuminated, though the news was not fully confirmed till towards night. The Light Infantry company hastened to show their appreciation of the event, and were soon marching through the streets, with a band of music. Fireworks gleamed in every direction, and the whole city seemed aroused. A bonfire blazed on Sadler's Rock the entire night ; and the material of which it was composed being heavy tarred paper its remains were clearly visible more than fifteen years after. Old High Rock, also, lighted up the adjacent country with her fiery crown.

One week after the above day of rejoicing, namely, April 10, the people were again jubilant, and this time, over the crowning event of the war — the surrender of General Lee, commander of the Confederate forces. The weather, however, not being favorable, the proposed proceedings were somewhat abridged. A procession, composed of military and fire companies, various civic associations and patriotic individuals, moved through the thronged streets, with music and banners. One or two individuals who were reputed to entertain secession views, or who had indulged in expressions favorable to the rebel cause, were visited with rough threats, and forced to display Union flags. It was proposed to hold a meeting, in the evening, in Lyceum Hall, for speeches and other congratulatory proceedings, but the exhausted condition of some of the leaders and the drenching rain made it expedient to dispense with that part of the programme.

The conspicuous and rather picturesque little wooden building on the summit of High Rock, known as the Observatory, was

(17)   2

burned on the night of April 19; perhaps the work of some
patriotic incendiary who took that way of celebrating the anniversary of the first battle of the Revolution.

News of the assassination of President Lincoln was received
in Lynn on Saturday, April 15, and was followed by becoming demonstrations of profound sorrow. The Mayor issued a
request that all business places should be closed at noon, which
was readily complied with, and mourning drapery was freely
displayed. The City Council convened early in the afternoon
and adopted resolutions expressive of a deep sense of the nation's
bereavement. On Sunday the churches were draped in mourning, and appropriate services held. The city authorities attended
the First Methodist church.

At Swampscott, on the arrival of the news of the President's
death, one individual, of alleged strong secession proclivities, was
so indiscreet as to manifest his satisfaction in such strong terms
as to kindle the wrath of his patriotic neighbors, who seized him,
and after bedecking him with a coat of tar and feathers set him
forth on a compulsory march through the town, bearing a Union
flag, large numbers following in procession. He afterwards
brought a civil suit for damages, persistently declaring that his
expressions were misinterpreted, and recovered judgment for $800.

There were five photographic establishments in Lynn, this year,
at which were taken the aggregate number of 38.500 pictures.

An idea of the extent of the lobster trade in this vicinity may
be gathered from the fact that during the year ending May 1,
there were taken at Nahant 150.000, and at Swampscott 37.000,
which were valued, as taken from the traps, at an average of six
cents each.

The fine mansion on Ocean street, for some time, and until
his death, the summer residence of William H. Prescott, the historian, was destroyed by fire on Sunday morning, May 7. It
belonged to the widow of the historian at the time of its destruction, but was unoccupied.

Mrs. Mary Kirby was killed by falling into a culvert on the
Eastern railroad, near Market street, June 14.

On Tuesday afternoon, June 20, the bodies of John S. Joyce,
aged 12, and his sister Isabella, aged 14, were buried in one
coffin, from St. Stephen's church, where they had been Sunday
school scholars. These were the children whose terrible death
sent such a thrill through the community. ' They were found
murdered in a piece of woods, in West Roxbury, near Boston,
whither they had gone for an afternoon's recreation. No trace
of the murderer was discovered.

Daniel Ames, of Lynn, in a sportive wrestling contest with
Edward Gibson, at Nahant, June 17, received injuries from which
he died two days after.

Independence was this year celebrated, in Lynn, with more than usual pomp, all parties joining. There was a grand procession, music, speeches, and in the evening a fine display of fireworks. A balloon ascension was to have taken place from the Common, in the afternoon, but an unfavorable wind rendered it expedient to postpone that, till the sixth, when it took place in a manner highly satisfactory.

The taxation of Lynn, this year, under the United States revenue laws, was $626.993.12, being chiefly, of course, on manufactures. There were then but about 20.000 inhabitants.

In July, several sharks appeared in Lynn harbor, to the terror of bathers and boatmen. And it may be stated in this connection that the ferocious species known as man-eaters, some times make their unwelcome visits to these waters. In 1819 a boy was fishing near the mouth of Thomas Newhall's creek, so called, at Saugus river, when one of those desperate rovers suddenly sprang towards him with such a momentum as to ground himself. The affrighted boy, by his shouts attracted the attention of a couple of men at work on the marsh, and they, hastening to the scene with their pitchforks, succeeded in despatching the monster.

A considerable number of whales were observed at different times during the summer moving about in the offing.

During this year there began to be seriously felt the need of a larger number of dwelling houses, especially those suitable for the accommodation of working people. Capitalists had invested so largely in government securities, and in enterprises promising greater returns — these being times rather fruitful of speculative schemes — comparatively little was devoted to the erection of tenement houses. A large number of workmen were obliged to come into town in the morning rail-road trains, labor during the day, and return to their distant homes by the evening trains. And the inconvenience was felt for several years.

The number of individuals attached to the Sunday schools of the different religious societies in Lynn, this year, was as follows: First Methodist, 623. St. Mary's (Roman Catholic,) 500. First Universalist, 429. Boston Street Methodist, 322. St. Paul's, (Union Street,) Methodist, 300. First Congregational, 283. High Street Baptist, 225. South Street Methodist, 213. Friends' 200. First Baptist, 190. Second Universalist, 190. Maple Street (Glenmere,) Methodist, 183. Central Congregational (Silsbee Street,) 182, Christian, 160. Tower Hill Chapel, (Congregational,) 159. St. Stephen's, (Episcopal,) 110. Chesnut Street, (Congregational,) 110. City Mission, 73. Unitarian, 70. Third Baptist, (Wyoma,) 70. Second Advent, 30. These numbers include officers, teachers and pupils.

Richard S. Fay, of Lynn, died in Liverpool, England, on the

6th of July. He owned and for a number of years occupied the celebrated Mineral Spring estate, in the northeasterly section of the city. Being a gentleman of culture and large means he highly enjoyed life in his romantic retreat, which he greatly improved and beautified. He was a graduate of Harvard, and for some years practised law. In agricultural pursuits he took great interest, imported improved stock, and engaged in many useful experiments. He was affable and generous, and merited and received the esteem of all classes. During the war he contributed largely for the Union cause. At the time of his death he had just completed a European tour, and was expecting to return in the steamer which brought the news of his death. The death stroke fell upon him while passing in the street.

Edward Pranker, well known as the proprietor of a large woolen factory, near the site of the old iron works, in Saugus, died, August 14, at the age of 73. His death was very sudden, he having retired for his accustomed afternoon nap, and being found, a few hours after, in his room, dead. He was a native of Wiltshire, England, and came to this country while quite a young man, to seek his fortune; was very successful in his enterprises, after becoming able to begin business on his own account, and accumulated a large fortune.

The number of apple trees in Lynn, this year, was 17.400 and of pear trees, 21.900; yet the aggregate value of the fruitage did not exceed $16.000.

On the morning of August 31, as a couple of gentlemen were passing from Market street towards Central square, they discovered that the inner clothing of a lady before them was on fire, and informed her of the fact in time, probably, to avoid serious injury to her person. How the fire was occasioned remained a mystery.

There were this year owned in Lynn, 720 horses, the average value of each being $140.

During the month of August, the shoe business of Lynn exceeded that of any previous month. The total value was $1.200.000; and the internal revenue tax for the month was $77.099.62. Business was very active, and would have shown a still greater increase had it been possible to procure a sufficiency of material and workmen.

Gen. Alonzo G. Draper, of Lynn, died on the night of Sept. 3, at Brazos de Santiago, Texas, at which post he had been in command. He was shot from his horse, while riding out, as was supposed by a stray ball from a great distance, no battle being in progress at the time, and lamented by his brethren in arms as a brave and efficient officer. His body was brought to Lynn, and buried in Pine Grove Cemetery, on the 27th, with becoming honors. He was a native of Brattleborough, Vt.

Very destructive fires raged in the woods of Lynn, Lynnfield, and Saugus, during September, the weather being unusually warm and dry. The woodlands hereabout, as well as in other parts of the country, have, from the period of the early settlements, been occasionally swept over by fire, which sometimes originated in the most unaccountable manner. In early colonial years severe laws were made against smoking tobacco in the woods, and various other precautions taken ; yet the fires would occur. Once in a while, it is possible, lightning may have been the cause of the mischief. But recently a French philosopher has suggested that the globules of pitch which exude from the pines may sometimes act as burning lenses and so concentrate the sun's rays that they will produce flame. There is little doubt, however, that in these days the careless use of friction matches is the cause of many of these fires. Very few are aware of the rapidity with which a fire once lighted in the dry litter of a pine forest will spread and get beyond control.

An extraordinary drought prevailed this year. It continued from July 25 to October 15 ; and had not been equalled for eighty-one years, as meteorologists claimed.

The corner stone of the new City Hall, at the east end of the Common was laid on Tuesday, November 28, in presence of the Mayor, a committee of the City Council, and a small number of other spectators. There was no display. A proposition had been made to have the event marked by grand masonic ceremonies, but some of the old anti-masons energetically protesting, they were dispensed with.

The number of deaths in the city during the year was 477.

1 8 6 6 .

On the morning of February 5, Pranker's brick woolen factory, in Saugus, was nearly destroyed by fire. The town having no fire-engine, the flames had gained almost uncontrollable head-way before one could arrive from Lynn.

Dr. Abram Gould, the oldest practising physician in Lynn, died, February 27, aged 58. He was a man of thorough education and much more than ordinary skill, and had gained an extensive practice. His residence was on Boston street, nearly opposite Cottage.

On the afternoon of June 25, there was a heavy shower, which flooded the streets of Lynn, though Nahant and even Long Beach escaped the visitation. And on the afternoon of the 30th a copious shower took place in the eastern section of the city, while in the western there was scarcely a sprinkling.

General Sherman passed through Lynn on the morning of July 16. An enthusiastic crowd rapidly collected in Central square, and most cordially greeted him. Some climbed upon the cars in their eagerness to grasp the hand of the hero of the grand march through the very bowels of the rebellious Confederacy. His stay, however, was but momentary. The day was excessively warm, the thermometer in the course of the forenoon reaching to 100 degrees, in the shade.

A rattlesnake, measuring four feet in length, and having ten rattles — thereby showing his age to be thirteen years — was killed in Dungeon pasture, July 29. The reptile attempted to strike his assailant before being despatched.

James R. Newhall succeeded Thomas B. Newhall as Judge of Lynn Police Court, his commission bearing date August 24.

The Central Church edifice, on Silsbee street, was entirely consumed by fire early on Sunday morning, September 9. Nothing of value was saved. It was of wood, built in 1850, and was insured to the amount of $15.000, exclusive of $2.000 on the organ and $500 on the pastor's library. The structure being on elevated land and the spire tall, when the flames enwrapped the whole, the scene was very striking.

On an evening in September, a lady, who was sitting at a window in a house on Ocean street, observed a brilliant meteor descend and strike near the house. She immediately went to the spot and discovered the strange visitant to be white and smelling strongly of sulphur. On being examined by an experienced naturalist of Boston it was pronounced to be a genuine aerolite.

A great meteoric shower was predicted to take place on the night of November 12, and public notice was given that the church bells would be rung to awake the sleepers, if the celestial visitants appeared. But nothing unusual was observed here during that night, though the sky was very clear. In some parts of the world, however, especially in England, a brilliant display occurred, at about the time indicated. At Greenwich, some 12.000 meteors were seen on the morning of the 14th. At Washington, on the same day, at about noon, an extraordinary exhibition took place. In this vicinity, at about the time, an unusual number of "shooting stars" appeared.

1867.

A terrific snow storm occurred on the 17th of January. No storm within twenty-five years bore a comparison to it for severity, with the exception of that on the 18th of January, 1857, when the terrible shipwreck of the Tedesco, at Swampscott, took place, at which time the cold was more intense. The mail carrier between Lynn and Nahant, for ten years, failed in traversing his route only on the occurrence of these two storms.

There was an exceedingly high tide on the 21st of January. It was higher than at any time since the awful night of April 15, 1851, when Minot's Ledge lighthouse was carried away.

On Sunday, March 24th, Rev. Mr. Woods of the Boston Street Methodist Society, and Rev. Mr. Biddle, of the First Universalist, exchanged pulpits. The leading doctrines taught by these two divines being so directly opposite, a good deal of surprise was manifested, and not a little feeling on the part of some of the more rigid Methodists. While it was regarded by some as a commendable instance of christian courtesy, by others it was looked upon as a marked instance of waning denominational integrity.

A strange reptile was killed near the head of Sluice pond, in May. It was something more than four feet in length, and in the largest part nearly as thick as a man's wrist. Its back was covered with a horny coat resembling that of a crocodile, the bone making a perceptible ridge.

On the 27th of May, a man, in digging a post hole, in Summer street, exhumed some human bones, which were in such a position as to indicate that a body had been buried there, in a sitting posture. An arrow head and one or two implements and ornaments were found with the bones, leading to the conclusion that they were Indian remains.

The new house of worship of the First Baptist Society, a neat structure of wood, in Gothic style, on North Common street, corner of Park, was dedicated June 20.

A beautiful mirage was observed from Long Beach, about noon, on Sunday, June 23.

On the 24th of June — St. John's Day — 30.000 persons were carried over the Eastern Rail-road, without an accident. It was the day of the great masonic celebration, in Boston, when the new temple was dedicated.

A balloon ascension was made from Lynn Common on the afternoon of the 4th of July. The descent was into the water off Swampscott, but the excursionists escaped injury.

Sagamore building, Union street, was nearly destroyed by fire on the night of July 13, it being the third time that it had come near being consumed.

Immense quantities of mackerel appeared in the offing, in July, affording rare sport for amateur fishermen and profitable employment for professional. A whale, some fifty feet in length, and two or three others somewhat smaller, were several times seen ranging about, evidently bent on securing their share. Several voracious horse-mackerel, with keen appetites, also made their appearance.

A fire occurred in Wyoma village, on the morning of August 3d, on the premises occupied by T. L. Brown and Company, for the wool-pulling business. Property to the value of $18.000 was destroyed.

A swing-tail shark, fifteen feet in length, was taken off Swampscott, in a net, August 10, and sold to Professor Agassiz for fifty dollars.

On the morning of Aug. 10, a flock of flying-fish, some twenty in number, appeared off Nahant, darting about and eliciting much observation, such visitors being very uncommon in this region; some even declaring that they were never seen here before.

A sun-fish, of the estimated weight of two hundred pounds, was observed sunning himself near Egg Rock, in August.

The encampment of the Second Brigade of Massachusetts Volunteer Militia, commenced at Swampscott, on the 3d of Sept. and continued five days.

A Second Advent Camp Meeting, so called, that is a camp meeting of those who believed that the second advent of our Lord would surely take place this year, commenced in Lynn, Sept. 10, and continued a week. On the last day of the meeting considerable excitement prevailed, as some of the more sanguine were confidently expecting that before another day the Son of Man would visibly appear.

Avis Keene, widow of Josiah Keene, died in Lynn, Oct. 13, aged 87. She was an accepted preacher of the Friends' society for some sixty years; was a graceful and influential speaker, and by her blameless life, amiable disposition, and active charities, endeared herself to a very extensive circle of those who did not as well as those who did come within the sphere of her public ministrations.

Richard Gregg, a sober, industrious man, aged 62, was killed on the Eastern Rail-road, near the Pleasant street crossing, on the evening of Oct. 17. He was walking towards home, on the track, and was struck by a locomotive, which broke his skull and caused immediate death.

An interval of beautiful Indian summer, of more than ordinary duration, was experienced in October.

The new City Hall, at the eastern end of the Common — the site being at the time about the centre of the city, both geographically and as regards population — was dedicated on Saturday, Nov. 30. The whole day, was very generally spent as a holiday. Crowds were in the streets, and about the building from morning till near midnight. The day was pleasant, so far as a clear sky and sunlight could make it so, but otherwise so far as a boisterous northwest wind and clouds of dust could make it.

The tower and other parts of the building were decorated with flags, and the Lynn band was in attendance to dispense their enlivening music at suitable intervals. A good deal of care was taken to have as large a number of the elderly men present as possible, and as many as seventy, whose births dated back to the last century, were gathered, Epes Mansfield, born in 1783, being the oldest.

A little before noon, the exercises commenced in the vestibule, with a prayer offered by Rev. J. W. F. Barnes, of the First Methodist Church. Mayor Roland G. Usher then delivered an Address, which was followed by a Poem by Cyrus M. Tracy. The Tablet, facing the main entrance, was then unveiled. Next came a brief address, retrospective and prospective, by James R. Newhall, which closed the forenoon exercises.

A liberal collation was served in the basement, which was partaken of by a multitude of citizens and many visitors from other places. Subsequently a number of prominent citizens addressed the crowds in the Council Chamber and other convenient parts of the building. Among these speakers were John B. Alley, James N. Buffum, George H. Chase, Charles E. Kimball, Peter M. Neal, and Thomas B. Newhall. There were likewise several speakers from abroad.

The entertainment was continued till late in the evening, the large company of ladies and gentlemen, young and old, promenading whithersoever they would, about the beautiful apartments, and enjoying themselves in decorous ways of their own choice. At the instance of the Mayor, about ten o'clock, the whole company were called to join in singing "America." And after that the majestic strains of the Doxology, in Old Hundred, floated upward. This closed the interesting exercises. As this is not the place that requires any thing beyond a mere statement of facts, it would perhaps be unwise to volunteer censure even if there were points that might justify it, or to offer laudatory remarks where they are not needed. The addresses and the poem were published in the newspapers of the day, and afterward in a neat little volume ; and they can all "testify of themselves." It need only be remarked here that the proceedings throughout were received with liberal applause.

The cost of the building, in round numbers, may be stated at $312.000. Some claimed that it was an unnecessarily elegant and costly structure, and of course, after the usual custom, indulged in a little harmless grumbling. But it was soon apparent that its superior conveniences would save expense in many ways ; and that it was giving an improving tone to the architecture of the city, a thing that had been long and sorely needed. Before a year had passed, there were few who did not take a real pride in pointing to it as the great lion of the city, or who entertained any lingering regrets that it had been reared. It certainly marks a period when a wonderful advancement in the architectural aspect of Lynn commenced.

The first number of the Lynn Transcript, a weekly newspaper, established by Rufus Kimball, Thomas P. Nichols and Abel G. Courtis, appeared on Saturday, Dec. 21, from the office on the southwest side of Market street, near South Common.

There were born in Lynn, during the year, 664 children —
334 male and 330 female — 385 of native parentage, and 279
of foreign. December was the most prolific month, and April
the least — 77 being born in the former and 35 in the latter.

1 8 6 8 .

On the evening of January 13, a meeting of naturalized citizens
was held in a hall on Washington street, preparatory to forming
an organization to promote their interests, as a class, and for
mutual benefit. It seems doubtful whether such organizations,
or the former ones aiming to place the administration of affairs
solely in the hands of natives, are really productive of permanent
good ; that is, so far as public policy is concerned. The endeavor to effect a general union of interests and to avail of the best
talent, of whatever derivation, would appear to give the highest
promise. Nevertheless, there are many cases in which, other
things being equal, it is eminently proper to give preference to
natives. There has long been complaint that the people of Lynn
are too much disposed to place new comers in positions of trust
and authority. Admitting that it is so, it must be said that
occasionally at least the good fortune of the party is aided by
ignorance of his past life.

Nahant this year numbered 95 polls, and had a valuation
of $1.054.37.

On the night of March 3, the thermometer stood at 12 degrees
below zero. On the 7th, the harbor was so frozen that loaded
teams could pass over to the beach. A day or two after, however,
the ice broke up. The ice harvest of 1867–'8 was superior to
any other known for many years, both in quality and quantity.

The interesting ceremony of strewing flowers on the graves
of the fallen heros of the civil war, took place on Saturday afternoon, May 30, under the auspices of the local Post of the Grand
Army of the Republic. A procession visited the different burial
places, and at Pine Grove Cemetery, where a large concourse
were assembled, appropriate services took place, with music and
speaking. Comrade T. C. Vassar, minister of the First Baptist
Church, delivered an appropriate address. The ceremonies were
in accordance with a general order issued at Washington, by
General Logan, Commander-in-chief of the association ; which
order is here introduced, as explaining the character and purpose
of the observance :

I. The 30th day of May, 1868, is designated for the purpose of strewing with flowers
or otherwise decorating the graves of Comrades who died in defense of their country
during the late rebellion, and whose bodies now lie in almost every city, village and
hamlet churchyard in the land. In this observance no form of ceremony is prescribed,
but Posts and Comrades will in their own way arrange such fitting services and testimonials of respect as circumstances may permit.

We are organized, Comrades, as our Regulations tell us, for the purpose, among other things, 'of preserving and strengthening those kind and fraternal feelings which have bound together the soldiers, sailors and marines who united to suppress the late rebellion.' What can aid more to assure this result than cherishing tenderly the memory of our heroic dead, who made their breasts a barricade between our country and its foes? Their soldier lives were the reveille of freedom to a race in chains, and their deaths the tattoo of rebellious tyranny in arms. We should guard their graves with sacred vigilance. All that the consecrated wealth and taste of the nation can add to their adornment and security, is but a fitting tribute to the memory of her slain defenders. Let no wanton foot tread rudely on such hallowed grounds. Let pleasant paths invite the coming and going of reverent visitors and fond mourners. Let no vandalism of avarice or neglect, no ravages of time testify to the present or to the coming generations that we have forgotten as a people the cost of a free and undivided Republic.

If other eyes grow dull, and other hands slack, and other hearts cold in the solemn trust, ours shall keep it well as long as the light and warmth of life remain to us.

Let us, then, at the time appointed, gather around their sacred remains and garland the passionless mounds above them, with the choicest flowers of spring time; let us raise above them the dear old flag they saved from dishonor; let us in this solemn presence renew our pledges to aid and assist those whom they have left among us as a sacred charge upon a nation's gratitude, the soldier's and sailor's widow and orphan.

II. It is the purpose of the Commander-in-chief to inaugurate this observance with the hope that it will be kept up from year to year, while a survivor of the war remains to honor the memory of his departed Comrades. He earnestly desires the public press to call attention to this Order, and lend its friendly aid in bringing it to the notice of Comrades in all parts of the country in time for simultaneous compliance therewith.

Such was the origin of "Memorial Day" — or "Decoration Day," as it is as often called — May 30. And the custom, so appropriate and so interesting, thus suggested, became at once established.

The brick house of worship, of the Central Congregational Society, on Silsbee street, was dedicated on Thursday evening, June 11. There was a large attendance notwithstanding the prevalence of a severe easterly storm.

Jonathan Buffum died at his residence in Union street, June 22, aged 74 years. He was a native of Salem, but came to Lynn in early life. For many years he was active in town affairs, and held responsible offices; was a painter by trade, though for some years engaged in shoe manufacturing. In early life he belonged to the Society of Friends, but seceded from the faith; indeed he was one of those engaged in the disturbance at their house of worship, in 1822, an account of which appears in these Annals, under the proper date. During the prevalence of anti-masonry, he was one of the most zealous and conspicuous in the party, and owned the Lynn Record, which was the party organ. He was a man of marked character, firm in conviction, determined in purpose, and of unswerving integrity. He was an early and consistent advocate of the anti-slavery cause, of temperance, and of moral reforms in general. He also gave full credence to the doctrines of the spiritualists. He married Hannah, daughter of James Breed, and had five children.

A successful ascension was made from the Common, on the afternoon of July 4, by John H. Hall, of Lynn, in the balloon

"City of Lynn," which was manufactured by Parker Wells of this city.

Out-door religious services were held at High Rock and other public places, during the warm season, by clergymen of different denominations.

On Tuesday, Aug. 11, the Trenton Hose Company, of Trenton, N. J., accompanied by a Newark band of music, was received in Lynn, by the Empire Fire Association, the whole fire department indeed participating in the proceedings in honor of the visitors. An extensive procession traversed the streets, and other festivities followed, rendering the whole a very enjoyable occasion. The visitors remained several days, and were entertained in the most hospitable manner, being conducted over some of the largest manufactories, and to places of interest in the vicinity. For some years the fire companies of different places had been in the habit of interchanging such visits, to the promotion of much brotherly feeling, thus superseding, almost entirely, the old military campaigning.

A farmer in Lynnfield killed thirteen rattlesnakes during the summer of this year.

James Purinton died, August 31, aged 92 years. He was a member of the society of Friends, and had worked on his bench, as a shoemaker, for seventy-two years.

Mary Phillips died, Sept 12, aged 98 years, being the oldest person then in Lynn, with the exception of Mary J. Hood, a colored woman, aged 103. Mrs. Phillips was a member of the society of Friends, and retained her faculties in a remarkable degree, her clear memory embracing a history of the eastern section of the town for more than two generations. She was the widow, for many years, of Jonathan Phillips.

On the afternoon of Wednesday, Sept. 30, the granite monument erected in Pine Grove Cemetery to the memory of Rev. Parsons Cooke, late minister of the First Congregational Church, was dedicated, with appropriate services.

Edward O'Baldwin, known as the Irish Giant, and Joseph Wormuld, an Englishman, noted prize-fighters, were arrested by the police, just as they had commenced a battle, in Lynnfield, on the morning of Oct. 29. A crowd of those who delight in such demoralising contests had assembled, from Boston and neighboring places, but they very suddenly dispersed, in dismay, when the police appeared, zealous to act their part. O'Baldwin and Wormuld were arraigned before the police court, and bound over to the superior court. The former was finally sentenced to the house of correction for two years ; but the latter escaped, forfeiting his bail.

Died, in his lonely residence, at Dungeon Rock, November 10, Hiram Marble, aged 65. He was widely known for his perse-

vering labors in the rock just named, where he worked some seventeen years, and died without a realization of his ardent hopes
and unwavering expectation of exhuming jewels and gold, according to the promises of his unseen allurers. He remained a
spiritualist to the last, and the mediums of the vicinity were
invited to be present at the funeral services which were held at
the rock on the forenoon of Wednesday, November 11. He was
a native of Charlton, in Worcester county, and thither his remains were conveyed for burial. An account of the fruitless
task he undertook may be found in these Annals, under date
1658.

Quite a rage for velocipede riding prevailed here and indeed
all over New England about this time. Several schools for instruction were opened, and convenient structures erected for
their accommodation. Many young men became quite expert
riders, as well as a few ladies. But the difficulties of managing
the novel contrivances and balancing the body on them, was a
great draw-back to their use. They had two narrow wheels, and
those set fore and aft, with the little padded seat between, the
crank producing the forward motion being turned by the feet,
while the steering was done by the hands; by which means
both hands and feet had constant occupation. It was literally
working one's passage. And there was very little to mark the
machine as an improvement upon the condemned affair of generations before. There was a velocipede race in Boston, July 5,
1869, at which George W. Buzzel, of Lynn, took the second
prize, of $20. He rode a mile in two seconds short of five minutes.
Horses were liable to be frightened by them, and they soon went
out of fashion. After a few years, however, a kindred contri-
vance, the bicycle, came into use, among young men especially.
This had one large wheel, and a diminutive one to steer by, and
required somewhat less skill and labor in the management.

On the night of Christmas day, the most disastrous fire that
had ever occurred in Lynn, took place. It commenced in Lyceum building, on Market street, corner of Summer, entirely
destroying that, and then leaping across Summer street, it destroyed the fine large new brick blocks belonging to Lyman B.
Frazier and Samuel M. Bubier, and damaged other less valuable
structures. The Central National Bank was in Lyceum building,
but the vault withstood the flames. The Post-office was in Frazier's block, but every thing of value there, was saved. Some
of the occupants of the buildings lost heavily, notwithstanding
large insurances. Lyceum building was erected in 1841, at
a cost of about $10,000. Frazier's block cost some $60,000,
and Bubier's about $65,000. The whole loss by the fire was
reckoned at not less than $300,000. The destruction of these
fine structures was much lamented by the people generally; but

they were soon replaced by others still more valuable. Odd Fellows' Hall, three years after, occupied the site on which Lyceum Hall or Lyceum Building, as it was indiscriminately called, stood. This last named was a wooden structure and not very comely in its proportions. It was, however, for years, much in use for lectures, shows, and meetings of all kinds, being centrally situated and almost the only eligible place in town for such purposes. The light of this conflagration was distinctly seen in Gloucester and Lawrence.

LYCEUM BUILDING, LYNN,
Erected in 1841 — destroyed by fire, in 1868.

1 8 6 9 .

Mary J. Hood, a colored woman, died at her residence, near Floating bridge, January 8, at the great age of 104 years and 7 months, as appeared by well authenticated records.

On Monday night, Jan. 25, another destructive fire took place in Lynn, destroying property to the amount of some $170.000. It commenced in the large brick shoe manufactory of Edwin H. Johnson, in Munroe street, destroying that and the manufactory of Harrison Newhall, and other adjacent buildings, and greatly damaging several in the neighborhood.

The shoe manufactory of Rufus A. Johnson, near the East

Saugus rail-road depot was burned on the morning of Feb. 20, with a considerable amount of stock.

Died, in Newton, Mass., Feb. 25, Dr. Edward A. Kittredge, a native of Salem, aged 58. He was for many years a practising physician in Lynn ; was of a genial and kind disposition, but rather eccentric manners. He was a frequent contributor to the newspapers, and his articles were always readable from their conspicuous humor and under-current of good sense. His education was good, and though trained in the old allopathic system, he finally adopted the hydropathic, or water-cure, system, having visited some of the water-cure establishments in Europe to study the theory. His remains were brought to Lynn and interred in the Eastern Burying Ground, after appropriate services at the First Universalist church.

From the 13th to the 17th of March, it was very cold. Only three days before St. Patrick's the thermometer reached 10 degrees below zero.

There was a magnificent display of beautifully tinted aurora borealis on the evening of April 15, during which a meteor of great brilliancy shot across the eastern sky.

The number of children in Lynn, between the ages of five and fifteen years, on the first of May, was 5.674.

The North Congregational Church was formed in the spring of this year, chiefly by members withdrawing from the First Church. The organization was recognized by a council held May 6.

May 10 was the day on which the last spike was driven, in completion of the first continuous rail-road line connecting the Atlantic and Pacific. It was an eventful occasion, far away there in the Rocky Mountain shadows, and drew together many prominent persons from different parts of the country. The spike was of solid gold, and what renders the occurrence of interest to people here is the fact that it was driven by David Hewes, a native of Lynnfield, and a contractor on the road. It was, however, soon withdrawn and deposited in a museum in San Francisco, under the apprehension that if allowed to remain some straying traveller, curious or covetous, might appropriate it.

Memorial Day was celebrated on Saturday, May 29. The principal address was delivered by Dr. Bowman B. Breed ; but Mayor Buffum made some appropriate remarks.

The famous Peace Jubilee commenced in Boston, June 15. It was the greatest musical entertainment that had ever been held in this country, the chorus singers alone numbering 10.528. It was attended by lovers of music from all parts of the Union, and from foreign countries. The average number of persons carried daily through and from Lynn, by the Eastern Rail-road, during the week, was about 11.300, and the receipts from the sale of tickets to the various concerts, amounted to $300.000. Lynn furnished her quota of performers in the association known as the Chorus Class, which, under the name of Choral Union, was continued, much to the benefit of musical education among us. And the whole affair gave a sensible impetus to musical interests in all parts of the country.

Benjamin H. Jacobs, for more than thirty years undertaker for the Old Burying Ground, near the western end of the Common, died June 16, aged 76. He was a native of Littleton, Mass., was faithful in his office, and took great pains to keep the venerable resting place in order and give it a pleasant aspect. And there his own remains were deposited. His son Edwin S., who long acted as his assistant, died on the 27th of the same month, aged 45.

The picturesque cruciform Episcopal church at Nahant, built in 1868, was consecrated June 27.

The public drain through Shepard street was constructed this year, in compliance with the strongly expressed desire of many residents of the vicinity. But it dried up so many wells in the neighborhood that some began to question its utility. The little pond on the Common, likewise, met the fate of the wells. But notwithstanding the temporary inconvenience, there is no doubt of the value of such works. Lynn had for many years felt the necessity of a system of drainage, which was at about this time energetically commenced. Other localities soon went through experience similar to that of Shepard street.

A caricature celebration of independence took place this year under the auspices of the "Antiques and Horribles," with discordant music by the "Old Canaan Band." Some parts of the procession were rather picturesque and some of the hits good.

Jeremiah C. Stickney died, August 3, aged 64. He was a native of Rowley, Mass., graduated at Harvard, with the 1824 class, immediately applied himself to the study of law, with Judge Cummins, of Salem, and in 1827 was admitted to the bar. He soon settled in Lynn, and was presently in active and successful practice, in which he continued for forty years. He was postmaster from 1829 to 1839, and again from 1853 to 1858; but having little ambition for office he was less in public life than was desirable for one of his ability. He declined the office of United States District Attorney for Massachusetts, when offered him, during the administration of Gen. Jackson. He however served in the lower house of the Massachusetts Legislature in 1839 and '40. When the city form of government was adopted, in 1850, his legal advice and assistance proved of great value ; and when in 1853 the office of City Solicitor was established, he was promptly elected to fill the position. It was the

privilege of the writer to be for some time associated with him
in professional partnership, and he would not pass silently by
this opportunity to remark that he can hardly speak in too high
terms of his constant affability and gentlemanly traits, or of his
reputation for legal attainments.   He was endowed in a large
degree with that invaluable power which few really possess,
though many claim — the power to discern the real sentiments
and motives that so often underlie the professed — a power which
is sure to raise the lawyer above the common ranks.   He was
not a man to blindly follow the dictation or direction of any
client when he saw that envy, hatred, or malice gave coloring to
his story.   In his investigations he was thorough, to the court
always respectful, and to his professional brethren courteous.

At the time Mr. Stickney commenced practice, the two other
lawyers here were men of mark if not eminence — Robert W.
Trevett and Isaac Gates.   They were both graduates of Harvard
and well read in the law.   A brief notice of Mr. Trevett appears
on pages 409 and '10 and of Mr. Gates on pages 435 and '6 of the
1865 vol.   By reference to those notices the reader will gain some
knowledge of the antagonists with whom Mr. Stickney had to
cope in his early professional days.   But they and he knew well
what was becoming to the character of gentlemen.   It was,
according to Mr. Rogers, a great consolation to Mr. Trevett,
when "in poverty and distress," to be able to say, "No matter
what I am now ; I take a great deal of satisfaction in reflecting
that I was once the principal lawyer in Lynn ;" — thus giving a
sort of reverse turn to the Shakespearean "All 's well that ends
well."

For many years Mr. Stickney owned and resided on the beautiful estate known as Forest Place, which under his hand was in
a great measure transformed from a mere rough pine-clad hill
into one of the most tasteful and picturesque places within a
score of miles.

On Christmas day, 1829, Mr. Stickney was united in marriage
to Miss Mary Frazier, daughter of John Frazier, of Philadelphia.
Three children were born to them ; namely, Charles Henry,
born Sept. 29, 1830, John Buffinton, born May 25, 1832, and
Martha Anne, born September 5, 1834.   The two sons entered
the legal profession.   John B. removed to Florida, where he for
some time filled the office of United States Marshal.   Martha
Anne, in 1868 became the wife of Capt. Stephen H. Andrews,
of Lawrence, Kansas, and removed thither.

A very severe gale took place on the afternoon of Wednesday,
Sept. 8.   Nothing like it had been felt since the historically
famous gale of September 23, 1815, and many old people thought
it exceeded that in violence, as it certainly did in the damage

3

done. The morning was still and sultry. About ten, a breeze
sprang up from the southwest, whence it continued to blow with
some vigor, and with dashes of rain, till about three in the afternoon, when it suddenly veered to the southeast and continued to
blow with increasing violence, till about half past six when it had
attained the character of a perfect hurricane, with torrents of rain.
Chimnies fell in all quarters, and several buildings were levelled.
But the most visible destruction was among the trees. Multitudes were uprooted — some of the largest along the streets ; and
few escaped dismemberment. Until the authorities had time, on
the next day, to remove the fallen ones, some of the sidewalks,
particularly that of North Common street, were dangerously obstructed. Several houses were much damaged by the falling of
the trees against them. During the height of the tempest, the
tall spire of the First Baptist Church yielded to the blast and
fell crashing through the roof, demolishing also the westerly side
of the edifice. A new two-story house in Essex street was raised
from the underpinning and completely prostrated. The extensive
green-house and conservatory of the Marquis de Lousada, near
King's Beach, was almost totally destroyed. No less than four
hundred and thirty shade trees, in different parts of Lynn, were
prostrated, and very few of those that withstood the gale escaped
unharmed. In the woods, the fallen trunks were beyond numbering. And the fruit trees were almost stripped of their unripe
fruit. Great havoc was made among the yachts and other small
shipping at Swampscott, but there was remarkable freedom from
loss of life or personal injury.

A field meeting of the Essex Institute was held here Sept. 23.
The day was pleasant, most places of interest were visited, and
numerous specimens in different departments of natural history
collected.

A blue heron, a very rare bird in this region, was shot in
Swampscott woods, Sept. 29. Its height, when standing upright,
was nearly four feet, and its spread wings measured some five
feet from tip to tip.

There was a fearful explosion of a part of the steam apparatus
at a building in Spring street, on the morning of Oct. 11. Capt.
Robert H. Reeves, of Salem, who happened to be in the room,
and a young man named Frank Alley, lost their lives.

A very perceptible shock of an earthquake was felt at about
half past five on the morning of Oct. 22. Beds oscillated with
sufficient violence to awake sleepers.

An association under the name of The Lynn Board of Trade
was formed in the fall of this year. It soon numbered a hundred
of the most prominent business men, and its beneficial influence
was felt particularly in the interests of shoe manufacturing.

The brick grammar school houses on Ireson and Warren

streets were built this year ; the former for the Whiting school, so named in memory of Rev. Samuel Whiting, settled over the First Church, from 1636 to 1680, and the latter for the Shepard school, so named from Rev. Jeremiah Shepard, minister of the same church, from 1680 to 1720. The Whiting was dedicated Sept. 4, and the Shepard Dec. 15.

The Turnpike through Lynn, from Salem to Chelsea bridge, became a public highway, this year, by legislative enactment. It was opened in 1803, and until the building of the Eastern Rail-road, in 1838, was the avenue by which the great bulk of Lynn travel reached Boston. The stock paid large dividends, for many years.

On the 8th of December water from the Flax Pond, to be used in cases of fire, was let into the pipes that connected with the hydrants in various parts of the city. See page 39.

The new Town Hall, at Nahant, was dedicated Dec. 24.

There were forty fires in Lynn, this year ; most of them slight. Eleven were in Munroe street, leading some to fear that that was a doomed locality.

To show the extent of the use of illuminating gas in Lynn, it may be stated that the gas company during the year manufactured something over 3.000.000 feet.

An act more stringent than any that had before existed, for the prevention of cruelty to animals, was this year passed by the Massachusetts legislature, and the many prosecutions under it, in Lynn, had a manifestly salutary effect.

1 8 7 0 .

The winter of 1869–'70 was unusually mild, so much so that a good deal of out-door work, such as plowing, digging of gardens and setting of fences, was done. February and March, however, did something to redeem the character for violence. There was a severe snow storm as late as March 13, when about a foot fell. The ice-cutters reaped but a scanty harvest, and the price became high in the succeeding summer. Our ponds had now for so many years continued to furnish a supply, that the article had come to be regarded rather as a necessity than a luxury, and the partial failure was seriously felt.

The City Hotel, at one time called Columbian House, a large wooden structure on Western avenue, near the Summer street crossing, was destroyed by fire on the morning of Monday, Jan. 3. It had for many years been kept as a public house, though not of the first class.

A remarkably beautiful display of aurora borealis took place early on the morning of Jan. 3. Shafts of red, white, and purple shot upward till the whole heavens were nearly covered. And waves of light rolled up occasionally from the north, as if from a radiant fountain below the horizon. On the afternoon of the following Thursday, there was the unusual appearance of two sun-dogs, and a circular rainbow. Another extraordinary auroral display took place in August, when emerald green was added to the other colors. And on still another night a well-defined red arch extended across the heavens, from southeast to northwest. About the middle of January, the planet Venus could for several days be distinctly seen, at noon, by the naked eye.

A small piece of land near the Central depot was sold in the early part of this year for five dollars the square foot. This was in the most valuable locality, and the highest price land had sold for in Lynn, up to that time.

A little son of Thomas Saxton, on the 5th of February, while playing around a stove, sportively inhaled the steam from the nozzle of a kettle of boiling water, and died the next morning from the effects.

The Young Men's Christian Association was incorporated March 31, though it was formed in August, 1868. Its object was to promote among young men, piety and the christian virtues, as well as social and mental improvement. Devotional meetings were frequently held, visiting and missionary work performed, temperance and other lectures delivered, and assistance rendered to strangers and others, in procuring employment and suitable homes. Rooms were furnished with books and periodicals, and for the holding of meetings, social intercourse and rational amuse-ment. The quarters were made attractive and every one was welcome. Similar associations were formed in most of the large places throughout New England, always with highly beneficial results.

About midnight, on Sunday, April 3, the Fred Bliss, a brig of 338 tons, was wrecked on the Swampscott shore, near the old Ocean House estate, a few rods from where the unfortunate Tedesco met her fate, in 1857, when all on board perished. The crew of the Fred Bliss were in much danger, but all were saved. The wreck continued for days to attract numerous visitors. A touching instance of animal sympathy is said to have taken place on the occasion of this disaster. A dog, and a cat with two kittens, were on board. By some mishap the cat and one of the kittens were killed. The dog, seeing the other kitten neglected, seized it and swam ashore, holding it up carefully in his mouth. On reaching the shore he dug a nestling place in the sand and kept vigilant watch over it till some one took it in charge.

A delegation of about seventy-five of the colored citizens of Lynn attended the celebration of the ratification of the Fifteenth Amendment of the U. S. Constitution, in Boston, on the 14th of April. They were in citizens' dress, but wore badges and were accompanied by the Lynn Band.

The Exchange Insurance Company, of Lynn, was organized April 23. It was afterwards removed to Boston, though still controlled by gentlemen of this city, and was ruined by the great fire of Nov. 9, 1872.

May 30, the Soldiers' Memorial Day, was duly observed. The address was by Rev. A. H. Currier, of the Silsbee street church.

The first regatta of the Lynn Yacht Club — an association recently formed by young men fond of the healthful exercises indicated by the name — took place June 17. The wind and weather were not very favorable, but the animating contest drew together a goodly number of spectators. On the 4th of July another regatta took place, and the weather being propitious it passed off very satisfactorily.

John E. Gowan, having returned to Lynn from his successful undertaking in raising the ships sunk in the harbor of Sebastopol, during the Crimean war, presented to the Light Infantry a Russian twelve-pound brass field-piece which he brought with him as a remembrancer of his arduous labors.

The publishers and printers of Lynn this year formed an association for social and fraternal purposes. An annual fishing trip down the bay, in summer, and perhaps a general meeting and modest banquet in the winter, served to keep alive the good feelings of the craft.

A general meeting of the qualified voters of Lynn was held in the vestibule of the City Hall, on the afternoon of Thursday, Sept. 1, being the first meeting ever called in accordance with the section of the City Charter which provides that on the requisition of fifty qualified voters, such meetings shall be warned by the mayor and aldermen, "to consult on the public good." The meeting had special reference to the laying out of Central avenue, which some prominent parties deemed uncalled for by any public exigency or interest. The City Council had ordered the laying out, and this meeting was called in the hope of obtaining such an expression of public opinion as would induce a reversal of the order. The meeting was large, and several prominent men took part in a warm discussion, which diverged to other questions of public concernment. A decided majority appeared against the measure, and strong resolutions were passed accordingly. But the government, having thoroughly examined the matter, were not led to reconsider their resolution.

The Park, at the east end of the Common, which had heretofore been so low as to be occasionally incommoded by standing water, was this year raised in grade some fifteen inches, over its entire surface.

The severest shock of an earthquake felt for many years, in this region, took place in the forenoon of Thursday, Oct. 20. In several instances persons in different parts of the city were so alarmed by the swaying of the buildings that they rushed into the streets. This was the case, especially, at the large brick factory at the corner of Western avenue and Federal street. No serious damage, however, was done.

The brick market house, on Central avenue, was opened for the first time for the sale of commodities, on Saturday, Nov. 19. In the evening, a large crowd gathered.

At the municipal election held Dec. 12, six ladies were elected members of the school committee, this being the first instance of the election of ladies to public office in Lynn.

Music Hall, on Central avenue, was first occupied on Thursday evening, Dec. 22. A fair, by the High street Baptist society, was then held there.

Early in the evening of Sunday, Christmas day, the large wooden house of worship of the First Church, on South Common street, corner of Vine, was entirely destroyed by fire. The afternoon service had closed but a short time before the fire broke out, and so rapidly did the flames progress, that it was impossible to arrest them. The illumination was striking, and seen as far inland as Lawrence. Portions of the fixtures and furniture were saved. The house was erected in 1836, but could not lay claim to great architectural beauty. The interior, however, had within a few months been much improved, by repairs and embellishments. The fire commenced in the eastern wall, no doubt from a defect in the heating apparatus. From the same cause it had taken fire during service, on Sunday, Oct. 6, 1867, when timely discovery prevented serious damage. There was an immediate offer to the bereaved society, by several of the neighboring churches, of the use of their houses of worship, and much christian sympathy was expressed.

Gold Fish Pond, on Fayette street, near Lewis, was this year greatly improved; in fact changed from a weedy, bushy sort of shallow lakelet, uncomely to the eye, though to some extent useful for the watering of cattle, to one of the chief ornaments of that quarter of the city. It was formerly known by the local name of "The Swamp;" and was likewise called "Ingalls's Pond," from the circumstance that near it Edmund Ingalls, one of the first settlers, established himself in the year 1629. About 1840 it began to be called Gold Fish Pond, the name originating in the fact that there had then appeared in it numerous gold fish. And these were supposed to have been the offspring of five of the species which some boys procured and let loose there, in 1837. They became so abundant, in a few years, that the youth of the neighborhood gained many a shilling, every season, by catching and peddling them about town. The cost of the improvements of this year, which gave the little pond so picturesque an aspect, was about $3.700.

The number of arrivals at the port of Lynn, this year, was 704; and among the imports were 18.872.961 feet of lumber, 44.205 tons of coal, 2.509 cords of wood, 651.000 bricks, 161.511 bushels of grain, and 2.460 bushels of potatoes.

The shoe business of Lynn, for 1870, seemed, on the whole, to have been quite satisfactory. The number of pairs manufactured was about 10.600.000, their value being some $17.000.000, many being of superior quality. It should be remarked that shoes vary in kind, quality, and price, from year to year, a circumstance sufficient to account for apparent inconsistencies in estimates.

The population of the city having become so large, it had for several years been manifest that means for a supply of water for domestic, mechanical, and fire purposes, beyond the primitive resource of wells, must speedily be devised. The great fires in the winter of 1868-'9 spurred to immediate action. Capacious reservoirs, had, indeed, been constructed in different sections, at considerable expense; but they were far from being inexhaustible. After a good deal of discussion in the city council, and out, an arrangement was effected whereby water for fire purposes was to be taken from Flax Pond. Pipes were accordingly laid along some of the principal streets, and the water was first set flowing, on the afternoon of Dec. 8, 1869; that being the first time the city received a supply from any source, by aqueduct, for any purpose. The Flax Pond arrangement being temporary, the subject matter was still further promptly acted on in the council. An accomplished engineer was employed to examine the several sources in the vicinity from which a supply might be obtained — Flax, Sluice, Humphrey's and Breed's ponds, and Saugus river. He made an elaborate report, and strongly recommended the purchase of Breed's Pond, which he claimed would yield sufficient for all necessary purposes, at least, for the time being. The city authorities, being satisfied of the value of the recommendation, soon made the purchase. But Breed's Pond was an artificial one, and depended on the dam at Oak street for its very existence. The dam had never appeared perfectly tight and safe. Indeed during the terrific storm of April 15, 1851, when Minot's Ledge light house was destroyed, such breaches had been made that all the water rushed down into the meadow. Immediately after the purchase, work was commenced on the dam; and the other necessary labor at the pond was vigorously pushed forward. The pipes, also were laid as rapidly as possible. And on Monday, Nov. 21, the water was sent coursing down into the city, announcing its arrival on the Common by leaping up at the fountain jet to the height of a hundred feet. The first cost of the Breed's Pond property, was $21.500, exclusive, of course, of the repairs and laying of pipes, but inclusive of several dilapidated wooden buildings. The reasonable apprehensions that had disturbed many minds, as to what could be done in case of a sudden conflagration, were now allayed, and a point attained when time could be taken for further deliberation on the question as to what source should be turned to for a permanently sufficient supply for all necessary purposes. The surveyors had determined that Humphrey's Pond would be insufficient; that Breed's Pond would supply 1.000.000 gallons per day, on the average; Flax Pond, with its adjuncts, 3.000.000; Saugus River, 5.500.000. Careful estimates were further made as to the probable amount of population in Lynn at certain future periods. And the conclusion was reached, that by the year 1900, the city would require 4.000.000 gallons daily. So that, at that comparatively near period, no single source, excepting Saugus River, would be adequate. The different waters were analysed, for the purpose of ascertaining their relative purity; and it was found that Sluice Pond was the purest; next came Breed's Pond; next Saugus River; and last, Flax Pond. In future pages of this volume will be found an account of what was subsequently done in relation to the water supply.

For several years there had existed among the Lynn people a good deal of dissatisfaction at the unsuitable and insufficient depot accommodations furnished by the Eastern Rail-road Company. The uncomely brick structure, in Central square, which was the principal station, and which was erected in 1848, in a few years became entirely insufficient for the increased traffic.

EASTERN RAIL-ROAD STATION, CENTRAL SQUARE,
Erected in 1848, taken down in 1872.

It may, perhaps, be well to mention, in passing, that this was not the first depot. The one erected at the opening of the road, was a diminutive one story wooden structure, standing on the northerly side of the road, without any roofing or other shelter over the track. As soon, however, as the Company manifested a willingness to supply the need, a somewhat warm sectional feeling sprang up, which, to say the least, afforded an excuse for delay. Those who had invested in property, or had established their business in the Square or its immediate neighborhood, naturally enough could not appreciate the claims of those who advocated the removal to a site farther westward. Others, not so circumstanced, claimed that it would be vastly more convenient for the people in general to have the new erection on the westerly side of Market street. There was much discussion and loud talk, success seeming to lean now to one side and then to the other. The legislative arm was invoked, and on the 29th of April, 1865, it was strangely enough enacted that " No rail-road corporation shall abandon any passenger station or depot which is on its road in this Commonwealth, and owned by said corporation, and which has now been or shall hereafter have been established for five years, except by the consent of the legislature ; and the accommodation furnished by the stopping of trains at such stations shall not be substantially diminished, as compared with that furnished at other stations on the same road." This was an unexpected and staggering blow to the Market street party, as it was called. And it seemed as if the Company was inclined to take it as an excuse to delay the erection of a new depot in either that street or Central square. But the matter was kept seething, and in 1868 the legislature sent out a committee to examine into the rival claims. They made a report, and on the 11th of June an act was passed requiring the Company to erect a suitable station on the old site in Central square ; with a provision that if they failed to do so, the Supreme Court should have power to appoint commissioners and compel specific performance. Still the Company did nothing, taking the lofty ground that the act was unconstitutional. Then the question of constitutionality went to the Supreme Court, and that august body determined that it was constitutional, and appointed commissioners to proceed with the work of erection. But before they had had time to accomplish any thing, an appeal was taken to the United States Court. But this little stirring episode in Lynn's rail-road history need not be pursued farther than to say that the good people presently came to realise the folly of so illustrating the fable of the Dog in the Manger. And the result was that in 1872 two handsome and costly stations were erected, one in Central square, where it still stands, and the other in State street, a few rods from Market, where it remained some months, and was then

demolished ; thus leaving the old Central square site the permanent one. A little wooden building, sufficient for the shelter
of waiting passengers, however, was erected on Market street,
where some of the daily trains were made to stop. This "depot
war," as it came to be called, has its lesson. It shows how a
whole community may be made to suffer inconvenience, year
after year, and its business be damaged, by the persistent disagreement of a few whose pecuniary interests are at stake. Had
the good citizens whose tenacity so long prevented the erection
of a new depot in either place, been content to yield a little for
the public good, the Company would have had no excuse for delay
in providing the much needed accommodations.

1 8 7 1 .

Rev. Joseph Cook, who for the time being was stated minister
of the First Church, during the early part of this year delivered
a series of Sunday evening lectures in Music Hall. They were
of a somewhat sensational character and drew very large audiences.
One in particular, "On the Moral Perils of the Present Factory
System of Lynn," elicited warm discussion, and was denounced
by many considerate people as giving an altogether unwarrant-
ably dark picture of the culture and morals of the young men and
women who labored in the shoe manufactories ; and as unjustly
assuming that there was almost, if not entirely, criminal laxity in
the management of the establishments. In style, he seemed to
emulate his sturdy predecessor, Rev. Parsons Cooke, often employing language any thing but choice and denunciations far
from gentle. The lectures also appeared in print, and caused
much acrimonious comment. Mr. Cook, some years after, delivered lectures in Boston and other large cities, where they were
attended by very great audiences, and met on the one hand with
the warmest applause and on the other with the most vigorous
tokens of disapproval.

Died, in Swampscott, Jan. 21, Capt. Thomas Widger, a native
of Marblehead, aged 80 years. He commenced a seafaring life
when but nine years old, shipping at that time for a fishing
voyage to the Grand Banks. He afterwards sailed on merchant
voyages to foreign ports, and early in the war of 1812 was taken
prisoner by the British, and remained a year in a prison ship,
when he was exchanged. Subsequently he sailed from Salem in
the privateer America, on a cruise during which several prizes
were captured. After the war he was again in the Grand Bank
fishery. In 1832 he settled in Swampscott and continued to
follow the seas ; finally, as age pressed upon him, employing
himself in the humble capacity of a dory fisherman. His habits
were temperate, and through life he enjoyed remarkably good

health, and never required the use of spectacles in reading the finest print. An interesting incident in his stirring life, and one indicative of his horror of inhumanity in a sailor, was his joining in the famous feat of tarring and feathering " Old Floyd Ireson," which remarkable performance has been so often celebrated by historian and poet. It should, however, be kept in mind that it was long since positively denied that Skipper Ireson was guilty of the "hord horted" act of refusing assistance to the wrecked crew, which was the occasion of his ignominious treatment, but suffered from false accusation.

Between one and two o'clock on the morning of Feb. 20, a fire occurred in a building on the Osborne estate, on Walnut street, near the Saugus line. Mr. John M'Kenney, with his wife and five young children, occupied a tenement in the building. The alarm was sudden and the fire spread rapidly. Mr. M'Kenney perished in the flames and the others barely escaped in their night clothes. One little fellow of six years fled barefoot upon the ice and snow, with a younger child upon his back, bravely struggling on for about a quarter of a mile, till he reached a place of safety.

The month of March was unusually mild — stated by meteorologists to be the warmest for forty-seven years.

There was a brilliant auroral display on the night of April 17. A beautiful arch of several hues rose in the north, and by its constant changes in form and color afforded a most interesting spectacle.

The fine brick building on the northeast side of Exchange street near Broad, was completed in the spring of this year, and immediately occupied by the Lynn Institution for Savings and the First National Bank.

The first lighting of street lanterns on Nahant, was on the night of May 9.

Four of the clergymen of Lynn were this year travelling in Europe.

The little pond near the centre of the Common and its neat surroundings were completed about the middle of May, and the sparkling little fountain then threw up its picturesque jets.

A reputable citizen reported seeing, as he passed Gold Fish pond, early on a May morning, a singular contest between hostile parties of frogs and toads. They were engaged in a fierce battle, which terminated in victory for the frogs. He declared that the poor toads were actually drowned by having their heads forced under the water and there held by the frogs, it requiring in some instances two frogs to overcome one toad. The victory was celebrated by exulting croaks. What the occasion of the reptile war was, did not appear.

On Tuesday, May 30, Soldiers' Memorial Day, fitting ceremonies took place.   The oration was delivered by J. K. Tarbox, Esq. of Lawrence.

The corner stone of Odd Fellows' Hall, on the site of the old Lyceum Hall, on Market street, corner of Summer, was laid on Monday, June 12, with appropriate ceremonies.   Preparations had been made for a grand display, and organizations from abroad had been invited.   But the unpropitious weather interfered with many details.

It is an old belief, traces of which may be found reaching back to periods long before European settlement commenced here, that shell fish, clams especially, are poisonous during the warm season, or, as it is usually expressed, during every month that is spelled without an R.   Many, however, have contended that the bivalves are as healthy for food at one time as another.   But an incident occurred here, on July 6, which was accepted by many as confirmatory.   Four men went over to Pines Point, and there ate rather bountifully of raw clams.   They were soon taken sick and hastened homeward.   Immediately after their arrival two died ; but the others, after much suffering, recovered.   Such a meal, however, might be accounted sufficiently dangerous for any stomach, irrespective of the idea of poison.   An incident similar to the foregoing occurred in June, 1848.

A singular case of spontaneous combustion took place in August, in a body of some four hundred tons of Sydney coal, on a wharf running from Broad street.   It appears to have smouldered for a few days, when, on the 11th, it set fire to the shed under which it lay.   A steam fire engine was employed in the attempt to extinguish it, but it was necessary to throw a portion into the dock, to save the remainder.   About sixty tons were lost.   The combustion appeared to have been caused by rain and the heat of the sun.

An unusually long drought occurred in the summer of this year.   No rain fell for forty-two days.

Five tents of Indians — about the number who usually appear here when the summer visitors arrive — encamped on the Beach, near the foot of Beach street, and remained a month or two, plying their humble trade in baskets and bead-work.

A terrible disaster took place on the Eastern Rail-road, at Revere, on the evening of Saturday, Aug. 26, the weather being damp and foggy.   An accommodation train from Boston reached the Revere station soon after eight o'clock.   The passengers for that place had landed and the train was just beginning to move forward when an express train, with a terrific crash, dashed down upon it, the locomotive fairly burying itself in the rear car, which was crowded with passengers, their number being not less than a hundred, many of whom were standing.   By this appalling casualty thirty persons were killed, eleven of them of Lynn, and some seventy-five injured, fifteen or twenty seriously. The venerable Dr. Ezra S. Gannett, a Unitarian minister of Boston, and long a colleague of the celebrated Dr. Channing, who was on his way to Lynn to preach in the Unitarian church, the next day, was among the killed. Mr. Thomas F. Bancroft, a deacon of the First Church of Lynn and an extensive shoe manufacturer, was also among the killed. He had but recently made the long journey to and from California, over the Pacific Rail-road, without meeting with an accident. Large claims for damages were made against the road, and they were honorably settled.

There was a violent storm on Sunday evening, Aug. 27. Several small buildings and numerous trees were prostrated.

The Odd Fellows of Essex county had a great parade in Lynn, Sept. 29. The weather was favorable and the members appeared in their rich and showy regalia.

The Electric Fire Alarm was first operated through all the circuits, on the evening of Oct. 2.

Something of an idea of the passion for out-door social gatherings, or pic-nic parties, as they are called, at this period, may be formed from the fact that thirty-seven were held in the single locality of Echo Grove, during the summer ; and that grove is but one of several similar places of resort within or about our borders. Many of the parties were from neighboring towns ; and on the other hand many Lynn parties went to other places.

Died, at his place of residence, South Common street, corner of Commercial, Oct. 11, David Taylor, aged 68. He was not a native of Lynn, but came here at an early age, friendless and poor. By industry and business tact, however, he took rank, while yet a young man, among the first of our shoe manufacturers. In January, 1833, he met with a serious loss by fire, his manufactory, which stood on the corner of Elm and Ash streets, being burned, with a large amount of stock. But he was soon again in prosperous business and largely engaged in the southern trade. He took considerable interest in political affairs though not an office holder, and in 1838, in connection with Charles Coolidge established the Lynn Freeman, a large and well-appointed political weekly newspaper of the Whig stamp. His connection with the paper, however, was not of long continuance. He established a business house in New Orleans, and for several years spent a large part of his time in that city. A newspaper writer said of him, " He was a fixture in the New Orleans market, and was as well known there and up the river as the most popular boat that came and went. We can see him now as he used to appear, with his portly person, his partially bald head, his genial countenance, his neat dress, and his massive gold fob-chain and seal." The war of the Rebellion found him in the south, a staunch Union man; and he suffered severely, in a pecuniary way. After the close of the war, he was able to gather up something from his scattered fortune, and passed the remainder of his life in Lynn, in comfortable though not affluent circumstances. He was accustomed to take a practical view of life, and for his reading chose the more solid works. And having been in contact with all classes and travelled in various parts of the country, with an observing eye, he was enabled to impart much useful information. The house in which he died was the same which he had in process of erection at the time of the burning of his manufactory, in 1833. "Taylor's Building," on the corner of Elm street, and adjoining the western extremity of "Healey's Arcade," which was, at the time of its erection, probably the most costly building in Lynn, and considered by many to be quite beyond the requirements of the times, remains as evidence of his enterprise.

By the great fire in Chicago, which commenced on the night of Oct. 7, it was for a time feared that some of our business men would suffer materially, the shoe and leather dealers there being indebted to Lynn manufacturers to the amount of some $150.000. But the real loss, happily, proved inconsiderable. A meeting in aid of the sufferers by the calamity was held in Music Hall on the evening of October 10, at which resolutions of sympathy were adopted, and arrangements made for systematic contributions of money, clothing, and all articles of prime necessity. The contributions in money amounted to something above $17.000. And some forty cases of bedding, clothing, boots and shoes, &c. were likewise gathered and forwarded.

President Grant passed through Lynn on the morning of Oct. 16. A large crowd had assembled in Central square to greet him, but he merely stepped out upon the platform of the Pullman car in which he was journeying eastward, bowed to the multitude, and bad them good morning.

The autumn foliage this year presented unusually rich and varied tints. It was a rare treat even to one accustomed to these annual displays to witness the brilliant show, and many a fair lady could be met on a pleasant day wending her way from the woods with leafy gatherings of almost dazzling brightness.

Two human skeletons, supposed to be aboriginal remains, were exhumed, in Ocean street, Nov. 2.

A very violent easterly storm commenced on the evening of Nov. 14, and continued through the 15th. The wind was very high, and drove the sea in with great fury. Much damage was done along the coast. The lower part of Beach street was overflowed to the depth of something more than two feet, and the condition of the wharves indicated a tidal influx as great, within a few inches, as during the memorable storm of April 15, 1851. A great concourse, among whom were many women, gathered all about the headlands and in the vicinity of the beaches, to witness the grandeur of the scene, heedless of the pelting of the storm. The embankment along the seaward front of Ocean street was much damaged, and the Eastern Rail-road track was rendered impassable for some hours. The stone monument on Bowditch ledge, off Marblehead, was carried away, after having withstood the stormy assaults of thirty years.

On the night of Nov. 17, a shocking death occurred in a house on Howard street. Mrs. Jane Clinton, wife of John G. Clinton, a barber, was found dead on the kitchen floor, the body bearing such marks as at first led to the supposition that she had been murdered, and an attempt made to conceal the crime by setting fire to the premises. Suspicion fell on the husband, and he was arrested. A coroner's inquest was held, and the result of their examination was that she was burned to death by the breaking of a kerosene lamp. The jury also found that both husband and wife had been intoxicated and engaged in a quarrel during the afternoon. They ascribed to the husband no direct agency in the death of the wife, but added that had he been sober, and attended to his duty, the death might not have taken place.

A fire occurred on Lamper and Brother's wharf, at the foot of Pleasant street, on Wednesday evening, Dec. 13. A large stable and wagon shed, with a quantity of hay, were consumed. But the most lamentable feature of the disaster was the perishing of sixteen valuable horses.

A startling tragedy took place on Saturday forenoon, Dec. 16, in which William Vennar, known also as William Brown, a man about thirty-six years of age, and a native of Maine, but who had resided here a few months, was chief actor. He came to Lynn with a woman who appears to have been the wife of Thomas Jones, of Washington, Me., but who had abandoned her lawful husband to live with Vennar, who seems to have had a wife in Washington. They were boarding, temporarily, with Mrs. Sarah Roundy, on Adams street. He was intemperate, and, especially when in liquor, of ferocious disposition. The two had many quarrels, but were represented to have appeared unusually loving on the morning of the murder. A Mrs. Conway, who resided in another tenement in the same house, at about half past nine, hearing terrific screams, hastened to the door, and saw Vennar clutching his victim by the hair, and with a large dirk knife actually butchering her. Having accomplished his purpose, by nearly severing the left jugular vein and wholly severing the carotid artery, he washed his hands and fled. But Mrs. Conway had, as soon as she recovered from the first shock of horror, given the alarm, and persons were fast gathering. Vennar, however, escaped, and gained a patch of woods on Farrington's hill, on the north side of Western avenue. Here he was surrounded, and kept at bay till others arrived, among them the city•marshal and several police officers. Vennar now took a defiant attitude, brandishing his still bloody weapon and threatening death to any one who dared approach. By direction of the marshal, officers Thurston and Whitten endeavored to disarm him, but did not succeed. Finally, officer Thurston, in an attempt with a club to strike the arm that held the knife, lost his footing. Vennar then sprang to him, and with the utmost fury began to stab him. That was the decisive moment, it being evident that Thurston's life was in imminent peril, and that instant action alone could save him. And the marshal proved himself equal to the emergency. With promptness and coolness he levelled his pistol and fired two shots. And Vennar fell dead. The coroner's verdict, as well as public opinion, fully justified the act of the marshal.

During the winter of this year the frost penetrated to an unusual depth ; in many places five or six feet. There was little snow, and many days of intense cold.

During the three months ending Dec. 31, the Swampscott fishermen brought in 1.140.000 pounds of cod. At two cents a pound, which was rather a low price for that year, the value would be $22.800. Some $3.000 worth of oil was also obtained during the same three months.

The number of passengers carried over the Eastern Rail-road during the year was 4.635.482 ; and the tons of freight, 378.199. The rate of speed per hour, including stops, was as follows : freight trains, 15 miles ; accommodation passenger trains, 20 miles ; express trains, 28 miles.

The number of feet of lumber imported into Lynn during the quarter ending with December, was 8.443.000. About 50.000 tons of coal were brought in during the year.

The number of persons carried to and from Boston, by the horse cars, during the year, was 122.000.

There were 392 marriages in Lynn, this year. The ages of the oldest couple were 66 and 46 years, and the youngest, 18 and 16 years. The largest number solemnized by any one minister was by Rev. Patrick Strain, of St. Mary's Roman Catholic church.

This year and the two preceding years were remarkable for the little rain that fell. It was a common remark that we experienced a three years' drought. The winters set in with extremely low springs.

So many cases of small-pox occurred in Lynn, this year, that some alarm was occasioned, and measures were taken to have a general vaccination.

1 8 7 2 .

The new Methodist Meeting-house on the corner of Maple and Chesnut streets, Glenmere village, was dedicated on the afternoon of February 15.

The schooner Champion, of Swampscott, on Friday and Saturday, Feb. 16 and 17, with a crew of twelve men, stocked 30.000 pounds of fish, which sold for four cents the pound — $1.200. For Friday's catch the crew realized $72 each.

A two story wooden building, on Willow street, formerly standing on the north side of Central square, and known as the Bay State Building from the circumstance of its being that in which the Bay State newspaper was printed, was nearly destroyed by fire on Sunday morning, Feb. 25.

The City Hall bell was raised to its position, on Saturday, March 2. Its weight is 4.937 pounds.

During the early part of March there were several extremely cold days. Ice was formed from Swampscott to Nahant. On the 7th the fishermen were able to do what they had not done before for nineteen years, that is, walk on the ice to their vessels at the moorings. A great many garden evergreens and hardy shrubs were killed. The average temperature of the month, at sunrise, was twenty-one and a half degrees, which was three degrees colder than the average temperature of January.

On Thursday, March 14, the trim little steamer Meta, commenced running to and from Boston, making two trips daily, each way, with passengers and freight. In July, the Carrie was added to the line, and the two together then made six trips each way, daily. But the line was soon discontinued.

86.000 lobsters were taken during the three months beginning with Jan. 1, by the fishers of Nahant. Fears began to arise, and calculations to be made as to the probable extermination of the species, if the great destruction were not checked. It was shown, at least to the satisfaction of many, that in forty years lobsters would become unknown upon the coast, if some restrictions were not enforced. The apprehensions became so lively that the legislature was induced to interpose, and in 1874 passed a law that " Whoever sells, or offers for sale, or has in his possession with intent to sell, either directly or indirectly, any lobster less than ten and one half inches in length, measuring from one extreme of the body to the other, exclusive of claws or feelers, shall forfeit for every such lobster, five dollars." The fears for the fate of the lobster were by no means groundless ; yet one is reminded of the appeals of some of the early settlers who were sorely apprehensive that the old iron works would consume all the wood that grew hereabout.

A meeting of the City Council was held in the common coun-

4

cil chamber on the evening of Tuesday, April 16, to join in testimonials in honor to the memory of Professor Morse, the inventor of the electric telegraph, who had recently died. Appropriate resolutions were passed, and ordered to be entered on the records of both branches, and were also immediately sent forth, on the wires, to the meeting at the same time convened in the national representative hall, at Washington. Brief addresses were made by the mayor and several of the city clergymen ; and the whole proceedings were highly eulogistic of the deceased.

Died, at his residence on Western avenue, April 21, Dr. James M. Nye, aged 53, a native of Salisbury, Mass. He was a practising physician here, some thirty years, was highly respected as a citizen, and for skill and promptitude in his profession. In scientific pursuits and all educational matters, he took great interest, and was not remiss in labors for the moral elevation of the community. For many years he was a prominent and useful member of the First Baptist church.

The Lynn Homœopathic Society was formed, April 23, by the resident homœopathic physicians.

May 30, was, according to the now established custom, celebrated as the Soldiers' Memorial day. The address was delivered by ex-Governor Fairfield of Wisconsin, in the vestibule of the City Hall, the inclemency of the weather interfering with the contemplated out-door proceedings.

The fine brick building in Franklin street, erected for the Cobbet school, was dedicated May 31. Besides the usual intellectual entertainment, a banquet was provided, to which ladies as well as gentlemen were invited. The Cobbet school received its name from Rev. Thomas Cobbet, settled here in 1637, as colleague of Rev. Mr. Whiting.

There was a heavy thunder shower, June 12, during which the lightning struck in five places in Lynn, and considerably disarranged the telegraphic fire alarm.

On the 17th of June, a regatta took place under the auspices of the Lynn Yacht Club, which afforded much gratification to the large company assembled.

The great musical entertainment known as "The World's Peace Jubilee and International Musical Festival," commenced in Boston, June 17, with its chorus of 20.000 voices and its orchestra of more than 1.000 instruments, its great organ, mammoth drum, and belching cannon, and continued some fifteen days. Many ladies and gentlemen of Lynn lifted their voices in the chorus. Among the most notable features of the whole occasion were the grand performances of the instrumental bands from Europe — the English, Irish, French, and Prussian. The weather was excessively warm most of the time, and the crowds of people in and about the Coliseum, and indeed around the city generally rendered a visit though highly interesting, subject to many discomforts.

Died, in Saugus, June 19, Joseph Cheever, aged a hundred years and three months. He served as a representative in the legislature in 1817, and for several terms in subsequent years, his last service being in 1835.

The first Roman Catholic church on Nahant was built this year, and occupied in July.

The National Association of Morocco Manufacturers, composed chiefly of the principal persons engaged in the trade, in the Middle and New England States, visited Lynn, July 11. They were hospitably entertained by the brethren of the trade here, and taken to Nahant, where they partook of a dinner, and then to Swampscott, where a supper was provided. During the day opportunity was taken to discuss matters pertaining to their branch of business, which had risen to be of commanding importance in the country.

A company was formed this year for the manufacture of Frear stone. They established a factory in Essex street, and among their first contracts was that to furnish the trimmings for the Baptist church, about that time in process of erection at the corner of Essex and Washington streets. Door-steps, memorial stones, garden urns, and a variety of other articles were made, which it was claimed were quite as durable and in some respects preferable to manufactures from natural stone. The company, however, were not successful, pecuniarily, and operations were soon discontinued.

On the 18th of July, there was a considerable gathering under the auspices of the Lynn manufacturers, of persons engaged in the shoe and leather trade in different parts of the country. The portion of the company assembled at Lynn rode to Nahant in procession, and were there joined by others who came from Boston by steamer. The occasion was rather designed for social enjoyment than dry business purposes, and a band of music was employed to enliven the occasion. Every provision was made for table gratifications, and speeches, humorous and sedate, were delivered. Various sports were engaged in, and the interesting spectacle of a regatta provided. The latter, however, proved rather a failure, as a dense ocean mist rolled in.

A comical little incident occurred to some of our grave city officials on a certain balmy summer day. The question of a new almshouse had been agitated in the council, and afterwards, in committee, the style of the proposed building was considered. In the course of the discussion it was represented, on newspaper authority, that a model institution had lately been erected in Hartford. Upon the information, such high authority not being questioned, three or four officials went forth on a tour of inspection. Arrived in Hartford, they forthwith waited on the mayor and proceeded to unfold the purpose of their visit. They were hospitably received, but without circumlocution and with manifest astonishment informed that no such building as they came to inspect, existed. The polite attentions were calculated to alleviate their chagrin, but not to abate the unspoken maledictions upon the disseminator of the false information that induced their fruitless journey.

The lamps placed along the beach road leading to Nahant were lighted for the first time on the evening of July 24. They proved not only a great convenience, but quite a picturesque feature, as viewed from the heights.

A Crispin strike, so called, took place in Lynn during the summer. The organization known as the Knights of St. Crispin had been in existence several years and embraced a large portion of the operatives in the shoe business. For a year or two they had been working at prices agreed upon between themselves and the manufacturers ; but the time to which the arrangement was limited had expired, and the employers were not all disposed to continue to pay the same prices, in every department, some of them proposing to make a small reduction in the price of work on a particular part of the shoe, where it was alleged such facilities had lately been introduced as to justify such a step. This was met by the peremptory order of the Crispin "Board of Arbitration," that all members who were at work in the shops where the reduction was made, should cease work on Friday, July 26, as well those who were not called to suffer a reduction as those who were. The manufacturers did not propose to reduce the prices generally. In compliance with the official order, the Crispins in the shops alluded to, ceased to work ; the great body of the associates were soon idle ; and some of the largest manufactories were brought to a "stand still," as the phrase was. To indulge long in such a course, it soon became apparent, would not only be damaging to individual interests, but seriously detrimental to the prosperity of the city. Some prominent manufacturers made preparations to move their machinery to other places, where they would not in future be embarrassed by the action of such organizations. A good many Crispins who had been satisfied with their situations and rates of pay, were forced by the order of their Board of Arbitration to remain idle for weeks, much to the injury of themselves and their families. It happened to be a season when business was not brisk, so that the manufacturers felt the better able to take a persistent stand against the demands of what they deemed an unjust and unreasonable organization. The Crispins, being generally dependent on their daily labor, and, with perhaps the exception of a few hot-heads, really considerate and fair-minded, began to see the greater evils that must follow, if things remained in that position, or if the business were driven out of the city. On the evening of August 2, the manufacturers held a meeting at which it was resolved " That it is for the best interests of the city of Lynn that every manufacturer manage his own business, irrespective of any organization." The following agreement was then drawn up, and received the signatures of some fifty of the principal individual manufacturers and firms : " We the undersigned, manufacturers of the city of Lynn, hereby agree that on and after Saturday, Aug. 10, we will employ no person subject to, or under the control of, any organization claiming the power to interfere with any contract between employer and employee." They claimed that they had a right to make their own bargains, and had decided to make them with such only as were free to bargain for themselves. The Crispins received notice of the determination of the manufacturers, and though at first there seemed to some extent a disposition to refuse compliance, the organization in reality soon ceased to claim control over its members in the vexed matter of bargaining for wages. And then, when business revived, all hands went cheerfully to work. On the whole, perhaps, this movement was beneficial in its results, for it was taken notice of throughout the country, and elicited discussions touching such organizations which were calculated to prove widely useful. And here, at home, the good and evil features of the local organization were canvassed in a manner that may have a permanent influence for good. There was an unusually small amount of personal acrimony exhibited during the proceedings, the troublesome questions being mostly met, by both sides, in a forbearing, manly way. Possibly the circumstance most to be lamented was that some of the enterprising manufacturers withdrew portions at least of their business from Lynn and established factories in other parts of the State, in Maine and New Hampshire. Some distant towns, availing themselves of the posture of affairs here, offered large inducements in the way of remission of taxes and assistance in various forms to such as would commence establishments within their borders.

Early in the evening of Aug. 13, the large box factory building of S. O. Breed, near the southerly end of Commercial street, was struck by lightning and set on fire. It was totally destroyed, together with a small building in the rear. The bolt was seen by several persons when it struck.

The summer of this year was remarkable for its excessive heat and the frequency and severity of its thunder showers. It was also remarkable for the abundance of winged insects, particularly mosquitos and house flies. From April to Nov. much rain fell.

The brick house of worship of the First Congregational Society, on South Common street, corner of Vine, was dedicated on Thursday evening, Aug. 29; sermon by Rev. Mr. Dennin. An auction sale of pews was held on the evening of Sept. 18, and $3.000 raised. The highest bid for choice was $250. The corner stone was laid on the afternoon of July 10, 1871.

The capacious and elegant Ingalls school house, on Essex street, was dedicated Aug. 31. Ingalls school was so named from Edmund and Francis Ingalls, the first settlers.

Died, in Swampscott, Sept. 25, Joseph Harding, aged 97. He was supposed to be the oldest free-mason in the State, having joined the Adams lodge, in Wellfleet, in 1800.

William F. Mitchell, having been chosen City Missionary by representatives of the different religious organizations, entered upon the duties of the office in September. He served faithfully for five or six years, and then the distinctive office was discontinued.

From May 19 to Oct. 6, inclusive, on all the Sundays, twenty-one in number, the weather was pleasant.

So famed had Swampscott become as a watering place that during this year it was estimated that there were between 10.000 and 11.000 visitors. The fashionable time for driving was from four in the afternoon, till dark ; and at that time the fine drives in the vicinity afforded as much elegance and as great diversity in turn-outs as could be seen any where. The gay nag pranced with the lordly equipage, and the raw-boned roadster with his rattling gig. There is probably no place on the New England coast with a more salubrious climate, or affording better facilities for the comforts and enjoyments of a temporary summer residence. Yachting, rowing, fishing, bathing, and in short all kinds of marine exercise or sport, can here be indulged in to the heart's content. Here, too, all the fashionable in-door recreations and diversions — games, music, dancing, social converse — may be pursued in the most genial company. And then the magnificent and ever changing ocean views, by sunlight and moonlight, and the charming landscape scenes are never wearying to the cultivated eye.

During the warm months of this year and the three preceding years there was great activity in real estate transactions, and prices advanced wonderfully, not only in the central sections but in the remote outskirts and rough highlands. Indeed they were rank speculative times. Many who owned small estates near business centres found themselves suddenly rich — and it should be added that if they invested their sudden gains in other real estate, and continued to hold it a couple of years, they probably grew just as suddenly poor again, for an equalizing depression followed the inflation.

Odd Fellows' Hall, on Market street, corner of Summer, was dedicated on Monday, Oct. 7. During the afternoon there was a parade, in regalia, which attracted much attention, and a dinner was partaken of at the Kertland House. The dedicatory services, held in the evening, were of a highly interesting character, and at the close the officers partook of a supper at the above-named house. Soon after the dedication a great Fair for the benefit of the lodge was held in the new building, and the sum realized was a little over $5.000. The Bay State Lodge of Odd Fellows, in Lynn, was instituted in 1844, and at the time of the dedication numbered a membership of 680.

ODD FELLOWS' HALL, LYNN; ERECTED IN 1872.

Cheap rail-road trains, intended particularly for the benefit of working men, commenced running on the Eastern Rail-road, between Lynn and Boston, in November. Twenty tickets were sold for a dollar, which made the fare about half a cent per mile. A train left Lynn at half past five in the morning and Boston at half past six in the evening.

The great fire in Boston commenced on the evening of Saturday, Nov. 9, and continued to rage sixteen hours, destroying property to the value of $70.000.000. During the night, from the hights about Lynn the flames presented a grand and startling spectacle, and the light was seen by passengers on board the steamers as far off as Long Island Sound. Detachments of the Lynn firemen hastened to the assistance of their unfortunate neighbors, taking with them a couple of our steam fire engines, and were afterwards by the Boston officials publicly thanked for their efficient services. A number of the business men of Lynn were large sufferers by the calamity. Between fifty-nine and sixty acres of the heavy business portion of the city were burned over.

During the latter part of the autumn of this year a singular disease prevailed among the horses here and all over this region of country. It seemed to be a sort of catarrhal fever. Epizootic was the name usually applied. Scarcely a horse in all Lynn escaped, though it proved fatal in but few cases. It was, however, disabling, and evidently painful. So extensively did the disease prevail that for some days the accustomed noise of wheel carriages almost entirely ceased to be heard in our streets. Hand-carts and wheel-barrows were put in requisition, and oxen, cows, goats and dogs were put to new duties. Odd and comical turn-outs were every where seen. In some instances teams of from three to six men were seen hauling along loads. The trips of the horse cars to Boston were suspended, and only occasionally was one made through Lynn. Public request was made by the authorities for the citizens to hasten, in case of an alarm of fire, and assist in dragging the steam fire-engines. In Boston, the United States mails were carried to and from the post-office in ox teams. The ministers in many instances took up the matter as the theme of their Sunday discourses ; and the whole community began to realize our dependence on the equine race. In many cases the recovery was slow, and the exhausting effects were felt for months.

The brick and iron station of the Eastern Rail-road, on Central square, was built this year ; also the brick and iron station on State street ; which latter was soon taken down. On pages 40, 41, and 42, may be found a brief account of the " rail-road war," so called, which took place about this time. The number of daily passenger trains running from Lynn to Boston was forty ; and the number from Boston to Lynn was the same, including five from East Boston. Ten years before but twelve ran each way.

The Reservoir, on the northerly slope of Second Pine Hill was built this year.

The whole number of streets in Lynn, this year, was 236 ; and the number of courts and alleys 75 ; together making about ninety miles in length.

1 8 7 3 .

The pumping engine at the public water works, on Walnut street, was first put in operation on the afternoon of January 14, sending up the water from Breed's pond into the Pine Hill Reservoir. And on the 27th of February the water was let into the distributing pipes. It was, however, soon discovered that serious leaks existed in the reservoir, and it became necessary during the ensuing summer to puddle the entire bottom. Measuring on a depth of fifteen feet the reservoir has a capacity of 2.000.000 gallons, and is 177 feet above the sea level. The depth is 18 feet, and the water surface about five acres.

PUMPING ENGINE HOUSE,
Walnut Street, Lynn. (Rear View.)

On the night of March 7, a fire commenced in the hardware store on the corner of Washington and Munroe streets, by which property to the amount of $3.600 was destroyed.

This year Lynn had five organized bands of music, and few public parades of any note took place without the services of one at least.

On the morning of April 9, the keeper of Egg Rock light shot two wild geese which had alighted on the rock for rest on their migratory journey northward.

Several of our enterprising Lynn residents sent specimens of their manufactures to the "World's Exposition" which was this year in successful operation at Vienna, in Austria. Specimens of boots and shoes, of elastic car wheels, and steam gauges were forwarded, and elicited favorable notice.

On Soldiers' Memorial Day, May 30, Col. C. B. Fox delivered the address.

English sparrows made their appearance in Lynn, this year — probably the progeny of those imported into Boston a few years before in the hope that they would, in a measure at least, preserve the trees from the ravages of canker worms and other destructive insects. Bird houses were placed in the trees on and about the Common and on many private grounds for their accommodation.

A singular and almost amusing instance of forgetfulness happened to one of our Lynn ladies this year. When about going away on a visit, she concealed, in a rag-bag, divers valuables in the shape of notes and bank books, representing some four thousand dollars. Some time after her return she sold to a travelling rag gatherer the contents of her bag, entirely forgetting the concealed treasure. But the alarming fact soon after occurred to her, and she hastened to attempt the recovery of her treasure. She traced the rag gatherer to Salem, found the place in which he deposited his musty chattels, and there regained her valuables.

On the morning of Aug. 16, John Cuzner, aged 34, while at work, with two others, on the northerly side of the tower of the Washington street Baptist church, then in course of erection, was precipitated to the ground from a height of seventy-eight feet, by the fall of the staging, and so injured that he died in an hour. The two others were seriously injured. Charles L. Savage, a mason, who worked on the same building, lost his life on the morning of July 1, also by defective staging.

A serious fire occurred in Union street, on the morning of Aug. 25, commencing in French's furniture store, near the Sagamore hotel, the latter barely escaping. Four hundred thousand gallons of water were used in extinguishing the flames, and the water in the new reservoir was lowered four inches.

Died, Aug. 27, William S. Boyce, aged 63. He was greatly respected for his many excellent qualities. His native place was Portland, but he came to Lynn when about nine years of age, and by industry and diligence accumulated a respectable fortune. He was a member of the Society of Friends, upright in his dealings, intelligent and liberal ; was officially connected with several monetary institutions, and for the last seven years of his life was president of the First National Bank. His death was tragical. He called at the United States Hotel, in Boston, and retired to a bathing room. Remaining so long as to excite alarm, the door was forced open and his lifeless body found, in such a condition as to leave no doubt that his death was voluntary. His garments were found disposed in neat order, and every thing indicated premeditation. No satisfactory reason could be given for the act, though he had somewhat failed in health and become depressed in spirits. On the day of his funeral respect was shown for his memory by the closing of a number of prominent business places, and the attendance of many friends.

The Soldiers' Monument, in Park square, was dedicated on Wednesday, Sept. 17. The day was pleasant, and Lynn perhaps never before witnessed a grander demonstration. A long procession, consisting of military organizations, associations of various kinds, and the fire department, marched through the principal streets, along which many buildings were beautifully decorated, the City Hall especially exhibiting a profuse array of flags and streamers, with various emblematic devices. The dedicatory exercises were held on a platform erected for the purpose, in front of the City Hall, and consisted of music by the military bands, singing by the Lynn Choral Union, prayer by the Rev. Mr. Biddle, an oration by Col. E. P. Nettleton, and a poem by Mr. E. P. Usher. The monument, allegorical and classic, was designed by John A. Jackson, a native of Maine, but resident of Florence, Italy. The casting was executed at Munich in Bavaria, and the whole cost was $30.000.

SOLDIERS' MONUMENT,
Park Square. Dedicated Sept. 17, 1873.

The new stone and brick house of worship of the First Universalist society, on Nahant street, was dedicated on the 11th of September, the sermon being preached by Rev. Elbridge G. Brooks.   The corner stone was laid May 27, 1872.

Concrete crossings began to be laid in the streets this year.

The branch of the Eastern Rail-road, from Swampscott to Marblehead, was opened for travel, Oct. 20, its length being four miles.

There was a grand masonic parade in Lynn, Oct. 22, on the occasion of constituting the Olivet Commandery, installing the officers, and dedicating the hall.   The day was fair, and the proceedings attracted much attention.

October of this year was found to average the warmest in forty years ; but the next April averaged the coldest in fifty years, rain or snow falling on thirteen days, and there being but nine clear days.

In the course of local discussions and disagreements as to the source from which the public supply of water should be drawn, a good deal of false alarm was created during the summer and fall.   Some asserted that an extraordinary amount of sickness had prevailed in the previous year, and that it was in part at least attributable to the impurity of the water of Breed's pond, which at that time furnished the supply.   This induced the Lynn Medical society to publish the result of their investigations, which they did in the following terms : " Whereas, it has been generally reported that the last year has been unusually sickly, and the use of the water lately introduced has been assigned as the cause, therefore, *Resolved*, That the past year has been unusually healthy, and probably the improved health of our city is in some measure to be attributed to the use of water more wholesome than that of wells, many of which are contaminated."

The Friends' Biennial Conference was held in Lynn this year, commencing Nov. 19.   A large number from all parts of the country were present, and the meeting-house, in Silsbee street, being inadequate for their accommodation, some of the meetings were held in the First Universalist church, on Nahant street, which was courteously tendered for their use, other houses of worship being also offered.   Many leading members of the denomination, male and female, were present to give their testimony, to advise, and to discuss ; and it was considered a season of much spiritual profit as well as social enjoyment.   The attendants from abroad were hospitably entertained by our people of all denominations, and on their departure expressed much satisfaction.

The three masted schooner Robert Raikes, of Provincetown, from Digby, N. S., struck on the "outer ledge," Swampscott, near midnight, Nov. 17, during a severe storm, and was completely wrecked. All on board perished. The fatal place was near where the Tedesco was wrecked, in 1857, and also the Fred Bliss, in 1870. There were five persons on board the Robert Raikes. The captain's name was John Ellis, and his brother William was also on board. And it was a rather remarkable coincidence that another brother, attached to another vessel, was lost during the same storm. Capt. Ellis's body was not recovered till Nov. 30.

A prize fight was interrupted by the police at the Half-way House, on the Turnpike, on the morning of Dec. 31. The principals were from Providence, R. I., and Boston, and most of the company were from those places. The principals and several others were made prisoners. The fight was going on in an apartment of the house, and it was with great skill and caution that the officers eluded the sentinels and made the captures.

Three masted coasting schooners, which for some years had occasionally appeared in our harbor, began now to be quite common, that style of vessel proving to be much more readily and economically worked than the square rigged of equal tonnage.

During the year, 515.952 mail letters and 39.162 drop letters were delivered in the city by post-office carriers.

Birch Pond was formed this year, for the purpose of securing an additional supply of water, by building a dam across Birch Brook valley, on the east of Walnut street, near the Saugus line. The pond was made to cover about sixty-seven acres.

1 8 7 4 . `

On the morning of January 10 a fire commenced in the stable of the Glenmere line of stages, on Chatham street, and consumed the building, several tons of hay, and other property. The most serious matter, however, was the death of ten horses. The whole value of the property lost was $2.500.

George W. Keene died suddenly in the St. Nicholas Hotel, New York, Jan 27, aged 58. He was a native of Leicester, in Worcester county, but from his early youth, with the exception of one or two brief intervals, was a resident of Lynn ; and his sudden death created more than ordinary sensation, for he was widely known as an active business man as well as for his genial manners and benevolent disposition. He belonged to a Quaker family, his mother being the accredited preacher spoken of under date 1867 ; but he early adopted the Unitarian faith and held fast to it to the end of his life. He was a member of the Masonic and Odd Fellow fraternities and attained to high ranks in the lodges ; had a cultivated mind and took considerable interest in literary and educational affairs ; was thoughtful, and in his meditations and reasonings did not always pursue the beaten track.

He became an adherent of the doctrines of the spiritualists, though perhaps in a modified form, and held a newspaper discussion on some points of their faith, with President Felton of Harvard college. For almost the whole of his business life he was engaged in the manufacture of shoes, the great staple production of Lynn, and by his enterprise in seeking out new inventions and introducing the most approved machinery did his full share in elevating the trade from the position of ill-requited toil to one of profit and commanding importance. The circumstances of his death were peculiarly afflictive to his friends. He left home on Monday, accompanying a niece to New York, and on Tuesday evening, having taken lodgings at the St. Nicholas, as he was passing through the entrance hall, fell, and in a few minutes expired. He was buried in Pine Grove Cemetery, in the original purchase, laying out, and dedication of which, he took a lively interest. The funeral services were held in the Unitarian church, on the corner of South Common and Church streets, on a day of intense cold and amid the buffetings of a raging snow storm. Mr. Keene married a daughter of Hon. Isaiah Breed, and by her had eight children, five of whom died in infancy. One daughter, Mary B., and two sons, William G. S. and Frank, survived him.

The act incorporating the Lynn " Home for Aged Women," was passed Feb. 6, the institution being " for the purpose of providing for the support of aged indigent females, not otherwise provided for." The institution was opened with a banquet and informal reception, on the evening of April 20, 1876, a large company assembling.

The Irish organizations of Essex county joined in a grand celebration of St. Patrick's day, March 17, in Lynn. The procession was long, and quite imposing — pronounced by some to be one of the three finest ever seen here, eight bands of music enlivening the long march, and the showy regalia and banners attracting much attention. A number of buildings were handsomely decorated. The weather, however, was very unfavorable.

A lady in Lynnfield gave birth to three children, at one time, in March, making up a family of four infants, under the age of thirteen months, and eight children, all under twelve years. The parents not being in very flourishing pecuniary circumstances, were deservedly the recipients of many useful gifts.

Comrade George S. Merrill was the orator on the Soldiers' Memorial day, May 30.

In the summer of this year, some workmen in digging a cellar on Pine street, in Swampscott, exhumed what were undoubtedly the remains of an Indian, probably of the ancient Naumkeag tribe. Their situation showed that the person was buried in a sitting posture. Other remains, supposed to be Indian, were found a short time afterward in the same vicinity. Aboriginal remains, as they undoubtedly were, were also dug up in Lynn, near the corner of Ocean and King streets.

The act incorporating the Flax Pond Water Company was passed June 2, being granted by the legislature for the purpose of supplying with pure water "the city of Lynn or any city or cities, town or towns." It enabled the corporators, their associates and successors, for the purpose named, to purchase and hold the waters of Flax, Sluice and Cedar ponds in Lynn, and Nell's pond, in Lynnfield, together with the tributary streams and a suitable width of land around to preserve the purity of the water, and such other lands as might be required for the necessary works.

Died, in Peabody, June 6, Oliver B. Coolidge, aged 76. He was for many years a resident of Lynn and an acting justice of the peace, in which capacity his services were much sought for, as his judgment and discretion were greatly relied on. For several years he was ticket-master at the Central rail-road station, for which position his patience and urbanity well qualified him. He was a native of Woburn, and seven years town clerk there, likewise representing the town in the General Court. One of the most notable points in his life was his association with Mr. Goodyear in his early attempts to vulcanize India rubber; and it was interesting to hear his details about the experiments on an old cooking stove, amid poverty and every sort of annoyance and discouragement.

The brick house of worship of the Washington Street Baptist Society, corner of Washington and Essex streets, was dedicated on Wednesday evening, June 10, the corner stone having been laid on the afternoon of Saturday, Oct. 5, 1872.

A comet, with what is popularly called a feather tail, was visible this year, in the northwest, being brightest about the middle of July.

Base-ball had, for the last few years become so popular a sport in different parts of the country as to be spoken of as the national game. Many of our active young men formed themselves into clubs and played match games with those from other places, some times from other states. Lynn Common was frequently the scene of these friendly contests, which called together crowds of spectators, before whom, in their often rather picturesque costumes, and repeatedly in the fervid heat of summer, they exhibited their skill and prowess. But this year a convenient ground for the games was enclosed on the south side of the old Turnpike, a short distance east of Saugus river.

Died, Sept. 2, John B. Wormstead, aged 85. He was a native of Marblehead, but long a resident of Lynn. In the war of 1812 he was a privateersman, and assisted in the capture of seven prizes. One of the vessels had a large amount of specie on board, designed for the payment of British troops, and while under convoy for an American port, Mr. Wormstead, being on guard over the prisoners, discovered a mutinous movement, just in time to prevent the disasters of a recapture.

The crew of the fishing schooner Laughing Water, of Swampscott, on the 11th of Sept. captured, off Boon island, a sword fish, weighing, when dressed, six hundred and ninety pounds.

John H. Smith, aged 23, driver of Empire steam fire engine No. 5, was killed on the evening of Sept. 18, by being run over by a hose carriage when starting at an alarm of fire. His head was crushed by one of the wheels. He was buried from the Washington Street Baptist Church, on Sunday, the entire fire department attending, and also one or two societies of which he was a member.

Wong Chin Foo, a native Chinese, lectured in Odd Fellows' Hall, on Sunday evening, Oct. 11, to a large audience. He appeared in native costume, and his subject was "Confusius, the Founder and Teacher of the Chinese Religion." He spoke good English, and his lecture, giving a very favorable account of his countrymen, was listened to with much interest. He considered the religion of Confusius more promotive of the good of the four hundred millions of people by whom it is embraced, than any other could be, if indeed it were not the best for the whole world. He endeavored to remove from the minds of his hearers the false belief that his was a nation wholly given to idolatry, and to impress upon them the fact that multitudes of profound scholars and philosophers were to be found there, that moral science was cultivated and virtuous living enforced.

During the last week of October the tides ran lower, as was calculated, than at any time for forty years. The cause was, partially at least, without doubt, the long-continued mild weather and off-shore winds.

A fire commenced in the furniture establishment of G. B. French, in Union street, on the night of Nov 9, destroying large portions of several stocks of goods. The premises were the same on which a fire occurred Aug. 25, 1873.

A mechanics' fair was opened in the building in Market street, adjoining Odd Fellows' Hall, and known as the Academy of Music, then just erected, Dec. 22. Many useful mechanical contrivances and interesting mechanical productions were exhibited by Lynn artisans and tradesmen, and by others from abroad. One rather peculiar feature was the introduction of dramatic entertainments during the evenings.

For two or three years, business affairs in Lynn were in a greatly depressed condition; indeed the same was true of almost every part of the country. There were quite a number of failures among the prominent shoe manufacturers, as well as among the smaller tradesmen and mechanics. Many operatives were out of employment for long intervals, and it was generally believed that some families of honest mechanics and laborers suffered, especially in winter, for what were commonly considered the necessaries of life. Real estate declined very much in value, rents fell, and many tenements were vacant. Yet the cost of most articles of family consumption remained high. The better kinds at least of bread stuffs and butcher's meat, sold at prices nearly as high as those of war time ; and the same may be said of articles of clothing. The whole history of the country shows that such seasons of depression follow seasons of great apparent thrift, or inflation, as perhaps they might in most instances be properly called, as surely as night follows day, mainly attributable, no doubt, to the extravagance induced by the prosperous intervals. Extravagance in dress, among women, was a notable feature of the time, and many a conscientious though possibly timid young man doubtless avoided a matrimonial connection from sheer apprehension that he would be unable to supply the demands upon his purse.

About this time there were a great many vagrant wayfarers, called Tramps, homeless wanderers, drifting from place to place, seeking food by day at the hand of charity, and at night lodging in police stations, poor-houses, or other similar retreats. During the winter of this year an average of something rising four hundred a month were thus entertained in the basement of the City Hall — provided with a supper and lodging, and a frugal breakfast to start on in the morning. Lynn enjoyed a good reputation among the fraternity, as appeared by a memorandum found on one of them, detailing his experience of the hospitalities of different places, and giving a sort of bill of fare by which they were entertained. The lodgings here were described in the memorandum as being warm, and the food better than in most cities ; facts which in a measure, no doubt, accounted for the favor of repeated visits from some of them. Occasionally rare characters appeared among the motley crews. One evening a hatless orator rose up and entertained the crowd of "brother tramps," as he called them, with an address containing many sensible as well as humorous points, and delivered in a style that showed he had been trained to a different course of life. An artist of more than common skill and taste also appeared one stormy night. Several off-hand sketches that he made were very spirited and attracted much attention. But the entertainment of the increasing numbers of this questionable class began to be intolerably burdensome in many places, and early in 1875 the legislature interposed to abate the nuisance, passing a law enabling cities and towns to

5

require all tramps to perform a reasonable amount of labor in return for food and lodging. This, together with the fact that our city authorities somewhat reduced their rations and assigned them less enjoyable lodging quarters had a tendency gradually to reduce the number who sought relief here, though it was some years before there was any really great decrease, as appears by the following showing for eight years : Number of tramps lodged in Lynn in 1871, 1.392. In 1872, 1.017. In 1873, 2.132. In 1874, 3.294. In 1875, 2.958. In 1876, 2.825. In 1877, 2.901. In 1878, 2.500.

Christmas was very generally observed this year ; indeed for many years the observance of the day has been gaining in popular favor, over the strange old puritanical prejudices. In 1856 it was made a legal holiday by legislative enactment. The festival of Easter, too, has come to be celebrated by most of our religious societies in a manner calculated to rejoice the hearts of all good churchmen, the floral decorations of the churches in some instances being superb.

A rather novel kind of recreative exercise was inaugurated during the winter of this year, in the form of spelling matches. Large classes of old and young, male and female, would meet in churches or other convenient places, with spelling masters and umpires and engage in orderly contests, each member, on missing a word ignominiously retiring, and those successfully passing the orthographic ordeal receiving prizes. These healthful memoriter exercises afforded much amusement, and were sometimes quite productive in a pecuniary way, an admission fee being usually required of spectators.

For many years, Fairs, as they were called, had been frequently held in public halls, church vestry rooms, and other convenient places, at which a great variety of the lighter articles of clothing, musical instruments, and all kinds of fancy articles, together with flowers and refreshments were disposed of for the benefit of some benevolent enterprise, in aid of church funds, or other worthy object. All the ordinary enticements of young lady solicitors, music, and occasionally a merry dance were resorted to. But seriously objectionable features by degrees crept in, till games of chance and lotteries so extensively prevailed that it became necessary to do something to prevent the many serious breaches of the law, and of fair and honest traffic. Most of the principal clergymen of the city during the winter of this year signed an earnest protest which was published in the newspapers, and for a time the more objectionable doings were discontinued ; but by degrees, as generally happens in such cases, similar evils, under other names, began to appear.

One thousand and thirty-eight dogs were licensed in Lynn this year.

1875.

Dedicatory exercises were held in Trinity (Methodist) Church, Tower Hill, Jan. 13, though the main body of the house remained uncompleted.

During the latter part of January, Eliza Ann, the nineteenth wife of the Mormon seer, Brigham Young lectured in Lynn on her "Life in Bondage." The peculiarities of the Mormon religion and the practice of polygamy as it existed in the Salt Lake Canaan were dwelt upon. The picture she drew was a sad one, both in its moral and social aspect. But why she should have accepted the nineteenth marital position and then claimed that all the wrong was on the other side did not seem to be satisfactorily explained.

On Sunday, Feb. 21, the eighty-fourth anniversary of the formation of the First Methodist Society of Lynn was observed. Appropriate services were held in the old Common street meeting-house, that being the first Methodist house of worship in New England.

A codfish of the extraordinary weight of ninety-six pounds was caught in the offing, March 30.

The Lynn Hospital was formally opened, March 31. The old Phillips mansion, on Waterhill street, the salubrious situation of which strongly recommended it, had been procured and fitted up in such a manner as to make it convenient for the purpose. A number of prominent citizens attended the opening and some made appropriate remarks.

The centennial celebration of the battle of Lexington took place on Monday, April 19, on the territory where the battle occurred. Mayor Lewis and several members of the city government attended, all, however, bearing their own expenses, the city council having refused to make any appropriation. The Lynn Light Infantry, accompanied by a full band, also attended, as well as a multitude of private citizens. President Grant and some other prominent officials from Washington were present. The day was pleasant, excepting the prevalence of a high, chilling wind. Such an immense concourse assembled that all the public conveyances were excessively crowded, and a great many were compelled to go hungry as the supply of provisions was altogether inadequate.

A demonstration was made in Lynn, May 22, in favor of the Boston Revere Beach and Lynn Rail-road, the first narrow-gauge line in this vicinity, which was then in process of construction. A considerable number of men, young and old, volunteered the work of half a day with shovels and picks. A procession was formed under the leadership of Col. John Nichols, one of the oldest men in town, and accompanied by a platoon of police officers and a couple of bands of music, moved through several streets, reaching the scene of their labor about the middle of the afternoon. After performing a small amount of work — the main purpose, no doubt, being rather to show good-will towards the enterprise, than to help much otherwise — they gathered, in number about a hundred and fifty, in a hall in Munroe street, and there partook of an entertainment, after which speeches were made and many good wishes towards the road and congratulations on its fair prospects were expressed.

The great travelling show, known as the hippodrome of P. T. Barnum, the most noted showman of the age, visited Lynn on Saturday, May 29. It is not probable that any exhibition of the kind ever exceeded this in attractiveness. The multitude of male and female performers and attendants, decked in unique and showy costumes, the numerous trained and wild animals, the historic and classic equipages and appendages, which appeared in the long procession that traversed the principal streets on the pleasant morning of their entrance, called forth throngs of spectators, old and young. The magnitude of this aggregation of circus, menagerie, and spectacle could warrant exhibition only in the cities and larger towns. The tents were pitched in the Fairchild field, so called, on Boston street, extending back to the vicinity of Lover's Leap, and the principal one was said to be sufficient to accommodate 12.000 persons. Great numbers attended, not only of our own people, but from other places. A special railroad train was run from Salem and Marblehead. During the afternoon a balloon was sent up, and after a short, successful trip, came down in Lynnfield.

Decoration day, May 30, was duly observed. Gen. A. F. Stevens, of Nashua, N. H., was the orator.

On the 17th of June, the great centennial celebration of the battle of Bunker Hill, took place in Boston. The Legislature had made it a legal holiday, the weather proved remarkably favorable, and there was an almost entire suspension of business in Lynn. Extra rail-road trains ran and multitudes visited the city to see the grand military and civic processional display. On the preceding night some famous bonfires were lighted here, the most conspicuous ones on High Rock and Reservoir Hill. The light of the illumination in Boston was distinctly seen in Lynn. This celebration, by the popular voice, both north and south, was pronounced to be more effectual than any other occurrence since the civil war, in reestablishing the old brotherly feeling between the different sections of the Union.

The corner stone of St. Joseph's (Roman Catholic) church, in Union street, was laid on Sunday, July 4.

The Boston Revere Beach and Lynn Rail-road was formally opened for travel on Thursday, July 22. After the directors and invited company had passed over the road, a collation was had at Odd Fellows' Hall, at the close of which speeches were made and congratulations interchanged. The regular hourly passenger trains commenced running July 29, on which day 1.075 passengers were conveyed. A few interesting Indian relics were found during the excavations.

The famous sea-serpent was alleged by several credible persons to have been seen by them, during August, not far from Egg Rock. He was described, so far as his form could be discerned, to be of glossy black, with some white on the under parts ; the head resembling that of a lizard, long, flat, and from twenty-four to thirty inches across ; the mouth large and occasionally widely opened ; the eyes large and staring. He sometimes raised up his head six or eight feet and then suddenly submerged it. Some accounts gave the appearance of a flipper or sort of foot, which strongly indicated some such animal as the supposed extinct ichthyosaurus or plesiosaurus. He was also alleged to have been seen again in the waters of Lynn and Swampscott in November. An account likewise appeared in the newspapers of a furious combat between a serpentine monster and a whale, as witnessed by the officers and crew of a vessel on the southern coast.

A General Convention of Universalists of the United States commenced a session in Lynn, on Wednesday, Oct. 20, and continued three days. The weather was favorable and the attendance large. Delegates were present from all parts of the country, one hundred and forty ministers constituting the clerical representation. Much christian courtesy was extended by people of all denominations. Among the speakers on the closing day of the session was a full-blooded Delaware Indian, an accredited missionary residing in Canada, with settlers of his tribe.

A blackfish, ten feet in length, and weighing three hundred and fifty pounds was found stranded on Long Beach, Nov. 2, having probably ventured too far towards the shore during the night.

1876.

This, the Centennial Year of the Republic, will be remembered for the fervor with which it was observed by all classes, and the magnificence of the displays, military, industrial, and indeed of every kind that enlivened patriotism could devise. Yet it was a year during which there was great business depression throughout the country. Had times been prosperous and means abundant it is quite possible Young America would have overleaped his proprieties. The most important enterprise, perhaps, that marked the year, was the World's Exposition, at Philadelphia, which continued open six months — from May 10 to November 10. Great crowds attended. "Excursion parties" were formed in all parts of the country, and hastened on to Philadelphia in a pleasant and economical way. The whole great undertaking was eminently successful, all the principal foreign countries heartily joining with splendid contributions. The Lynn exhibit, though not very large, was varied and satisfactory, pertaining almost exclusively to the shoe and leather interest. The specimens were much admired by visitors from all parts of the country and from abroad. Some twenty-five manufacturers had their goods displayed in an elegant case, over which was this announcement : " Lynn, Mass., greeting : The Shoemanufacturers of Lynn desire to open trade with foreign countries, and are ready at any time to receive orders from Cuba, South America, Mexico, West Indies, or any other market. We make the very finest and the cheapest shoes made in this country. We claim that our facilities, with our methods, organization and machinery, are not excelled for producing all grades of sewed shoes at the smallest possible cost. We make what is called for." Awards were made by the Exposition judges to several Lynn manufacturers.

The City Item, a weekly newspaper, was commenced on Saturday, January 8, by Horace N. Hastings.

A cat show, said to have been the first in the country, though not uncommon in Europe, was opened in Exchange Hall, Market street, Feb. 29, and proved to be quite interesting. A number of the feline specimens were really beautiful, some showed remarkable traits of sagacity and cunning, and others wonderful progress in training. The weight of the heaviest was fifteen and a half pounds. Prizes were awarded.

A grand exhibition of babies took place in Music Hall, Central avenue, March 4, including only those of three years old and under. Much interest was excited, and though arrangements were made for only fifty, the applications were more than a hundred. There was a great crowd of spectators, and prizes were awarded for the youngest, the fattest, and the handsomest babies. Among the latter was a sprightly little mulatto. On the 27th of the same month another similar exhibition took place in Odd Fellows' Hall, on Market street, at which seventy-two entries were made.

A violent storm — the " equinoctial " — which suddenly set in on the evening of March 20, did much damage. Three or four of the fishing jiggers were wrenched from their moorings and driven upon the shore or wrecked upon the rocks, at Swampscott. It was called as violent a storm as any within twenty years.

The beautiful summer residence of Charles W. Galloupe, at Swampscott, called Bay View Cottage, was totally destroyed by fire, April 2. Loss, between $50.000 and $60.000.

A hair seal, weighing ninety-five pounds, was taken off Swampscott, in April.

"Let us plant a Centennial Tree," was a greeting that this year was heard in all quarters, and heeded by many. On the afternoon of Saturday, May 13, a party assembled in the little square at the junction of Ash and South streets, for an object so indicated. They procured an elm, some thirty feet in height, and put it in position as the stirring tune of Yankee Doodle was being played. A large number were present, patriotic remarks made and songs sung. Several enthusiastic ladies assisted in shovelling in the earth. It became necessary, however, soon to substitute another, as the original tree began to wither.

May 30, Decoration Day, was duly observed. Gen. W. W. Blackmar, of Boston delivered the oration.

From the commencement of the shoe trade in Lynn, a good deal of the manufacturing was done at establishments on either side of the Common, but in June of this year the only remaining factory was removed, the tendency having been, ever since the building of the rail-roads, to concentrate in other quarters. The manufactory of James Purinton and Son, which stood on or very near the site of the old Academy, was the last to leave, being removed this year.

Dom Pedro, Emperor of Brazil, passed through Lynn, by the Eastern rail-road, on the evening of June 9. He did not leave the car, and but few had a glimpse of the royal party, during their short pause at the Central station.

That much-dreaded insect known as the Colorado beetle, or potato bug, first made its appearance here in the summer. It soon came to be a most destructive pest, descending or ascending in countless numbers and in a few hours making such havoc with whole potato fields, as to render it necessary to replant.

Probably not since the adoption of the constitution was the anniversary of the Declaration of Independence so generally celebrated throughout the country, as on this, the centennial year. In Lynn, however, there was no celebration under the auspices of the municipal authorities. Discordant views among the members of the council, and disagreements as to the suitable sum to be appropriated to meet the expenses, were the direct cause of the failure. But the patriotism of the people could not be suppressed, and the day was observed in various becoming ways. Before the morning dawn, bonfires blazed on several of the most commanding heights. There was a grand one on High Rock; but the most noticeable was on Reservoir Hill. The old two-story wooden house, on Boston street, at the south-west corner of North Federal, known as the Hart house, a part of which constituted the dwelling of Richard Haven, one of the very early settlers, and head of the great Haven family now spread all over the country, was, by the willing hands of Young America, and consent of the owner, torn down, a day or two

before, and the combustible part of the material transported to
the hill just named, and there reared in a pyramid some forty
feet in height. As soon as the midnight hour had struck, the
pile was lighted, and amid the shouts and cheers and songs of
the sleepless young spirits who kept vigil around the centennial
sacrifice, it disappeared in a glorious blaze. Morning dawned ;
and soon after daylight, there was a parade of the Antiques and
Horribles, as such have come to be called ; in other words, a
caricature display. The procession marched through the principal streets and afforded much amusement to the early risers by
the grotesque decorations and costumes, sarcastic hits, and ludi-
crous turn-outs ; some members of the city government who
were not in favor of an appropriation for celebrating the day,
being remembered in a manner that created considerable mirth.
A successful semi-religious celebration was held in the First
Methodist meeting-house, in the forenoon, under the general
direction of Rev. Charles D. Hills, minister of the society worshiping there. The principal feature of the exercises consisted
of brief addresses on the following topics and by the following
named persons : The Day We Celebrate, by ex-Mayor Thomas
P. Richardson ; The United States of America, by John B.
Alley, ex-member of Congress ; Christianity and Our Country,
by Rev. Daniel Steele ; The American Public Schools, by Nathaniel Hills, Principal of the High School ; The American Ju-
diciary, by Thomas B. Newhall, ex-Judge of the Police Court ;
Massachusetts, by George H. Chase, ex-Postmaster ; The Centennial History of Lynn, by James R. Newhall, Judge of the
Police Court ; Our Army and Navy, by Capt. George T. Newhall.
And Mrs. Abbie L. Harris was appointed to read the Declaration
of Independence. At evening, there were many fine displays of
fireworks, at private residences. The "Centennial Memorial,"
published soon after, by order of the City Council, contained an
Historical Sketch, by James R. Newhall, and brief Biographical
Notices of all the Mayors, with Portraits and other Illustrations.
It formed a volume of 204 octavo pages, and was issued in a
style perhaps as creditable to our printers and binders as any
book from the Lynn press up to that time. The volume was
prepared in compliance with a recommendation of Congress.

A serious fire occurred on the southwest side of Market street,
July 26. The principal losses were — by R. A. Spalding & Co.,
dealers in dry goods, some $5 000 ; Mrs. Lancey, millinery and
fancy goods, $2.000 ; W. T Bowers, photographer, $2.000.

July and August of this year were uncommonly hot. Visitors
at the World's Exposition, in Philadelphia, suffered much ; especially those from northern countries.

Died, December 17, at his residence in Park street, Jacob
Batchelder, for many years a well-known and much-respected

resident. He was born in Topsfield, July 10, 1806, graduated at Dartmouth college in 1830, and came to Lynn in 1835, commencing his labors here as principal of the Academy. In that position he continued till the establishment of the High School, in 1849, of which he became the first principal, and remained till 1856, in which year he went to Salem to take charge of the High School of that city. In 1861 he returned to Lynn, and took his former position in our High School, remaining, however, but about a year, and then closed his labors as a teacher, after pursuing the vocation for a little over a quarter of a century. In 1862 he was appointed librarian of the Lynn Free Public Library, and that office he continued acceptably to fill till the time of his death. He was Town Clerk in 1847, and collector of internal revenue several years. His remains were buried from the Unitarian church, on South Common street, where he had worshipped many years, and the funeral service was attended by a large number of the most venerable citizens. The lives of his two sons, Charles J. and George W., were lost in the war of the Rebellion, as noted under date 1862. Mr. Batchelder was a man of clear understanding, genial manners, and great industry, and should be long remembered as one who really did much for the advancement of the community in which he dwelt.

A splendid meteor passed over the city about six o'clock on the evening of December 20.

The fine brick fire engine house, in Federal street, was built this year.

1877.

The Lynn Home for Aged Women was dedicated February 15. It was the eligible building on North Common street, erected in 1832 for Nahant Bank, and had been fitted in a very comfortable manner for the reception of those who were to make it the home of their declining years.

The new and picturesque Town House in Saugus, centre village, was dedicated March 1. Wendell Phillips was chief orator, and all the exercises were appropriate and interesting. The corner stone was laid Oct. 17, 1874, ex-Governor Banks delivering an address on the occasion.

Died, March 13, at his residence on Western avenue, Charles Merritt, aged 72 years. He was born in Bowdoinham, Me., and was a son of Rev. Timothy Merritt, one of the early ministers of the Methodist itineracy. Almost the whole of his long life was spent in Lynn. He was a Deputy Sheriff for the county, about forty years, and performed the perplexing and often disagreeable duties of his office in a highly satisfactory manner. Before the adoption of the city form of government he held several of the most important municipal offices, including that of chairman of the Selectmen ; and after Lynn became a city, was called to continue in the public service — was an Alderman in the second year's board, and City Clerk five years. He was also a Representative in the General Court, and United States Revenue Assessor. For many years he was an honored member of the South street Methodist church, and always maintained an unblemished character. His wife was a daughter of William Breed, a father in the Quaker faith, and they reared a respectable family, eight sons and three daughters having been born to them. Few men, after so long and active a life go to their final rest more worthy of grateful remembrance.

The velocity of the wind in and about Lynn, during a storm, March 9, was seventy-two miles an hour.

The annual session of the New England Conference of the Methodist Episcopal Church, commenced in Lynn, in the old historic Common street Methodist meeting-house, April 4, and continued one week, Bishop Foster presiding. The first session of the Conference here was held in 1795, in an unfinished chapel which occupied the same site.

Sweetser's brick block, a substantial four-story building, at the junction of Central avenue and Oxford street, was burned on the morning of April 7. It was well fitted with machinery and other appliances for the prosecution of the shoe business, on a large scale, and there was considerable stock in the different lofts. The loss, including that of an adjacent three-story wooden building, amounted to some $115,000.

The last building on Market street occupied exclusively as a dwelling was removed in the spring of this year. It stood on the southwest side, between Tremont and Summer streets, and was first owned and occupied by Dr. Coffin.

Some excitement prevailed in the spring of this year regarding mad dogs, and continued many months. Two or three fatal cases of hydrophobia occurred. The city authorities ordered that no dogs should be permitted to go at large unmuzzled, and many canine lives were sacrificed. Samuel A. Parker, of Saugus, a worthy man, of middle age, died of hydrophobia, April 17, having been bitten by a rabid dog, January 15.

A marked religious revival took place in the various evangelical societies of Lynn, in the spring of this year, and many were added to the churches. At St. Joseph's (R. C.) meetings in charge of four Jesuit fathers, from Chicago, were held, commencing May 20, which excited much attention and were attended by crowds.

Captain Johnson, the intrepid fisherman who did his part in celebrating the centennial year by crossing the Atlantic in his little fishing dory "Centennial," exhibited his memorable craft in Munroe street, in April. He is said to have declared that a million of dollars would not tempt him to again undertake such a fool-hardy feat.

Died, in Oakland, Cal., May 2, John B. Felton, a native of Saugus, aged 48. While a young man he was a tutor in Harvard college, but settled in California and became a conspicuous lawyer. He was twice a Republican Presidential Elector, was Mayor of Oakland and a prominent candidate for the office of U. S. senator.

On the evening of May 28 there was an unusually brilliant display of aurora borealis. Many honest and observing persons declared that they could distinctly hear a rustling of the coruscations. Imagination, however, probably had something to do with the auricular demonstration. "It has often been asserted," says Mr. Payer, the late Austrian arctic explorer, "that sound accompanying the aurora has been heard in the Shetland Isles and in Siberia ; but all scientific travellers protest against this."

Memorial Day, May 30, was pleasant, and the usual services took place. Rev. Mr. Biddle, of the First Universalist society, was the orator.

An unsuccessful attempt was made in the Legislature of this year, by some of the business men of the east village of Saugus, to have their portion of the town united to Lynn.

During this year, the old belief that light, passing through blue glass, has wonderful power in developing life, both animal and vegetable, and in curing diseases of almost every kind, was revived, and extensively prevailed. Many dwellings had a few blue panes set in the windows, and greenhouses were liberally supplied with the supposed life-giving appliances. The idea was started, at this time, by General Pleasanton, of Philadelphia, and seems to have been, that the electro-magnetism produced by the sun's rays passing through that medium, receives some mysterious and extraordinary power. While the excitement continued, the glaziers in Lynn, as elsewhere, had an abundance of orders. Ladies wore blue veils, and cerulean tints were decidedly in the ascendant.

On the evening of July 1, a severe thunder storm passed over the city. Between nine and ten o'clock a terrific peal startled the dwellers in the western section and a bolt struck the dwelling of J. M. Tarbox, at the junction of Myrtle and Walnut streets. Its instantaneous work was strange and destructive, the interior walls being torn and pierced, and the furniture broken and thrown about in the most extraordinary manner. No person, however, was injured further than suffering a temporary shock, all the inmates being in bed. And herein appears additional evidence that the recumbent position, especially if a little elevated, is the safest, on such occasions. From the peculiar appearance of what looked like real " witch-work " about the house, it seemed not unreasonable to conclude that the bolt had an upward course. The house of Mr. Tarbox is within a stone's throw of the rock which was struck in 1807, a portion weighing some twelve tons being thrown two hundred feet.

The first boy church choir in Lynn, was organized this year, in St. Stephen's, and commenced taking their part in the public services, in the summer. Boy choirs, though comparatively new in this country, are an ancient church institution. In the history of St. Margaret's of King's Lynn, England, mention is made of the choir boys as early as 1478, a bequest or two having been made for their teaching and maintenance.

The British Consular Agency at Lynn, was this year discontinued, the insignificance of British trade here not warranting its continuance.

A rattlesnake, fourteen years old, as the number of rattles showed, was killed in Lynn woods, July 5. And on Aug. 4, a huge one swam across Lily pond, Boston street, and as he glided into the yard of John M. Newhall, was killed by a son of Mr. N., a lad of 14 years. This reptile was between four and five feet in length, and some two years older than his courageous destroyer.

For some ten days, in September, at night, the waves dashing along our shores, exhibited an extraordinary phosphorescent glow. The spectacle was grand, strong easterly winds bringing in heavy seas.

On the fifth of October, at about one o'clock in the afternoon, Alderman Aza A. Breed, of Lynn, was attacked by two ruffians, in Belcher lane, Boston, knocked down, and robbed of the large sum of $8.000. A light carriage with a man in it stood near the scene of the assault, and the robbers, after securing their booty, jumped in, and the three rode off. Mr. Breed gave chase, and was fired on from the carriage, three times, one of the pistol shots taking effect in his hand. The robbers escaped. The money belonged to the Central National Bank, and was in Mr. Breed's care, for delivery in Boston. A question as to whether Mr. Breed or the bank should bear the loss arose; but a settlement was made, the bank agreeing to sustain the principal share.

1878.

At the beginning of this year rather serious labor troubles existed in several of the large manufactories. Disagreements between workmen and their employers, in the matter of wages, were the cause of the difficulties, but mutual concession and temperate negotiation finally resulted in satisfactory adjustments.

The new bell on the First Congregational meeting-house, on South Common street, corner of Vine, was raised to its place, March 28. It may be interesting to mention that the bell which was raised on the Old Tunnel, in 1816, and the one which at the same time was raised on the Common street Methodist house, were cast at the old Paul Revere foundry, and that the present one was turned out by Revere's successors in that historic establishment. When the Old Tunnel was removed from the centre of the Common, in 1827, and wrought into the house now on the corner of Commercial street, the bell went with it, and remained in the modest belfry till it was taken down, this year, and recast, the city paying for the recasting, in consideration of its having for more than sixty years faithfully marked the hours of twelve at noon and nine at night, as well as having rung out its fire alarms and jubilant peals, besides attending to its other duties of calling together worshipping congregations and announcing the bearing away of the dead for burial. Its Methodist coadjutor still survives and sends forth its sonorous calls from the steeple of the new brick edifice in Park square.

A singular custom has for many years prevailed in Lynn, the origin of which it is hard to determine, namely the blowing of tin horns, by the youth, on May-day. From dawn till night, in all directions, these discordant instruments may be heard ; but especially are morning slumbers disturbed.

The services on Memorial Day, May 30, were interesting, though the inclemency of the weather somewhat disarranged the proceedings. Rev. C. D. Hills, of the Common street Methodist society delivered the address.

On the 12th of June, twelve gentlemen, mostly quite aged, and all lovers of old-time customs, set out from Newburyport to enjoy a ride to Boston in the old-fashion four horse stage coach of their boyhood. The driver was a veteran of the road, and eighty-one years of age. The start was propitious and the ride enjoyable, till they reached Lynn, when, near the junction of Western avenue and Washington street, an axle broke and the stage was overturned. Two or three of the passengers were seriously injured, and the aged driver received a severe shock to his system besides painful bruises.

On the fourth of July there was a successful balloon ascension from Park square, Alderman Aza A. Breed, City Marshal Charles C. Fry and Frederick Smith, a Boston newspaper reporter, accompanying the æronaut. A landing was made at Hamilton, in this county. There was to have been a display of fireworks on the evening of the day in question, but a singular accident prevented. They had been loaded at the laboratory, preparatory to transportation hither, but by means of fire or friction, they went off in one general explosion. Others, however, were prepared, and on the evening of the 18th a successful exhibition took place.

Dennis Kearney, a radical agitator and "sand-lot orator," so called, from California, addressed a large collection of people, on the Common, on the evening of August 12. He was coarse and intemperate in his language, and fitted to make little impression on intelligent minds. He was escorted from Sagamore hotel, on Union street, by a large procession of working men, and a band of music.

Thursday, August 10, was a bright day, and a memorable one for the people of the east village of Saugus, it being that on which the public water was introduced from the reservoir of Lynn. A public celebration was held, with music, speeches, processional displays, illuminations and fireworks. Among the most interesting features were the performances of a detachment of the Lynn Fire Department, with their steam engine, hose, and ladders — demonstrating to the good people the value of their new acquisition.

The Lynn Light Infantry had a 'veteran parade" and banquet on the 11th of October, which had probably never been exceeded in interest since the organization of the old company, in 1812, and elicited much commendation as a genuine and hearty civil-military demonstration. The procession included a number of prominent citizens and military persons from abroad. The march was long, and so interrupted at different points by the acceptance of invitations to pause and partake of refreshments that it was after dark when Exchange hall, in which the banquet was prepared, was reached. After the gastronomic duties had been attended to, music, toasts, and speeches were in order, the latter abounding in cheery hits and entertaining reminiscences.

The brick fire engine house in Broad street was built this year. And the iron railing was placed around the Park.

It may be mentioned as a singular fact among the curiosities of temperature, that at midnight, Dec. 2, the thermometer ran higher in Lynn and vicinity than in any other part of the whole country — six degrees higher than in New Orleans, La., seven higher than in Savannah, Geo. and St. Louis, Mo., nine higher than in Charleston, S. C., and ten higher than in Jacksonville, Florida.

On the 17th of December, for the first time in sixteen years, gold stood at par ; that is, $100 in gold were worth just $100 in greenback government notes. The extreme of variation was in July, 1864, when $100 in gold were worth $285 in bank bills. The difference in the relative values then began to decrease. In 1870 it averaged 114.9, in 1877, 104.7.

1879.

Some 30.000 tons of ice, of remarkably good quality, were cut on Flax pond during the cold season of 1878 and '79.

On the afternoon of February 27, an old trunk was discovered on the margin of Saugus river, near Fox Hill bridge, containing the mutilated remains of a young woman. The nose had been severed, among other evident attempts to prevent identification. A great deal of excitement soon prevailed, and the newspapers, far and near, teemed with sensational articles. Hundreds came, many from distant places, to view the remains, some hoping to identify them, but the greater number probably from morbid curiosity. Untiring efforts were made by the police and others to solve the tragic mystery, and it was finally determined that the remains were those of a young woman of the name of Jennie P. Clarke, whose death was occasioned by the mal-practice of parties in Boston. Miss Clarke was a native of Milton, Mass., but at the time of her death was a resident of Boston Highlands, and would have been twenty years of age the very day on which her lifeless body was found. The illegal practice which resulted in her death took place in Lagrange street, Boston, and the offenders were tried in the superior court of Suffolk county. Caroline C. Goodrich was convicted as principal, and received a sentence of ten years in the house of correction, and Dr. Daniel F. Kimball, as accessory after the fact, was sentenced to six years in the state prison. The body was buried from the First Universalist meeting-house, in Nahant street.

The brick house of worship of the Common street Methodist society, on Park square, was dedicated on Thursday, February 27, Bishop Foster preaching the sermon.

Died, at his residence on Boston street, March 29, Henry Moore, aged 52, a native of Brighton. He was a graduate of Amherst college, and principal of the Cobbet grammar school, some twenty-four years ; was a faithful and highly esteemed teacher as well as citizen.

Memorial Day, May 30, was observed in the usual manner, the address being delivered by Comrade W. G. Veazie, of Rutland, Vt.

The most notable occurrence this year was the celebration of the Two Hundred and Fiftieth Anniversary of the Settlement of Lynn — [1629-1879] — which took place on the 17th of June. The day was very pleasant and the temperature agreeable. There was a grand procession, an oration by Cyrus M. Tracy, and other appropriate exercises at Music Hall, and a banquet at Odd Fellows' Hall, followed by toasts, addresses, and music. Several friendly and highly interesting communications from prominent officials and others of King's Lynn, England, were read by George H. Chase. Attractive performances and out-door sports, of various kinds, designed to suit different tastes, were held in several localities, and in the evening a grand display of fireworks took place on the Common. A neat volume of 224 octavo pages, was printed by order of the City Council, containing a full account of the proceedings, with an Introduction and a Second

Part, by James R. Newhall, embracing historical, topographical,
statistical and other matter relating to Lynn. It not being
certain on what particular day of June the settlement commenced — nor indeed certain beyond a doubt that it was in
June — after some discussion the City Council fixed on the historic 17th, as the proper day for the observance, and in April
appointed a committee to have general supervision of the proceedings. This committee consisted of Mayor George P. Sanderson, Aldermen N. D. C. Breed, and Nathan A. Ramsdell, and
Common Councilmen, President Charles E. Kimball, Charles E.
Harwood, Josiah F. Kimball, and Alfred P. Flint. This committee decided to invite the cooperation of the citizens ; and the
Mayor, on the 30th of April, issued an invitation to the citizens
generally to assemble in their several ward rooms, on the 5th
of May, to select five persons from each ward, to act with them.
The ward meetings were accordingly held, and the following
individuals selected : Ward 1. John L. Shorey, William Lummus,
Breed Bacheller, John R. Jordan, George W. Vincent. Ward 2.
Oliver Ramsdell, William H. Rood, Sylvester H. Mansfield, John
Marlor, C. H. Ramsdell. Ward 3. Amos F. Breed, J. Frank
Lamphier, Ebenezer Beckford, Jacob M. Lewis, William B. Phil-
lips. Ward 4. George T. Newhall, A. B. Martin, James N.
Richardson, W. A. Clark, jr., L. A. May. Ward 5. T. P. Rich-
ardson, Otis L. Baldwin, S. M. Bubier, N. M. Hawkes, George
C. Neal. Ward 6. Gardiner Tufts, James W. Switzer, Wallace
Bates, Frank J. Douglass, William Snell. Ward 7. William
Shepard, Richard C. Lawrie, William F. Brackett, jr., Alonzo
Penney, John Dougherty. The City Council appropriated $3.000
to defray the expenses of the celebration, and liberal individual
contributions aided in various ways. Of the city appropriation,
$750 were devoted to the juvenile part of the procession, $525
to music, $350 to fireworks, $150 to the rowing regatta, $100 to
the antiques and horribles, $50 to dory and tub race, $10 to
bicycle race. The balance was absorbed by carriage hire, the
banquet, and various incidental expenses.

Rollin E. Harmon succeeded in office James R. Newhall,
whose resignation as Judge of the Lynn Police Court took effect
Aug. 24. The business of the court had a steady increase, as
population increased, from the time of its establishment, in 1849.
The earlier records having been destroyed, at the burning of the
old Town House, Oct. 6, 1864, no exact statement can be made
as to the business during the earlier years. But in the thirteen
years during which the now retiring justice presided, namely,
1866 to 1879, the number of cases disposed of was twenty thousand, one hundred and twelve — criminal, 12.971, civil, 7.141 —
exclusive of a large number coming under the juvenile jurisdiction
and poor debtor laws. The entire term of the retiring justice, in

the court, was thirty years — seventeen as special and thirteen as standing justice.

John A. Jackson, the designer of the Soldiers' Monument, in Park square, died in Florence, Italy, in August, aged 54 years. He was a native of Bath, Me.

On Tuesday and Wednesday, Sept. 30 and Oct. 1, the annual exhibition of the Essex Agricultural Society was held in Lynn, for the first time since 1848. It was the society's sixty-first yearly exhibition. Hon. George B. Loring, of Salem, delivered the address, in the Central church, and dinner was served in Odd Fellows' Hall. The weather was pleasant but very warm, and there was a large attendance. The receipts were found to be $1.937.50, and the net profits $659.37.

St. Joseph's (Catholic) Cemetery, was consecrated, Oct. 16, Archbishop Williams conducting the ceremonies.

The newly-invented telephone came into use in Lynn, this year, especially for business purposes.

Sherry's building, in Munroe street, was built this year, and was the first full six-story brick building erected here.

Anthony Hatch, aged 67, a farmer of Cliftondale, Saugus, died Nov. 19, from injuries received from an infuriated bull which he was driving to pasture, on the Sunday previous.

Benjamin F. Mudge, died on Friday evening, Nov. 21, at his residence in Manhattan, Kansas, aged 62. He was born in Or-rington, Me., but at an early age came to Lynn ; was our second Mayor, having been inaugurated June 16, 1852. He had made a brief visit here within a few months of the time of his death, receiving the cordial greetings of many old friends ; and while here delivered one or two very acceptable lectures on scientific subjects. A biographical sketch appears in our "Centennial Memorial," of 1876.

The extraordinary occurrence of a clear sky, all over the United States, from the Atlantic to the Pacific, happened Nov. 24, as reported by the U. S. Signal Corps.

A flock of wild geese, estimated to be half a mile in length, and flying very low, passed over Dungeon rock, Dec. 2.

The length of pipes for the conveyance of the public water, in Lynn, was this year fifty-three miles, and the average daily con-sumption of the water was 1.268.000 gallons.

The number of streets in Lynn, this year, was 480, measuring, in the aggregate, some 125 miles. The increase in the number, in ten years, was 125 ; in twenty years, 208.

This year, after a long season — some seven years — of busi-ness depression, affairs began to assume a much more cheering aspect. Business of all kinds, in all parts of the country, began to revive, and every thing to look promising. Lynn had her full share of depression, and was among the first to feel the rising

6

tide of prosperity. Under date 1874 appear some remarks concerning the then state of things.

From the following statements an idea may be had of the provision for the poor. During the year, 523 families received assistance from the public treasury, the number of individuals being 1.992. The average number of paupers in the almshouse was 52, and the cost of each, per week, for food and clothing, was $1.35. The number of tramps furnished with food and lodging, was 1.757, the average cost of each being 14 cents. Some account of the latter class may be found under date 1874.

The number of volumes in the Free Public Library, at the close of this year, was 27.804. The average daily delivery during the year was 461 volumes.

The appropriation for the free education of the youth of Lynn, for 1879, was $83.000, which, with certain receipts, brought the whole amount devoted to school purposes up to the generous sum of $86.816.88. The number of schools was as follows : 1 high school, 7 grammar and 55 primary schools, and 1 evening drawing school. Whole number of pupils in all the day schools, on the first of May, 5.413. Average daily attendance of pupils in all the day schools, 4.667. The expenditure for school purposes, for each inhabitant of the city between the ages of five and fifteen years, was $15.66.

As noted under date 1864, the first steam fire-engine procured for the city, arrived that year. And now, 1879, we have four of those efficient machines, and the fire department is, in other respects, well equipped. It has more than twelve thousand feet of hose, and there are distributed about the city, some four hundred hydrants, twenty capacious reservoirs, and a number of public wells. The department is also provided with one large four-wheel double tank chemical fire-extinguisher and seven hand extinguishers. In former years Lynn has been, emphatically, what is termed a wooden town, almost every building being of wood ; and had it not been for the fact that there was no really compact part, serious conflagrations would probably have occurred. Lately, numerous capacious brick structures have been erected, and as land increased in value, some of the business streets have become as compact as those of any city. It can hardly be expected that in the future we shall be as free from disasters by fire as we have been in the past ; yet, with the improved facilities for grappling with the flames, and the improved modes in the construction, heating, and lighting of buildings, there is reasonable ground for hoping that our good fortune may continue. The telegraphic fire-alarm, which was established in 1871, has proved extremely beneficial, saving an immense amount of confusion and delay on the occurrence of a fire.

Speaking of the later style of building, and the more compact

character of some of our streets, leads to the remark that the
great change in the mode of manufacturing shoes has been the
principal cause of this, at least so far as relates to buildings
erected for business purposes. It is quite within the recollection
of our middle-aged people — as the writer had occasion to remark
in the little book giving an account of the proceedings on our two
hundred and fiftieth anniversary — that shoes were made by hand,
not by machinery. The shoes were cut in the manufacturer's shop,
which was generally a small wooden structure, and thence taken
by the workman to his own premises, made up, and returned.
A great many, however, were carried by express-drivers to country towns, to Maine, New Hampshire and Vermont, and there
made up, by workmen whose regular occupation was, perhaps,
farming, but who resorted to the shoemaker's seat in winter
and other unoccupied times. The work of some of these un-
skilled operators was very poor and occasioned much complaint
and annoyance ; but still a great deal of work went out of town,
and a great deal of money went to pay for it. But the introduction of machinery wrought a great change. Large factories,
often of brick, began to supplant the small cutting shops, and
the little work shops of the journeymen began to disappear.
The new factories were built in a thorough and substantial
manner, as the ponderous machinery required ; some were tastily
ornamented, and remain really fine specimens of architecture.
To the factory it was now necessary that the workman should
go to perform his labor. The work of making a shoe was divided
among several, each having his particular part to do ; and the
labor of all became so interlinked, that each depended much on
the skill and promptness of the others for his own success.
Rules were necessarily established for the guidance of all ; regular hours of labor, especially, being required ; and efforts were
made to place the whole business on a permanent basis. And
so the business continues, every day developing fresh energies
and evidences of thrift. New factories are constantly rising, and
though there is some abridgment of the old-time freedom of the
workman as he whistled over his work in his rude little shop,
he yet gains by the comfort, order, and sometimes forced industry of the factory.

The number of deaths in Lynn, during the year, was 680,
which, taking the increase of population into view, was about
the usual rate of past years. The most fatal disease was consumption, by which 120 died. The next most fatal was diphtheria, by which 65 died. Consumption was the most fatal among
adults, diphtheria among children. In 1876 there were 121
deaths by diphtheria.

The number of marriages during the year was 429. And the
number of births, 717.

With the year 1879 it was at first thought advisable to close
our Annals, the first two hundred and fifty years of our municipal
existence being then completed.   Yet it seemed as if that reason
was hardly sufficient to refuse space for the occurrences of one
or two additional years that would elapse before the volume could
be presented to the public.   It was therefore concluded to proceed till a time nearer that of publication.

1 8 8 0 .

A generous sum was contributed in Lynn, early this year, for
the suffering poor in Ireland, our Irish residents being especially
liberal.

The winter of 1879 and '80 was uncommonly mild, so far as
temperature was concerned.   Far less ice than usual was cut on
the ponds, and in consequence, the price during the succeeding
summer was much higher than during any late preceding year.
Yet the number of snow storms was above the average, there
being thirty-four in number, and the aggregate depth of snow
five feet and three and a half inches.

Edwin Marble, who succeeded his father Hiram Marble in
the strange search for treasure in Dungeon Rock, as spoken
of under date 1658, died January 16, aged 48 years, leaving a
widow but no children.   He had been out of health many months,
occasioned, no doubt, by his persistent labors in the dark, damp
cavern, though the immediate cause of his death was paralysis.
He was a man of good character and agreeable disposition, a
firm believer in spiritual manifestations, and a patient laborer
under supposed supernatural direction.   He was buried near the
foot of the rock, on the southwestern slope, it having been his
expressed desire to be interred near the scene of his hopeful
though fruitless labors.   A considerable number of friends, perhaps fifty, most of them of the spiritualistic faith, were present
at the burial service, which was simple and affecting ; and held
there, deep in the forest, amid the winter scenery, was peculiarly
touching.   At the close, the hymn " In the Sweet By and By,"
was sung.

May 29 was observed as Memorial Day, the 30th falling on
Sunday.   The address was delivered by Col. T. W. Higginson.

On the evening of Wednesday, June 2, " Summit Villa," the
fine mansion on the Galloupe estate, in Swampscott, was entirely
destroyed by fire, with most of its contents, the loss, in the
aggregate reaching about $15.000.   It was rented to Commodore
Hutchins, of New York, for $3.000 for the summer.

James McMahon, aged 50 years, a resident of Blossom street,
was alleged to have been bitten on the arm, by a black spider,

June 29. Deeming it a trivial matter, he made no application, till, on the second day, it became swollen and excessively painful. Medical aid was sought, but the progress of the poison could not be arrested, and three days after receiving the bite he died. It should be remarked that this is given as reported at the time ; but good authorities declare that no spider bite can cause death or even much pain. In the physician's return the cause of Mr. McMahon's death is stated to have been malignant erysipelas.

By the summer arrangement of the Eastern rail-road, this year, there were one hundred and twenty-four regular passenger and freight trains entering and leaving Lynn, each week day. Besides these, there were thirty-eight out and in trains on the Boston, Revere Beach and Lynn steam rail-road, and the hourly cars of the Lynn and Boston horse rail-road.

Ex-Mayor Hiram N. Breed and his wife Nancy Stone Breed, on the 3d of July, the 4th falling on Sunday, celebrated the "golden" anniversary of their marriage, they having been united on the 4th of July, 1830. There was a large and cheery gathering of descendants and other relatives and friends, a number of city officials, and six ex-mayors.

Independence was celebrated on Monday, July 5, in a moderate way. Explosives, as usual, made their demonstrations, early and late, bells were rung, and out-door sports engaged in. In the evening there was a successful display of fireworks, to witness which it was estimated full 10.000 persons assembled.

Adam Hawkes was among the first settlers of Lynn, as we find him here as early as 1630, located in what is still known as the Hawkes neighborhood. He had five sons, and many descendants remain, scattered all over the country, and adorning various professions and callings. Several are yet found in the vicinity of the early family home, and among them Louis P. Hawkes who occupies a part of the original farm, in what is now known as North Saugus. And there, on the 28th and 29th of July, of this year, gathered from various quarters, distant and near, an interesting company of representatives of the family, to the number of about three hundred and fifty. They met with cordial greetings and brotherly sympathies ; and the weather proving favorable, the most agreeable anticipations were realized, all the exercises and entertainments, literary, social, athletic and gastronomic, giving much satisfaction. Hon. Nathan M. Hawkes, of Lynn, was master of ceremonies.

Died, in Saugus, July 30, George W. Phillips, aged 70. He was a native of Boston, a brother of Wendell Phillips the "silver tongued" orator, and a graduate of Harvard college, with the 1829 class. He was a good lawyer and long in large practice, interested in town affairs, but steadily declining to hold office. For some years he was a partner of Franklin Dexter, and managed many important cases. During the last thirty years he was a resident of Saugus, was thrice married, and his last wife survived him. His death was very sudden. Returning from Boston early in the afternoon, and seeing his men pitching hay, he said, pleasantly, "Boys, would n't you like to have me up there with you?" He mounted the hay-rigging, and was presently observed to totter and fall, death almost instantly following. The funeral services were held in Saugus, Rev. James Freeman Clarke, Dr. Oliver W. Holmes, and one or two others of his Harvard classmates being present and making remarks.

A fire commenced on the morning of August 6, in the three story wooden building numbered 2 and 4, Central avenue, owned by S. P. Miles, and resulted in the loss of property to the amount of about $2.500, largely in stock.

On the afternoon of Wednesday, August 11, a meeting of the wardens and vestry of St. Stephen's Church was held for the formal reception of the stone from the ancient walls of St. Margaret's Church, in Lynn Regis, England, which had been sent with its friendly inscription by the authorities of that venerable shrine, to be incorporated in St. Stephen's Memorial Church, then in process of erection on South Common street. Resolutions were passed warmly acknowledging the courtesy of the brethren of St. Margaret's.

Sunday night, August 22, was one of the most beautiful conceivable. The full moon rose between seven and eight o'clock and pursued a cloudless course through a sparkling sky. The air was soft, the westerly breeze very light, and the woody hills, rocky shores, and quiet sea defined with marvellous clearness. But this record would be common-place were it not for the additional and uncommon fact that at midnight, as on the 24th of November, 1879, the weather was clear throughout the whole United States, though there were considerable variations of temperature. In this vicinity the thermometer stood at about 70° ; but proceeding southerly, it grew warmer. At Savannah, Geo., it reached 82 degrees.

Tubular wells having been sunk by the city authorities on the south side of Boston street, between Cottage and Bridge, in the hope of obtaining large quantities of pure water, for public use, pumping from them into the Pine Hill reservoir commenced on the 4th of September. One effect, soon felt, was the draining of wells on estates more than half a mile distant. In the first forty-five hours that the pump was in motion 1.250.000 gallons were drawn.

The cattle show and fair of the Essex Agricultural Society was again held in Lynn, on Tuesday and Wednesday, September 28 and 29. There was a large attendance and highly satisfactory exhibition. Lieut. Col. D. W. Lowe delivered the address.

The entire fire department had a parade, Oct. 20. The display
was very fine and to the participants an occasion of much
enjoyment. At the close of the march dinner was served in Odd
Fellows' Hall.

In the autumn of this year a great sensation was produced in
political circles all over the United States, by the appearance, in
a New York paper, of a letter purporting to have been written
by General Garfield, the Republican candidate for the presidency,
and addressed to " Henry L. Morey," of the " Employers' Union,"
of Lynn. It was in the interest of cheap labor, and in pursuance
of the purpose, favored Chinese immigration. The Pacific coast
people, especially, became highly indignant at the drift of the
letter, and the name of Morey and of Lynn were heard in every
quarter. But the letter was soon proved to be a base forgery,
concocted to damage the prospects of General Garfield ; and it
would, without doubt, have had a serious effect, had not timely
evidence of the unpardonable fraud been discovered. It was
satisfactorily shown that no such person as Henry L. Morey and
no such association as the Employers' Union existed in Lynn.

Early in the forenoon of Oct. 28, a fire occurred on the south
side of Broad street, near the foot of Market, which destroyed
the steam planing mill of James N. Buffum and Company, together with several neighboring buildings, the entire loss being
some $93.500.

Soon after the burning of the planing mill, as above noted, it
was concluded to rebuild on a site some six or seven hundred
feet southward. The great brick chimney, nine feet square at
the base, and ninety feet high, had been left standing in solitary
grandeur, and was removed, in its erect position, without accident,
by the skillful management of Boston contractors.

On the 22d of November a beautiful mirage appeared in the
bay.

The district of Lynn, Nahant, and Swampscott, returned, as
the product of their fisheries for the quarter ending Dec. 3, as
follows : codfish, cured, 300.000 lbs ; mackerel, 400.000 lbs. ; her-
ring, salted, 100.000 lbs. ; lobsters, 7.000 lbs. ; fresh fish, daily
catch, 315.000 lbs. ; fish oil, 3.200 galls. Total value, $44.141.50.

A rather singular, though not serious, accident happened to
ex-Mayor Buffum on an evening in December. He was in the
store of Mr. Barton, on Market street the door of which was
composed of a single plate of glass. Observing his horse, which
had been left standing in the street, suddenly start, Mr. B. hastily
and without realizing that the door was not open, but transparent,
dashed through, causing one or two uncomfortable cuts upon his
face and other parts of his head.

The United States census, taken this year, gave Lynn a population of 38.284. 18.255 males, 20.029 females.

1881.

The Young Men's Christian Association Building, on the corner of Market and Liberty streets, was dedicated on Monday afternoon, January 17. There was a large attendance, and among the notables was Governor Long, who delivered a short address. The cost of the building was a little rising $57,000. The corner stone was laid on Thursday, April 8, 1880, the principal address on that occasion being by Russell Sturgis of Boston.

On the morning of Wednesday, January 19, a fire occurred on the westerly side of Market street, near Broad, destroying property to the amount of $155,500. Augustus B. Martin and Co., morocco manufacturers, C. B Lancaster and Co., shoe manufacturers, and Skinner and Golder, were the principal losers. For a time there was danger of a more extensive conflagration, and assistance in arresting the flames was received from Salem and Marblehead.

A fire took place on Sunday morning, January 30, in the carriage manufactory of E. J. Leslie, on Boston street, near Myrtle, by which property to the amount of $3,500 was destroyed.

Dr. Daniel Perley died at his residence in Breed street, January 31, at the age of 77, leaving a widow, two sons and a daughter. He commenced practice here in 1836, and became highly esteemed as a physician and citizen. He was a native of Boxford, Mass.

The government weather signals, on High Rock, were shown for the first time, February 23.

A fire commenced in the rubber factory of Melcher and Spinney, in Broad street, near Market, March 31. The flames spread so rapidly that one of the workmen to save his life was obliged to jump from a second-story window. Total loss on building and stock, about $3,700.

On the night of May 2, a fire occurred in the morocco factory of Henry Beyer, rear of Spring street, doing damage to the amount of $3,400.

The pond on the Common was this year stocked with gold fish from Gold Fish pond.

The address before the General Lander Post No. 5, of the Grand Army of the Republic, the City Government and others, was delivered in Music Hall, on the evening of May 31, by Gen. James Carnahan of Indiana. It was postponed from the preceding evening on account of a violent thunder storm. Memorial Day, May 30, was this year made a legal holiday by the legislature.

Mr. Eugene F. Forman, editor and proprietor of the Lynn Daily Bee and Weekly Reporter, came to his death by a strange and terrible accident, at the Sagamore hotel, in Union street, where he boarded, at about one o'clock on the morning of September 3. He was at the open window of his room in the fourth story, and by some means lost his balance and fell a distance of about forty feet, to the street pavement, in his descent striking upon an iron railing attached to the basement of the building. He survived, at times suffering great pain, till about six o'clock in the evening. He was a young man of more than ordinary promise in the journalistic profession, of good education, and seemed destined to make an enduring mark in the community. He was born in Nantucket, on the 16th of February, 1852, and was unmarried. The several printing offices in the city were closed, in respect to his memory, at the hour of his funeral.

On the 6th of September, soon after sunrise, the atmosphere began to assume a yellowish hue — brassy, as the phrase employed generally was when speaking of it — and by the middle of the forenoon, there was a very unnatural appearance. People began to wonder what was coming. At noon the obscuration was so great that artificial light was needed for most in-door employments. The blaze of a lamp was no less noticeable than the other phenomena, for it was strangely brilliant and remarkably white. The greatest darkness was at about three in the afternoon. At that hour it was difficult to read common print by the daylight; the faces of people were of a light saffron hue; blues were changed to green; the grass and foliage had a beautiful golden tinge; and every thing wore a sort of weird aspect. Domestic animals and fowls seemed to notice that something unusual was going on, but manifested no alarm. The day was close and warm, and the smell of smoke very perceptible. The wind was southwesterly but very light. Towards night a gentle westerly breeze sprang up, and before sunset nature had assumed her wonted condition. Several theories were proposed to account for this "yellow Tuesday," as it came to be called; but there seems to be little doubt that it was occasioned by smoke arising from fires in the woods, some of which were perhaps as far off as Canada. The writer very well remembers that when he was a small boy, probably in 1817 or 1818, he was surprised on going out one Sunday morning to see how yellow everything looked, and called the attention of the family to the appearance. But by "meeting time" the strange hue had nearly passed off. Like a good boy he was drawn by the sound of the bell to the venerable Old Tunnel, and clearly recollects hearing a knot of men at the door commenting on the "brassy" appearance of the morning; and one of them remarked that it looked just as it did on the morning of the great dark day of 1780.

On the night of September 12, between eight and nine o'clock, there was a singularly beautiful appearance in the heavens. A band of dense mist skirted along the horizon, but above, the sky was clear and the stars bright. Suddenly there appeared what may not inaptly be compared to two immense comets, one at the southeastern and the other at the northwestern horizon, sending up their broad and sharply defined tails, to meet at the zenith. The arch, if such it may be called, formed a striking spectacle, and was so transparent that stars were visible through it. · It retained its most perfect proportions about twenty minutes, and then, sweeping off in a southerly direction, soon faded away. At the Signal Office, in Boston, it was judged to be the corona form of aurora borealis ; but some, professedly wise in such matters, contended that it was a nebulous belt which had made a near approach to the earth. It was described as of a "reddish yellow" tinge as it appeared in some places ; but as it was observed by the writer, it was of a beautifully clear white, and at the time thought to be without doubt the aurora. One scientific observer, who called it a "nebulous band," claimed, in a newspaper communication, that it is recurrent, and is every season to be seen, always in the same direction, and always between the 25th of August and the 20th of September. One of our Lynn papers referred to it as something hardly worthy of remark. But the circumstances under which the writer of that paragraph saw it must have been very unfavorable, or he could not have seen it during the short time of its greatest brilliancy. As seen from the piazza of the stone dwelling at the junction of Walnut and Holyoke streets it was certainly a very striking and beautiful object.

About midnight, September 19, the church bells were tolled, announcing the death of President Garfield. The effect was very solemn.

On Wednesday, September 21, "The Exploring Circle," a voluntary association of ladies and gentlemen of culture held a "Camp Day," on a romantic elevation perhaps a mile northward from Dungeon Rock, and as was calculated about the centre of Lynn woods. They had previously held similar meetings in the forest, and consecrated and given appropriate names to some of the other hills which still remain unknown to most of our people, but which would richly repay the visits of every lover of the wild and weird, the romantic and lovely in nature. The occasion under notice was the consecration of "Mount Gilead," one of the most interesting spots within our borders, and from which the view, though chiefly of forest, is grand in the extreme. The services were highly pleasing, music, both vocal and instrumental, lending its charms to the picturesque ceremonials. There were also brief addresses, and the substantial addition of a pic-nic entertainment. The day was very pleasant, and several noted individuals from abroad were present. The "Circle" entertains the laudable hope of initiating such measures as will prevent the

entire destruction of our noble forests by the relentless woodsman's onward march, and perhaps ultimately secure a suitable
tract for a public park.

Memorial sevices on the decease of the President were held
in the First Methodist church, in Park square, on the 26th of
September. Some public and many private buildings were
appropriately draped.

The Hon. Enoch Redington Mudge died very suddenly, on
Saturday, October 1, at his beautiful summer residence in Swampscott. He was at his place of business, in Boston, on Friday,
and towards night called to inspect the concluding work on St.
Stephen's Memorial Church. Up to the time of retirement he
appeared to be in his usual health ; but on Saturday morning,
before rising, was seized by a severe pain in the head. Medical
attendance was promptly summoned and every effort made for
his relief, but all without effect, and before noon he had breathed
his last. The death of no one in this community has produced
more wide-spread and unfeigned sorrow, for he was universally
respected for his integrity as a business man, his great liberality
in the furtherance of all good works, and for his christian principles, and genial manners. By diligence, enterprise, and uncommon business capacity, he had accumulated a large fortune,
which he evidently regarded as entrusted to him for the benefit
of his fellow-men. For many of the latter years of his life he
was extensively concerned in cotton and woolen manufacturing
though in earlier manhood his attention was directed to other
employments.

That he was a man of cultivated taste, and a true lover of the
beautiful in nature and art, his delightful home at Swampscott,
in its surroundings and interior appointments, abundantly testified. And in St. Stephen's Memorial Church future generations
will behold enduring evidence not only of his liberality, parental
love, and christian faith, but also of his elevated conception of
grace and adaptation.

Mr. Mudge undoubtedly regarded the erection of St. Stephen's
as the crowning work of his life. And that elegant structure will
long remain his noblest visible monument. It is gratifying to
think that he lived to see the work well-nigh completed, though
we may lament that in the ways of a mysterious Providence he
was not spared for a few additional days that he might witness
the solemn ceremony of consecration ; a consummation he so
devoutly contemplated. His sudden decease sent a thrill through
the community such is rarely experienced. And the numerous
meetings that were held in Boston and elsewhere by the business
men and by public associations, and the eulogistic addresses and
resolutions of sympathy, showed that one held in far more than

ordinary esteem had passed away. And it spoke well for the
elevated tone of society that such appreciative tributes were so
spontaneously offered to the memory of such a man.

In person, Mr. Mudge was of full medium size, remarkably
well formed, dignified in manners, and always attentive to those
who addressed him, whether high or low. He was quick of apprehension, self-possessed, decided in his views, and able at all
times to give a reason for the faith that was in him. It was
impossible for one to have intercourse with him for an hour and
not perceive that he was a man of superior mental endowment.
And those who had fellowship with him in church work were at
once impressed with his fidelity to his clearly-defined principles,
his bright, cheerful anticipations, and his freedom from bigotry.

For political honors he did not aspire, though at one time he
served in the State Senate. Yet he took commendable interest
in public affairs, labored and expended liberally for the advancement of enterprises that he believed were for the public good.
He manifested especial interest in the young business men —
they who were soon to take the places of the generation of which
he was a member — gave lectures to them, in Boston, and improved every opportunity to urge upon them the formation of
habits of strict integrity, industry, and moral rectitude, as the
ground on which alone permanent prosperity could rest. Though
he made no pretensions as an orator, he was yet a very effective
speaker, and one who always secured the close attention of his
auditors. His style was earnest and indicative of his own deep
convictions. His language was well chosen, his points concisely
presented, and his arguments effective from resting on a basis
of sound common sense.

The burial service over the remains of Mr. Mudge was held in
St. Stephen's Church — then just on the verge of completion —
on Tuesday, October 4. It was the first service ever held within
those walls, was simple, and in strict accordance with the rubrics.
The edifice was entirely filled, large numbers of distinguished
persons from abroad, and many of the clergy being present. And
the large attendance of our own citizens of all classes, afforded
grateful assurance of the wide-spread sympathy for the bereaved
family. The remains were conveyed to the cloister garth, and
there, with prayer, and sacred melody, and words of heavenly
promise, and amid the tears of loved kindred, committed to their
final resting place.

Mr. Mudge was born in Orrington, Me., on the twenty-second
of March, 1812, and was a son of Rev. Enoch Mudge, a native
of Lynn, of whom a brief biographical notice may be found in
our 1865 edition of the History of Lynn. At an early age he
was united in marriage with Miss Caroline A. Patten of Portland,
Me., and they became the parents of seven children, the mother,

INTERIOR OF ST. STEPHEN'S CHURCH, LYNN.

ON A leaf preceding the title-page of this volume is a good view of the exterior of this fine edifice. For an historical sketch of Episcopal worship in Lynn, see page 259. For a biographical sketch of Mr. Mudge, donor of the Church, see page 91. And for consecration services. see page 93.

one son, and two daughters surviving him. His eldest son, Charles Redington, a lieutenant-colonel in the Union forces, was killed in the battle of Gettysburg, July 3, 1863, and his eldest daughter, Fanny Olive, died July 23, 1879. And in memory of those beloved children the costly tablets in the south interior wall were placed at the time of the erection of the church.

A fire occurred early on the morning of October 27, in the stable of A. H. Bosworth, on Willow street, destroying property to the amount of $600.

The National Security Bank of Lynn commenced business on Tuesday, November 1, Benjamin F. Spinney, president, David J. Lord, cashier ; capital, $100.000. This is the fourth bank of discount in Lynn.

St. Stephen's Memorial Church was consecrated on Wednesday, November 2, and the services, conducted according to the prescribed order, were extremely impressive. Many distinguished clergymen and others from abroad were present, and there was a large attendance of our own citizens. Bishop Paddock of the Massachusetts Diocese and Bishop Neely of Maine, took parts in the exercises ; and Bishop Huntington of Central New York, delivered the sermon. The beautiful edifice was erected by Hon. Enoch Redington Mudge, for the use of St. Stephen's parish, and had become doubly hallowed by his own sudden decease and burial within its walls. What wonder then that a large and sympathetic concourse should have gathered. The corner stone was laid on the 19th of May, 1880. There were present on that occasion also a large number of prominent clergymen. Bishop Paddock delivered an address ; and under the stone was placed an engraved copper tablet stating that the building was to be reared as a thank-offering to God and in memory of a deceased son and daughter ; to remain a house of worship, for the use of St. Stephen's parish, in conformity to the rites, ceremonies, usages and canons of the Protestant Episcopal Church of the United States. The edifice will be known as St. Stephen's Memorial Church. But the design of the donor was not merely commemorative of his deceased children, dear as they were. His greater object was to do something noble for the spiritual elevation of the community in which he felt such a glowing interest ; and had his children lived he would have done some great work for that end. But his martial son had laid his life on his country's altar, and the thought came of a Christian soldier's most befitting monument.

The Sanborn School House, in Ward 2, (Glenmere,) was dedicated on Monday, December 5. The name was in honor of Jeremiah Sanborn, a former teacher in the ward.

As noted under the proper date, horse rail-road cars first began to run in the streets of Lynn, Nov. 29, 1860. They were found to be of very great convenience, especially to working people whose employment was in the manufactories in the central parts. And though for some time the pioneer company did not realise much from their pecuniary investment, by perseverance, fair dealing, and efforts to accommodate, they gained the confidence and good-will of the community, and finally secured to themselves generous returns. As exigences seemed to require the lines have been extended to different neighborhoods, and come to be considered very important auxiliaries to our prosperity. The cheap lands in the suburbs afford opportunities to many of limited means to secure pleasant homes, free from the damaging necessity of frequent removals ; and by such the street rail-way is highly appreciated.

Some of those wise prognosticators who may always be found endeavoring to disturb the equanimity of naturally apprehensive minds, predicted that the year 1881 would be distinguished for remarkable and disastrous occurrences if indeed it was not to witness the end of all earthly things. Dire celestial phenomena, atmospheric disturbances, calamities by fire and flood, were among the promised woes. As far as certain parts of the world were concerned there was a verification of some of the predictions, hurricanes, floods, and conflagrations, attended by startling incidents, taking place. The number of shipwrecks was remarkably large, and the loss of life by their means and by conflagrations was appaling. But in this favored region nothing of a very extraordinary nature took place. A couple of rather pale comets decorated the heavens in the latter part of the summer ; indeed not less than seven of those erratic wanderers were reported as appearing within the range of telescopic vision during the year. A rattling thunder storm occupied the evening of Decoration Day. And a few uncomfortably sudden changes of temperature took place. Then there was the "yellow day," September 6, and the beautiful aerial phantom on the night of September 12. These were about the sum of our share of wonders. We had no severe drought, steam-boat or rail-road disaster, no great conflagration, hurricane, or flood. Still, in many unreflecting and superstitious minds there lingered through the whole year vague apprehensions of brooding evil. The literary forgery known as "Mother Shipton's Prophesies," purporting to have been made in 1448, and to foretell at least one event of some importance that was to happen in this pregnant year 1881, strangely enough, created real alarm in minds that would have been supposed far above such influences. The matter was rather cunningly devised, and to the unthinking mind that entertained no doubt of the genuineness of the predictions, the allusions to steam, the electric-telegraph, iron ships, California, the British premier Disraeli, &c., must have come with alarming force. But let us give place to a few of the occult lines, for it is not unlikely that the "Prophesies" may in the future, with a modification or two be presented afresh. It does seem as if every generation must have some such mysterious chapter to ponder over.

> "Carriages without horses shall go,
> Around the world thoughts shall fly
> In the twinkling of an eye.
> Iron in the water shall float
> As easy as a wooden boat.
> Gold shall be found, and found
> In a land that 's not now known.
> Fire and water shall more wonders do,
> England shall at last admit a Jew.
>
>   *   *   *
>
> The world then to an end shall come
> In eighteen hundred and eighty-one."

In concluding these remarks on what may be called some of the popular vagaries of the day, it may be well to add that in various parts of the country professed scientists, who are expected to keep an eye on nature as she pursues her marvelous developments, propounded new theories and claimed extraordinary discoveries. It was alleged, for instance, by an Ohio astronomer, that in consequence of "the change in the parallelism of the axis of rotation of the earth, which took place during a superior planetary conjunction, October 11, 1877, the United States are now in the torrid zone." Finally, we may as well record our own "prophecy;" which is that all such predictions as the foregoing will fail in the future, as they have failed in the past.

—

In closing our chapter of Annals, it is not deemed necessary to occupy space with a formal recapitulation. The matter has been so arranged that it is thought anything in the book can be readily found by reference to the index. Such statistical items as seemed most aptly to exhibit our progress and condition at different periods, and most interesting to the general reader, have been given. But for many details, useful and interesting to a class, but dry and useless to others, resort may be had to published municipal documents.

In the matter of business energy and enterprise, Lynn stands among the foremost in New England. But for some reason her reputation abroad for intellectual development and scholarly attainment has not been enviable. We must work for a change. It is not easy to give any reliable data on which an accurate judgment of the progress and condition of intelligence and mental discipline among us, can be predicated. Our people are great readers ; but the quality of the reading should be taken into account before a proper estimate of its usefulness can be made. The Free Public Library has now about 30,000 volumes, and the average daily delivery amounts to about 500. This is a large circulation, and to a considerable extent lies with the young work-people, who, in some sense as a relief from daily toil, peruse the lighter works, which, though by no means positively pernicious, are liable to usurp the place of those which would be more conducive to mental health and growth. It may be said that if the class to whom we refer cannot procure the desired books they will not read any thing; and in that light it is perhaps well to keep up the supply, looking to reformation in the future, which may gradually come about, for the shelves are well provided with attractive works of solid character. The circulation of newspapers in Lynn has increased with astonishing rapidity within a dozen years. Almost every one must now have his daily paper, and if all those connected with the editorial profession would maintain the dignity of the press, avoiding the merely sensational and frivolous, what an influence they would have in elevating the tone of society and shaping its destinies. At this time there are not probably less than 14.000 daily papers circulated in Lynn, and of other publications large numbers; and while, for the most part, they are of a character worthy of commendation, a few could be spared without detriment. All that it seems necessary to say of our 65 public Schools, appears elsewhere. They are doubtless in good condition as measured by the apparent requirements of the day and as compared with institutions of similar grade in other places; but future times will have other views and demands.

BIOGRAPHICAL SKETCHES.

INTRODUCTION.

It is proposed to give, in this Chapter, Biographical Sketches — or perhaps it should rather be said in regard to many of them, brief Personal Notices — of some of the people of Lynn who have become more or less strongly marked by their integrity of character and their efforts to promote the best interests of the place ; or even, peradventure, of those who by their abnormal ways have afforded useful allurements or warnings ; for, from the delinquences and miscarriages, the buffetings and failures of some, as well as from the fidelity and success of others, we may as certainly receive useful guidance as may the mariner from the occasionally lurching as well as from the ever-constant buoy.

As the parent survives and continues an extended existence in the lives of his offspring, so the good member of society lives an extended life in the enduring influence of his deeds and example, often accumulating power as time recedes. There is a fascination in the tracing of family connections. In so doing, to be sure, one sometimes falls on an individual who does no credit to his lineage ; but such may be silently passed by ; and it must be a very low-conditioned family that in the course of generations can present no honorable example. But how little do we know of the estimation in which an individual who lived even a few years

(97)   7

before ourselves, was held by his cotemporaries. The prominent features of character survive; but the minor lights and shades are obscured; the petulance of the churlish and the vagaries of the conceited have faded away in the lustre of their better qualities.

The plan adopted in the 1865 edition of our History of Lynn, will not be so closely followed, here, as has been done in the chapter of Annals, as it is thought that some variations will be improvements. As alphabetical arrangement is always convenient, that will be pursued. And to make the whole as plain and comprehensive as possible, the names of a class of individuals, who were not natives, will appear, with references to the dates in the Annals under which some account of them may be found. In short, it is proposed to give in the following pages what will enable the reader to refer to any biographical notice, whether of a native or otherwise, or whether it is to be found in this volume or in that of 1865. In a few instances, too, notable persons spoken of under different dates in the Annals will receive brief connected notices. And furthermore, lest the reader who may not fully observe our plan, should discover a seemingly unwarrantable omission, here and there, it is thought proper to introduce a few names with references to accounts in other places than the regular History; for instance to the Mayors, of whom sketches, with portraits, are given in the "Centenn al Memorial."

In our many notices we shall endeavor to give fair glimpses of character, not unreasonably magnifying mediocrity nor unjustly exhibiting blemishes. The more prodigal one is of his compliments, the more he lessens their value; and unjust censure recoils upon himself. It will not be inferred that the individuals here brought to notice are the only ones spoken of in our Annals. Many more are there named and their meritorious doings alluded to, as a reference to the indexes will enable any one to perceive. Mere genealogies of families, of course, are not to any extent given. They are but skeletons without flesh; interesting, indeed, to the near kindred, but not to the general reader Of course the names of a great many worthy people do not appear at all in the connection, as it is by no means intended to present an annotated directory. But it is sought to introduce a meet representative or two from the various walks of life. No person living has not, in addition to his modest self-appreciation some friend to whom he would be glad to see a tribute paid. But in a work of this kind it devolves on the author to discriminate, and endeavor to present, within reasonable limits, what seems, on the whole, to be likely to result in the greatest good.

An attempt to delineate character is always a delicate task, and especially so when a cotemporary is the subject ; for we necessarily view our travelling companions along life's road in different lights and from different stand-points ; and hence what one might pronounce a faithful delineation, another might look upon as distorted. Some look deep down for the principles from which actions spring, while others look only to surface indications. But there is a kind of fellow-traveller whose companionship very few of us much esteem ; namely, the one who is prone to make those about him uncomfortable by unnecessary complaints, ill-formed conceits, and irregularities of temper. To his cotemporaries he is always disagreeable ; and if he be a man of real genius and worth must look to future generations for a just estimate of his merits, they not being tried by his vaporings. This reflection, perhaps impertinent, forced itself upon the writer as the image of one of whom a sketch has already been prepared, came up before his mind. We will call him Mr. G. He long since passed away, and his name is now among the choicest in the keeping of our people. A little anecdote will serve to illustrate our meaning as well as the degree of honor awarded him in his own time ; though it is not to be denied that there were those who, while he yet remained among us, duly estimated his superior endowments, having power to penetrate the sometimes repulsive haze that obscured his better nature. On an afternoon, nearly forty years ago, the writer, in passing through Central square observed mounted on a wagon that stood there an individual well known throughout the town as a half-lunatic, but shrewd, observing, and fond of indulging in sarcastic remarks. He was delivering a rambling oration to the motley assembly gathered around. Just then Mr. G. came along. The orator caught sight of him, and suspending his discourse called out, "Here, here, Mr. G——, I have something to say to you. Pray stop a moment and hear me." This salutation was of course unheeded, and Mr. G. moved along with his accustomed dignity.

The other repeated the call, but with no better success; and then, with an air of mingled chagrin and contempt, added, "Well, well, my friend! so you won't notice me, will you? I suppose you call yourself up in the world and think I 'm down, do n't you? We all know you 're up-ish, and I 'm derry-down. But before heaven I do n't believe there 's much to choose between us. We both act like the devil!" The shout that went up from the crowd at that sally may be imagined. After the explosion, the orator calmly resumed his harangue, and the whole assembly seemed to feel that the popular mind had been expressed. But the time has now arrived when the displeasing foibles of Mr. G. are forgotten, and his name stands high on the roll of those we delight to honor. His many worthy deeds are gratefully remembered; his minor blemishes, which so annoyed those of his own generation, are buried with him. As there are among the individuals of whom we shall speak, some of like characteristics, this illustration may not be without its use in making up our judgment. It will, however, be borne in mind that moral defect is to be regarded in a very different light from mere social indecorum.

With these remarks and explanations we proceed to give our imperfect notices.

ADAMS, Rev. BENJAMIN, minister of Lynnfield parish twenty-one years, including the trying period immediately preceding the Revolution, and the opening stages of the conflict. He was patriotic, though less stirring and conspicuous than the two other ministers — Roby and Treadwell — then settled in Lynn. The ministers of the country parishes, very generally, manifested commendable zeal in the provincial cause, and in their ardent exhortations frequently exhibited a spirit that would ill-accord with modern views of the sacred vocation. The ultimate success of the cause is in no small degree attributable to their urgent and persistent appeals. The Lynn ministers certainly did their part. See Annals, date 1777.

ALLEY, HUGH and JOHN. These two settlers, who appeared here as early as 1640, were farmers, and located in the vicinity of Market street. From them descended the numerous persons of the name who have for many years been numbered in our population. Some of these descendants have made favorable marks in their generation. Solomon Alley was one of the "Flower of Essex," in Lathrop's command, and was killed in the Indian massacre at Bloody Brook, in 1675.

In former years many of the family were members of the Quaker society, which may in a measure account for their not more frequently appearing in public life. In the letter of the Quakers of Lynn, to Governor Dudley, dated "22th 4m° 1703," giving a list of those of the faith here, appears the name of Hugh Alley, who was probably a grandson of the one whose name stands at the head of this notice. There was a Captain Hugh Alley who commanded a small schooner-rigged vessel running from Lynn to Boston, which seems to have been very successful in his day of limited carrying trade. He continued in the business some years, the land route being circuitous, rutty and rough. Hon. John B. Alley, the first Congressional Representative from Lynn is of this respectable lineage. John Alley, father of the last named, was a very stirring and thrifty business man, though not without conspicuous eccentricities. He built the Railroad House, opposite the southern end of Market street ; also the dam near the foot of Pleasant street, thus forming the capacious mill-pond. He was, in his earlier years, a member of the Quaker society ; participated in the troubles there, in 1822, and subsequently seemed quite unsettled in his religious views ; yet he maintained a high character for integrity and neighborly-kindness.

The christian names Hugh and John seem to have prevailed in the Alley family for many generations. Hugh Alye, "citizen and wever, of London," died in 1533, leaving a son John and daughter Elizabeth. He was buried in Saint Mildred's, and "Maude Croumwell, late wife of Richard Croumwell" was executrix of his estate. See Annals, 1640 and other early dates.

ARMITAGE, JOSEPH. This individual figures somewhat largely in our early history. He made his appearance here in 1630, and was a tailor by trade. In those primitive times, however, the permanency of fashions, the scarcity of material, and the necessity of household economy, conspired to make the calls for the exercise of his artistic skill quite limited, and we are not surprised to find him turning his attention to occupations that promised more satisfactory returns.   In him was exemplified that fruitfulness of resource which lies at the foundation of at least one leading trait of true Yankee character ; and very likely, had a wider field opened for the exercise of his peculiar talents, he might have attained a more conspicuous position, and been more thrifty in a pecuniary way ; as, after all, notwithstanding his industry and frugality, he lived and died a poor man.   There is, indeed, little art in financiering, for whoever lives within his means and pays his debts is successful.   And this simple rule applies as well to nations as individuals.   But the speculative mind is not content to take this rational view, and must experiment among doubtful projects.

The ill-success of Mr. Armitage, however, may, in part at least, have been attributable to his fondness for lawsuits, than which hardly anything can be more detrimental, directly and indirectly, to the interests of the average citizen.   The law is an extremely hazardous resort ; and it may be safely said that if some among us who waste their substance in pursuing it, would only apply the means thus squandered to the payment of their honest debts, they would not pass their whole business lives on the verge of bankruptcy, nor be always forced to confront the claims of charity with the argument of an empty purse.   The writer once knew two brothers in the very neighborhood where the humble dwelling of Mr. Armitage stood, who began life as prosperous farmers, and soon, with what they inherited, possessed enough to call themselves moderately rich.   But unfortunately, from some unaccountable cause, both became fascinated by the law and were seldom without a suit or two on hand.   When they were well along in years, the writer asked one what made him waste so much time and money in such unprofitable business. "Why," said he "it is the best amusement I have.   It is an exciting game of chance, and I like it.   I sometimes gain and sometimes lose.   My brother likes it, too ; and when we cannot get up a lawsuit with any one else we can with each other."   Both of these sturdy yeomen are now dead ; and they died poor ; they had the music and paid the piper.   It is safe to conclude that there is something wrong about the man who is always engaged in lawsuits.

As the first landlord of the Anchor Tavern, Mr. Armitage is best known, he having opened that famous house of entertainment when it must have been a seriously doubtful enterprise, considering the limited number of travellers. But it was not a Fifth Avenue establishment, though great men were sometimes entertained there. He was licensed to "draw wine," and perhaps hoped to derive most profit from that questionable source, though his hopes could hardly have been realized, if he was often so indiscreet as to render himself liable to be fined for neglect of duty, as he appears to have been on one occasion in 1651, which occasion is indicated by the following entry on the Court records : " In ans' to the petition of Joseph Armitage ffor an abatement of a fine of five pounds, imposed on him for not acquainting the counstable of a psons being drunke in his company, as the law requires, the Court sees no cawse to abate the petitioner any part of that fine."

The houses of entertainment, of those days, though useful and even necessary for the accommodation of travellers, were not probably to be much prized for their neighborhood influences, as they were often the resort of the lazy and gossiping townsmen who there passed hours of idleness over their tankards of flip, in the haze of tobacco smoke. Yet, when the presiding spirit himself happened to be of high character and able to gather around him kindred spirits they no doubt became meeting places for the discussion of matters of the greatest importance.

It is evident that Mr. Armitage was a stirring if not a meddlesome man, and did not confine his attentions to any particular class or calling. And upon the Court records here and there appear indications that he was one of the many who find it difficult to see how the public good can be reached excepting by the road that leads to their own personal advantage.

The Armitages — for Joseph was not the only one of the name who appeared in Lynn during the early days — seem to have belonged to a family of some note in the old country. Here, however, though not what would be called a shiftless, they were yet a shifting race. Godfrey, mentioned in our Annals, under date 1630, removed to Boston ; and Thomas, whose name does not appear in the Annals, but who, according to Savage, was for a time commorant here, and who came from Bristol, in the ship James, in 1635, a fellow passenger with Richard Mather, was one of the Sandwich settlers, in 1637; from there he went to Stamford, then to Oyster Bay, on Long Island; and in 1647 he appeared among the Hempstead settlers.

Returning for a moment more to Joseph and his destructive lawsuits, we will transcribe the testimony of one of the witnesses in an action brought against him by John Ruck, administrator, at the June term of the Essex County Court, in 1671 : " The testimony of Christopher Lawson, of Boston, aged 55 years or Thereabouts: This Deponent saith, that haueing beene acquainted these five or six and twenty years with the dealings betweene Mr Thomas Ruck of Boston, deceased, & Joseph Hermitage of Lyn, & haueing beene seuerall times at the transacting of them, as appears by my hand to diuers papers subscribed, I doe very well remember that the said Thomas Ruck hath giuen him credit from time to time & ye said Hermitage promised to pay him thirty pounds in money in London, of this debt, and the remainder of the same in New England, to his content. But in the year 1669 coming to Boston, Mrs Eliz. Ruck, then widdow, made a sad complaint to me, & said she could gett nothing of ye said Hermitage, whereupon I spoke with Joseph Hermitage & agitated the business with him, in the widdows behalfe ; his answer was that he would not wrong ye widow nor fatherless, but would do that was right in the sight of God & man ; he would not wrong her of a penny, with many solem p'testations. In fine, the said Joseph Armitage & Mrs Ruck bound themselues in a bond to stand to ye arbitration of Capt. Roger Spenser & Christopher Lawson. We heard both their pleas & allegations & found Joseph Armitage debtor to Mrs Rucke, upon all Accounts to ye value of aboute Eighty pounds sterling, which we thought was more than he was able to pay ; we found likewise a bill of exchange to England for Thirty pounds protested, & nothing paid of his debt in New England, save something in Wharfe wood as he calls it. Whereupon we called them both in & desired Mrs Rucke to take twenty pounds giueing him some tyme to pay it & forgiue him the rest, which 20*l* he should pay at Boston in money, or goods at money price within such a tyme,

as appears by the Arbitration in writeing, and yet none of this
was performed that euer I heard off. This is the true state of
ye case, as I hau beene acquainted with it from first to last, to
my best knowledge. Taken upon oath : 29 — 4mo 71 [June 29,
1671.] Wm Hathorne, attest :" This, however, appears to be
simply the old, old case — " I owe but cannot pay " — and perhaps
involves no element to the especial discredit of Mr. Armitage.

We here copy an ancient document which will in these pages
be a number of times referred to as " The Armitage Petition "—
a petition of the wife of Joseph for permission herself to keep
the ordinary, he having receded into the back-ground. It is
inserted not so much for anything of special interest it contains
as for the autographs of a number of the early settlers which are
appended, fac-similes of which are given — among them that of
Godfrey, brother of Joseph. The petition itself, we have little
doubt, is in the hand-writing of Captain Robert Bridges.

To THE RIGHT WOR^LL THE GOUERNOR, DEPUTIE GOUERNO^R &
THEIR HONORED ASSOTIATS :

The humble peticon of Jane, wife of Joseph Armitage :

Humbly sheweth that whereas the indigent and low estate
of your poore peticonesse is evident not to a few, in as much as
her husbands labours & indeauo^rs haue beene blasted and his
ames & ends frustrated by a iust hand, beinge also made incapable of such other ymploym^t as hee is personally fitted for by
reason of the sensure vnder wch for the p^rsent hee lyeth & alsoe
being outed of such trade & comerce as might haue afforded
supportacon to his familie consistinge of Diuers p^rsons & small
Children in comiseracon of whom, togither with yor peticonesse,
the inhabitants of o^r town were .pleased (as farr as in them lay)
to continue yor poore peticonesse in the Custodie of the said
Ordinary & that benefitt wch might accrew from the same to
take towards makeinge of theire liues the more comfortable ;
wherevpon & by reason whereof yor peticonesse said husband
procured the most convenient howse in Lynn for the purpose
albeit itt was very ruinous & much cost bestowed respecłinge
his p^rsent condicon in repaireinge & fittinge vp of the same
accordingly : And also whereas some of his Credito^rs haue of
their clemencie and gentle goodnes furnished him wth Comodi-
ties apt for the mainteyning of an ordinary to the intent some
benefitt might redound towards the maintenance & liuelyhood
of his familie & reedifieinge of his ruined estate in case the same
may bee obteined : and that thereby wee may bee enabled to

pay our debts, in regard of which the name of god now suffers.
May itt therefore please this Honored Assembly to
take the p^rmisses into tender consideracon & w^th
bowells of comiseracon to way the lowe estate of yor
said Peticonesse & her familie and to reconfirme the
Custodie of the said Ordinarie to yor peticonesse
duringe the winter season & further as shall seeme
good in yor sight vpon the well demeano^r of yor Peticonesse in the said place, &c.

Voted &
granted
Octob. 26th
[1643]

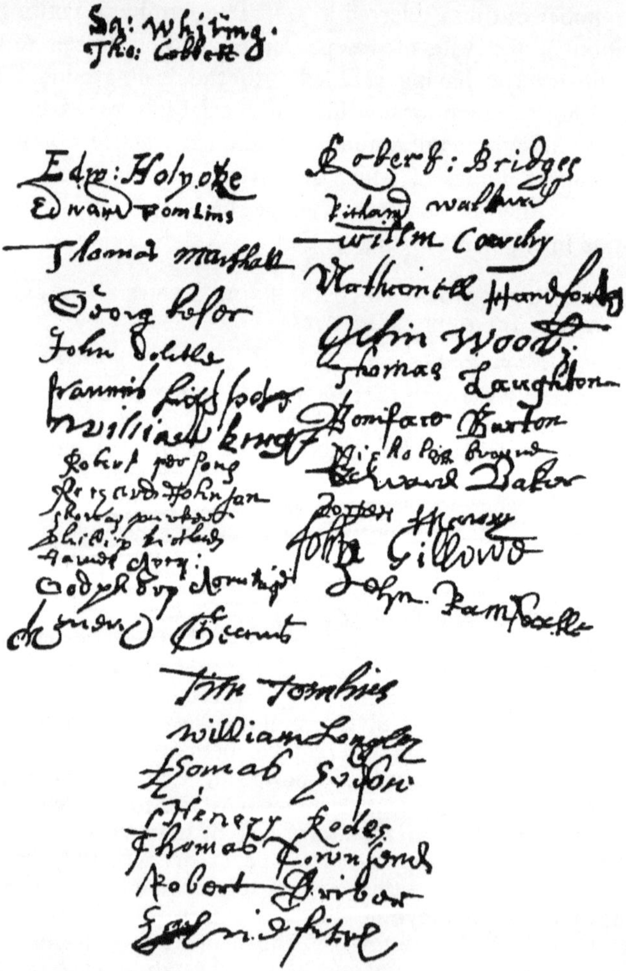

The foregoing is what will be referred to as " The Armitage

Petition." Some of the autographs being rather obscure, we give the names in letter-press, as follows — arranged very much as they stand on the original petition — coupled with the remark that most of the individuals will be found noticed in alphabetical order in these pages of sketches.

Sa : Whiting.
Tho : Cobbett.

Edw : Holyoke,
Edward Tomlins,
Thomas marshall,
Georg keser,
John Dolitle,
frauncis Ligtfoote,
William king,
Robert persons,
Richard Johnson,
Thomas parker,
Phillip Kirtland,
James Axey,
Godphrey Armitage,
Henery Eeames.

Robert : Bridges,
Richard walker,
Willm Cowdry,
Nathaniell Handforth,
John Wood,
Thomas Laughton,
Boniface Burton,
Nicholas Browne,
Edward Baker,
Robert Massey,
John Gillowe,
John Ramsdalle,

Tim Tomlins,
William Longley,
Thomas Godson,
Henery Rodes,
Thomas Townsend,
Robert Driver,
Zachrie fitch,

The names of Robert Persons, Richard Johnson, Thomas Parker, Philip Kirtland and James Axey look very much as if written by the same hand. If they were, it could not have been because the individuals did not know how to write but because it was more convenient to have some one else attach their names. On the Colony Records, under date Sept. 7, 1643, is the entry, " Goody Armitage is alowed to keepe the ordinary, but not to draw wine." Upon the margin of the petition is seen the memorandum, " Voted & granted Octob. 26th, [1643.]" This is by a different hand, and was probably made at a subsequent session. The 1643 being in brackets denotes that it may have been a considerably later insertion. The "clemencie and gentle goodnes ," of some of Mr. Armitage's creditors, certainly indicate that he had friends, though under censure for something not stated.

It has been remarked that Mr. Armitage, after his long and laborious career, passed his latter years in poverty. This is apparent by his curious petition, presented in 1669, for the payment of some trifling scores which certain colonial dignitaries ran up at his tavern about twenty-five years before ; a specification

of some of which charges may be found in our Annals, under date
1643. On his decease his estate was appraised at £6 2s. 6d.
Other incidents in the career of this typical individual may be
found in the Annals of early dates.

ATTWILL, THEODORE. Mr. Attwill died of Bright's disease,
December 9, 1880, in the 55th year of his age. He was a native
of Lynn, and for many years enjoyed a reputation for intelligence
and probity attained by few. The surname was not unknown
here before the beginning of century 1700, though there were
none of the kin among the first settlers. And there does not
seem to have been at any time a large number of the lineage
among us. The business of the subject of this sketch apper-
tained to the shoe-manufacture, and in it he was successful; but
beyond that he had a decided literary taste, and was a constant
reader of the better class of books, and quite proficient in mathematics and the languages. With Latin, Greek, French, Spanish,
and German, he was more or less familiar. His literary acquirements were appreciated, and for fifteen years he was called to
serve as a member of the School Committee, and for a like term
as a trustee of the Free Public Library. He was a member
of the Common Council four years, during two of which he was
president; and at the same time he filled various responsible
offices of a more private nature. In person Mr. Attwill was
of medium size and apparently possessed of a firm and healthy
constitution. His countenance was usually of rather a serious
cast; but he had a vein of genuine humor which would not
unfrequently assert itself to the enjoyment of appreciative friends.
He built the fine residence on Essex street, at the junction
of High Rock avenue, and there he died, leaving a widow, one
son, and three daughters.

AXEY, JAMES — was one of the first settlers, having appeared
here as early as 1630. He was a man of considerable importance
and possessed a fair estate for those times. He was a Representative in 1654; and in 1657, was one of the committee
appointed to lay out Nahant in planting lots. Axey's Point
the site of the present gas-works, perpetuates his name.
We are inclined to think that he had some share in domestic

trials, to which so many are exposed through the infirmities
of our common nature ; yet there is no conclusive evidence that
he did not, on the whole, live as peacefully with Frances his
spouse as is the ordinary experience, though she does appear to
have had a wakeful eye for the main chance. Her vigilance,
alert to the last, is shown by certain depositions still on file
in Salem, concerning his attempts to make a will. When drawing near his end, he proposed executing such an instrument ;
but her opposition prevailed, and he refrained. On his decease
she was appointed administratrix of his estate, but did not long
survive to enjoy any gain she possibly may have made by her
successful interference. He died June 7, 1669, and she a few
months after.

An extract or two from the quaint depositions filed in the case
will be sufficient to show that human nature has changed but
little since that time. Andrew Mansfield, aged about forty-nine
years, " Testifyeth y^t In ye tyme of the sickness of James Axey :
I being severall tymes with him, one off which tymes was, to my
best memory, about three weeks before hee dyed, hce signifyde
his desyrd to make his will, his wife being present ; & hce began
to Declare his intent toward John Pearson, declareing hee would
leve him to have the greater Lott, and then his wife spoke as
houlding out to my understanding y^t she would have him to make
noe will, saying can not you confide in me y^t I will perform what
yeo mind is, but you will give awaye all. He answered I intend
to give nothing from you whilst you Live except some suche
legasye or Legasyees ; shee then replied hee might if he would
make his will. but [he] sayd I will not, you cannot consent to it ;
and I replyed it was an Apoynted of God to sett his house in
order, and instanced that of Hezekiah : sett thy house in order
for thou must dye, and did declare to him y^t I hoped God would
guide him in soe doeing ; but she replying, hee alsoe replyed,
saying I can dispose of none of my estate, &c. ; and being
troubled, wee then got him to bed. . . . " Joseph Rednap
and Samuel Johnson testified that " they Being att ye house of
James Axey ten days before he dyed, the wife of James Axey
asked him, before us, what he ment by those words which he
spake the last night ; which was you said I bequeath my spirritt
to God and estate to John Pearson, and took him by the hand

and said, Love, is not your mind as it was formerly agreed between you and I : and he said yes ; and he sed by my estate to John Pearson I meane he should looke after it for you." Samuel Tarbox testified that "beinge in the house of James Axey about two nights before hee dyed and Nathaniell Kirkland and John Pearson was there the same time, and Nathaniel Kirkland s^d to John Pearson, I marvell yoo do not Ask your maister how hee hath disposed of his goods. And James Axey hearing their discourse said, brother Kirkland I will satisfy you concerning it ; I had thoughts to have made a will and to have disposed of some things att my death, but my wife was not willinge, for I would not cross her, but leave it to her." Mr. Kirkland added that he did not remember the words "leave it to her." In another deposition of Andrew Mansfield, which was given sometime after the death of both Mr. and Mrs. Axey, he says : "being with James Axey in the time of his last sickness, which was, to the best of my memory, aboute three weekes before his death, his wife and Joseph Fiske being present, his wife oposing the s^d James Axey, her husband, in order to the making of his will, according as in my first testimony which is in Court, the said James Axey before his wife and Joseph Fiske solemlye Left it with mee that if any should aske why hee did not make his will I should tell y^m hee would have done it but his wife would not Let him, and I was then to have written it." See Annals, 1630 and other early dates. Mr. Axey's signature may be seen appended to the Armitage Petition.

BACHELOR, Rev. STEPHEN — first minister of the first church in Lynn ; an active and prominent divine, but possessing such eccentricities of charaĉter that his early removal became expedient. He was born in 1561, and lived to reach his hundredth year. See Annals, 1632, 1636, and other early dates.

BAKER, CHRISTINE — a maid and matron of various fortunes ; an Indian captive ; a ward of the French Catholics, in Canada ; a returned wanderer. See Annals, 1630.

BAKER, DANIEL C. — third Mayor of Lynn. See biographical sketch, page 566 History of Lynn, 1865 edition. Also notice with portrait, page 151 Centennial Memorial. He died in New Orleans, La., July 19, 1863, aged 46. A fac-simile of his signature follows.

BAKER, EDWARD — ancestor of the numerous family of the name hereabout. His autograph appears on the Armitage Petition. See Annals, 1630.

BARKER, Dr. CHARLES O. — a reputable physician. He died January 8, 1843, aged 41. His wife was a daughter of Rembrandt Peale, the celebrated painter. He left no children. See Annals 1843. His residence was on Western avenue, near Mall street. An amusing anecdote about his introduction to Dr. Hazeltine may be found in our notice of the latter.

BASSETT, WILLIAM. Mr. Bassett died very suddenly on the night of June 21, 1871, aged 68 years. He was a native of Lynn, and well-known from having been much in public life. And for his many virtues and kindly sympathies he was as widely respected as known. At the time of his death he was cashier of the First National Bank, and had filled that office for eighteen years. He was quite active and efficient in the labor of putting the new municipal machinery into successful operation when the City Charter was adopted, and for the first three years was City Clerk. He was a zealous and intelligent laborer in the cause of education and the moral and social reforms of the day, and in early manhood sought by actual experience and observation to determine the value of various "community" systems then existing; for he was well convinced that the condition of our social life might be greatly improved by some radical changes in the domestic economy. Yet he did not appear to have had his hopes verified, and returned to the home of his youth to remain till the close of his life. Although bred in the orthodox Quaker faith he became a Unitarian, and for a long period was a faithful and useful member of the society here. Indeed he was faithful

and useful in every position he filled. He was patient in investigations, accurate in conclusions, and affable in manners ; a
good penman and careful recording officer. On the day of his
burial some of the principal business houses were closed in token
of respect ; and though the weather was very inclement, a large
concourse attended. Some prominent persons from abroad were
present ; among them Wendell Phillips the orator and William
Lloyd Garrison the anti-slavery reformer. His remains were
interred in Pine Grove Cemetery, in the original laying out of
which he took an active part. In our Annals, under date 1640
may be found a genealogical sketch of the family A fac-simile
of his signature is here given.

BATCHELDER, JACOB — first principal of Lynn High School,
and for some years librarian of the Free Public Library. He
died December 17, 1876, aged 70 years. See Annals, 1876.

BENNETT, SAMUEL. The name of this early settler is perpetu-
ated by the extensive swamp near our northern border. He was
a considerable real estate owner, many of his acres lying in the
vicinity of the ancient iron works, near which he resided. He
was one of the early members of the Ancient and Honorable
Artillery, in good circumstances, public spirited, and withal
possessed of considerable independence of character — a little
wilful, perhaps. In 1644 he was presented by the grand jury as
a " common sleeper in time of exercise," and fined two shillings
and sixpence. And for one or two other offences of equal enor-
mity he suffered punishment. He seems to have been once fined
for a breach of the law forbidding the sale of commodities at too
great a profit ; and on petitioning for a remittal of the fine
received this rebuff from the Court. It is found on the Colony
Records under date May 15, 1657. "In answer to the petition
of Samuell Bennett, humbly craving the remittment or abatement
of a fine imposed on him by the County Court, for selling goods
at excessive prizes. the Court hauing pervsed, and by theire
comittee examined, the papers in the case presented, together

wth the allegations & pleas of the peticoner & others, by him produced, vnderstanding, by what appeared, the peticoner received of George Wallis about forty pounds or vpwards meerely for the release of the bargaine made betwixt them, . . . see it not meete to graunt the petition in whole or in part." Mr. Wallis had also been fined "fivety pounds" for "selling goods at excessive prizes," and petitioned for a remittal ; and the same Court judged it "meete to remitt the fine all to tenn pounds ;" which remittal was made in consideration of his being necessitated "to be at the losse of about forty pounds or more to attayne a release of the bargain betwixt him & Samuell Bennett." It seems to have been what is vulgarly called a "game of sharps," between Mr. Bennett and Mr. Wallis ; but the Court, while endeavoring to render an equitable judgment, were not disposed to see invaded the wholesome law forbidding the selling of goods at exhorbitant prices.

There is a deposition of the noted Samuel Maverick of Noddle's Island, as East Boston was called till within a comparatively late period, touching a certain agreement of Mr. Bennett relative to the marriage of his son, which has been quoted for one or two purposes. It is as follows: "Samuel Maueric, aged 63 yeares or thereabouts, deposeth that sometime last yeare, having some speech wth Samuell Bennet, sen^r of Lynn, as to a match intended betweene his son Saml Bennett, Junr & a dau. of Capt. Wm Hargrave of Horsey doune, Marinar, The s^d Bennett, sen^r did promise that if his sonne should marry wth s^d Hargraues dau. he would make over to him the house he now liues in with barns, stables, lands, &c. belonging to s^d farme & £80 of stock ; wth this prouisoe that s^d Bennet, Junr should yearly pay his father during his life £20 if he needed it or demanded it ; and to the best of my remembrance he wrote so much to Capt. Hargraue. He also tyed his sonne not to alienate the premises w^{th}out his consent durcing his life. Thus much he testifieth, and further saith not. Boston, Decr 7th 1665. Taken upon oath the 8th Dec. 1665. Samuell Maverike. Before Thomas Clarke, Commiss."

Various facts of interest concerning Mr. Bennett may be found recorded in Annals, running on from date 1630. Few of the settlers within our borders were better adapted to keep things in lively trim than Mr. Bennett.

8

BLANCHARD, AMOS. Master Blanchard, as he was always called, was for some ten years teacher of the western district school, and the house in which he taught was a small square one story wooden building, with hipped roof and unoccupied belfry, standing near the latitudinal centre of the west end of the Common, within a stone's throw of the eastern end of Healey's Arcade. The pay of common school teachers, in those days, was meagre, not often, in country places, exceeding a dollar a day ; and Master Blanchard, having a wife and twelve children to provide for, at times found it extremely hard rubbing. But in addition to his day school he received from minor auxiliary employments a little help. He taught a private evening school at different seasons ; from his skill in penmanship, for he wrote a beautiful hand, he derived something ; from the exercise of his musical talents he received a pittance ; and his "grateful coun- try," in return for his services as a fifer in the revolutionary army granted him a small pension. Nevertheless, he lived and died a poor man — poor in purse only, however ; for he was rich in the respect of his fellow townsmen. The pay for "literary services," to use a favorite expression of his, was at that time small, as just remarked, and having before us at this moment a re- ceipted bill of his that shows something of his prices, there seems no objection to inserting it just as it stands :

> "1821. Mr Benja Newhall, To A. Blanchard,   Dr
> To the Instruction of your son, 6 weeks,   1 20
> To the Instruction of your Daughter,   30
> _____
> 1 50
>
> Sept   Recd payment,   AMOS BLANCHARD."

The barbarous old laws allowing indiscriminate imprisonment for debt were then in force, and it is not remarkable that a man circumstanced as Master Blanchard was should once in a while find it necessary to procure a substitute to take his place in the school, for thirty or sixty days. But he bore his misfortunes with complacency and never yielded to the misanthropic mood. In music he always found a solace, and upon its wings his spirits could rise in the darkest hour. He was one of the most accom- plished musicians ever resident hereabout, and composed several pieces which took rank among the approved compositions of the day. He led the singing at the Old Tunnel, from 1811 to 1824, and played the bass-viol with an unction that was inspiring. With the doctrines taught in that venerable sanctuary he was in full accord and did all in his power to advance both the temporal and spiritual interests of the society. In some of her darkest hours his hopeful voice was raised.

For a few years before the date of the above receipt, 1821, the writer attended his day school, and with a recollection of the routine of study comes a feeling remembrance of the discipline. The rod was not spared, in those days, though Master Blanchard was not given to its severe use. But yet, when in the morning he announced that any boy who misbehaved during the day would be "made an example of," we all felt that there would be squalls before night, and our forebodings seldom failed of being realised. Reading, spelling, defining, writing, ciphering and a little grammar were taught ; and there were other important things impressed upon us which seem to be too much neglected in the schools of the present day ; namely, good manners, and correct deportment, as well out of school as in, as well in the street as in the parlor ; and especially was respect for superiors in age inculcated.

Master Blanchard at one time lived in the old Merry house, which stood on the north side of Boston street, nearly opposite the foot of Mall. And in fancy the writer can at this moment see him, of a balmy summer morning, wending his way towards the scene of his scholastic labors, his whole air expressive of the combined dignity of classic and musical erudition, his long, light calico gown swaying in the breeze as proudly as if it were a Roman toga investing some grave senator.

As before remarked, Master Blanchard was the father of twelve children, ten of whom came with him when he removed hither from Exeter, N. H., in 1811. The other two were born here. His daughter Levina became the wife of John Lovejoy, for many years a successful morocco manufacturer and resident of Market street, whose descendants remain.

Such men as Master Blanchard leave an enduring impress upon a community. The influence of the good principles he enforced — for besides the routine of study, he usually devoted an hour or two every week to lecturing us on morals, manners, or

some didactic subject, closing with a fervent prayer — has not
ceased to this day, either in this community or in many other
fields to which his restless flocks became scattered.   Yet, his
was not what would be called a pronounced character, but
one of those we are apt to speak of as "non-committal."   In
discussion he did not like to offend, and hence did not, on many
occasions, press his views with a vigor commensurate with their
value.   In manners he was genial, in habits social, in morals
strict.   He was intelligent, and ready and interesting in conversation but not much given to humorous diversions.   He died on
the 25th of May, 1842, at the age of 78 years.

BOWLER, THOMAS.   Mr. Bowler was born in Lynn, on the 3d
of January, 1786, and died July 22, 1867.   He led an unostentatious life, and no one stood higher as a consistent Christian than
he.   Adhering to the earlier Methodist views and usages, he
often saw cause to lament over the worldly tendencies of many
of the faith, especially the young, particularly in matters of dress,
amusements and display.   In 1831, when the anti-masonic party,
of which he early became an adherent, gained the ascendancy in
Lynn, he was elected Town Clerk, and held the office sixteen
years.   His records were kept in a careful and neat manner, and
those of us who remember him in his official capacity can bear
testimony to his accuracy, uniform courtesy, patience, and disposition to oblige.   His manners were gentle, his voice low, and his
aspect subdued ; but his spirit was far from cringing.   He was
married in 1807, and became the father of eleven children, none
of whom, with one or two exceptions, lived beyond middle life.

BOYCE, WILLIAM S. — president of the First National Bank —
died August 27, 1873, aged 63.   See Annals, 1873.

BREED, ALLEN — ancestor of our fifth and ninth Mayors.
" Breed's End" took its name from him.   The surname was in
old times spelled Bread.   See Annals, 1630 and other early
dates.   A fac-simile of his signature is appended.

BREED, ANDREWS — was the fifth Mayor of Lynn. He died in Lancaster, Mass., April 21, 1881, at the age of 86 years ; and as a notice of him, with a portrait, may be found in our Centennial Memorial, little need be said here. But of one or two of his ancestors, not elsewhere under notice, a word may properly be said.

His father, who bore the same christian name was keeper of Lynn Hotel, at the west end of the Common, for a number of years onward from 1813 ; and under his supervision the house attained an enviable reputation, especially for the excellence of its table and the promptness with which the largest demands of guests could be met. He was a very stirring man, and recognised by every one in the streets, as he sallied forth on his brawny roadster, in his yellow top boots and coat of sporting cut. In addition to his large business at the Hotel he did a good deal of farming, and many of us can well remember the jolly husking parties which in autumn assembled at his bidding to divest the yellow ears of their rustling robes, and at evening receive their reward at the banquet of baked beans and Indian pudding, with relays of apples and cider. He was not a man who could pass noiselessly through the world, or who could yield much to what he deemed the unreasonable demands of those about him ; in short, he was of what is called an arbitrary disposition, rather boisterous in language, and strict in his requirements of those in service under him. No lazy man's excuses weighed with him. Among his enterprises was the laying out of Centre street. He was a descendant of Allen Breed, the early settler who was father of the Breed family of Lynn.

Then there was the long celebrated " Madam Breed," grandmother of Mayor Andrews. She kept a school for very young pupils, on Water Hill, at the moderate charge for each of ninepence a week — a ninepence being the Spanish real, of the value of twelve and a half cents. There was at that time very little silver of American coinage in circulation. Spanish pistareens, reals and half-reals constituted almost the whole change we had. Madam Breed was of such queenly dignity that it was said she would not allow even her own children to be seated in her presence without permission. Where she would have ranked had the " Woman's Rights " question been agitated in her day it is not easy to determine. But she was a good woman, though her education was hardly sufficient to answer the demands for a modern high school position ; yet her practical view of the duties of life and conception of the dignity of the female character emi nently fitted her for the guidance of susceptible girlhood. Over her little subjects in the school room she had good control, and inspired in them a wholesome fear of the tingling little rod that lay menacingly on her table. But it seems as if her usefulness would have been greater in a higher sphere and among more mature minds. She loved children : and the writer has special cause for grateful remembrance of her ; for upon a certain Sun day morning, while posted on his accustomed seat in the Old Tunnel Meeting-house, he was startled by a sudden punch in the back, and on turning about beheld, thrust through the little creaking balustrade that adorned the pew, the hand of the venerable dame, displaying to his astonished gaze sundry yellow and red sugar-plums. His wonder at the condescension was so stupefying that he did not venture to seize the prize till a gracious nod assured that it was inten ed for him. And it is well remembered that more satisfaction was felt at the honor of the bestowal and on being referred to by his juvenile companions as "the fellow" to whom Madam gave the sugar-plums, than in the legitimate use of the gift.

As elsewhere remarked, the Breed family is one of the largest and most respectable among us, as it is one of the most ancient. Mayor Andrews Breed was a man of medium size, erect, well-proportioned, and active in his movements even after he had reached the age of eighty years. A fac-simile of his autograph is here given.

BREED, Dr. BOWMAN B. Doctor Breed died on the 16th of December, 1873, of Bright's disease of the kidneys. He was born in Lynn, February 29, 1832, and was a son of Hon. Isaiah Breed. After pursuing his elementary studies in Phillips Academy, Andover, he entered Amherst college, in 1853, and continued to maintain a creditable rank in scholarship till he graduated. He then chose the profession of medicine, and after a course of study here, visited Europe for study and travel. On his return he commenced practice in Lynn, continuing till the war of the Rebellion broke out, at which time he joined the Eighth Massachusetts Regiment, as surgeon. Subsequently he was put in charge of government hospitals and sanitary establishments in several places, and throughout his term of service acquitted himself with fidelity and success. After the close of the war he was appointed Surgeon of the Military Asylum at Augusta, Me., and there continued till the destruction of the place by fire. After that he resumed practice in Lynn ; but though skillful and devoted his health was such that he could not apply himself with the constancy necessary for the building up of an extensive business. He finally relinquished his profession, and for a year and a half was co-editor and proprietor of the Reporter newspaper. He was a member of the City Council for several years, and a Representative in the General Court. As a member of the School Committee, likewise, he was attentive and efficient. In short, he took commendable interest and discreet action in all that seemed most conducive to the highest good of his native place. Being a member of several organizations, benevolent, professional, and military, his funeral was attended by large numbers who had become attached by brotherly and social ties. By the City Council his decease was noticed in a manner that showed his loss to be regarded as a public calamity.

Dr. Breed married Hannah Pope, October 20, 1859, and by her had six children.

BREED, EBENEZER. A biographical sketch of this individual, popularly known as " Uncle Eben," whose marvelous good fortune at one period and distressingly adverse circumstances at another, have furnished many an impressive lesson, is given in the 1865 edition of the History of Lynn. He died in the almshouse, in 1839. The following is a fac-simile of his signature, at the age of 31.

BREED, HIRAM N. — the ninth Mayor of Lynn — is another creditable representative of the extensive family who trace their pedigree to the early settler, Allen Breed. A notice of him, with a portrait, may be found in the Centennial Memorial. He was born on the 2d of September, 1809, and is still, 1881, in active life. A fac-simile of his signature follows.

BREED, ISAIAH — was for many years an active business man, in the shoe-manufacturing line, and likewise took much interest in public affairs. He was one of the principal founders of the Central Congregational Society, and one of its chief supporters for a number of years. A brief biographical sketch of him may be found in the 1865 edition of the History of Lynn, page 541. He was born in 1786 and died in 1859.

BRIDGES, ROBERT. Mr. Bridges — or Captain Bridges, as he was usually called — because of his having been, as one may say, the father of the first iron works in America, if for no other reason, should be held in remembrance. It was in 1642 that he took specimens of the bog ore found in Lynn, to London, and succeeded in forming a company which soon after commenced operations here, erecting a bloomary and forge, the site of which is still shown by the "cinder banks," or heaps of scoria on the margin of Saugus river, in the vicinity of Pranker's mill. And although to its projectors the enterprise did not prove pecuniarily successful, it cannot be doubted that the result was of great and lasting benefit to the country at large, for it drew hither some of the most skillful workers in iron that England had produced, several of whom, even before the attempt had been abandoned, removed to other settlements and established works which under better management were highly successful, and added immensely to the general prosperity of the country. And it is a noteworthy fact that descendants of some of the operatives at these Lynn works, are at this day found among the leaders of the great iron trade of America. The iron turned out from the Lynn works was considered of very good quality, and it had a ready sale;

but the company was almost ceaselessly engaged in law-suits; which was enough to ruin any incipient enterprise.

The residence of Captain Bridges was in the vicinity of the works; and Edward Johnson, in his "Wonder Working Providence," says "He was endued with able parts, and forward to improve them to the glory of God and his people." And there is abundant evidence, from other sources, that his principles were of rigid puritanical stamp. He was an acting magistrate, and in that capacity did not always allow the kindlier sympathies to prevail when those brought before him dared to enunciate sentiments adverse to the prevailing faith or to question the authority of those appointed to guard against innovations. It was he who, in 1651, granted the warrants for the arrest of Clarke, Crandall and Holmes, the Baptist missionaries from Rhode Island, concerning whose advent here, an account may be found in our Annals, under the date just named. And in the Essex County files may be found the following record of his official action in the case of Thomas Wheeler, who appears to have been a man of character and some estate, and of whom a brief notice may be found in its alphabetical order in these pages: "4th mo. 1654. Thomas Wheeler, bound over to the Court by the worshipful Captain Bridges for sinful and offensive speeches made by him in comparing the Rev. Mr. Cobbet to Corah. It being proved by three witnesses, sentence of Court is, that he shall make public acknowledgment upon the Lord's day, sometime within a month after the date hereof, according to this form following, and pay the three witnesses £12 2s. 6d. and fees of Court: [I, Thomas Wheeler, having spoken at a town meeting in February last, evil, sinful, and offensive speeches against the Reverend Teacher, Mr. Cobbet, in comparing him unto Corah, for which I am very sorry, do acknowledge this my evil, to the glory and praise of God and to my own shame; and hope, for time to come, shall be more careful.] The constable of Lynn is to see it performed." Mr. Cobbet, it need not be added, was the colleague of Rev. Mr. Whiting in the ministry of the First Church; and the offensive words were probably spoken by Mr. Wheeler, in a heated town meeting debate, the ministers at that time being paid by the town, and the pastorate being regarded, in several particulars, as a town office.

It was in 1649 that the energetic protest against the wearing of long hair, "after the manner of ruffians and barbarous Indians," was promulgated, signed by the Governor and Assistants, of whom Captain Bridges was one. But the antipathy to the wearing of long hair, existing in those days, had a deeper significance than at first appears — a political tinge, indeed. In Cromwellian times, say for twenty years onward from 1640, the English royalists, cavaliers and high churchmen, delighted in "bravery of dress," and in long curling locks, while the puritans and parliamentarians were distinguished by their round hats and by their hair "cut round according to a cup." This perhaps suffi ciently hints at a reason for the singular protest. But the antipathy began to manifest itself even before the time named. By the Salem records, " 21th of the 6th month, 1637," it appears that John Gatshell of Marblehead was fined ten shillings, to be paid in two months, for building on the town's land without leave ; but the proviso was added, that "in case he shall cut off his long hair of his head into a civil frame, in the mean time," five shillings of the fine should be abated. It is said, however, that he refused to be shorn of his darling locks.

That Captain Bridges was a man of high character and very considerable attainment cannot be doubted. As a military officer he was in good repute ; as a diplomatist he was entrusted with important negotiations ; as a legislator he was for many years active in the public service, for ten years filling the responsible office of Assistant. In 1644 and '45 he was a Representative, and in 1646, Speaker of the House.

His curious deposition in the case of Taylor against King, so well exhibits the simplicity and some of the peculiar customs of the times, that it seems well to introduce it here, with the prefatory remark that the action was one brought to recover damages for the goring to death of the plaintiff's mare by the defendant's bull ; and Captain Bridges was a witness as to the vicious character of the bull. He says : " . . . myself being on horseback with my wyfe behinde me, ye s^d Bull stood in the high way as I was riding a Longe. When I came up to the Bull, not knowing whos beast it was, neither thinking of any opposition, I struck at the bull, wth my stick, to put him out of the way ; ymediately ye bull made att my mare, and placed his horne vpon her shoulder, and had well nigh overthrone both the mare and her riders ; and although I endeavored to shunne ye bull, yet he still so prest vpon mee y^t I cannot but conceave had not the nearcman bin att hand to beat him off that some hurt had bin done, either to o^{r}selves or my mare, or both ; but gods good hand better provided."

Captain Bridges was a member of the Ancient and Honorable Artillery, having joined in 1641. And in the codicil to the will of Robert Keayne, the eminent Boston merchant and first commander of that now historic corps, dated Dec. 28, 1653, this item appears : "I have forgott one Loveing Couple more that came not to my mind till I was shutting vp ; that is, Capt Bridges and wife, to whom I give forty shillings."

The foregoing is sufficient for a glimpse at various points in the character and career of one of the devoted men who so faithfully labored in laying the foundations of the social fabric which has become our inheritance — men honest, religious, persevering, hopeful, and brave. Yet it must be admitted that Capt. Bridges was not of a specially genial disposition ; nor could he have been very popular in some of his relations. He had hard points of character ; was arbitrary, exacting, unyielding, in the smaller concerns of daily intercourse, and perhaps not sufficiently regardful of the minor rights of those about him ; for we all love to have our rights respected even when they are of little value. In those days of difficulty and doubt minds were trained to meet the trials of life with a fortitude that amounted to heroism. Indeed, it was a favorite idea, that the afflictions men were called to endure were disciplinary ; that souls were purified by such means. This, however, was probably quite as much theoretical as otherwise, for the best of us would prefer to secure by observation rather than experience, the good that might be derived from pain and suffering.

In our Annals of early dates may be found many facts concerning Captain Bridges not here alluded to. The Petition of Dame Armitage, presented in 1643, for license to keep the tavern, established by her husband in the westerly part of Lynn, as before remarked, was, no doubt, written by him. He was a remarkably good penman ; and his name is conspicuous among the signers, as may be seen by reference to page 106.

BRIMBLECOM, Col. SAMUEL — an early and enterprising shoe-manufacturer, public spirited, intelligent, and of genial manners. He was an admirer of the works of some of the old English writers and of the poets of later date, especially delighting in the writings of Pope, from which he was accustomed often to quote. He lived on Western avenue near Franklin street, and died April 24, 1850, aged 81. See Annals, 1850. Brimblecom street, which after his decease was cut through a field belonging to the homestead estate, took its name from him.

BROWN, GOOLD — a famous grammarian and author — lived on South Common street, and died March 31, 1857, aged 65. See Annals, 1857.

BUBIER, SAMUEL M. — was the fifteenth Mayor of Lynn. He was twice elected to the office, his inaugurations taking place on the first of January, 1877 and the seventh of January, 1878. He is a native of Lynn, and was born in the Col. Mansfield house on Strawberry avenue, on the 23d of June, 1816. His whole business life has been connected with the shoe trade ; and he was a manufacturer for forty years, a considerable part of the time on quite a large scale. Few persons of his generation have done more to advance our staple industry than he, as he has ever held himself in readiness to introduce new and improved machinery, and to adopt any plan calculated to advance the interests of the trade. Some of the finest business buildings in the city were erected by him, and he has long been regarded as an enterprising, faithful, and meritorious citizen. On the 30th of October, 1844, he married Miss Mary W. Todd, of Topsfield, Mass., and became the father of three sons and one daughter. Mr. Bubier, during the last few years, has gradually withdrawn from active business. A fac-simile of his signature is here given.

Samuel M. Bubier

BUFFUM, JAMES N. Mr. Buffum was our twelfth Mayor, and twice elected to the office. His first inauguration took place on the 4th of January, 1869, and his second on the 1st of January

SAMUEL M. BUBIER. (Fifteenth Mayor of Lynn.)

1872. He was born in North Berwick, Me., May 16, 1807, and his wife was a daughter of Dr. John Lummus of Lynn. A biographical sketch, with a portrait, may be found in the Centennial Memorial, and a fac-simile of his autograph is hereto appended.

BUFFUM, JONATHAN. Mr. Buffum was for many years prominent in public life and active in business. He was intelligent, and in his opinions firm to the verge of obstinacy. He had keen sympathies for the oppressed, and in the anti-slavery cause was a zealous worker. He lived on Union street, opposite the head of Washington, and died June 22, 1868, aged 74. See Annals, 1868.

BURRILL, Hon. EBENEZER — a Crown Counsellor, and otherwise conspicuous, in provincial times. He lived in Swampscott ; was born in 1679 and died in 1761. A biographical notice, with some account of the Burrill family, may be found in the 1865 edition of the History of Lynn, page 492, et seq.

BURRILL, GEORGE — one of the first settlers, and head of the family once called the royal family of Lynn. He lived on the western slope of Tower Hill. See Annals, 1630. A fac-simile of his autograph follows.

BURRILL, Hon. JOHN — a Representative for some twenty years, and Speaker of the House ten years. He was highly respected by his associates, and extolled for his ability as a presiding officer. He lived at Tower Hill; was born in 1658 and died in 1721. A biographical sketch appears in the 1865 edition of the History of Lynn. He was a good penman, as the fac-simile of his signature here given shows.

John Burrill

BURTON, BONIFACE. This somewhat noted individual died on the 13th of June, 1669, at the age of 113 or 115 years as has been repeatedly asserted. But it is claimed by others that he died at about the age of 90. His autograph appears among those attached to the Armitage Petition, page 106. There was a propensity in early times to overstate the ages of elderly people ; yet we find no conclusive evidence that Mr. Burton's years were not as many as the largest number claimed. See Annals, 1630.

CARNES, Rev. JOHN — minister, magistrate, and politician. 'Squire Carnes, as he was called, lived on Boston street ; and Carnes street, which was opened through land belonging to his estate, perpetuates his name. His dwelling was of wood, two stories in height, and stood where the last named street enters Boston street. A couple of enormous buttonwoods, looking as if reared for gate posts, stood in front. It was once a somewhat pretentious residence ; but in its last years was shabby, and presented anything but an inviting appearance. He died on the 26th of October 1802, aged 78. See Annals, 1802.

CHADWELL, THOMAS. The Chadwell family is one of the oldest in Lynn, and has always had prominent and worthy members. Thomas, the above-named, was here as early as 1630, and settled as a farmer in the section known as Breed's End. There was also a Richard Chadwell here, in 1636 ; but the next year he went off with the Sandwich settlers. See Annals, 1630.

Lieutenant Harris Chadwell of the Revolution was a descendant of Thomas. So also was the late William Chadwell, for many years deputy sheriff of the county ; an officer in many respects well qualified for the performance of his often disagreeable duties.

He was convivial in his habits, active and mirthful. After his retirement from the office of sheriff he was for a time ticket-master at the Central Depot; and it was while he held this position that the depot safe was blown open and robbed, during a thunder storm, on the night of May 6, 1848. He was rather a strong political partisan; took an active interest in town affairs; and with many became unpopular by the ardor with which he opposed the anti-masonic movement. He was a member of the craft, and quite as zealous as discreet. But he was far from being deficient in good points of character; was companionable and unselfish; and as an officer, willing to exercise a reasonable degree of forbearance.

A vein of eccentricity seems to have cropped out here and there in the line, in former years, though we never heard of its assuming an offensive character. We remember one of the family who some sixty-five years ago was a hard working man, laboring somewhat at rough farming and in winter, when the swamps were frozen, cutting and teaming wood. He was long marked for his amusing vagaries of speech; especially for the curious discourses to his cattle as they jogged along their weary way. He would make the most extravagant promises to them as to the quality and amount of fodder they should receive in return for putting forth a little extra exertion. " Come, now, my friend, you off-ox, put in a little more of the tug and let us get home before sun-down, for it will be a dark night. You shall have a good supper of English hay; we 'll put off the old cow with salt hay rations; come, another strong pull and we 'll be over these hubbles; and you, old horse, you know where I keep the corn and oats, and if you 'll get us home by supper time, you shall have your fill, if it takes ten bushels and a half. It is meeting night, you know, and I want to be in my place. Come, come, now let us try that quick step. We 'll haul up at the Major's corner, a spell, and you can rest while I go in and get a little something warming; your treat will come when we get home." With such discourse, uttered in a voice so loud that the passer-by might conclude that he thought his animals deaf, was the tedium of the way beguiled by the kindly teamster, he really appearing, by his earnestness, to fancy that his cattle fully understood his proposals and promises; and what is quite as remarkable they seemed to have some comprehension of his meaning and be willing to exert themselves to merit his favor. It was Bayard Taylor, if we rightly remember, who claimed that there are minds which can establish intelligent communication with lower animals.   Perhaps there are, and that this Mr. Chadwell's was one of them.

CHASE, HEZEKIAH.   Mr. Chase was for many years a well-known and highly respected resident ; was first president of the Nahant Bank, and long identified with the business enterprises of the day.   His residence was on Western avenue, near the Summer street crossing ; and the grist, spice, and coffee mills, in that vicinity, so long known as Chase's mills, were owned by him, and from him took their name.   His death, which occurred on the 26th of March, 1865, was occasioned by injuries received on being thrown down by a sudden jerk of the cars as they started from the West Lynn depot.   His age was 72, and he was a native of Plaistow, N. H.

CHASE, JOHN.   Mr. Chase, at the time of his decease, was one of the few remaining old-time shoemakers, and had little practical knowledge of the recent improvements in the mode of manufacture, as well as little taste for them.   At the age of twelve, in accordance with the custom of the time, he finished his schooling and was put upon the shoemaker's seat.   And upon that seat he worked for seventy years, using the same lap-stone and several of the same tools, for that long period.   How many feet his labors must have helped to clothe during those many years, we need not pause to calculate.   He was an intelligent, worthy man, active in politics, and among the early advocates of the abolition of slavery.   For thirty years he was a member of the First Methodist church.   The old seat on which he worked and some of his tools have been preserved as relics that will be appreciated by curious inquirers into the earlier history of the great manufacture of New England.   He died on the 2d of October, 1876, aged 83 years.

CHASE, Rev. STEPHEN — minister of the Lynnfield parish some twenty-four years.   See Annals, 1755.

CHEEVER, Rev. EDWARD — first minister of Saugus parish. See Annals, 1747.

CHILDS, AMARIAH — manufacturer of a famous kind of chocolate. His mill was on Saugus river, at the Boston street crossing, and his residence on Boston street, nearly opposite Bridge. He died January 21, 1846, aged 80. See Annals, 1846.

CLAPP, HENRY — known during the latter years of his life as the "King of the Bohemians." He made his appearance in Lynn, in or about 1847, and while here kept up a pretty lively agitation on some of the reformatory questions of the day. He was a man of undoubted ability and good education, terse and bold as a writer, and eloquent as a speaker; but his utterances were often too reckless and extravagant to have the desired effect. He was editor of the Pioneer, a weekly newspaper, of which Christopher Robinson, a well-known shoe-manufacturer was proprietor, and of whom Mr. Clapp was a sort of protege. In his editorials were many striking and valuable ideas, but far too often there was a lurking venom or pungency of expression that overshot the mark and destroyed the good effect.

Mr. Clapp died in New York, early in 1875, and the newspapers here and abroad had much to say about his erratic character and career. It was he who said of Horace Greeley, that "he was a self-made man, and worshiped his maker." His literary efforts were chiefly confined to the newspapers, though the magazines were occasionally enriched by his articles. In the fifteenth volume of Harper's Magazine may be found a paper of his entitled "How I came to be Married," and in the sixteenth volume another, entitled "Love Experience of an Impressible Man." The latter volume also contains a poem of his entitled "My Illusions Spare," which is far above the average of magazine poetry, and may yet be garnered up as one of America's literary jewels.

The following, which appeared in a Boston publication soon after the decease of Mr. Clapp, furnishes a comprehensive glimpse of him and the class to which he belonged.

With the death of Henry Clapp, long known as the "King of the Bohemians," fades the memory of one of the most peculiar cliques of roystering literary characters

9

ever known. Not long ago Ada Clare, the "Queen of Bohemia," died a victim of that strange malady, hydrophobia, and the rest of the colony that once met at Pfaff's beer saloon, on Broadway, to enliven the midnight hour with songs and jokes and reckless repartee, are either dead or dispersed, or turned respectable. The most brilliant lights went out some years ago, when George Arnold and Fitz James O'Brien died, and Clapp retired from the Bohemian throne. Others are still living, but the haunts that once knew them know them no more. There is Walt Whitman, a confirmed invalid; "Doestick" still lives, but the unction of his humor has passed with the increasing obesity of his body; Ned House is in Japan, connected with the educational department of the government; and Willie Winter has subsided into a taciturn and sedate, though bright and vigorous critic. There were women in Bohemia besides Ada Clare. There was Jenny Danforth, who is dead, or in obscurity almost as complete as death; Dora Shaw, who claimed the authorship of "Beautiful Snow," but could not maintain the doubtful honor; and Mary Fox, still lively and sharp-witted, the "M. H. B." of the St. Louis Republican. But then Bohemia is completely dead, though there are Bohemians enough of a straggling sort in Gotham yet, God wot. But the Bohemia over which Clapp presided, the bright, witty and wicked circle of writers in the basement beer saloon, whose quips and cranks were as sparkling and as evanescent as the foam on their glasses, is a thing of the past. It required a peculiar genius to call together and keep together such a company, and its existence and its opportunity are not likely to occur again in the present generation.

The life of Henry Clapp was a strange one. He was born in Nantucket, and in his early life was a sailor. Afterwards he appeared as a temperance lecturer and an ardent advocate of the abolition of slavery, travelling extensively in the cause of reform. He was for some time in Paris, and after his return he made translations of some of the prominent socialistic works of Fourier. His first journalistic experience was in editing an anti-slavery paper in Lynn, but he was best known as the founder of the "Saturday Press," and "Vanity Fair," in New York. Both of these were too bright and too impracticable to last. Many of the brightest of the Bohemians were contributors to Vanity Fair, but all their wit could not keep it alive. Clapp afterwards became well known as "Figaro" of the Lander, a paper at one time owned and edited by Mayor Hall, and latterly he obtained a precarious livelihood by writing paragraphs for the Daily Graphic and sending occasional contributions to dramatic and musical journals from a New Jersey farm-house. His talent was essentially that of the French Feuilletonistes, bright, keen and witty, but unsubstantial and ephemeral. In character he was of the essence of Bohemia, reckless and witty, caring and thinking little of the serious concerns of life, but living as those who say, "Let us eat, drink and be merry, for to-morrow we die." That to-morrow of death has come for Henry Clapp, and no one can have the heart to throw anything but the mantle of charity over his bier.

There would, perhaps, be little reason for introducing Mr. Clapp in this connection, were it not that he played so conspicuous and sensational a part while here. He fraternized with the "Comeouters," though guiltless of the extremes that characterized the conduct of some of the earlier ones, as noticed in our Annals, under date 1841. And it may be pardonable to add that the writer was well acquainted with him, and in common with others esteemed him highly for his generous and genial qualities. It was likewise our fortune, while a resident of New York, to very well know one or two of the other " Bohemians " named above. The fact is, that "clique of roystering literary characters " led a sort of dual lives — now in the society of the better class of literary workers, supplying, with amazing facility, elaborate papers and high-toned critiques, and anon at some Pewter Mug rendezvous, bandying quibs and relating wild adventures. Their condition and appearance were attributable to utter improvidence. They could earn money, and some of them did get high prices for magazine articles and editorial assistance ; but what did they do with their earnings ?

The writer one day, during a later visit to the city, on passing down Fulton street met one of the " Bohemians " named in the foregoing extract, whom he had not seen for months, and the greeting was cordial. The meeting happened to be near a restaurant and it was about noon. " Come, come," said he " now let us step right in here, and I 'll order something for the encouragement of the inner man ; and over the supply we 'll have a talk." " But I can't," was the reply, for I am now on the way to a steamer, and cannot delay." " Well, then, good-by ; and perhaps," he added with his old air of mock gravity, " it is about as well that you declined my generous invitation, for six cents is the grand sum-total of my funds." But he forsook the Bohemian life, is yet living, and his fame as a writer is second to that of but few either here or in Europe.

COBBET, Rev. THOMAS — was settled over the Lynn church, in 1637, as colleague with Rev. Mr. Whiting. He was a marked character among the early New England divines. His autograph is attached to the Armitage Petition, page 106. Cobbet school, Franklin street, takes its name from him. See Annals, date 1656.

COFFIN, Dr. EDWARD L. — physician, scientist, and writer. He lived on Market street, and died March 31, 1845, aged 50. A biographical notice appears in 1865 edition of History of Lynn.

COLLINS, MICAJAH — minister of the Friends' society, and teacher of the Friends' school. He was born in Lynn, in 1764 and died in 1827.   In the 1865 edition of the History of Lynn, appeared a biographical notice.

COOK, REV. JOSEPH — for a short time minister of the First Church — a pungent preacher and popular lecturer in America and Europe.   See Annals, 1871.

COOKE, REV. PARSONS — minister of the First Church, twenty-one years ; a rigid Calvinist, and warm controversial preacher and writer — born in 1800, died in 1864.   See Annals, 1864.

COOLIDGE, OLIVER B. — well-known in various public positions. He died June 6, 1874, aged 76.   See Annals, 1874.

COWDRY, WILLIAM — whose autograph may be seen among those appended to the Armitage Petition, page 106, came here in 1630, but did not remain many years.   He became one of the first settlers of Reading, and was very conspicuous there ; was a deacon of the church, a representative, selectman and town clerk from the beginning of the settlement till his death, in 1687, at the age of 85.   He was born in 1602, and was a farmer.

CURTIN, ENOCH — a poet and prose writer.   He lived in the eastern section of the town ; was born in 1794 and died in 1842. For biographical sketch, with poetic specimens, see 1865 edition of History of Lynn.

DAGYR, JOHN ADAM — famed throughout the province as a fashionable shoemaker.   He died in the almshouse, in 1808. See Annals, 1750.

DAVIS, EDWARD S. — the eighth Mayor of Lynn.   For Biographical notice, with portrait, see Centennial Memorial.

DEXTER, THOMAS — one of the most enterprising and noted of the early settlers. See Annals, 1630, et seq. The following represents his signature.

DOAK, BENJAMIN F. Mr. Doak died at his residence, corner of Atlantic and Ocean streets, on the 8th of November, 1876, aged 50 years. He was a native of Lynn though of a Marble-head family, and after receiving a fair common school education, in early manhood began business in a small way as a shoe-man-ufacturer. By industry and shrewd management he soon attained a position among our first class business men. He was a con-spicuous and highly respected member of the First Universalist Society, and a much esteemed citizen and friend. At various times he filled positions of public trust, and on the day of his burial a number of large business houses were closed in token of respect for his memory. By will, he bequeathed " to the City of Lynn, the sum of ten thousand dollars to be invested by the City as a separate fund, the income thereof to be expended by said City for the benefit of its poor, in such manner as the City Council may direct." This bequest is what is now called " The Doak Fund." Mr. Doak was for some years known as Benjamin F. Doak, 2d, there being two others of the name, in the vicinity, his seniors.

DOOLITTLE, JOHN — a settler of some note ; was one of the appraisers of the estate of Edward Holyoke. He removed to Boston, and was a constable in 1653. The Armitage Petition, page 106, bears his signature.

DOWNING, ELIJAH — an early and zealous Methodist ; an acting magistrate and one interested in town affairs. He was born in 1777 ; was a cabinet-maker ; lived on North Common street, corner of Park ; died in 1838. See History of Lynn, 1865 edition, for a biographical notice.

DOWNING, Rev. JOSHUA WELLS. Mr. Downing was one of the most promising young men Lynn has produced, and by his early death she no doubt lost one who would have done much to extend her fame.   He was born here on the fifth of March, 1813, and was a son of Elijah Downing, named next above.   At the age of seventeen he entered Brown University, and graduated in 1834.   His original design was to adopt the legal profession as the business of his life ; but being brought to a deep sense of the greater dignity and importance of a profession that more nearly touched the higher concerns of men, he soon directed his attention to the ministry, and in June, 1835, was received into the New England Methodist Conference, and stationed at Randolph, in Norfolk county.   The next year he was appointed to the Salem charge, and in the short space of two years after, that is, in 1838, had attained such a reputation as to be placed in charge of one of the oldest and most opulent churches of the denomination in New England — the Bromfield Street Church, in Boston.   And in that charge, secure in the affections of his people, and with an ever increasing reputation in the community at large, he remained till the time of his death, which occurred on the 15th of July, 1839.   About one year before his death he married May Ann, a daughter of Daniel L. Mudge, who survived him ; but he left no children.   His brother, the Rev. Elijah Hedding Downing, now a minister in the Protestant Episcopal Church, and who is a graduate of Bowdoin College, prepared a very sympathetic and interesting memorial volume, which was published in New York, in 1842.   The sermons and addresses embodied in it evince a remarkably pure, well-trained, and earnest mind, and are composed in a terse, vigorous, and attractive style.

DRAPER, ALONZO G. — a commander in the war of the Rebellion ; shot from his horse, apparently by accident, in Texas, September, 1865.   See Annals, 1865.

DRIVER, ROBERT.   Respectable descendants have sprung from this early settler, though not much is known of him.   His autograph is on the Armitage Petition, page 106.   He died in 1680, aged 87.   See Annals, 1630.

FAY, RICHARD S. — owner of the beautiful Mineral Spring estate — (Lynnmere).   He died June 6, 1865.   See Annals, 1865.

FITCH, ZACHARY, whose autograph is last on the Armitage Petition, had "30 and ten acres" allotted to him in the land distribution of 1638. He moved to Reading, in 1644, and became a deacon in the church there. Fitch's Hill, so called, was a part of his estate. Few of his descendants are now found here.

FLACG, Dr. JOHN — a highly esteemed physician and revolutionary patriot ; lived on Marion street ; born in 1743, died May 27, 1793. See Annals, 1793.

FLORA — a pious negro woman of touching history ; died in 1828, aged 113 years. See Annals, 1828.

FORMAN, EUGENE F. — editor of the Lynn Daily Bee. His death was occasioned by a singular and distressing accident, September 3, 1881. See Annals, 1881.

FULLER, JOSEPH — first Senator from Lynn, and first president of the first bank here — was born on Water Hill, March 29, 1772. See History of Lynn, 1865 edition, page 505.

FULLER, MARIA AUGUSTA — poetess and prose writer — was born in Lynn, Dec. 9, 1806, and died January 19, 1831. A biographical notice, with specimens of her writing may be found in the 1865 edition of the History of Lynn. A fac-simile of her signature follows,

Maria A Fuller

GARDNER, Dr. JAMES — a physician of high standing, and much respected for his good judgment and benevolence. He died December 26, 1831, aged 69. His residence was on Boston street, near Bridge. See Annals, 1831.

GARDNER, JAMES H. — was born in Lynn July 29, 1796, and died in Richmond, Va., September 10, 1877. He was a son of Dr. James Gardner, just named, and a grandson of Dr. Flagg, who occupied the "Billy Gray" house. He became a resident of Richmond in early life, and for many years carried on a large and successful business there, maintaining a character for integrity and liberality attained by few. The Richmond Despatch, in an obituary notice, said of him, "There was no man who was more worthily loved and respected, and no man whose life was more exemplary." He always entertained the highest regard for his native place, and until the infirmities of age overtook him, made an annual visit, encouraging her public enterprises and liberally bestowing in charity, from his large means, which, however, became sadly reduced by the calamities of the civil war, an occurrence which he deeply deplored. He was an active member of the Protestant Episcopal communion, and even as far back as 1819, when the first attempt was made to establish a church here he looked hopefully forward to the time when her benign influence would pervade the community ; was a strong and helping friend to St. Stephen's in her darkest hours, and happily lived to see her in comparative prosperity. A memorial window has been placed in the church at Richmond, where he worshiped, and in which he was a vestryman and Sunday school superintendent many years.

GATES, ISAAC — a shrewd but eccentric lawyer. His office and residence were on Market street, that street then being chiefly occupied by residences. He died Nov. 9, 1852. See Annals, 1852.

GILLOW, JOHN. There were several Gillows here at an early period, but it does not appear that any of their descendants remain. The John whose autograph is to be seen on the Armitage Petition, page 106, was doubtless the shrewd individual who so successfully turned the tables on a pestilent fellow who sued him for the loss of a cow. The case occurred in 1638, and is thus related by Winthrop : "A remarkable providence appeared in a case which was tried at the last Court of Assistants. Divers neighbors of Lynn, by agreement kept their cattle by turns. It fell out to the turn of one Gillow to keep them, and as he was driving them forth another of these neighbors went along with him, and kept him so earnestly in talk, that his cattle strayed and gate in the corn. Then this other neighbor left him, and would not help him recover his cattle, but went and told another how he had kept Gillow in talk, that he might lose his cattle. The cattle getting into the Indian corn, eat so much ere they could be gotten out, that two of them fell sick of it, and one of them died presently ; and these two cows were that neighbor's who kept Gillow in talk. The man brings his action against Gillow for his cow (not knowing that he had witness of his speech;) but Gillow, producing witness, barred him of his action, and had good costs." Mr. Gillow died in 1673.

Gould Dr. Abraham — A skillful physician, of large practice. His residence was on Boston street, a furlong east of Tower Hill, and he died February 27, 1866, aged 58. See Annals, 1866.

Gray, George — the Lynn Hermit — lived on Boston street, nearly opposite the entrance to Pine Grove Cemetery, and died February 28, 1848, aged 78. See Annals, 1848.

It was natural enough that many wonderful stories touching the career of such a mysterious personage as Mr. Gray should have gained currency. The writer had occasional interviews with him, and knew that he was well aware of the gossiping indulgencies of his neighbors. But he was shrewd enough never to admit or deny the truth of anything that was said about him. Among the most interesting incidents in his veritable or imaginary history was his alleged connection with the fate of the French Dauphin, Charles Louis, son of Louis XVI and Maria Antoinette. It is easy enough to see how in a fertile imagination such an alluring connection may have been suggested by the following facts : A number of years ago the Rev. Eleazer Williams, a respectable clergyman of the Protestant Episcopal Church, who had for a considerable period been laboring as a missionary among the St. Regis Indians visited Lynn. An article had about that time appeared in Putnam's Magazine, a periodical of high standing, presenting quite an array of evidence tending to show that this Mr. Williams was in truth the scion of royalty whose death history had all along informed us took place in 1795, through the cruel treatment of Simon, into whose relentless custody the revolutionary miscreants had resigned him. There were many, however, who did not feel assured that history, in this instance, spoke the exact truth.

Mr. Williams, during his visit to Lynn, which was brief, called on the writer, for the chief purpose of obtaining a specimen of the handwriting of the Hermit ; and no doubt he had interviews with others. That he felt confident that he really was the Dauphin may not be disputed, the theory being that he had become well nigh demented by the heartless treatment of Simon — his memory and power of observation almost extinguished — and in that condition was secretly taken from that austere custody, brought to the wilds of America, and given in charge of a woman of the St. Regis tribe, who nurtured him lovingly. He believed that he had always been kept in sight by French partisans, and mentioned the fact that the Prince de Joinville, when in this country sought him out and had an interview at Green Bay, but was shy about stating the object or result of the interview. The magazine article, however, intimated that the Prince had enjoined conditional secresy, and added that Louis Philip himself, after the return of his son, wrote to Mr. Williams. The almost idiotic condition to which the Dauphin had been reduced was urged as a reason why Mr. Williams had no clear recollection of things that happened before he attained the age of thirteen or fourteen — only a few dream-like catches. It was likewise mentioned as a significant fact that in the reign of Louis xviii the name of the Dauphin was omitted in the funeral solemnities for the deceased Bourbons. The Indian woman was said never to have claimed that the child was her own ; and it is asserted that when Professor Day placed before him a portrait of Simon, he gave a shudder ; and further, that he recognized a portrait of Madam Elizabeth as the likeness of one whom he had seen. It was also said that the ambassador Genet declared that the Dauphin was alive, in New York state, in 1817, though it is not known that he located him in St. Regis, which is in that state, and that a Frenchman named Boulanger, who died in New Orleans, in 1848, on his death-bed declared that he had a hand in bringing the royal child to America.

These circumstances, in connection with the fact that Mr. Williams was so anxious to obtain a specimen of the handwriting of the Hermit furnished a basis for a very interesting superstructure. And it was soon claimed — on what authority we have yet been unable to determine — that Gray was in France, a red republican, during the most sanguinary days of the revolution, and was one of those who brought hither the ill-fated boy.

What the truth in this mysterious matter is, it is now probable will never be known ; and though it may detract something from the romance of the narrative, we feel bound to add a few facts of a different aspect touching the identity of Mr. Williams. The name Williams has been long known in the St. Regis tribe, for it will not be forgotten that the minister of Deerfield who with his family was taken captive among others on the terrible night of the savage attack on the settlement, in 1703, was the Rev. John Williams. The captives were, with a few exceptions, finally redeemed. But his daughter Eunice had become so enamored of Indian life that she could not be induced to return to civilization, though she occasionally visited her early friends. Now we find it stated in the Historical Collections of New York, that this very Eleazer Williams was a grandson of Eunice who adhered to the surname of her father, and that he was educated by her Christian friends. For many years he was a devoted missionary in the tribe, and did much to ameliorate their condition. A late chief of the tribe bore the name of Williams, and was, no doubt, another descendant of Eunice. Assuming that these statements are all authentic, they would preclude a belief that Mr. Williams was the French Dauphin. But there is no conclusive evidence on the point, his own recollection being entirely at fault. He possessed one physical feature which was quite observable, namely, an unmistakable Bourbon nose.

We remarked that when here Mr. Williams was anxious to obtain a specimen of the handwriting of the Hermit ; but he seemed to desire it for use in efforts then being made to secure the property left by Gray, who had lately died, for a claimant in whom he felt an interest, but whether one connected with old French affairs is not known. The following is a fac-simile of the Hermit's signature.

GRAY, WILLIAM — best known by the inelegant sobriquet "Billy Gray" — an eminent merchant, and Lieut. Governor of the State. He was born in the Dr. Flagg house, Marion street, and died in Boston, November 3, 1825, aged 75 years, leaving many descendants. Rev. William Gray Swett, who was installed minister of the Unitarian society, January 1, 1840, was a grandson of his ; and Chief Justice Gray, of our Supreme Court, and later an Associate on the Supreme Bench of the United States, was likewise a grandson. For biographical notice see 1865 edition of History of Lynn.

HALSEY, THOMAS. Not much will be found in our Annals, relating to this individual, though he was allowed a hundred acres in the land distribution of 1638, for he became interested in the Long Island enterprise, and was one of the settlers of Southampton. In his new location he became prominent and comparatively wealthy. Among his numerous descendants, scattered all over the country, several have won their way to distinction and useful positions. Among the few from the eastern part of Long Island who joined the Continentals on the opening of the Revolution, was Jesse Halsey, who, on hearing of the battle of Lexington, started for the scene of conflict. He left his horse at Sag Harbor, crossed in a boat to New London, and after a tedious journey reached Boston just too late for a part in the battle of Bunker Hill. He became a Captain in the Continental forces, and as is stated by Mr. Howell, in his History of Southampton, was standing near General Lee, at the battle of Monmouth, when Washington rode up, foaming with indignation, and demanded, " In the name of God, Lee, what do you mean ?" and these, he ever afterwards declared, were the exact words of Washington as distinctly heard by him on that momentous occasion. Daniel Halsey, another descendant, was born in the latter part of the last century, on the estate of his fathers, and became of some note as a poet. He had a good education, and enjoyed a high reputation as a teacher. The following opening stanza of a spirited ode written by him for a fourth of July celebration will remind some of our more elderly readers of the lyrical fire and patriotic sentiment pervading the productions of Enoch Curtin, furnished for similar occasions :

When the Goddess of Liberty found not a place
Where the sole of her foot in the old world could rest,

> She directed the daring Columbus to trace
> A path to the new world unknown in the west ;
> In the wilds which she chose
> An empire arose,
> As by magic, of freemen redeemed from their foes,
> Redeemed from the hand of oppression and wrong,
> To the rights which by nature to all men belong.

There is preserved another effusion of Mr. Halsey, written at the request of a tavern keeper for an appropriate inscription to be put upon his sign-board. It is rather suggestive, and reads as follows :

> Rum, whisky, brandy, cordial, porter, beer,
> Ale, applejack, and gin, are dealt out here,
> Diluted, raw, or mixt, in any measure,
> To all consumers : come and act your pleasure,
> The above specifics will, in time, God knows,
> Put to a period all your earthly woes ;
> Or would you bring life to a splendid close,
> Take double swigs, repeating dose on dose ;
> A panacea this for every ail ;
> 'T will use you up ; 't was never known to fail ;
> Use up your property, ere scarce you know it,
> Use up your character, or sadly blow it,
> Use up your health and strength, and mind repose,
> And leave, mayhap, your carcass to the crows.

And the following fragment, smooth in expression, and charged with wholesome truth, may be well worth the space it occupies :

> Hear when the widow and the orphan cry,
> And with a liberal hand the poor supply ;
> Nor with an envious eye the rich behold ;
> None are the better for their sums of gold.
> A virtuous mind should be our only test ;
> He is the worthiest man who is the best.
> Wealth can no real happiness bestow ;
> How few in higher life contentment know ;
> Then to the will of Heaven be thou resigned,
> Enjoy thy fortune and contentment find.

HANDFORD, NATHANIEL. This is the " honest old man " who saw the wonderful apparitions in the air on a Sunday evening in March, 1682, when looking for a new moon, after a violent storm of wind, hail, thunder and lightning, as noticed under that date, in our Annals. From the account given by Rev. Mr. Shepard it is concluded that he was of an apprehensive and superstitious cast of mind ; but perhaps not more so than was

common in those days. And that in his latter years he felt like
retiring from life's combats, its cares and vexations is evident
from the fact of his conveying the chief part of his estate to his
kinsman Nathaniel Newhall, on condition of his providing a
suitable home for him and his good wife Sarah, for their closing
years. And we hope the trust was more faithfully executed than
is sometimes the case at this day. Some passages in the deed
of conveyance exhibit a meek, pious and trustful spirit, though a
little weak withal, and may interest the reader: "To all Christian people to whome this present Deed of Gift shall come,
Nathaniel Handford of Lynn in ye County of Essex, Gentl^m and
Sarah his wife doe send greeting: . . . . Know ye that wee y^e
said Nathaniel Handford and Sarah his wife being well stricken
in yeares and thereby waxen weake and not fitt to continue alone
and dwell by ourselves as wee haue done for a long space nor
able to doe one for another as wee should in duty & loue would
still bind us and should did not our natural strength faile us which
we belieue ye Lord our good God and Sauiour in Jesus Christ
will accept in and through him and not impute sin unto us but
ye consideration of ye premises and duty bindeth us to take y^e
most effectuall course that wee can for our more easy and comfortable liuing while our time is appointed which wee willingly
wait on God for: And Seeing it hath pleased god to raise up
our beloued kinsman Nathaniel Newhall of ye same Towne and
County aforesaid a ship-carpenter who had his name Nathaniel
giuen to him in his Infancy for our sakes by his parents now
Serjeant John Newhall Secundo and his now wife and our neer
kinswoman and this said Nathaniel Newhall hauing shewed us
kindness already and hath taken as wee Trust a good wife and
hath obtayned a good and comfortable house to entertaine us
and a convenient roome for us to liue in our old age together
where wee shall not be troubled with too much company and our
said cousins are very willing to haue us to leaue our solitary
place and condition and to remoue our selues into our Cousin
Nathaniel Newhall aforesaid his house where he and his wife
now dwelleth. . . . . Wherefore for and in consideration of y^e
premises and being willing to free our selues of ye Troubles and
cares of ye world and ye better to prepare our selues for our
great and solemn change wee doe therefore accept of ye kind

loue of our cousin Nathaniel Newhall and Rest his now wife."
. . . . And then follow the proper terms of conveyance for the
purpose shadowed forth in this excursive preamble. The instrument bears date March 31, 1687.

The Nathaniel Newhall to whom the conveyance was made
removed to Boston, a few years after, probably because his business as ship-carpenter was better there, and there he died, in
1731. His grave-stone may yet be seen in Copp's Hill burying
ground. He was born in 1658, and was a grandson of Anthony
Newhall, brother of Thomas, from whom most of the present
Newhalls of Lynn descended.

Mr. Handford was a haberdasher from London. See Annals,
1635 and 1682.

HANNIBAL — sexton of the Old Tunnel — a pious and worthy
man — once a slave. See Annals, 1780.

HART, SAMUEL. Some uncertainty exists as to the precise
time when this individual first appeared in Lynn ; but he probably came in or about 1643, and was employed at the iron works.
The Harts became a noted family. Among the descendants of
this sturdy settler not elsewhere spoken of, was Captain Ralph
Hart, for many years a prominent and influential resident of
Boston. He was born in Lynn, June 12, 1699, and was, we think,
a grandson, though he is in some genealogical accounts set down
as a great-grandson, of Samuel. In 1742 he was commissioned
by Governor Shirley as " Lieutenant of the foot company of the
Town of Boston," and in 1754, as Captain of the Ancient and
Honorable Artillery. He married Mary Hudson of Lynn, Nov.
27, 1722, and she died August 2, 1733, aged 34. His second
wife, Lois, died November 5, 1751, aged 46. Their grave-stones
are still to be seen in Copp's Hill burying ground, in Boston,
bearing little or no mark of injury by the ravages of the British
soldiers during their occupation of the town. A daughter of his
married Joshua Bowles, who belonged to a highly connected
family, and was brother-in-law of Benjamin Lynde, Chief Justice
of the Province. Their son, Captain Ralph Hart Bowles, served
faithfully during the whole of the Revolution ; and after the war
was over, settled on the outskirt of civilization near the Maine

frontier. His wife was distinguished for refinement, elegant manners, and true dignity and strength of character; and her influence in molding the social condition of the little wilderness community was excellent and enduring. She died in 1847, at the age of 82, and her remains were entombed at Mount Auburn, in the lot of her son Stephen J. Bowles. Samuel Bowles, so long conspicuous and influential as editor of the Springfield Republican was a descendant.

Then there was Edmund Hart, the skillful naval architect, a native of Lynn, who lived in the Lois Hart house, on Boston street a few rods west of Federal. The famous frigate Constitution was built at his ship-yard, in North End, Boston; and as a good view of the yard could be had from Noddle's Island, now East Boston, hundreds went over from the town to see the launch. But the land which the ship-yard occupied does not seem to have been well chosen, as it was found that the ways were liable to sink. Two unsuccessful attempts were made before the frigate took kindly to her destiny. Sometime before the Revolution, Admiral Montague favored the project of having a British navy yard at the island, remarking that " the devil had got into the government when they fixed the navy yard at Halifax," for " God Almighty made Noddle's Island on purpose for a dock yard." But if it was preferable to Charlestown why did not our own government establish the navy yard there? Had a British dock yard been established there, in provincial times, instead of at Halifax, how different would probably have been the series of events that followed, and how different the condition of the whole country at this day.

The Hart family is extensively distributed over the country; and it seems quite certain that they did not all come from one family of immigrants. There was a John Hart, a Quaker preacher, who came with William Penn, and settled in Pennsylvania, having purchased a thousand acres of land before coming over. He left male descendants, one or two of whom, having abjured the faith of their fathers, became conspicuous as military leaders in Indian conflicts and in the Revolution. The similarity of christian names, however, rather indicates that all came from the same stock, not many generations back. " Honest John Hart," a well-to-do New Jersey farmer, whose name appears on that world-famed instrument, the Declaration of American Independence, and who for his temerity in thus employing his autograph, was subjected to great hardship and loss, will never be forgotten. And a grandson of his, living in West Virginia, had five sons in the Union army during the war of the Rebellion.

A neat volume of six hundred pages, embracing a genealogical history of Deacon Stephen Hart and his descendants evidently prepared with a good deal of care by Alfred Andrews of New Britain, Ct., was published a few years since ; and in the introduction is given a roving view of the family at large, which embraces some gatherings of much interest. In it are found the names of thirty-one authors, with the titles of their principal works ; among them Francis Bret Harte, the rollicking humorist, author of " Luck of Roaring Camp," &c. Then there are the names of twenty-seven physicians, twenty-five clergymen, and of soldiers who have served their country in various wars, two hundred and thirty. Few families can show a better record than the Hart. The earlier and more prominent of those in Lynn, seem to have located along Boston street, especially in the vicinity of Federal. Joseph Hart, a farmer, owned and occupied the ancient Richard Haven house that stood on the south-west corner formed by the two streets just named, and was for many years noticeable from the huge buttonwood standing in front. This house was the same that disappeared in a patriotic blaze on the morning of July 4, 1876, the centennial anniversary, as noticed in our Annals under that date. And upon the lot next west was the home of Edmund and Ralph Hart. There too lived their near kinswoman, Lois Hart, a strong-minded woman of the rougher sort — rough in speech and manners — made so, perhaps, in some degree, by the hard fortune to which she was subjected.

There is some doubt as to when the first person of the family name appeared in Lynn. There was an Isaac Hart here in 1640, who is said to have afterwards removed to Reading. And if, as seems probable, he was the individual referred to in the following entry found on the Colony Records under date July 30, 1640, there was some reason for his removal, and no cause for lamentation at his departure : " Isaack Hart bound himselfe in 20*l.* to bee of good behavio^r, and Mr Robt Saltonstall bound himselfe in 10*l.* for the said Isa: Hart his good behavior, till he dep^t out of the plantation, or bring a note from . . . . that he is free from fear." It does not appear what the rogue had done or left undone; but it looks as if he was put under bonds for some sort of a threat. For genealogical tracings see Annals, 1650. The name has prevailed to some extent in Lynn for considerably more than two hundred years. And if there is an ambition to connect it agreeably with old-world associations, it may be mentioned that Shakspeare's sister Joan married a Hart, and that the illustrious bard left legacies to his three nephews, her children, the bequests being in these words : " *Item:* I give and bequeath unto her three sons William Hart, [Thomas] Hart and Michael Hart, five pounds apiece, to be paid one year after my decease."

HAVEN, RICHARD. Mr. Haven was ancestor of the large family of the name now scattered all over the country. His wife, Susanna, was a sister of Thomas Newhall, the first white person born in Lynn, and they had twelve children. He lived in the old house that stood till 1876, on the south-west corner of Boston and Federal streets, when it was consumed in the centennial bonfire, on Reservoir Hill. Bishop Gilbert Haven and his cousin Bishop Erastus O. Haven, of the Methodist church, were lineal descendants of his. Samuel F. Haven, LL. D., a son of Judge Haven, who died in Worcester, September 5, 1881, at the age of 75, having served forty-three years as librarian of the American Antiquarian Society, was also a descendant ; and a son of the latter, a surgeon of great merit, who was attached to the Fifteenth Massachusetts Regiment, in the civil war, was killed in the battle of Fredericksburg. See Annals, 1640, and other early dates.

HAWKES, ADAM. This individual was one of the first comers, and located upon our inland border, in what is now known as North Saugus, having a grant of land which included the territory containing the ore first used at the iron works. Possessing rather a lively suspicion that the company were inclined to encroach upon his rights, he was not always at peace with them ; and to him and his neighbor Dexter is no doubt to be attributed somewhat of that harrassing legal warfare that proved so disastrous to the enterprise. A large and interesting gathering of his descendants was held on the original farm, on the 28th and 29th of July, 1880, of which a notice may be found in the Annals of that year. See also Annals, 1630.

HAZELTINE, Dr. RICHARD. Doctor Hazeltine was one of those staid and sober gentlemen who have great weight in a community; whose movements, professionally and socially, are well-considered, and who are not liable to be swayed by notions instead of principles. He was kind in manners, but very precise, and came to be popularly regarded as a strait-laced old-school gentleman. In short, he was just one of those persons who enjoy the respect but not always the love of those by whom they are surrounded. For professional dignity and propriety he was a great stickler; a characteristic aptly illustrated by a little occurrence which took place when Dr. Barker came here, in 1832, and which the latter himself described to the writer in his inimitable semi-serious way. He had located near Lynn Hotel, into the hospitable public room of which gentlemen from all quarters of the town were accustomed to drop, to look over the newspapers — for no dailies were then distributed by carriers — and hear the gossip of the day. Deacon Field, as we all called him, was the managing spirit though not the proprietor of the establishment. He was active and polite, and indefatigable in his endeavors to make his domain attractive and his visitors at ease.

One morning, while Dr. Barker, who had been very kindly received by the four or five other physicians then resident here, was in the room, Dr. Hazeltine dropped in, and the Deacon availed himself of the opportunity to effect a formal introduction. Dr. H. as soon as he heard the name of Dr. B. assumed one of his lofty looks — and he was so tall that he could look over the heads of most people — and without offering his hand, remarked, " Ah, yes, I have heard of a Mister Barker coming to Lynn, as a physician; but having examined the Medical Society's catalogue without finding his name I feel constrained to withhold professional recognition till further informed." Doctor Barker, naturally enough, not knowing the peculiarities of the other, felt a little nettled, and tartly replied, " But, Dr. Hazeltine, your examination was not thorough, or you would have seen by the errata that my name was accidentally omitted in the proper place." "Very well, Mr. Barker," rejoined Dr. H., "I will impose upon myself the duty of a further examination. In the mean time allow me to welcome you as a new resident of our town, and to bid you a very good morning." A few days after, Dr. H. called on Dr. B., informed him that he had re-examined the catalogue, found the fact as claimed, and with great cordiality welcomed him as a professional brother. And that he was sincere and retained his good feeling is abundantly shown by entries in his journal.

Dr. Hazeltine also served as a magistrate, and his judgments bore the impress of careful and conscientious investigation and consideration. His copy of old "Dickinson's Justice," with its many marginal notes, in his clear and compact hand-writing is now in possession of the writer. But of course the great business of his life was the medical practice. In that he was faithful and trustworthy though some thought him a little too strongly bound by old customs and traditions. He had great faith in the virtue of hops, especially in the simple form of a tea, and so frequently prescribed the infusion that some were so impolite as to call him "the hop-tea doctor." Indeed certain libelous articles touching this peculiarity of his appeared in the Mirror, written, it is believed, by Enoch Curtin, in a playful mood. The editor was proceeded against, and the jury awarded the Doctor a considerable amount in damages; but he, as the editor long after informed the writer, very readily relinquished all but his actual costs, and continued to treat him as if no occasion for difference had occurred.

The books of daily charges kept by Doctor Hazeltine, were, a number of years ago, placed in the hands of the writer; and a few extracts, which can harm no one, will no doubt be interesting as showing the scale of professional charges, and at the same time exhibit the precise and detailed manner in which he was accustomed to record his transactions. The first book of the series bears the inscription, "Richard Hazeltine's Day Book He removed with his family from South Berwick to Lynn, May 30, 1817." He however must have been here himself some time before he brought his family, for the first charge to a patient is under date May 13, and stands thus: "Samuel Chase, Dr. to 18 visits; i. e. 2 visits a day from Sabbath the 4th inst. to yesterday, including both, and sundry articles of medicine, such as [enumerating,] 10.25."

The Doctor must have soon secured a large practice, judging from the number of his charges; but to a physician of this day his fees would seem amusingly low, a fact which in a great . measure may account for the statement that he made a little before his death, to the effect that his profession had scarcely yielded enough to pay expenses during his whole residence in Lynn. A much greater proportion of "bad debts" no doubt accumulated in those days than in later times, in all professions. But let us present the promised samples of the Doctor's every day entries.

1817. Aug. 2. George Hamlin, credit by 2 phials and med. returned, .13.

1817. Aug. 6. Frederic Newhall, Dr. to calling and waiting some time to see your sister, 1.00.

1819. Feb. 21. Enoch Mudge, Dr. to calling from the meeting-house and extracting a tooth for yourself, .50.

1819. March 6. James Lewis, Cr. by a fresh fish, weighing 8 lb. at 2 cents a pound.

1819. March 21. Peter Shott, Dr. to calling to see you this morning, .25.

1819. April 9. Benjamin Burrill, Dr. to a visit, and making lint for your sore, .50.

1819. June 10. Stephen Oliver, Dr. to a three dollar bill, for one that I borrowed of you, last week.

1819. July 21. Jonathan Connor, credit, by six cords of wood, taken on the wharf, at $6 a cord, to be paid for in 60 days.

1819. Sept. 1. John Newhall, Dr. to calling to see your aunt Nabby, 0.25.

1820. March 4. Abel Houghton, Dr. to a visit for yourself, .25.

1820. March 8. Rufus P. Hovey, Esq. Dr. to a visit and a phial and vin. ipecac for yourself, 84.

1820. March 13. Henry A. Breed, credit by 1 lb. 8 penny and 1 lb. 6 penny wrought nails, at 18 and 22 cents, .40.

1820. April 10. Henry A. Breed, credit, by 1 gal. Lisbon wine, at $1.50, and 1 1-2 pint of brandy, 33, $1.83.

1820. April 15. Miss Lydia Stackpole, credit by your assistance in my family since Monday morning, before breakfast, till this morning, after breakfast.

1820. April 28. Preserved Sprague, Dr. to a visit, making lint, &c., and dressing your wound, and to a piece of bandage. .75.

1820. May 16. Jonathan Buffum, Dr. to a visit this morning and to 10 oz. of tamarinds, sent this evening by my boy, 0.42.

1821. March 5. This evening Mr. Trevett borrowed Hannah More's St. Paul, Dr. Worcester on Baptism and Medical Dissertations.

1821. March 28. Mrs. Mary Carter, Concord, N. H.: Her little son William Franklin Carter came to my house last Monday evening, to board and go to school. I am to board him for his schooling [?] and what services he will render in my family. This morning he gave me sixty-five cents in cash, which he brought with him, and for which I am accountable to his mother.

1821. July 10. Abel Houghton, credit, by mending my boot a little, yesterday, .06.

1821. Nov. 2. Amos Breed, credit by a barrel of cider [I found the barrel] and by 6 hoops and paying for setting them — hoops 2 cents each, setting 4 cents each, .36; cider, 2.50. 2.86.

1821, Nov. 3. Enoch Curtin, Dr. to a visit early this morning and another at 11 o'clock, and assisting in moving you, 1.50.

1821. Nov. 28. Thomas Hamlin, credit, by repairing my chaise apartment door, i. e. putting on hinge, .06.

1822. Jan. 3. Abner Alley, Dr. to a visit, post m. for your daughter, she having injured her hand by striking on a hair comb, .50.

1834. March 3. Mrs. Mary Mailey, Dr. to a visit this a. m. for yourself, .25.

1834. March 7. Charles Chase, Dr. to a visit this a. m. for your daughter Mary, 0.25.

1834. March 8. Mark Alley, Dr. to a visit this evening and 12 pills for Mrs. Alley, .38.

1834. March 11. David Ellis, Dr. to a visit this evening in co. with Dr. Barker, for your little boy, 1.00.

1834. March 19. John B. Chase, credit by a five dollar bill paid me this a. m. equal to six dollars, because paid within sixty days.

1834. March 24. Abel Houghton, Dr. to visit this a. m. and 9 small p. ip. for yourself, 0.42.

1834. March 28. Levi Frost, credit, by repairing chaise harness, .06.

1834. March 29. Alonzo Lewis, Dr. to a visit this morning and another this p. m. 2. pil. and some vin. ant. for yourself and some cal. added in the morning to two former powders, .92.

1834. April 7. Alonzo Lewis, Dr. to a visit this morning for yourself, .25.

1835. Feb. 18. Capt. Charles Merritt, Dr. to 12 pills delivered yourself this a. m. at the postoffice door, and consilium, .25.

1836. May 6. Nathaniel Ingalls, Dr. to cash paid you to-day, 67 cents. Credit, by assisting Mr. Merrill, the carpenter, about putting down some posts for fence, for me, yesterday, at Woodend, 67 cents.

1836. May 21. Daniel Moulton, credit, by 2 hours' assistance, at 8 cents an hour, .16.

1836. May 21. Esquire Daniel Henshaw, credit, by making out my last will, to-day, and attending to its signature, &c., 2.09.

The *Abel Houghton* named in two or three of the foregoing items, first, under date March 4, 1820, lived in Pearl street. He took great interest in horticulture, and it was from him that the Houghton Horticultural Society took its name. To him, also, we are indebted for that superior gooseberry known as the Houghton seedling. *Rufus P. Hovey,* named under date March 8, 1820, came to Lynn in or about 1816, and opened an office near the Hotel. He was a young lawyer of good education and fine abilities but destined soon to close his life. He died of consumption before attaining the fame and honorable position which his friends fondly believed awaited him. Under dates March 13 and

April 10, 1820, appears the name of *Henry A. Breed.* This gentleman, who is still among us, active and genial, was then a young
business man.   At the time of the transactions recorded he kept
a " West India goods and variety store," in the west wing of the
Hotel.   A few years after, he became extensively engaged in .
building and other semi-speculative enterprises, some of which
were on a large scale.   Possessing a sanguine temperament and
great physical activity, he did more than almost any other to give
" a start " to the Lynn of that period, and is deserving of the
gratitude of many now living for personal aid.   But he has had
his ups and downs ; his share of praise and censure ; and has
shown himself neither a fawner nor a misanthrope.   We can
hardly call to mind one who has more reason to keenly feel the
disregard of some now in prosperity who owe the foundation of
their good fortune to him.   *Preserved Sprague,* who is charged
by the Doctor with a visit on April 28, 1820, was a farmer, and
lived on Nahant street.   He wore a long beard, which excited
the wonder, if not the admiration of almost every one he met, as
it was the fashion, at that time, for men to be close-shaven ;
mustaches, especially, being an utter abomination.   Esquire
Daniel Henshaw, who under date May 21, 1836, is credited with
writing the Doctor's will — at a price which would make a lawyer
of this day stare if it did not induce some ejaculation indicated
by a verb that rhymes with stare — was a legal practitioner who
settled in Lynn, in or about 1833.   He had a classical education ;
but being one who had that rigorous sense of justice which for-
bids the advocacy of any cause of even doubtful right, and being
withal of a retiring disposition, never had much of an active
court business.   He was a good writer, with very little of the
picturesque in his style, and as editor of the Lynn Record —
the first paper of that name here — then under the proprietor-
ship of Jonathan Buffum, produced articles that were extensively
quoted and deservedly praised.   The Record was an energetic
advocate of the anti-masonic cause, of temperance, and anti-slavery.   It was to the house of Mr. Henshaw that the guard
of ladies conducted George Thompson, the English anti-slavery
orator, from the First Methodist meeting-house, when violence
was threatened by the excited crowd ; an account of which
occurrence may be found in our Annals, under date, 1835.   Mr.

Henshaw was a man of strong religious principles conformable to the old Calvinistic faith.

Several other prominent residents whose names appear in these book charges will be remembered by our elderly people. But as something concerning most of them may be found where they are introduced, in alphabetical order, in this volume, it is unnecessary to go into details here. The *Enoch Mudge* for whom the Doctor drew a tooth, Feb. 21, 1819, being called from the meeting-house, was Rev. Enoch Mudge, father of the late Hon. Enoch Redington Mudge, and a most worthy minister of the Methodist denomination. *Stephen Oliver*, to whom $3, borrowed money, were paid, June 10, 1819; *Jonathan Connor*, who sold the Doctor six cords of wood, July 21, 1819; and *Jonathan Buffum*, who had 10 ounces of tamarinds, May 16, 1820, were all among the best-known business men in the place. Mr. *Trevett*, who borrowed the books, March 5, 1821, was Robert W. Trevett, the lawyer, who was at that time among the foremost of the Essex bar, and could understand the value of a good book as well as any man in town. *Enoch Curtin*, who was so sick as to require two visits, Nov. 3, 1821, was the poet whose pen was the one usually in requisition for odes, hymns, and other occasional pieces. *Alonzo Lewis*, who also needed two visits, and medicine, March 29, 1834, was the Lynn bard and historian. Capt. *Charles Merritt*, who was supplied with pills, Feb. 18, 1835, at the postoffice door, was the deputy sheriff who so acceptably filled that disagreeable office for forty years.

The items quoted above from the books of Doctor Hazeltine are quite enough to show his exactness and methodical way of doing things even in those minor details which to most people appear frivolous. But that orderliness, no doubt, saved him from much of the tedious ransacking of the memory and many of the petty disputes to which less careful persons are constantly subjected ; and it was certainly an improvement on the method of keeping accounts adopted by another Lynn physician, well known to the writer, who made his charges on all sorts of odd scraps of paper, which he thrust indiscriminately into a bag, to which he resorted and drew out for collection when money was wanted. Some of the extracts may look as if selected for their quaintness or merely as curiosities ; but we have no such object.

The design is to show the Doctor's great conscientiousness and care, as well as something of the state of things at that time.

In his religious connections, Dr. Hazeltine ranked with the Calvinistic Congregationalists. He was rigid and consistent, but yet too high-minded not to deferentially regard the opinions of others. His only daughter, Phebe, a very intelligent and alert lady, though not without noticeable peculiarities, became an Episcopalian ; and we have some recollection of her once remarking that her father expressed approval rather than disapprobation of her sentiments. His religious tendencies were not merely theoretical, for there was evidently an earnest desire to give them a practical bearing upon the daily walk. His first book of charges is prefaced by two pages of "*Precepts to be read and duly regarded before charging.*" They are chiefly taken from the Scriptures, and if lived up to, would make an almost perfect man. The twenty-ninth appears as a dictate of "conscience," and reads in this wise : "In all thy endeavors to alleviate human misery, be careful by no means to increase it, either by negligent, careless, or unfeeling attention to the sick, nor by extravagant charges for thy services, nor by oppressive or inhuman measures in collecting thy demands." That he was truly conscientious, and never disposed to thwart the kindly endeavors of nature to restore health, by uncertain experiments, cannot be doubted.

The house in which Dr. Hazeltine lived during the whole of his life here, is still standing on the south side of Essex street, between High and Pearl streets. It was for many years one of the best and most conspicuous in town, and no other building was near enough to obscure the very commanding view. The site was for a hundred and fifty years the chosen seat of a line of worthies of the healing art. Dr. John Henry Burchstead, who came from Silecia, in 1685, settled here ; after him, his son, Dr. Henry Burchstead, lived on the place, and it is thought built the present house, which was subsequently the residence of Dr. Peter G. Robbins, who came in 1805. From the latter, Dr. Hazeltine had it, in 1817, probably at first, as a tenant, the earliest entry in one of his books being a charge against Dr. Robbins for money paid Micajah Cutler for whitewashing and laying a hearth. It is now so hemmed in by other buildings that a passer-by would hardly notice it.   For many years it was known as the house with the great whale bones for gate-posts, and more often inquired for by strangers, than any other house in town, as the cottage of Moll Pitcher, the celebrated fortune-teller, stood on the opposite hill-side, and the stealthy visitor thus sought to conceal the real object of his inquiry.   Dr. Robbins was father of Rev. Chandler Robbins, a prominent Unitarian minister, in Boston, and Rev. Samuel D. Robbins, the third minister of the Unitarian society in Lynn ; and in that house the reverend brothers were born.

Dr. Hazeltine was born in Concord, N. H., Nov. 28, 1773, and died July 10, 1836, as noted in our Annals of that year.

HENCHMAN, Rev. NATHANIEL — minister of the First Parish, forty-one years ; settled in 1720; died in 1761, aged 61.   His residence was on North Common street, a few rods east of Mall. See Annals, 1761.

HENTZ, CAROLINE LEE — an accomplished prose writer.   See Annals, 1680.

HITCHINGS, Major EZRA — was born April 15, 1765, in what is now Saugus, and died at his residence in Lynn, Nov. 26, 1829. For many years he was one of the most marked characters in the town and had great influence, though not generally in the most prominent offices.   His military title was conferred by the position he held in the militia regiment of Lynn.   He was also a freemason, a member of the old fire-club — a voluntary organization for mutual assistance in case of fire — and one or two other brotherhoods, social or benevolent.   He loved music and with his neighbor, Master Blanchard, and his bass-viol, no doubt passed many an enjoyable evening hour.

But the image of the Major looms up most conspicuously at his West India goods store, on Boston street, at the corner of Federal.   There he was to be found at all reasonable hours, ready to deal out his commodities, even to the cent's worth, to discuss religion with the minister or deacon, politics with 'Squire Carnes, Amos Rhodes, the elder, Benjamin Massey, Samuel Mulliken, Daniel Collins, or any town notable ; or to sally forth with measuring rod in hand at the beck of any teamster with his load from the woods. And, shifting the scene a little, we behold him if it be a day of military parade, standing at his door, intently watching the evolutions of a straggling militia company in the elaborate exercise of whipping-the-snake, or some similarly picturesque manœuvre, in the little square fronting his premises.

The business of the Major yielded him a comfortable maintenance, but nothing more, for the multiplicity of bad debts, in those days, was a sad draw-back to the retail trader. It was a day of small things. The shoe-manufacturers did a limited business, drew orders on the retailers, and in some cases made periodical failures. He was a careful purchaser and avoided all dishonest tricks of trade ; would not even water the rum he sold ; and could not comprehend the exalted morality of those virtuous brethren in the trade who, with consciences as weak as their own "extended" liquors, sought to convince him that to reduce the drink was a mercy to the poor deluded toper.

The Major was in many ways a most valuable man for any neighborhood ; sound in judgment, liberal in opinions, and ever ready to give his best advice to those who sought his counsel. He was not much given to hilarity or jets of humor, but rather inclined to the dignified and thoughtful mood, though by no means unsocial. With his stern sense of duty he had kindly sympathies, though occasional bluntness of expression might give a false coloring to his real feeling. Elderly people paid much deference to him, but from some cause, he failed to secure the good-will of the juvenile fraternity. In short, the boys had little love for him, though it is not believed that any were inclined to manifest their dislike in a rough way. His dignity of bearing was enough to have prevented any thing of that sort. It was probably difficult for him to come down to their level, if, indeed, he had power to discern where they stood. Some of us were inclined to think he never could have been a boy himself. One day a little fellow went into his store and asked for something for Mr. Benjamin Newhall, and was met with the repellent ejaculation, uttered in a voice not the most placid and with an air any thing but winsome, " Why do'nt you say your father ; don't you suppose I know who you are, and who your father is ; I hope I know neighbors who have always lived next door." The same lad had occasion presently again to go to the store, and remembering the admonition was careful to say "for my father." "And who is your father?" was the quick response, in the old inclement voice; "do you suppose I know every boy in the street, and who his father is; why do'nt you give your father's name?" That boy was pretty sure, ever after, to say, "for my father, Mr. Benjamin Newhall." These remarks are not made for the purpose of casting reflections on a really worthy man, or to unnecessarily exhibit his foibles, but for the opportunity of suggesting that most of us might profit by the example. It is easy to win the good-will of the juvenile legion by whom we are surrounded, and quite as easy to lose it. And is it not much better to have the sympathy and friendship of those who are growing up around us, and on whom we shall surely be more or less dependent, than to have their ill-will and opposition? But he was not blessed with any children of his own; yet he adopted several, whom he brought up in the most creditable manner. In this matter, however, he was seconded by his excellent wife who was undoubtedly entitled to a large share of the praise due for such commendable benevolence.

The Major was one of the early and active members of the Unitarian society, did what he could in a pecuniary way, but more efficiently aided by his exemplary life. His wife was of the same faith. She was a sister of Col. James Robinson, the first postmaster, and acted well her part in the management of their hospitable and happy home. She was a woman of much force of character, lively and sensible; and her conversation, even in old age, was not only cheerful, but marked by a vein of attractive humor, and replete with pleasing reminiscences.

HOLYOKE, EDWARD — a farmer and large land-holder; ancestor of the respectable Holyoke family of New England; a man of note in the Colony and honored in her councils. See Annals, 1630, and other early dates. His autograph is on the Armitage Petition.

HOOD, GEORGE — the first Mayor of Lynn — was twice elected to the office, and inaugurated May 14, 1850, and April 7, 1851. He died June 29, 1859, aged 52. For biographical notice see

1865 edition of History of Lynn. See also Centennial Memorial for notice with portrait. A fac-simile of his autograph follows.

George Moode.

HUMFREY, JOHN — an original Colonial proprietor and Lynn settler — eminent for his attainments, respected for his high social position, and honored for his wisdom in council. See Annals, 1634, 1641, and other early dates. The following represents his signature. *Jo: Humfrey*

HURD, Rev. ISAAC — minister of the First Parish — settled in 1813. See Annals, 1816.

HUTCHINSON, JESSE, of the Hutchinson family of singers. The picturesque stone cottage at High Rock, was built by him, in 1847. He died in 1853. See Annals, 1853.

HUTCHINSON, JUDSON J. — also of the family of singers. He died at his residence, High Rock, Jan. 11, 1859, aged 38. See Annals, 1859.

INGALLS, EDMUND and FRANCIS. " The first white men known to have been inhabitants of Lynn, were Edmund Ingalls and his brother Francis." So states Mr. Lewis ; but it is quite certain that others came with them. At the celebration of the two hundred and fiftieth anniversary of the settlement — June 17, 1879 — the names of these pioneers were heard on every side, and much curiosity was manifested to view the vicinity wherein they first pitched their tents. The grand procession, in its march through Woodend, halted to enable those who desired, to take a near look at the spot on which stood the humble habitation of Edmund, near Gold Fish pond. At the celebration, too, were read letters from John J. Ingalls, United States Senator from

Kansas, and Rufus Ingalls, an officer in the United States service descendants of Edmund. Many of the lineage have held useful and honorable positions here in the family home, and a number are now counted among our most worthy citizens. See Annals, 1629, and other early dates.

IRESON, SAMUEL EDWIN. Mr. Ireson died of consumption on the 7th of September, 1875, at the age of 44 years. He was a son of Samuel J. Ireson, and a well-educated lawyer, as well as classical scholar, having graduated at Harvard, with the 1853 class. After completing a regular course of legal study, he commenced practice in Boston, but subsequently took an office in Lynn, his native place, and continued with a growing reputation and business, till failing health intervened. In 1873 and 1874 he was City Solicitor ; but his health still declining, he was induced in the spring of 1875, to visit the West Indies. Receiving no substantial benefit, he returned, to close his life in a few months. He was a man of genial manners and liberal views ; had a fine literary taste, and wrote a few poems which were much admired. His funeral took place from the Unitarian meeting-house, which had been his place of worship from childhood, and was attended by the chief officers of the city, by the brethren of the legal profession, and by many friends. He left a widow, but no children.

JACOBS, BENJAMIN H. — undertaker at the First Parish for thirty years. He died June 16, 1869, aged 76. See Annals, 1869.

JENKS, JOSEPH. From all that appears, Mr. Jenks came hither from Hammersmith, England, as an operative at the iron works. But he was not destined long to remain in an obscure position, for his skill and ingenuity soon commended him to the notice of the Court and the country at large. And well may he be called the pioneer inventor of America. For his ingenious contrivances he was granted several patents, and one or two have hardly been improved upon to the present day — notably his scythe. It is said that the dies for the famous pine-tree coins, which all bear date 1652 — though they were struck in different years — were made by him. In our Annals, under date 1654, it

is stated that the selectmen of Boston agreed with Joseph
Jenks "for an Ingine to carry water in case of fire," and that
this was the first fire-engine made in America. The order of the
town was in these words : " The Select men have liberty to agree
with Joseph Jynks, for Ingins to carry water in case of fire,
if they see cause so to doe." This order, it will be observed, is
permissive rather than imperative ; and there has been a question
whether they did contract for an engine, or if they did, whether
the contract was ever fulfilled, for it is asserted that Boston had
no engine till after the great fire in November, 1676, at which
time some forty-six dwellings were destroyed, besides shops,
warehouses, and "a meeting house of considerable bigness."
An opportune rain is mentioned as having done much towards
arresting the flames, and some buildings were blown up. But
nothing is said about an engine being there. Pemberton seems
to have thought that as late as 1711 Boston had no fire-engine.
Yet, on the 9th of March, 1702, the town voted that the Selectmen should "procure two water engines suitable for the extinguishing of fire, either by sending for them to England, or otherwise to provide them." This must have been in addition to one
before had, for it was on the same day voted that " The Selectmen are desired to get the Water Engine for the quenching
of fire repaired, as also the house for keeping the same in." Now
might not the one referred to as needing repairs in 1702 have
been manufactured by Mr. Jenks on the order of 1654? It
would have been an old "machine," to be sure, but was no
doubt constructed in a thorough manner, and not very frequently
called into use.

Mr. Jenks was ancestor of a rather remarkable line. Joseph
Jenks, Governor of Rhode Island from 1727 to 1732, and who
was not only applauded for his executive ability but renowned
for his personal appearance, being seven feet and two inches tall,
was a grandson of his. The late Rev. Dr. William Jenks, an
eminent scholar and author, was likewise a lineal descendant.
See Annals, 1662, and other early dates.

JOHNSON, CALEB. Mr. Johnson is well entitled to be called
one of the patriarchs of Nahant — Nahant, that charming "little
dukedom," which so warmed the imagination of Secretary Ran-

dolph, some two hundred years ago, and inflamed his thirst for its possession. He was born in that section of old Lynn, in December, 1778, and there passed his whole life, with the exception of two years, which he spent in another part of the town, as an apprentice at the trade of shoemaking ; and there he died, in 1867. At the time of his birth there were but three houses on Nahant, and no other house was erected there, till he had attained the age of twenty-two, at which time Capt. Joseph Johnson built a large house on the western part, which was kept as a hotel, and which was destroyed by fire, on Sunday morning, August 28, 1803.

Years passed on, and Mr. Johnson remained in the seclusion of his peninsular home, now and then, during the warm season, entertaining individuals or parties who resorted thither for health or recreation, occupying himself chiefly in farming and fishing, by which he gained an ample livelihood.

By-and-by Mr. Tudor and other gentlemen of taste and culture, appreciating the delights of the place, went thither for summer sojourn, and a refined society accumulated. By the rise in the value of lands Mr. Johnson became comparatively wealthy ; and being surrounded by a promising family, possessing a social disposition, and uncommonly good health, he had many sources of enjoyment. In 1791 he married Olive Hartwell, of Charlemont, and by her had ten children — seven sons and three daughters. His sixth son, William Frederic, was Mayor of Lynn in 1858, and a Senator in 1862 and '63.

JOHNSON, OTIS. Mr. Johnson was a son of Enoch Johnson, by his wife Elizabeth Newhall, and was born in Lynn, in 1802. At the early age of sixteen he left his native place for Petersburg, Va., where he remained till 1820, when he removed to Savannah, Ga. ; and there, by diligence and enterprise was able, by middle life, to accumulate a moderate fortune. His business at the south was successfully continued till 1860, when he returned to his native place for permanent residence. In the mean time, however, he had erected a fine mansion on the westerly side of Federal street, and embellished the grounds with rare flowers, and other tasteful adornments. And every season he busied himself with various experiments in the pleasant and instructive

OTIS JOHNSON MANSION, LYNN.

mysteries of horticulture. He did much to foster a taste for decorative gardening and the raising of choice fruit ; and for his highly beneficial influence in that direction is certainly worthy of being long remembered. He was not ambitious of the ephemeral distinction conferred by public office, though he held positions of trust and responsibility ; among them that of director in the City Bank, from the time of its establishment, in 1854, till his death.

In 1824 Mr. Johnson married, at Savannah, Miss Virginia, daughter of Capt. R. G. Taylor, and by her had ten children, four only of whom survived him. He met death, with Christian serenity, at his residence, in Federal street, on the 17th of February, 1870, aged 68, and was mourned for as a man of kindly sympathies, unswerving integrity, and a good citizen. His widow died on the 5th of February, 1881, aged 78.

JOHNSON, RICHARD. Mr. Johnson was ancestor of the large and worthy family of the name still among us. His homestead estate was at the east end of the Common, and included the site of the present City Hall, together with a number of acres in and about Johnson street, a thoroughfare that perpetuates his name. His eldest son, Samuel, who was born in 1640, and died in 1723, and whose gravestone, though in a dilapidated condition, still remains in the Old Burying Ground, was known as Lieutenant, and earlier as Cornet Johnson. He and his brother Daniel served in the King Philip war, 1676, and both joined in the petition for remuneration presented in 1685. His name likewise appears as one of the official grantees in the Indian deed of Lynn, executed in 1686. The house which he, Samuel, built was a sort of semi-garrison, to which the neighbors might flee in case of any savage demonstration, and will be remembered by many now living as having stood where the present brick house of worship of the First Methodist Society now stands, on the northeast side of Park square.

Nothing more than a glance at our pages of Annals will be needed to show that the Johnson family has all along presented examples of high character and great usefulness. The autograph of the patriarchal settler, Richard, appears on the Armitage Petition, page 106. See Annals, 1635 and other dates.

11

JOHNSON, WILLIAM F. — seventh Mayor of Lynn — born on Nahant, July 30, 1819. For notice, with portrait, see Centennial Memorial. A fac-simile of his signature is here given.

KEENE, AVIS — a preacher in the Friends' Meeting, some sixty years. She died Oct. 13, 1867, aged 87. See Annals, 1867.

KEENE, GEORGE W. — a conspicuous business man and active in public enterprises. He died March 27, 1874, aged 58. See Annals, 1874.

KERTLAND, PHILIP — the first shoemaker here. His name appears on the Armitage Petition, page 106. See Annals, 1635.

KEYSER, GEORGE — a tanner — called by Mr. Lewis a miller ; perhaps he followed both occupations. His autograph is on the Armitage Petition, page 106. See Annals, 1630. It was in Mr. Keyser's tan-pit that a child of Thomas Newhall was drowned in 1665. "We Robart Potter and John Newhall: understandin by Too Testimonies," say a couple of witnesses in the case, "That Thomas Newhalls chilld was drounded in a pett which pett we heard George Keesar saye he digged: farther we doe Testifie that George Keser had a Tanfatt in that pett. I John Newhall doe furder Testifie that George Keyser did take up his fatt and left the pett open." This tan-pit was on the south side of Boston street, about where the tubular wells were driven, in 1880.

KING, DANIEL. By referring to our Annals, of early dates, various facts may be found concerning the King family, who were located chiefly about Swampscott, though they owned lands in other quarters. King's Beach perpetuates the name. They were an enterprising family, and in addition to farming and fishing, carried on a varied sort of commercial business, their traffic extending even to Barbadoes. Papers are yet to be found among our Essex County files, indicating to some extent the nature and course of their trade. In a memorandum dated May 6, 1653, Daniel King, jr. says : " I have Rec. of my cosen William Guy [of London] a parcell of goods amounting to the valew of fforty ffive pounds, ffourteene shillings nine pence starling money, which goods I have Rec : upon the account of Guy as an Adventure by him promising to doe my outmost indeuor for the sale of the aforesaid goods, and to make him returns by Chrismas next, if," &c. But such " ifs " seem to have intervened that a settlement was long delayed, and the matter finally got into court. Five years after, that is, in 1658, his father, Daniel King, makes the following statement : " Boston, this 14 of August, 1658. These presents Witnes that I, Daniell King of Lyn, Sener, doe aknowledge that Capt. Jnᵒ Peirce, Commander of the Ship Exchang, hath bene with mee and demanded of mee a debt of aboutt forty fiue pounds which my sone Daniell did Receive in goods of Mʳ Wm Guy, of London, haberdasher ; and my Answer is that my sone Daniel is gone to burbados and hath carried with him goods in order to the making the Returne much more then I can judge will Ballance that accᵒ. And I hope either by this time or very sudenly hee will Returne a satisfactory accᵒ."

Two years after the foregoing, namely, in 1660, Mrs. Elizabeth King, mother of the delinquent Daniel, jr., comes to the rescue of her son's credit and reputation in the following propitiatory epistle to her nephew Guy : " from Linn, in New England, Decembʳ the 28ᵗʰ, 1660 . . . . After Respeckts presented these earr to lett you under stand that yours wee have receued, Return you Manny thanks for your patiente lines But being much troubled that wee yett cannot Answer your ends According to your expecktations. Many ways wee have tryed, By Barbudoes, By Bills of Exchange, & By getting of Bever, for you, But as yet cannoᵗ proceure anny of them. But By the next shepping I hoape wee shall find out some way or other whereby you shall haue sattisfacktion ; my sonn Ralph & my sonn Blaenny douth Intend if pleas god the liue and doe well to com for England ; soe hoaping that you will bee pleased to Ad one mitt of patience unto your Aboundance which you have had soe.

" Resting and Remaining your Ever Loueing
Ante tell Death,
ELIZABETH KING."

The "sonn Ralph" was successful in his business, and accumulated quite a property for those times. The inventory of his estate, taken July 8, 1689, by Rev. Mr. Shepard, William Bassett, and John Ballard, gives an amount of £2365 4s. The inventory of the estate of Daniel King, senior, who died May 28, 1672, gives an amount of £1528 9s.

Ralph King's name appears first among the grantees in the Indian deed of Lynn.

KITTREDGE, Dr. EDWARD A. — a physician and humorous writer. He died in Newton, Feb. 25, 1869, aged 58. See Annals, 1869.

LAUGHTON, THOMAS. The name of this prominent settler, like the names of many others, was in old times spelled in various ways. He was elected Town Clerk in 1672, and remained in the office several years ; was likewise a Selectman for a number of years, and a Representative some ten. He held several other responsible offices ; was a farmer, and lived on Franklin street. Laighton street took its name from him. See Annals, 1635, and other early dates. His name is on the Armitage Petition ; and a fac-simile, taken from a signature of his made in 1668, follows.

Thomas Laughton

LEONARD, HENRY and JAMES. These brothers were connected with the ancient iron works on Saugus river, and became prominent in the iron manufacture of New England. See Annals, 1642.

LEWIS, ALONZO. A pretty full biographical sketch of Mr. Lewis the bard and historian, may be found in the 1865 edition of our History of Lynn. And in the Centennial Memorial a shorter sketch, with a portrait, may be found. It has been stated that Mr. Lewis, on one or two occasions, in early life, left his native place to seek his fortune elsewhere. His strong natural attachment to his home, however, always prevailed, and after a brief absence he was soon again among us. In 1832, at the age of 38, he removed with the determination, undoubtedly, to permanently reside abroad ; and the writer well remembers his emotion as he handed him the following touching lines for publication. But after an absence of a few months we were again favored by his presence ; and it is not recollected that he had, during the remainder of his life, any disposition to withdraw from the attractive scenes of his native place, its sunny hills and silvery streams, or to pitch his tent on any spot where the sound of old Ocean's harp could not be heard. We have always been impressed with the belief that the fourth stanza was founded on a singularly false apprehension, arising in an extremely sensitive mind. He had friends ; strong and loving friends ; and no real foes ; though there were those who could not avoid sometimes expressing annoyance at eccentricities which occasionally could hardly be called unobtrusive.

THE BARD'S FAREWELL.

Farewell ye streams, ye dear loved streams,
    Where I in childhood played,
Upon whose marge my youthful dreams
    Have blest the peaceful shade.
No more to hear your rippling song
    Shall I delighted bend,
Nor with the loved your banks along
    In twilight converse wend.

Farewell ye hills whose dewy brow
    These early feet have kist
While silent ocean lay below
    Half hid in sleeping mist.
Your sunny tops at distance far
    These anxious eyes may view,
But never shall the morning star
    Our vanished joys renew.

Ye early friends, to whom this heart
    Affection long has bound,
The day has come when we must part,
    And share affection's wound.
Your hopes o'er other joys may bloom,
    Your hearts with friendship swell ;
But mine shall give no other room
    To aught, except — farewell !

And ye, without a cause my foes,
    As o'er life's waves I glide,
May haply think upon the woes
    With which ye swelled the tide ;

The injured heart that would have died
        Your slightest griefs to quell,
Shall breathe from out its bleeding side
        Forgiveness — and farewell.

As when the purple ocean flower
        From off its rock is torn,
Submissive to the tempest's power,
        By which 'tis onward borne,
So shall my heart sustain the storm
        Its hopes in vain would quell,
And dying, breathe in accents warm,
        My friends — my home — farewell !

No extended notice of Mr. Lewis is required here, as the sketches already referred to will furnish sufficient information to meet all ordinary inquiries. But no more appropriate place will be found for the introduction of a pictorial view of the house in which he was born. It still stands on the north side of Boston street, nearly opposite Bridge. The writer well remembers it for at least sixty-five years, during which time the exterior has been a little modernized about the door-way, and the blinds have been added. The fence, likewise, is somewhat more artistic than the one Mr. Lewis built with his own hands, some forty years ago. We seem now to see him sitting in that door-way, just as he sat three score years since, in " contemplative mood," enjoying the cool of a summer morning, as we went whistling along towards the cow pasture.

BIRTHPLACE OF ALONZO LEWIS.

Mr. Lewis was born on the 28th of August, 1794, and died on the 21st of January, 1861. And it may be of interest here to reproduce a picture of the sea-side cottage in which he died, though it appears in our 1865 edition.

COTTAGE IN WHICH MR. LEWIS DIED.

Mr. Lewis was a fine penman, and somewhat ornate in his signature, as the appended fac-simile shows.

LEWIS, JACOB M. — the fourteenth Mayor of Lynn. He is a native of the place, was born on the 13th of October, 1823, and served in the mayoralty four terms. For biographical sketch, with portrait, see Centennial Memorial. A fac-simile of his signature is here given.

LIGHTFOOT, FRANCIS — whose autograph appears upon the Armitage Petition, page 106, was a man of small means, but respectable character. He died in 1646. See Annals, 1635.

LONGLEY, WILLIAM. This was no doubt the same individual who figured so strangely in the land claim spoken of in our Annals, under date 1638 ; and his name is on the Armitage Petition. The Longleys seem to have been often at war with their neighbors on account of land claims. Thomas Newhall, so often alluded to as the first white person born in Lynn, and who from all that appears was far from being of a quarrelsome disposition, was prosecuted in 1663 for assault and battery committed on the wife of this William Longley while assisting in running a land line. Among other evidence in the case was the following: " The testimony of Elizabeth Newhall ye wife of John Senier, and Mary Haven whoe sayth y^t Thomas Newhall Junier was desiered for to howld a poole for to rone a line between Will Longley and John Newhall : ye say^d Thomas Newhall stode on ye land of John Newhalls : then came ye two dafters of ye say^d Longley ; namely Mary Longley & Anna Longley and threue stons at ye say^d Thomas Newhall ; afterwards ye say^d Anna toke up a peace of a pulle & stroke ye say^d Newhall severall blows with it, & presently after ye wife of ye say^d Longley came with a broad axe in hir hand and cam to ye say^d Newhall and violently stroke at ye say^d Newhall with ye axe, but ye say^d Newhall sliped aside & soe ye axe mised him ; o^{r}wise wee cannot but thinke but y^t hee had bine much wounded if not killed : then presently after ye wife of Will Longley laid howld upone ye poole with hir two dafters to pull ye poole away from ye sayd Newhall : but ye sayd Newhall pulled ye poole from y^m. All this time ye sayd Thomas Newhall did stand upon ye land of John Newhalls. Taken upon oath, 28 1mo '63." The Longleys, in their version, of course gave the affair a different coloring. They testified that Newhall was on one side of their orchard fence, and they on the other ; that they were striving to get the pole from him, all having hold of it ; and one of the daughters goes on to say, " wee had almost pulled the poole out of his hands but his brother John came and helped him and pulled it from us, and after the said Newhall had got the poole again he strucke my mother scuerall blows with the poole so that one of her hands was black and blue severall dayes after." It must have been quite a spirited scene there at the orchard fence — the brothers Thomas and John in fierce combat with the sisters Anna and Mary, supported by their belligerent mother. And attention need not be called to the fact made apparent by this historical scrap, that then petty neighborhood quarrels, with their exaggerated details and strife-engendering tendencies furnished the same sort of unwholesome food for the inferior courts that they do in our day.

LOVERING, HENRY B. — the seventeenth Mayor of Lynn — was born in Portsmouth, N. H. April 8, 1841. He was inaugurated January 3d, 1881, and so satisfactorily performed the duties of the office that in December he was elected for a second term. He has been for nearly the whole of his business life connected in some way with the manufacture of shoes. And that he is deemed a citizen of ability and trustworthiness is sufficiently apparent from the responsible positions he has been called to fill. On the 25th of December, 1865, he was united in marriage with Abbie J., a daughter of Harrison Clifford, and has four children During the civil war he served in the Union army twenty-six months. While attached to the Third Massachusetts Cavalry, under Gen. Sheridan, he had the misfortune to lose a leg, at the battle of Winchester. A fac-simile of his autograph is here given.

LUMMUS, Dr. AARON — a skillful physician, who was in practice here nearly fifty years. He lived on Market street, and Tremont street was opened through his orchard. He died Jan. 5, 1831, aged 74. See Annals, 1831.

LUMMUS, AARON — familiarly known as "Judge Lummus" — was a son of Dr. Aaron just named, and his title "Judge," arose from his having long presided as a police magistrate. He was grave and deliberate in the examination of causes, but not over cautious in preventing the accumulation of small cases. His occupation as a trial justice was superseded by the establishment of the Police Court, in 1849. He was a Methodist minister before assuming the judicial office, and besides preaching was at times connected with denominational publications. He wrote considerable, but his writings, as a general thing, were didactic and better calculated to instruct than interest. As a preacher he was sound in doctrine, but not eminent in the way of oratory. We remember hearing his brother, Charles F., who will come next under notice, in his quaint way remark: "Well, there's my brother Aaron; he is a good exhorter, and that's about all." He died March 1, 1859, aged 62.

LUMMUS, CHARLES F. — the first Lynn printer. He died April 20, 1838, aged 37. For biographical sketch see 1865 edition of History of Lynn. A fac-simile of his signature follows.

MANSFIELD, ANDREW. Mr. Mansfield was, properly speaking, our first Town Clerk, and entered upon the duties of the office in 1660. He lived on Boston street in the section still known as Mansfield's end. The early dates of our Annals contain many references to him, as he was active and conspicuous. To him we are indebted for the preservation of a record of the land allotments of 1638, which he copied from "out of the Town Book of Records of Lynn," March 10, 1660. And the fac-simile of his signature here given is taken from his autograph appended to that copy.

MANSFIELD, Dr. JOSEPH. This individual, for many years a reputable practising physician in Groton, Mass., was born on the 17th of December, 1770, in the old Mansfield house, known also as the Moulton house, on the north side of Boston street, opposite the foot of Marion, and was a lineal descendant of Andrew Mansfield, the first Town Clerk. He graduated at Harvard college in 1801, and soon applied himself to the study of medicine, the practice of which he pursued as the business of his life, which terminated on the 23d of April, 1831.

Mr. Mansfield early exhibited poetic talents which bid fair to place his name among the foremost of American bards. But he seems not to have been ambitious of any such distinction and hence did not cultivate his rare gift. On the 8th of January, 1800, he delivered a poem in the chapel of Harvard college, for which he took the prize of eighty dollars, offered by the faculty for the best metrical produ&ion. The poem is entitled HOPE, and is two hundred and twenty-four lines in length. In reading it one is reminded of Pope's philosophical style ; though there are passages in a sentimental vein, and some in a playful. And as it was written at a period of intense political agitation, there are highly patriotic strains. The first and last stanzas, with a single intervening one will be here introduced.

> I am not blest, but may hereafter be :
> Who knows what fortune has in store for me ?
> This is the language common to mankind,
> Nor is to age, or rank, or sex, confined.
> Hope points to each some not far distant day,
> When every blessing will his wish obey ;
> When to possess, he only need require ;
> Fruition's self will supersede desire.
>
>   *   *   *   *   *
>
> See doting parents sedulously trace
> The opening beauties of their infant's face ;
> Commencing physiognomists, they find
> A world of wonders in its features joined ;
> The mother reads, and comments as she reads ;
> My child was born for more than mortal deeds ;
> Then *Hope* steps up and whispers by her side,
> You cradle in your arms creation's pride.
>
>   *   *   *   *   *
>
> We *hope*, long as the central orb attra&s,
> Long as the force of gravitation a&s,
> Long as the East is opposite the West,
> Long as the name of Washington is blest,
> Long as the atheist *hopes* to sleep in dust,
> Long as the sons of anarchy are curst,
> Long as the future differs from the past,—
> So long, Columbia, will thy freedom last.
> But should the monster Fa&ion break his chains,
> And fiery demagogues usurp the reins —
> We *hope* that future Washingtons may rise,
> Or rather make a visit from the skies.

An accident which happened to Mr. Mansfield, as narrated by Mr. John T. Moulton, was so singular as to merit notice here. "While bathing near Chase's mill he was seized with the cramp in his limbs and so disabled that he could not reach the shore, and when found by his companions, who were at work, haying, on the marsh near by, was supposed to be drowned ; but by the application of the proper means he was resuscitated and taken home, but did not regain his consciousness for some days. Then, awaking from sleep, he suddenly exclaimed, 'Mother, where have I been?' He seemed to have lost what knowledge he had acquired and his mind was like that of a child, so that it was necessary for him to begin and learn again his letters as he had done when a boy."

'It may not be inappropriate, in closing this notice, to remark that a poetic vein seems to have run in this family connection. Mr. John T. Moulton, who delivered the much-applauded poem at the reunion of the High School graduates, May 19, 1865, is one of the line ; and Solomon Moulton, of whom a biographical notice with specimens of his writing may be found in the 1865 edition of our History, and of whose poetic talents Mr. Lewis frequently spoke in high terms, was an uncle of John T. And this latter gentleman has, among his valuable collection, a number of poems, in manuscript, of Mr. Mansfield, the subject of this notice, which it is hoped may at some future time appear in print.

MARBLE, EDWIN — son of Hiram who in 1852 commenced, under supposed spiritual supervision, the excavation of Dungeon Rock. If possible, Edwin was more firm in the faith than his father. He died at the Rock, January 16, 1880, aged 48. See Annals, 1880.

MARBLE, HIRAM — a devoted spiritualist, who in 1852, undertook the herculean labor of excavating Dungeon Rock in search of gold and jewels supposed to have been secreted there by pirates, in 1658. He died at the Rock, November 10, 1868, aged 65. See Annals, 1658 and 1868.

MARSHALL, THOMAS — a jolly landlord of the old Anchor Tavern, in its palmy days ; and otherwise distinguished among his fellow-townsmen. His autograph adorns the Armitage Petition, page 106. See Annals, 1635, and other early dates.

MARTIN, Dea. GEORGE. Deacon Martin died on the 17th of December, 1868, aged 68. He was a native of Lynn and deacon of the First Church — Trinitarian Congregational — for the long space of forty-one years, and superintendent of the

Sunday school for twenty-five years. His death was by heart disease, and occurred without warning, during a prayer meeting in the vestry of the church, on South Common street, corner of Vine. He had just closed a fervent prayer, when he fell and expired. He was a man of intelligence, kindly feeling, and great integrity of character ; was industrious and unobtrusive, and by his example turned many to a better life. He was zealously engaged in the temperance cause and other reformatory enterprises of the day.

MARTIN, JOSIAH — an eccentric character, much given to " practical jokes," so called. He was landlord of the old Anchor Tavern, about the commencement of the Revolution. See Annals, 1782.

MERRITT, CHARLES — for many years a Deputy Sheriff of the county, and otherwise conspicuous in public office. He lived on Western avenue near the junction of Summer street, and died March 13, 1877, aged 72. See Annals, 1877. A fac-simile of his signature is here given.

MONTOWAMPATE — Indian Sagamore of Lynn. See History of Lynn, 1865 edition, page 36.

MOODY, Lady DEBORAH — a lady of great worth, wealth and influence, but being unsound in puritanical doctrine, was subjected to persecution and loss. See Annals, 1640.

MOODY, TRUE — a faithful sable out-door attendant at Lynn Hotel, in its palmy days — a man of scrupulous honesty and much favored by travellers. He died June 17, 1855. See Annals, 1855.

MOORE, HENRY — for more than twenty years principal of the Cobbet grammar school. He lived on Boston street, near Congress, and died March 29, 1879, aged 52. See Annals, 1879.

MOTTEY, Rev. JOSEPH — minister of the Lynnfield Parish, for many years. See Annals, 1821.

Moulton, Joseph. Mr. Moulton was a native of Lynn, and spent most of his life among us. On the maternal side he was a descendant from Andrew Mansfield, the first Town Clerk. For many years he owned and occupied the house on Boston street, nearly opposite the foot of Marion, in which he was born and in which he died, and which is supposed to be the oldest dwelling now in Lynn. A few of his earlier years were spent in Vermont and western New York, where his fortunes were varied and not always free from hardship and discouragement. But industry, self-reliance, and perseverance, carried him successfully through. He was a tanner and morocco-dresser by trade, and on his return to Lynn, in 1837, established himself in the latter branch, which he diligently pursued till it finally yielded him a competency; and his latter years were passed in quietude, and far above pecuniary want, though he was not exempt from a share of physical suffering, as cruel asthma long held its grip upon him. He was an accomplished antiquary; was for more than twenty years a member of the Massachusetts Historic and Genealogical Society and furnished some interesting papers for their publications. In viewing the memorials and contemplating the scenes of the past, he took unwearied delight. With English history and literature he was more than commonly familiar, and there was scarcely a point of New England history on which he did not possess almost exhaustive knowledge. On matters pertaining to our local history he was often applied to for information. And he possessed one trait especially, rare as it is valuable, namely, a readiness to admit ignorance when it existed, and an equal readiness to resort to patient investigation. Often have we heard him say to an inquirer, "Well, well, I declare to you I do not know; but will try to find out; come again." His reading, however, was by no means confined to historical works. Many delighted hours he spent over the volumes of the old poets, essayists and novelists; and his memory was so retentive that even in common conversation, he frequently quoted passages — sometimes in an amusing, always in a pertinent manner. He had a library, small but valuable, embracing a few rare works, and was not often deterred by any reasonable expense from gratifying his taste. The writer remembers one day meeting him with a couple of small volumes in his hand. "There," said he, "I have just received these little books from England, and they cost me thirty dollars."

He was an intelligent horticulturist, and took much pleasure in his garden, especially in experimenting with fruit trees, vines, and flowers, producing some valuable seedlings and some novel and interesting results by inoculation.

Soon after the breaking out of the civil war, he became the possessor of a bell which had done service on a Louisiana plantation, and this he sometimes, on occasions which seemed especially to call for the expression of patriotic feeling, sent clanging through the streets, mounted on wheels. He afterwards gave it to the trustees of Pine Grove Cemetery, and it now hangs in the tower of the keeper's house.

Mr. Moulton, while in Vermont, was united in marriage with Relief Todd, and by her had five children, to wit, Anne, James T., Charles H., John T., and Walter S. James T. and John T. inherit in a marked degree their father's love for antiquarian studies. He died, very suddenly, Feb. 10, 1873, aged 75 years.

MOULTON, SOLOMON — a writer of prose and poetry, of much promise. He died May 26, 1827, aged 19. For a biographical sketch, with specimens of his writing, see 1865 edition of the History of Lynn.

MUDGE, BENJAMIN. Mr. Mudge was born in Lynn, Sept. 1, 1786. He was the seventh child of Enoch Mudge, who was the father of fourteen children, and was in his turn the father of eleven. Till 1815 his life was passed in Lynn, excepting that for a short time he followed the seas under his brother Joseph. In 1808 he married Abigail Rich, who became the mother of all his children. She died in 1847, and the next year he married Miss Ardra Cobb, who, surviving him, died on the 14th of December, 1880, at the age of 92.

In 1815, with his family, Mr. Mudge emigrated to the then "far west," settling at Cincinnati, Ohio. The journey thither was at that time long and wearisome. At Laurel Hill, he had the misfortune to have his leg broken by being thrown from the top of a stage, the accident causing a tedious detention of some two months, and making a serious inroad upon his limited means.

He opened a shoe store at Cincinnati, which he continued till 1822, when he gave up and returned to Lynn, in anything but a satisfactory condition, pecuniarily. Possessing an active and enterprising mind, and being urged on by the requirements of a growing family, he industriously set to work, and for some years procured a livelihood by semi-literary pursuits. He was connected with Zion's Herald, the Masonic Mirror, and one or two other newspapers, appearing at one time as editor of the Lynn Mirror. In 1831, he commenced, in Lynn, the Essex Democrat, a weekly paper, warmly spiced with politics of what was then known as the Jacksonian stamp. This he continued about two years, and afterwards derived a moderate income from minor political offices.

In 1840 he was elected a Representative to the General Court. He was also an acting justice of the peace, county commissioner, and overseer of the poor. He was likewise postmaster from 1843 to 1849.

In 1854 he had the misfortune to fall near the rail-road track, in Ipswich, and before he could recover himself a train passed over his foot, so injuring it that amputation was necessary. Thus he became lamed for the remainder of his life.

When about seventeen years of age he connected himself with the First Methodist Church, of which his father and mother had long been members, and thence pursued an exemplary walk, through his long life.

He was Captain of the Lynn Artillery, from 1813 to 1816, and on a night during the war with England, on a sudden alarm instantly summoned his company and marched towards the quarter supposed to be in danger. It proved, however, to be a false alarm. His eldest son, Robert R., born in 1809, graduated from the West Point Military Academy, in 1833, and in 1835 was ordered to Florida, to take part in the Seminole war, as Lieutenant under Major Dade, and was killed at Withlacoochie, together with the whole company of one hundred and seventeen, with the exception of three.

Personally, Mr. Mudge was tall, well-formed, and erect ; active in movement, and of pleasant countenance. He died on the 21st of March, 1874, at the age of 87 years, and was buried from the First Methodist meeting-house, where he had so long worshiped

A large concourse gathered to take a last look upon the remains of one who in his various social, public, and business relations had maintained a high character for integrity and fellow-feeling.

MUDGE, BENJAMIN F. — the second Mayor of Lynn. He died at his residence, in Manhattan, Kansas, November 21, 1879, aged 62 ; and so great was the respect for him, that the citizens of that place erected a monument over his grave. See Annals, 1879. In the Centennial Memorial, is a biographical sketch, with a portrait. A fac-simile of his signature is hereto appended.

MUDGE, Rev. ENOCH — an esteemed minister of the Methodist connection, and a writer of some note. " Lynn, a Poem," published in pamphlet form, in 1826, was a production of his. His son Enoch Redington, was the donor of the beautiful St. Stephen's Memorial Church, erected in 1881. He died in Lynn, April 2, 1850, aged 74. In the 1865 edition of the History of Lynn may be found a biographical sketch.

MUDGE, ENOCH REDINGTON — son of the Rev. Enoch, just noticed, and the munificent builder of St. Stephen's Memorial Church. He died Oct. 1, 1881, aged 69 years. See Annals, 1881.

MUDGE, EZRA — a well-known citizen, much in public life. He died May 25, 1855, aged 75. In the 1865 edition of the History of Lynn, a biographical notice may be found.

MUDGE, EZRA WARREN. In the Centennial Memorial appears a biographical notice of Mr. Mudge, with a portrait. He died at his home, on Neptune street, September 20, 1878, aged 66 years. Few persons have ever left the busy scenes of our community more respected and beloved or more worthy to be held in grateful remembrance. His father, Hon. Ezra Mudge, was thrice married, and by the second and third wives each had seven

12

children, the first wife having died childless. Ezra Warren was the fourth child by the second wife. He received his education in the schools of Lynn, and in 1828 entered the dry goods store of Chase and Huse, near the west end of the Common. In this store, first as clerk and then as partner, he remained till 1849, at which time the Laighton Bank — afterwards the Central National — was established, and he was elected cashier, and continued to fill the office in a most satisfactory manner till his last sickness rendered it necessary to resign. He held various responsible positions under the old town government; was a Selectman, Town Treasurer, and member of the School Committee. And after the City Charter was adopted he was for six years City Treasurer. In 1856 he was inaugurated as the sixth Mayor, and administered the office two years, his administration being marked by prudence, integrity, and impartiality. During the civil war he was a member of the board of Aldermen, and with that body his opinions deservedly had great weight.

He had a taste for literature and took great interest in all educational enterprises, was identified with the Public Library, from its foundation, and at the time of his decease was president of the board of trustees. He had a well selected library, embracing, at the time of his death, some three thousand volumes ; and many an hour of pleasant retirement did he spend with those refreshing though silent companions.

In early manhood he married Miss Eliza R. Bray, of Salem, and became the father of nine children, four of whom survived him. His burial took place from the Second Universalist meeting-house, where he had for many years been a worshiper, and was attended by a large concourse of friends and citizens. His autograph, so familiar from its appearance on the bills of the bank with which he was so long connected, is here represented.

MULLIKEN, SAMUEL — third postmaster of Lynn. He died November 25, 1847, aged 86. See Annals, 1847.

MUNROE, Col. TIMOTHY. Colonel Munroe was not of a temperament to pass noiselessly through the world ; yet though for many years conspicuous as an ardent politician, and otherwise active in local affairs, he was most widely known by his military record. He was a native of Lynn, and died at his residence in Franklin street, on the 25th of May, 1873, at the age of 72 years.

He was for a number of years Captain of the Lynn Light Infantry, of which company he became a member as early as 1817 — a company which has ever maintained a high character for discipline. He was likewise commissioned as Colonel of the Eighth Massachusetts Regiment, and was in command at the time of the breaking out of the civil war ; at which stirring period his regiment was hastily summoned and departed for the scene of conflict, joining in the perilous march through Baltimore. He however continued in active service but a few months.

In his religious views he was a steadfast adherent of the Unitarian faith ; was one of the early members of the society here ; and from their meeting-house his remains were followed to their last resting place in Pine Grove Cemetery.

In early manhood he married Miss Rachel Lakeman, and became the father of five children.

Munroe street, which was laid out through his father's land perpetuates the family name.

NAHANTON — an Indian "wise man." See History of Lynn, 1865 edition, page 41.

NANAPASHEMET — an Indian Sachem of extensive jurisdiction. See 1865 edition of History of Lynn, page 34.

NEAL, PETER M. — the tenth Mayor of Lynn. For notice, with portrait, see Centennial Memorial. A fac-simile of his signature is hereto appended.

NEWHALL, ANTHONY.   See "Newhall, Thomas and Anthony."

NEWHALL, ASA T., of Lynnfield — an intelligent farmer, considerably in public life. He died December 18, 1850, aged 71. A biographical notice appears in the 1865 edition of the History of Lynn.

NEWHALL, BENJAMIN F., of Saugus — a man active in business, public spirited, and full of industrial resources, intelligent, and a frequent writer for the public journals. He died October 13, 1863, aged 61. For biographical notice see History of Lynn, 1865 edition.

NEWHALL, FRANCIS S. — was largely engaged in the shoe and leather trade, a Senator, and first president of Laighton — afterwards the Central National — Bank. He died Feb. 2, 1858, aged 62. See notice in 1865 edition of History of Lynn.

NEWHALL, HENRY.   Mr. Newhall was a lineal descendant from Thomas, one of the first settlers, and his father was Winthrop Newhall, who for many years successfully prosecuted the trade of tanner, his vats being on the west side of Market street, near where the Eastern Rail-road now crosses. The subject of this sketch, in company with his brother Francis S., just named, followed his father in the occupation, and added to it the manufacture of morocco. This was really the business of his life, though other pursuits to some extent engaged his attention, and he retired from active business with ample means but failing health. His habits were rather retiring than bustling, though he did not shrink from the performance of important public duties. He filled various municipal offices, was a bank director, and on the death of his brother Francis succeeded to the office of president of the Central National Bank, which he continued to fill till a few years before his death. His opportunities for education were limited, but he was fond of reading, and soon began to store his mind with information on almost every current topic, by no means overlooking the literature of the imagination. He was much esteemed for his gentlemanly manners and in rather a marked degree received the social deference so often

accorded to wealth. The Unitarian society, which was incorporated in 1822, counted him among its early members, and to the
end of his life he continued in the faith. He died July 15, 1878,
aged 81 years ; and his remains were interred on Linden avenue
in Pine Grove Cemetery, by the side of those of his brother
Francis, in accordance with the expressed desire of both, who,
having through life enjoyed uninterrupted brotherly attachment,
wished to lie near each other in their final rest.

NEWHALL, Dr. HORATIO. Dr. Newhall was born in Lynn, on
the 28th of August, 1798, and was a lineal descendant of one
of the first settlers. His mother was Lucy, a daughter of Col.
John Mansfield, who was commander of the Lynn regiment at
the time the Revolution broke out.

He fitted for college, at Lynn Academy, partly under the
tuition of Samuel Newell, who, with his wife Harriet, afterwards
became so famous for their missionary labors in India, and partly
under Solomon S. Whipple, subsequently a lawyer in Salem.
He entered Harvard College on his birthday, the 28th of August, 1813 ; and in his class were some whose names will long
remain conspicuous among the famous of our land ; among them
George Bancroft the historian, Caleb Cushing the jurist and
statesman, Rev. Dr. Tyng the divine, and Judge Emerson. He
graduated with honor, and soon applied himself to the study
of medicine, taking his degree in 1821. There had at that time
been an emigration of a number of families from Boston and its
vicinity to the then new State of Illinois ; and being in want of a
reliable physician, they applied to that distinguished professor
of the theory and practice of medicine, Dr. James Jackson, for
the selection of one ; and he cordially recommended Dr. Newhall,
who very soon after, with his letters of introduction, commenced
the long and toilsome journey towards the western border of
civilization, animated by youthful ardor and manly determination.

He reached the then little French village of St. Louis in just
one month, after travelling day and night. His place of destina-
tion lay some fifty miles beyond, and how to reach it was a
serious question, there being no public conveyance, and hardly a
possibility of securing a wheeled carriage of any kind. However,
he finally succeeded in obtaining a French pony and a sort of

light wagon.   And thus equipped he set forth with the phthisical
apprentice of a friendly shoemaker as a guide and companion,
and by whom the travelling equipage was to be returned.   During the first day they got lost on the prairie, but at night reached
a log hut, where they were hospitably entertained by the proprietor, whose name was Mather, and who proved to be a lineal
descendant of Cotton Mather the celebrated New England divine.
The next day they continued their journey over prairie lands
in splendid floral garniture, it being the eighth of June.   They
also saw herds of deer roaming in every direction.   The young
doctor was so inspired by the romance and beauty of the scene
that he shouted and capered till his poor companion was seized
with amazement and fears that he had become suddenly distracted.
In the afternoon he arrived at the border of the prairie, where
were a few settlers.   There he dismissed his companion with
good advice as to the treatment of the oppressive disease under
which he was suffering, and began to administer to his first
regular patient.

At Greenville, in Bond county, he immediately opened an
office, and soon found himself in a practice extending over all
the adjacent counties.   He was in no sense given to idleness ;
and besides being very industrious in his profession, was active
in public affairs, working diligently to promote the prosperity
of his new home.   In benevolent enterprises he took an unwearied interest ; and it may safely be said that to him are attributable the foundation and success of some of the most worthy
institutions that have proved such blessings to the great West.
And he was a man who never despised small beginnings.   In
March, 1825, the first Sunday school in Bond county, and the
second in the state, was established through his efforts, and of it
he was the first superintendent.   It was at about that period,
too, that he, together with a few other kindred spirits, succeeded
in establishing a Bible Society, and one in aid of Domestic
Missions.

In 1827 Dr. Newhall removed from Greenville into the midst
of the Indian country to the mining region.   He arrived at the
site of Galena, on the 31st of March, having occupied twenty-six
days in the tedious and dangerous journey from St. Louis.   For
a short time he turned his attention to mining ; but in 1828

resumed his medical practice, as more congenial. In 1830, he was stationed at Fort Winnebago, as an acting surgeon in the United States army. But in 1832 he returned to Galena and again went into practice there, and in the Black Hawk war, had sole control of a general hospital. The Asiatic cholera, during its devastating march over the country, a couple of years later, proved a great scourge to this region ; and when General Scott removed his head quarters from Galena to Rock Island, he wrote to Dr. Newhall, beseeching him to come to the latter place and exercise his skill in the endeavor to arrest the progress of the pestilence. It fortunately happened that he had made the disease a matter of careful investigation, and was able to render very efficient service.

During the civil war he did his utmost for the Union cause, though his advanced age was an impediment to his active participation in the stirring scenes of the field. In 1861 he was appointed physician of the United States Marine Hospital, at Galena, and continued to perform the duties till the institution was closed, in 1866.

The first newspaper published north of the Illinois river — the "Miners' Journal," commenced in 1827 — was edited by him. And the Galena Advertiser, first issued in 1829, was likewise under his editorial charge.

Having secured a comfortable home in the West, he became solicitous to share the blessing with a conjugal companion, and accordingly, in 1830, married Elizabeth P. P. Bates, a daughter of Moses Bates, of Richmond, Va. She was a superior woman ; of large and cultivated mind and amiable disposition. The union was a most happy one, and continued till 1848, when death deprived him of her endeared society. They had three sons and three daughters, all of whom survived their father.

The religious element was marked in the character of Dr. Newhall from an early age. In 1835 he joined the First Presbyterian Church of Galena ; some eight years afterwards was chosen an elder, and continued in the office during the remainder of his life.

From his extensive correspondence many papers of exceeding interest might be selected. But we are compelled to be chary of our space. The following letter to an old college class-mate,

however, which it will be observed was written but a few years
before his death, contains such points of interest as will fully
justify its insertion :

GALENA, JULY 8th, 1863.

Col. James W. Seaver, Boston:

DEAR SIR: Your note inviting me to meet the surviving members of the
Class of 1817, at the Revere House, on the 14th inst. is received. Absence from
home must be my excuse for not answering it at an earlier day. I could not realize
that a half century had elapsed since we entered college, until I reflected upon the
vast stride our country has made in its wealth and population during that period.
Since I became a resident of Illinois the population of the State has increased from
fifty thousand to two millions and a half. Then, I was on the frontier of civilization ;
now, my oldest son is a citizen of a State, two thousand miles farther West. It is
only twenty-five years since I hired a Sioux guide to conduct me to Carver's cave in
a wilderness where now is the beautiful city of St. Paul, the capital of Minnesota.
Thirty-three years ago, when I was stationed as surgeon at Fort Winnebago, I
passed through an Indian encampment of twenty-five hundred Winnebagoes on the
Four Lakes, where now is Madison, the seat of government of Wisconsin ; and I
have just returned from commencement at Beloit college, of which institution I am a
trustee. Thirty years since it was the hunting ground of the Winnebagoes. Less
than forty years have passed since this city (Galena) was the favorite dwelling place
of the Sacks and Foxes, and to-day we are celebrating the brilliant victories of our
townsman, General Grant, the great Captain of the age.

If I have been the means of aiding in moulding public opinion in this part of our
beloved country, I owe it, in a great degree, to the education I received at old Harvard. I should rejoice to meet my old class-mates on the 14th inst., but cannot leave
home at that time on account of the situation of my family. Give my fraternal regards
to those who may be present and believe me to be

Truly and Sincerely Yours,   H. NEWHALL

Dr. Newhall died on Monday, September 19, 1870. "Three
days after," says the record of an affectionate friend, "we were
present at the funeral which took place from the family residence.
There were many, very many stricken hearts on that solemn
occasion overshadowed with the gloom of the death presence.
A large concourse of relatives, friends, neighbors and acquaint-
ances assembled to express their sympathy with the living and
their reverence for the dead. The room and coffin were profusely
decorated with choicest flowers tastefully arranged. It was
fitting ; he loved them in life ; and in the fulness of life above,
he no doubt was enjoying the sweetness and beauty of those
that bloom fadelessly in paradise — the garden of blessedness.

" When at four o'clock on the 22d of September we affectionately and sorrowfully committed his remains to the earth — dust
to its kindred dust — we could not but feel, that, for his body,
worn out in the service of duty, there was to be a glorious awak-

ening and renewal by the Master, who said, 'I am the resurrec-
tion and the life ;' and there was deep solace in the Voice from
heaven, saying write, 'Blessed are the dead who die in the Lord.'
" Encircled in a garland of delicate flowers and green foliage
was a miniature sheaf of ripe wheat lying upon the coffin which
contained the inanimate form of the departed saint. The design
was appropriate and significant : 'Thou shalt come to thy grave
in full age, like as a shock of corn cometh in his season.' "

NEWHALL, ISAAC, of Mall street. By referring to page 540
of the 1865 edition of the History of Lynn, the reader will find a
notice of this individual, who was a native of the place, and established something of a literary reputation by his letters on Junius.
It is hardly probable that he anticipated the rank his little work
was destined to attain so soon after he had ceased to be moved
by anything the world could say of it or of him. The writer
well remembers that when the volume appeared, in 1831, it was
somewhat talked about, but probably not many copies were circulated in Lynn. The truth is, it was upon a subject concerning
which very few in our community knew much, and to most
of those few it had little interest. It was to the learned class
of statesmen and politicians, rather than to the mere partisan,
that it commended itself. But yet a sort of romantic interest
attended its advent, it being so unaccountable that a man of Mr.
Newhall's hum-drum vocation, could, while pursuing his daily
routine, be pondering on themes that agitated the minds of a
Burke and an Eldon.

In an address delivered by Hon. Charles W. Upham, of Salem,
before the Essex Institute, in 1868, appeared a warm recognition
of the success of Mr. Newhall, and interwoven were graphic allusions to his personal traits, habits, and pursuits. Said the
speaker : " Behind the counter of a retail store on Essex street,
[Salem] was to be found a person pursuing the daily routine of a
most unpretentious life, apparently thinking of nothing else than
the accommodation of customers, in the exhibition of his stock,
and measuring out, by the yard, linen, cotton, ribbons, and tape.
He was apparently beyond middle life, of a mild and courteous
demeanor, quiet, and of few words. There was, it is true, in his
mien and manners, a combined gentleness and dignity, that

marked him as differing from the common run of men, but nothing to indicate the tenor of his peculiar mental occupations The leisure hours of that man were employed in patient, minute, comprehensive and far-reaching researches in books, quarterly journals, magazines and political documents, guided by a cultivated taste, keen discrimination, familiarity with the best models of style and thought, and intimate acquaintance with the biographical details of all the prominent public characters of England, and their personal, family, and party relations to each other, that enabled him to grapple with a subject that was engrossing and defying the ingenuity of them all, and thereby to place himself as a peer among the literati of his day."

Mr. Newhall was not in any marked degree successful in life, as most people estimate success ; that is, he did not become rich ; but he lived in comfort, maintained a respectable position, and died in peace, at the old family mansion, on Mall street, in which he was born, and which has since been removed to give place for the fine modern dwelling of Mr. John T. Moulton. He was an elder brother of Dr. Horatio Newhall, a sketch of whom has just been given, was born on 24th of August, 1782, and died on the 6th of July, 1858.

NEWHALL, ISAAC, of Marianna street. Mr. Newhall died at his picturesque residence near the eastern border of the city, on the 22d of February, 1879, at the age of 65 years. He was a native of Lynn, and a direct descendant from one of the first settlers ; was a man of great decision of character and uncompromising integrity ; active in business and public enterprises ; not easily diverted from any course deliberately adopted, nor over-patient with those who undertook to thwart his plans ; was faithful to friends, and no time-server or selfish cringer. He loved to retire from the unsatisfying turmoil of business to his rural estate upon our eastern highlands, where he possessed many acres which he had brought from a rough and unproductive condition into rich bearing, there to enjoy the society of his affectionate family, and social intercourse with friends and neighbors. He was not much in public office, though he served as an Alderman. in 1851, and again in 1873. In his religious views he was liberal. Though of Quaker parentage, he in early life became attached to the Unitarian denomination. But in after years, with his family, he worshiped with the Methodists. By his own request, however, his remains were buried from the Friends' meeting-house, and the funeral services were attended by a large number of business men, as well as relatives and friends. For several years he suffered greatly from severe neuralgic attacks, which he bore with great fortitude, and for the relief of which he submitted to dangerous surgical operations. He made very free use of tobacco, insomuch that at one period of his life he was commonly spoken of as always appearing with a cigar in his mouth. Whether this habit occasioned or aggravated his terrible disease, was never, so far as the writer knows, determined.

Mr. Newhall was twice married, and left a widow and several children. An elder brother of his — John Bailey Newhall — was possessed of an observing mind and roving disposition, and had he lived no doubt would have made a mark in the literary world. It is not derogatory to compare him to Bayard Taylor. They were about equally educated, and commenced their travels a-foot not far from the same time ; and their letters were similarly interesting and graphic in style. As it was, though he died young he gave some attractive lectures about the Indians with whom he fraternized during his rovings beyond the western frontier ; and his epistolary accounts of pedestrian rambles in Europe were much read.

NEWHALL, JACOB — landlord of the famous tavern on the Boston road, in revolutionary times. He was born May 3, 1740, and died June 18, 1816. For biographical notice see History of Lynn, 1865 edition, page 494.

NEWHALL, JAMES R. — was born on Christmas day, 1809, in the old Richard Haven house, afterwards known as the Hart house, which stood on Boston street, corner of North Federal, till 1876, when, at the dawn of the great Centennial Day, July 4, it "ascended up" in a patriotic blaze. For biographical notice and portrait see Centennial Memorial.

NEWHALL, JOSEPH, mentioned on page 484 of the 1865 edition of the History of Lynn, was a man of considerable note in the town, and much respected. In 1696, the town granted him liberty to "sett up a pewe in yᵉ east end of yᵉ meeting house Between yᵉ east dowre & the stares; prouided itt does nott prejudice the going up yᵉ stares into yᵉ gallery, & maintains so much of the glas window as is against sᵈ pewe." He was a member of the General Court, and died while in office. And in this connection it may be remarked that the pay of Representatives and indeed of all public officers, was at a rate that did not encourage that degree of hankering for official position so lamentably prevalent in our time. Upon the records is found this item of account with Mr. Newhall: "Dec. 1706 to his serucing a Representative at the generall court in the year 1705, untill his death, 76 days at 3ˢ per day — 11£ 8ˢ 0ᵈ." True, the value of money was at that time very different from what it is at present; but the difference was not sufficient to make office the matter of anxious seeking that it now is.

Mr. Newhall perished while on his way from Boston to Lynn, in a great snow storm, in January, 1705-6. His grave-stone is in the Old Burying Ground, near the western wall; it gives his age as 47, and his title as Ensign. He had eleven children, all of whom survived him.

NEWHALL, JOSIAH — a prominent and public spirited citizen — born January 17, 1790, died November 7, 1842. His residence was at the east end of the Common. For biographical notice see History of Lynn, 1865 edition, page 533.

NEWHALL, Gen. JOSIAH. General Newhall was born in Lynn, in the district now constituting Lynnfield, on the 6th of June, 1794, and was a lineal descendant from Thomas, the early settler. His long and active life closed on the 26th of December, 1879. During several years of his earlier manhood he followed the profession of teaching but as time advanced retired to the more congenial employment of agriculture. He however retained his love for study, and became quite proficient in some branches, his attainments bearing his fame even to the other side of the Atlantic, where, in 1876, he received the honor of being elected a fellow of the Royal Historical Society of Great Britain. He served in the war of 1812, and was afterwards much interested in military affairs, attaining the rank of Brigadier General in the Massachusetts Militia. When General Lafayette reviewed the troops on Boston Common, during his visit to America, in 1824, he was present in command of a regiment.

Lynnfield was incorporated as a separate town, in 1814, and General Newhall was her first Representative in the General Court. He served also in 1826 and '27, and again in 1848. In the administration of President Jackson, he held an office in the Boston Custom House. He also at different times filled important local offices. But his most congenial and satisfying resort was the honorable occupation of farmer and horticulturist. There, the results of his experiments and suggestions were often of much value. He was kind-hearted, genial in manners, and ever ready to lend a helping hand to the deserving who needed assistance. The last time the writer had the pleasure of meeting him, was on the occasion of the celebration of the Two Hundred and Fiftieth Anniversary of the Settlement of Lynn, June 17, 1879. He seemed greatly to enjoy the proceedings, and as the open carriage in which he sat moved along in the procession, on that pleasant forenoon, was in fine spirits and highly interested in observing the many evidences of thrift and improvement.

His wife was Rachel C., a daughter of Timothy Bancroft, and they were the parents of nine children, only two of whom survived him.

NEWHALL, THOMAS and ANTHONY. These two individuals, who were among the earliest settlers of Lynn, were brothers ; and the first white child born within our borders was a son of the former, who, at his baptism, which took place immediately after the arrival of Rev. Mr. Bachelor, received the name of Thomas, a name which seems to have been a favorite in the family as far back as it can be traced. In the 1865 edition of our History of Lynn may be found such genealogical references as will enable many of the line living at this day, to trace their kinship. Dr. James A. Emmerton and Henry F. Waters, Esq., of Salem, a few years since, in their researches in the old country, found in the English archieves, the will of Thomas Newhall, dated in 1498, and proved April 22, 1499 ; and from that testator, it is concluded, the Newhalls of Lynn descended. The will is in

Latin, and names the testator's brother Hugo, his daughters
Margaret and Elizabeth, and other females, who may have been
married daughters. It also names William, Stephen, and Thomas
Newhall. To the latter, one cow is bequeathed. The executors
nominated are, "Thomas Newhall and Emmota my wife." That
the testator was a devout churchman is indicated by this bequest :
"My soul to God, the blessed Mary and all the saints, and my
body to be buried in the chapel of Witton." And to the "Abbat
and Convent of the Blessed Mary of Vale Royal, 5 marcas," are
given. If the worthy old yeoman could have anticipated the
extent to which his New England descendants would have
swerved from the faith he cherished, it is feared that he would
not have left the world in a particularly serene state of mind.

Oliver Cromwell seems to have been the owner of a manor
called Newhall ; and indeed the writer remembers to have seen
the names "Croumwell" and Newhall in some way connected
far back in English history. But the Protector, finding the
possession yielding but little, or perhaps being pushed for means,
in 1656 expressed a desire to dispose of the estate. The following
letter to his son-in-law, a photographic copy of which is in the
Mint Museum, at Philadelphia, is upon the subject : "Sonn ——,
you knowe there hath often beene a desire to sell New-hall,
because in these 4 years past it hath yielded very little or noe
proffit att all, nor ever did I heare you ever liked it for a seate.
It seems there may be a chapman had whoe will give 18,000*l.* it
shall be either layed out where you shall desire, at Mr Wallop's
or elsewhere and the monie put into Spoffer's hands in trust to
be soe disposed or I shall settle Burleigh wch yields me 1260 to
1300 *L.* besides the woods. Waterhouse will give you further
information. I rest y^r lovinge ffather   OLIVER, P.
"My love to y^r father and mother and your dear wife. May
29, 1656."

There has been a question whether the names NEWHALL and
NEWELL were originally identical. Many have contended that
they were not ; yet there is a will of Thomas New*ell*, proved 24
September, 1529, which mentions the testator's sister Margaret
New*hall.* Must not this same Thomas Newell have been the
son and executor of the Thomas Newhall before named, for we see
that he had a sister Margaret ? If the names were originally

separate, it is quite certain that they were sometimes used inter-
changeably, perhaps through ignorance, for it is not too much to
admit that in the course of generations there may have been
even in that brilliant family, an individual or two who might
ignorantly toy with the name. In " Traditions of Edinburgh,"
by Robert Chambers, it is mentioned that Sir Walter Pringle
was raised to the bench in 1718, and called " Lord Newhall."

In Copp's Hill burying ground, Boston, is a grave-stone bearing this inscription :

Here lies buried the Body of
NATHANIEL NEWEL
Aged 73 years decd Nov ye 29 1731

And upon another stone, in the same burial place is this :

Here lyes Buried the Body of
NATHANAEL NEWELL Junr
aged 26 years 10 mo & 15 days decd April ye
24th 1717

Now these persons were, without doubt, a grandson and great-
grandson of Anthony Newhall, who so early settled in Lynn.
Nathaniel the elder, who died in 1731 was born in Lynn, in
1658, and his son was born here, June 11, 1690 ; these dates
appear on the records, and clearly identify the persons, as the
family is known to have removed to Boston, in or about 1691,
and occupied a house in the vicinity of Copp's Hill. Yet it will
be noticed that on the grave-stone of the elder, the name is
spelled *Newel,* and on that of the younger *Newell.* And, more-
over, the christian names are spelled differently ; all which may
be attributable to the ignorance or carelessness of the stone-cutter,
in connection with the fact that even then not much importance
was attached to uniformity in spelling. It will be observed that
Nathaniel, jr. died young, but he left a widow. His father was a
ship-carpenter, and evidently a man of means and good character.
In our notice of Nathaniel Handford, page 142, for whom he
received his baptismal name, there appears evidence that great
confidence was reposed in him.

Having alluded to the favor with which the baptismal name
Thomas has been regarded in the family as far back as the line
can readily be traced it may be mentioned that among those
now bearing it is *Thomas A. Newhall,* of Philadelphia, a native
of Salem, Mass., a son of Gilbert, and grandson of Col. Ezra,

of the Revolution. He went to Philadelphia, in 1830, a lad
of sixteen years, having previously served for a while in the office
of Dana, Fenno and Bolles, money and note brokers, in State
street, Boston. In due time, by assiduity and business capacity,
he became prosperously established in the home of his adoption,
and yet remains there, enjoying the fruit of his industry and the
respect of an appreciative community. He is father of one
daughter and the patriarchal number of ten sons, several of the
latter being established in honorable business around him. Capt.
Walter S. Newhall, a commander in the Third Regiment of Pennsylvania Volunteer Cavalry, during the civil war, and who lost
his life in the service, was one of his sons, and one of six brothers
who were in the army at the same time, receiving high commendation for the spirit and discretion with which they discharged
their perilous duties. Lieut. Col. Frederic C. Newhall, another
son, was Assistant Adjutant General on the staff of Lieutenant
General Sheridan, and served during the entire war, from the fall
of 1861, when he entered the army as a Lieutenant, till mustered
out, at New Orleans, in 1865. This latter is the author of the
volume entitled "With General Sheridan in Lee's Last Campaign" — a work forming one of the most valuable contributions
to the literature of the war. His graphic description of the expi-
ring throes of the Confederate army are almost pathetic. During
Lee's invasion of Pennsylvania, six of the brothers were at the
front ; and the youngest, Charles, being at the Agricultural
School, in Centre county, wrote to his father that as there was
not time to wait for an answer to his request for permission to
"join the other boys," he should go, " knowing it would be all
right." Several of the brothers are well-known as among the
best American players of the good old English game of cricket,
which is still held in high esteem in and about Philadelphia and
New York.

In view of the facts stated regarding the family of Mr. Thomas
A. Newhall, and others of the surname spoken of in this volume,
it will be seen that some of the transplanted Newhalls of the old
Lynn stock, have so conducted as to reflect enduring honor on
the name, however delinquent we of the indigenous branches
have remained.

For many years our Philadelphia friend has taken much inter-

est in our family history, and for what he has done deserves the
thanks of the entire brotherhood. He was, as just remarked, a
grandson of Col. Ezra of the Revolution — the latter being a
great-great-grandson of Thomas, the first of European parentage
born here. He, Col. Ezra, was Captain of the Lynn Minute
Men at the opening of the Revolution, but in consequence of
the delay of Col. Pickering from Salem was not present at the
battle of Lexington. Nor was he present at the battle of Bunker
Hill, as he was attached to Col. Mansfield's regiment, as senior
Captain. Col. Mansfield, it will be borne in mind, was cashiered
for " remissness and backwardness in the execution of duty," on
that memorable occasion. Col. Ezra, in earlier life, was an
officer in the French war, under Col. Ruggles. Subsequent
to the battle of Bunker Hill, he was Major, then Lieutenant
Colonel in Colonel Putnam's Fifth Massachusetts Regiment,
and so continued to the end of the war. He was twice married.
His first wife was Sarah Fuller, of Lynn, and his second, Elsie
Breed, also of Lynn. After the establishment of peace, in 1783,
he removed to Salem, purchased an estate on Essex street, and
there resided till his death, which took place on Fast day, April
5, 1798, at the age of 66 years. He has always been spoken
of as a brave and prudent officer, and a worthy and beloved
citizen. There is abundant evidence that while in the army he
was very popular with his companions in arms. While the
regiment was encamped at Winter Hill, some dissatisfaction was
manifested concerning the rank of the captains and other officers,
as they stood on the brigade major's books. The captains therefore, on the 27th of August, 1775, held a meeting and voted to
" settle the rank of officers by lot, and abide thereby ; " at the
same time voting that Captain Ezra Newhall should rank as first
Captain.

It may be mentioned in this connection, that Mr. Charles L.
Newhall, of Southbridge, Mass., a few years ago undertook the
preparation of a genealogy of the Newhall family and collected
a considerable amount of material, but from some cause was led
to abandon his enterprise, and Mr. Thomas A. Newhall, of whom
we have been speaking, took measures to have the materials
thus collected placed in the hands of Henry F. Waters, Esq.
of Salem, who diligently followed up the researches, correcting

13

errors and adding new matter, till a very satisfactory result has been reached, and the whole will undoubtedly soon appear in print, some portions having been already given to the public among the historical papers of the Essex Institute.

The will of Anthony Newhall, who died in Lynn, January 31 1656, mentions his son John and grandchildren Richard and Elizabeth Hood. His house was on the east side of Federal street.

NYE, Dr. JAMES M. — a reputable physician and scientist. He died April 21, 1872, aged 53 years. See Annals, 1872.

OLIVER, STEPHEN. Mr. Oliver died at his residence on Blossom street, March 15, 1875, at the mature age of 89 years. He passed a busy and useful life, and under the old town government was much in public office. Being an active politician, and full of interest in passing events, and withal a ready and racy writer on current local affairs, he exercised considerable influence. During the earlier years of the anti-masonic excitement he was a stalwart advocate of the cause; was one of the most pungent writers in the old Lynn Record; and was a delegate to the national anti-masonic convention, at Baltimore, which in 1831 nominated William Wirt for the presidency. His zeal in the cause seemed sometimes to outrun his discretion, till it rather suddenly waned, and he became a warm adherent of the whig party. He strongly advocated the re-chartering of the United States Bank. In 1836 and 1840 he was a member of the State Senate; and for a short time, under President Harrison, postmaster. Being diligent and on the whole — though he had "ups and downs" — successful in business, he provided well for a large family, engaging at different periods in various occupations, but chiefly in the retail dry goods and shoe-manufacturing lines.

In one of so much versatility it could hardly be expected that literary aspirations would remain altogether dormant; and hence, in addition to his political newspaper writings, which, by the way, were usually timely and telling, he sometimes appeared as an essayist or lecturer; and in all his productions there was a vein of good sense and good nature that secured attention. In

verse, too, he occasionally beamed forth, one or two of his productions eliciting favorable comment ; but generally his efforts
at versification did not extend beyond the newspaper advertisement, where, being stimulated by the exigencies of trade, he was
quite felicitous, entirely out-doing a neighbor of his, who, being
a sort of rival in business, thought it meet to attempt to rival
him in the poetic arena.

Under some circumstances, there can be hardly a doubt, Mr.
Oliver would have become conspicuous in a field far more extensive than the county of his birth.   He was ready with tongue as
well as pen ; not lacking in assurance, shrewd and discriminating,
though perhaps a little too uncompromising as a partisan.

In person he possessed some noticeable features, was well-proportioned, and bore the marks of a firm and healthy constitution.
His residence was for a long time on South Common street, the
site being that afterwards occupied by the mansion of his son
Stephen, and later still by St. Stephen's Memorial Church.

He was of Quaker parentage, but on his marriage, which was
"out of the meeting," was disowned, though he continued to
worship with the society.   Six sons and one daughter, of his nine
children, survived him.

PARKER, THOMAS — lineal ancestor of Rev. Theodore Parker.
His autograph is among those appended to the Armitage Petition,
page 106.   He removed to Reading.   See Annals, 1635.

PARSONS, Rev. OBADIAH.   Mr. Parsons was minister of the
First Parish some eight years, having been installed February 4,
1785.   He preached in the house known as the Old Tunnel ; and
it was during his pastorate that the parsonage was erected,
though there were "parsonage lands," so called, before that
period.   The parsonage occupied the site now forming the south-
east corner of South Common and Commercial streets, the last
named street having been opened in 1832, at which time the
house was removed to its present location, at the south-west
corner of Commercial and Neptune streets.

Mr. Parsons was a man given to such irregularities and indulgencies, as was charged, that the spiritual condition of the parish
during his pastorate, was at a low ebb.   Grave suspicions were

afloat, touching his moral character, even before his settlement, and while here, some things occurred calculated rather to confirm than remove the suspicions. He was, at least, a man of such convivial habits as in our day would be likely to exclude one from the ministry; but then it was a time when such habits were indulged in by preachers as well as people. And an apt illustration of the prevailing custom occurred at the time of the erection of the parsonage, just referred to, a work in which Mr. Parsons took a lively interest. The story is, that a number of the parishioners of small means were surprisingly liberal in the amounts they subscribed in furtherance of the good object, though it was understood that their offerings would be received in the form of labor upon the premises, at a fixed price per day. The work went bravely on. The contributors were highly applauded for their generosity, and the building committee praised for their liberality in arranging with a neighboring retailer for a supply of "refreshments," as they might be called for. Cheerily and rapidly the work progressed to completion. And then — when the accounts were brought together, the contracting parties were astonished to find that the retailer's score for rum alone exceeded in amount all that class of subscriptions; to say nothing of the other " refreshments " in the shape of crackers and salt-fish. See Annals, 1792.

PATCH, CHARLES F. Mr. Patch died on the 24th of January, 1873, after a sickness of three days, aged 27 years, leaving a widow but no children. He was a son of Joshua Patch, who was long engaged in the lumber business here. The deceased was a young man of much promise, had been a member of the Common Council, and at the time of his death was on the second year of his service as City Treasurer. He was a freemason, and several lodges of the order attended his burial.

PERKINS, Dr. JOHN, of Lynnfield — an eminent physician and learned writer. He died in 1780, aged 85. See Annals, 1780.

PERLEY, Dr. DANIEL — a skillful physician and much esteemed citizen. He died at his residence on Breed street, January 31, 1881, aged 77. See Annals, 1881.

PHILLIPS, GEORGE W., of Saugus, a brother of the "silver tongued" orator, Wendell Phillips, and a lawyer of high standing. He died July 30, 1880, aged 70. See Annals, 1880.

PIERSON, Rev. ABRAHAM — a profound scholar, and father of the first president of Yale College. By reference to our Annals under date 1640, it will be seen that some doubt was entertained as to the place of residence of this individual. But it appears by both Savage and Sprague that he must have lived here ; or at least that his son Abraham, the college president, was born here in 1641. The chair in which president Pierson was accustomed to sit is still preserved among the college treasures, and a picture of it may be seen in Harper's Magazine, volume 17, page 2. There is no doubt that the church composed of Long Island emigrants, was formed at Lynn, in November, 1640, and that Mr. Pierson, the elder, was at the same time installed as its minister, the celebrated Hugh Peters taking part in the exercises. He appears to have come from Yorkshire, to have graduated at the University of Cambridge, and to have preached for a time in England under Episcopal ordination. He graduated in 1632 and arrived in New England in 1639, and hence could have been here but a short time before leaving for Long Island. That he was rigidly set, like many others of the early New England clergy, in his views touching ecclesiastical authority, maintaining that none but church members should be allowed to vote or hold civil office, is quite apparent. And it is likewise apparent that he was regarded by his cotemporaries as a man of high character and great usefulness. Mather says, "wherever he came, he shone ;" adding that "he left behind the character of a pious and prudent man and a true child of Abraham now lodged in Abraham's bosom." No doubt his influence was large in establishing some of the stalwart principles that long prevailed in the eastern section of Long Island and the neighboring Connecticut colonies, and which were figured forth in that imaginary but hardly exaggerated code known as the Blue Laws. The orders against drunkenness, lying, and kindred vices went quite beyond the conceptions of the most zealous reformers of our day. And the higher offences — of which even a suspicion was not to escape — were so signally dealt with that the severity of the punishment attached, sometimes operated as a virtual repeal ; for the magistrates could not always find it in their hearts to reject defences of a very doubtful nature, rather than impose the penalty that must follow conviction. For instance, one John Kelley, a carpenter, was complained of for endeavoring to enter into a supplementary matrimonial connection, declaring his wife was dead. It appeared on the trial that she was not dead ; but he defended against the original charge in some befoging way, and against the additional one of lying, by maintaining that his meaning was that his wife was dead in trespasses and sin. It is not intended to connect Mr. Pierson with any absurd or farcical proceeding, but to present a sort of by-way illustration. See Annals, 1640.

PITCHER, MARY — better known as Moll Pitcher, the fortune-teller. Her residence was on Essex street, opposite Pearl, and she died April 9, 1813, aged 75 years. See Annals, 1813. A fac-simile of her signature is here given.

Mary Pitcher

POMPEY — an African prince, stolen, brought hither and sold as a slave. See Annals, 1780.

POQUANUM — Indian sachem of Nahant. See 1865 edition of History of Lynn, page 40.

PRANKER, EDWARD, a woolen manufacturer, and proprietor of the mill bearing his name near the site of the ancient iron works, in Saugus. He died August 14, 1865, aged 73 years. See Annals, 1865.

PRATT, MICAJAH C. Mr. Pratt was for many years a prominent citizen, was a native of Lynn, and died on the 28th of January, 1866, aged 74 years. For the whole of his business life, which commenced as early as 1812, he was a shoe-manufacturer, struggling along during the protracted period when trade was depressed, by industry and carefulness sustaining his position, and gathering the experience which when better times dawned led on to fortune. He continued in business forty years, manufacturing the various kinds of shoes in demand for the southern and western markets, and at one period employing between four hundred and five hundred operatives, turning out some two hundred and forty thousand pairs a year, which was a very large business for a time before machinery had to much extent been introduced in the business.

Being a member of the society of Friends, he was but little in public life, though he held some positions of responsibility, where his integrity and business capacity appeared conspicuous. He was active in promoting the usefulness of the Institution for Savings, established in 1826; was president of the First National Bank of Lynn, and of the Lynn Fire and Marine Insurance Company. His manners were genial and his tendencies benevolent and social.

On the 26th of November, 1812, he married Theodate B. Brown, and by her had six children. His second wife, whom he married late in life, was Abby Newhall, by whom he had no children. His residence was on the north side of Broad street, a little east of Silsbee.

PRATT, SIDNEY BOWNE. Among the liberal and unassuming sons of Lynn may surely be reckoned this one. He was a son of James Pratt, who died in 1832, and who was a prominent shoe-manufacturer. The subject of this notice was born on the 14th of May, 1814, and died on the 29th of January, 1869. About the time of the opening of the Eastern Rail-road, in 1839, he engaged in the express business, and by faithfulness and assiduity soon found himself on the high road of success, and continued on, till the time of his death, always possessing the confidence of the public. He was at the head of the well-known firm of Pratt and Babb. His manners were affable, and his disposition to accommodate unvarying. Indeed he seemed to possess just those elements of character which are best calculated to ensure success in any business; and he was certainly successful in that which he chose. He was successful, too, in gaining an enduring name, by his liberal bequest to the Free Public Library, the first gift of the kind received by that institution, the amount being $10.000. His funeral took place from the Friends' meeting-house, on Silsbee street, and was attended by the Mayor and other members of the city government, and a large concourse of relatives and fellow-townsmen. He was never married. In the Public Library a very good likeness of him is preserved.

PURCHIS, OLIVER. The fame of Mr. Purchis extended far beyond our municipal limits. He was a man possessed of strong points of character, undoubted patriotism, and a pertinacity that sometimes might well be called obstinacy. During the Andros administration his energetic course in baffling the unwarrantable demands of the Governor and his unscrupulous Secretary, no doubt saved the town from loss and mortification, and received well-merited applause. His position as Town Clerk, at that trying period, afforded opportunities for the display of patriotic zeal and hatred of oppression well fitted to his temper. He came as early as 1635, and in his official capacity is named as a grantee in the Indian Deed of Lynn. For some ten years he was a Representative in the General Court; was agent of the iron company, and somewhat of a military character, though he was not a particularly bright star in the latter sphere. But his long and useful life appears to have ended in poverty and distress. On the Council records, June 19, 1701, is found this entry: " A resolve was sent up from the Representatives in the words following, vizt : ' Whereas, Mr Oliver Purchase, an ancient public servant in the government is fallen to decay and become very indigent and necessitous, not having whereof to subsist now in his age, and being rendered incapable of labour : Resolved, That in consideration of the good service done by s^d Oliver Purchase, he be allowed the sum of Ten pounds out of the public Treasury of this province for his necessary support.'—Which resolve being read at the Board was concurred with and his Honour the Lieut. Gov. gave his consent unto and signed the same." But the poor man, " deceasing before he had received s^d gratuity," it was resolved by the Council and House of Representatives, " That the aforesaid sum of ten pounds be paid out of the public treasury of this Province to Mr William Wilson of Concord, to be by him delivered to Mrs Sarah Purchis, widow, relict of said Oliver Purchis." It was in 1691 that Mr. Purchis removed from Lynn to Concord, where he died in 1701, aged 88 years. See Annals of early dates for many facts concerning him. A fac-simile of his signature is here given.

PURCHIS, THOMAS — a Maine fur trader. See Annals, 1678.

QUANOPKONAT — a prominent Indian resident of the territory of Lynn. See History of Lynn, 1865 edition, page 42.

RAMSDELL, ABEDNEGO. Mr. Ramsdell was one of the immortal four from Lynn, who fell at the battle of Lexington. It was said by an aged lady, that on the fatal day a woman in his neighborhood seeing him hastening along towards Lexington and being seized by an unaccountable presentiment of danger, called to him and warned him of her premonition. He bravely replied that he might be going to his death ; but it was a good cause, and he hoped by the aid of his musket to take a red-coat with him, if he fell. On he sped, and was killed immediately after reaching the battle ground. See Annals, 1775.

RAMSDELL, JOHN — one of the early settlers of Lynn. He was a witness in the famous case between the Town and Thomas Dexter, concerning the ownership of Nahant. Descendants of his are yet among us. His autograph is upon the Armitage Petition, page 106. See Annals, 1630.

RHODES, AMOS. Mr. Rhodes was born in Lynn, on the 24th of April, 1795, and died on the 15th of January, 1870. His father was Amos Rhodes, long a prominent business man, in the western section of the town, at that time the chief business part, his dwelling being the one still standing on the east side of Federal street, next south of the mill brook, which house was built by him near the beginning of the present century ; and he was the same Amos Rhodes named in the correspondence of Ebenezer Breed, given in the 1865 edition of the History of Lynn, page 523 et seq. The mother of the subject of this notice was Elizabeth, the eldest daughter of Rev. Obadiah Parsons.

Mr. Rhodes graduated at Harvard College with the 1816 class, and for a few years engaged in teaching, spending a part of the time at the south. His absence, however, was of short duration. In 1817 he was preceptor of Lynn Academy. He never prepared himself for entering either of what are called the learned professions, choosing rather to pursue a more sequestered path of usefulness. On the organization of the Lynn Institution for Savings, he was elected treasurer, and filled the office for more than forty years. And to his careful management, scrupulous fidelity, and unwearied vigilance, that institution is indebted for much of its early success. He was also for many years secretary of the Lynn Mechanics Fire and Marine Insurance Company In the reading of choice books, and in the conversation and society of the intellectual and cultivated, he took unflagging delight ; and ever seemed more desirous of doing what he could to promote the mental and moral elevation of those about him, than to aid in their struggles for the acquisition of mere wealth. For twenty years — 1830 to 1850 — he acted as librarian of the old Social Library, and no doubt succeeded, during that long period, in forming in many a youthful mind an enduring taste for the better class of reading, as his judgment in the selection of books came to be much relied on. He was a fast friend of Mr. Lewis the poet and historian, and of Mr. Lummus the first Lynn newspaper publisher. He however exercised his pen but little save upon the books pertaining to his daily business ; though his good taste, judgment, and acquirements made him a useful member of the little coterie who wrought in the literary interests of the Mirror during its most successful days.

Mr. Rhodes was among the early members of the Unitarian society, and before the introduction of church organs in Lynn aided the choir by his flute and bass-viol. In the Sunday school, also, he took an active interest ; and having labored for the society through all its days of weakness, had the happiness to see it strong and prosperous. But he lamented as much as any the tendency towards extreme rationalistic views, which some years ago began to manifest itself in various sections of the denomination. We remember how grieved he was at some of the sentiments enunciated by Rev. Theodore Parker in his famous sermon preached at South Boston, in or about 1841, and how pleased he appeared when his own minister, the Rev. Mr.

Swett, after reading a few passages, from the pulpit, in his clear voice and with striking emphasis, added, "If that is Unitarianism I am not a Unitarian."

On the second of December, 1834, Mr. Rhodes married Lydia, a daughter of Winthrop Newhall, but had no children. She survived him. Funeral services over his remains were held in the church where he had so long loved to worship.

RHODES, HENRY, whose well-written autograph appears upon the Armitage Petition, page 106, was among the early comers, and descendants of his are still among us. Not much is known of him, though he seems to have been a man of good habits, industrious, and respected. See Annals, 1640.

RICHARDS, RICHARD. Mr. Richards was a descendant from one of the early settlers, and was born in Lynn, in 1796. He was, perhaps, the most inventive genius, in a mechanical way, ever born here ; and though he never produced anything to establish a world-wide reputation, he yet originated some things that have proved of great usefulness, especially in the staple business of Lynn, and which furnished suggestions for still greater discoveries by other minds. He was a last-maker, by trade, and in pursuance of that occupation, contrived such improvements and adaptations of machinery as greatly facilitated the work and added to the finish and beauty of the products of his shop. He constructed a sole-cutting machine, for which, n 1844, he obtained a patent, and which was superior to any thing in use before that time. He also designed a peg-cutting machine, which was extensively used. A rail-road turntable which he invented has continued to be used, in some of its essential features, to the present time. And a number of minor inventions and improvements in machinery originated with him. But the sole-cutting machine was the only one for which he received a patent.

As a citizen Mr. Richards was much esteemed ; and he held various offices under the old Town government. He was also a Representative in the General Court, but never seemed to covet official position, preferring rather to pursue the even tenor of his mechanical employments. The enormous shoe, capable of con-

taining some twenty full-grown persons, which figured in proces-
sions, and created so much observation during the memorable
hard cider presidential campaign, in 1840, was a product of his
genius and handiwork.   He also constructed a miniature log
cabin, which, mounted on wheels and dragged along the streets,
excited much curiosity as a political adjunct in the same spirited
campaign.   He died on the 19th of December, 1851, aged 55.

RICHARDSON, JONATHAN.   Mr. Richardson was a native of
Lynn, and died here on the 28th of June, 1872, at the advanced
age of 87 years.   There was no particularly striking event in his
life, for he was content to plod along, unambitious to rise from
the operative's work-bench.   He was a shoemaker of the old
stamp, and quietly pursued his humble calling for full three
quarters of a century.   And his memory compassed a perfect
history of the wonderful progress in our staple business.   He
was one of the early members of Mount Carmel lodge of freemasons, and tyler for more than forty years.   Through the disturb-
ing reign of anti-masonry, when so many of his neighbors withdrew from the institution, he remained faithful ; and his burial,
which took place from the First Methodist meeting-house, was
attended by a large number of the brethren.

RICHARDSON, THOMAS P., was the fourth Mayor of Lynn.   A
biographical notice with a portrait may be found in the Centennial Memorial.   He died very suddenly on the evening of Thanksgiving day, November 24, 1881, aged 65 years.   The writer met
him at the door of Mr. Harrison Newhall's residence, on Park
square, at about seven o'clock.   After a cordial greeting, he
immediately said, " I 'm sick," sat down on a sofa, and within an
hour, breathed his last.   The funeral services took place at the
First Methodist meeting-house on the afternoon of Monday,
November 28, the large audience room being completely filled
with sympathising friends.   The remains were thence conveyed
to their last resting place in Pine Grove Cemetery.   Few have
passed out from the business ranks, from among the laborers for
the moral elevation of the community, or from social life, more
deservedly regretted than Mr. Richardson.   He had but a few
weeks before his decease taken up his residence in the fine

mansion which he had just erected on North Common street, opposite St. Stephen's Memorial Church. A fac-simile of his signature is here given.

J. P. Richardson

ROBBINS, Dr. PETER G., whose name appears in our Annals, under dates 1808 and 1810, was a conspicuous resident here, for many years. He came in 1805, and lived on Essex street, between High and Pearl, in the same house previously occupied by Dr. Henry Burchstead, and subsequently by Dr. Hazeltine. Dr. Robbins was much interested in the political events of the pregnant period in which he came here. Party spirit then ran high, and on the fourth of July, 1806, he was selected as orator of the Democratic party, there being likewise a celebration by the Federalists, whose orator was Hosea Hildreth, then preceptor of the Academy. In 1810, however, the parties united in celebrating the day, and Dr. Robbins was the orator. Rev. Chandler Robbins, D. D., for many years minister of the Second Church of Boston, (Unitarian,) and author of several erudite works, was a son of his, born in the house just designated, on the 14th of February, 1810, and graduated at Harvard in 1829. Rev. Samuel D. Robbins, settled over the Unitarian society of Lynn, in 1833, was also a son of his.

ROBINSON, Col. JAMES — a revolutionary soldier, and the first postmaster of Lynn. He died January 21, 1832, aged 75. His residence was on Boston street, corner of North Federal. See Annals, 1832.

ROBY, Rev. JOSEPH — minister of the third Parish (Saugus) for the long period of fifty-one years. He was a man of learning and held in high esteem as a preacher. Yet we find a flippant bit of doggerel, stated by Mr. Eaton, in his History of Reading, to have been written by a parishioner of the Rev. Mr. Hobby, therein named, which has been claimed to give the popular estimate of four neighboring divines. The allusion to Mr. Roby is certainly not over-complimentary :

Good Mr. Emerson (of Malden),
Proud Mr. Hobby (of Reading)
Silly old Carnes (of Stoneham),
And *Coxcomb* Roby (of Saugus).

" Proud Mr. Hobby " was the reverend gentleman referred to in our Annals, under date 1745, as having had the controversy with Mr. Henchman of Lynn, respecting the celebrated preacher Whitefield. Mr. Hobby went with the multitude to hear Mr. Whitefield when he preached on Reading Common, and was candid enough to afterwards say that he went to prick a hole in Whitefield's coat, but Whitefield had pricked a hole in his heart. He became a warm defender of the great preacher against the assaults of the alarmed clergy who with vigor and pertinacity opposed everything that did not accord with the old faith and their established usages. Mr. Roby died January 31, 1803, aged 79 years. See Annals, 1803.

SADLER, RICHARD. The lofty porphyry cliff near the junction of Walnut and Holyoke streets, from which some of our most extensive and charming views can be obtained, took its name of Sadler's Rock from this individual, who, at the land allotment in 1638, had two hundred acres assigned to him, and " the rock by his house." This enables us with certainty to determine in what neighborhood he settled. He was a prominent personage and well-known throughout the Colony ; and that his services at home were appreciated is indicated by the liberality of the grants to him. He was our first Clerk of the Writs, and a member of the Salem Court ; also one of the commissioners to run the bounds between Lynn and Boston, in 1639, Robert Keayne, the first captain of the Ancient and Honorable Artillery being a fellow-commissioner. He was a man of education, and it is presumed had remained a churchman, inasmuch as after his return to England, in 1647, he became a minister in the established church, though ecclesiastical matters were, about that period, so mixed up in England, that it was sometimes a problem with an individual where he should rank. He was here but about ten years ; and his return may have been hastened by want of sympathy with the rigid views and usages of this then puritanical community. A rude Memorial Stone was erected some years ago, by the writer, at the roadside near the foot

of the rock that bears the good old settler's name.   See Annals,
1635, and other early dates.

SANDERSON, GEORGE P., the sixteenth Mayor of Lynn, was
inaugurated on the 6th of January, 1879.   He was also elected
for a second term, and inaugurated on the 5th of January, 1880.
He was born in Gardiner, Me., on the 22d of November, 1836.
For most of his business life he has been engaged as operative,
agent, or manufacturer, in some department of the shoe trade,
chiefly in Lynn.   He has all along been identified with the
workingmen's interests, and as a leader, received the confidence
and support of his party.   He was a soldier in the civil war,
performed his duties faithfully, and was honorably discharged.
On the third of July, 1859, he married Julia A., a daughter
of William H. Mills, and has four sons.   A fac-simile of his
signature is appended.

SHEPARD, Rev. JEREMIAH, minister of the First Parish for
forty years.   Shepard street takes its name from him ; also
Shepard school.   He died on the third of June, 1720, aged 72.
See Annals, 1720.   His signature is shown by this fac-simile :

SILSBEE, HENRY.   This individual appeared in Lynn at an
early period and was the founder of a family which, though not
remarkable for numbers, has always been in creditable standing.
Silsbee street commemorates the name.   Dr. Emmerton in his
Gleanings from English Records says : " The name Silsbee is
one of the rarest in the records accessible at London." . . . " The
parish records of Olney, Bucks, dating from about 1666, gives
baptisms of a Samuel Slisby's daughters after 1670.   Mr. James
Stowe, the affable parish clerk, told me, while I was studying

the inscriptions on the gravestones in the churchyard, that the name had disappeared from Olney but still remained in neighboring villages. Mr. Stowe's interest in such matters was evinced by the care with which he had cleaned the inscriptions obscured by lichen and mold rather than age, for few, if any, antedated the eighteenth century. The records contain many entries of familiar Lynn names: Laughton, Collins, Townsend, Cooper, etc.; and though Farrington and Kyrtland had disappeared, I was more than ever inclined to the theory that Henry Silsby [the first of the name here] had removed from Salem and Ipswich to Lynn, in order to be near old country neighbors."

It may be added here, that Dr. Emmerton is a native of Salem but lineally connected with the Silsbees and Newhalls of Lynn. His great-grandfather, on the maternal side, was 'Squire James Newhall, who lived in the two-story frame house still standing on the north side of Boston street a little west of Tower Hill, and opposite the end of Summer street. He, the Doctor, in company with Henry F. Waters, Esq., recently visited England; and both being deeply interested in genealogical researches, discovered among the old records there, many interesting facts, some of which have already appeared in print. Mr. Waters was a son of the late Judge Waters. It is to educated, intelligent, and appreciative gentlemen like Dr. Emmerton and Mr. Waters that the student of the past and of family history is greatly indebted.

Several of the Salem branch of the Silsbee family became widely known; among them, Hon. Nathaniel Silsbee, United States Senator. In the spelling of the name similar variations and vagaries were indulged in as in the names of other early settlers; and hence we find Sellesby, Scylesbie, Sillsby, Silesbey, Silsby, Silsbee, Silsbye, Sylsbe, Scilsbey, Silsbe, Sillsbe, Sillsbee.

Henry Silsbee, the first of the name in Lynn, probably came in 1651, purchasing the house once occupied by Joseph Floyd, or Flud, or fflood, as the name was variously spelled, which stood on Fayette street, a few rods south of Essex. He seems to have possessed some means, and was called a "shooemaker," but very likely followed farming most of the time, as he owned a considerable quantity of land. A grandson of his named Nathaniel, whose father was a carpenter, residing in Salem, is traditionally reported to have taken the coffins in which some of the witches were buried, in 1692, to Gallows Hill, he being then a lad of about fifteen years. Dr. Emmerton has lately published " A Genealogical Account of Henry Silsbee and some of his descendants," which is or ought to be in the hands of the whole family connection.

SPARHAWK, Rev. NATHANIEL, first minister of Lynnfield Parish, settled in 1720. He died May 7, 1732, aged 38 years. See Annals, 1731.

STICKNEY, JEREMIAH C., a prominent lawyer in Lynn for forty years, and first City Solicitor. He died August 3, 1869, aged 64. See Annals, 1869. A fac-simile of his signature follows.

SWETT, Rev. WILLIAM G., fourth minister of the Unitarian society. He died January 15, 1843, aged 34. See Annals, 1843.

Mr. Swett was possessed of such rare and diversified qualities that to a superficial observer it might appear that in him were assembled downright contradictory characteristics. Out of the pulpit, he was lively, overflowing with wit, and not unfrequently with jocularity. But in the pulpit, nothing approaching levity was perceptible. His discourses were scholarly, pointed, and delivered in a distinct and finely modulated voice, without sensational gush or misplaced fervor. His style, indeed, was just such as is appreciated by thoughtful minds ; and it is not wonderful that so many of the more intelligent class of our people were attracted that his church became so filled as to render it difficult for new-comers to procure eligible sittings. He was notably free from what were known as transcendental and rationalistic tendencies, and so little inclined to make prominent any peculiar doctrine, that even one of broad evangelical views, as they are called, could seldom see anything to offend.

His sermons hardly ever exceeded twenty minutes in the

14

delivery ; and the writer has heard him remark that if a preacher
could not enforce at least one good lesson in that space he ought
to be ashamed ; and one good lesson at a time, he added, was
full enough for the digestion of most persons. His purpose
manifestly was to benefit his hearers rather than to enjoy any
oratorical triumphs of his own ; thus in a measure reversing the
example of some of our pyrotechnic friends in the sacred desk.
He was not a mere book student, but relied chiefly on his own
innate ability to interest and instruct ; and hence there was an
originality, a freshness and vigor pervading what he wrote, that
was remarkably telling. He had no collection that could be
called a library — hardly a book of reference. We remember
once hearing Rev. Dr. Peabody ask to be shown to his library
for the purpose of determining some point. " Well, Doctor,"
said he, " I have but a poor library, and it is all here," — pointing
to his head.

His health was not good, and he often expressed the belief that
he should not live to be old ; but he was active and much out
of doors.   For a good horse he had an almost sentimental fondness ; and the beautiful drives in our vicinity, held out, in pleasant weather, irresistible attractions ; but he frequently made his
own enjoyment subservient to duty, by taking out for an airing
some poor, aged, or infirm parishioner.

He had some pecuniary resources beyond his salary, and hence
was able to indulge in acts of benevolence in the quiet and secret
way which was his delight.   He was accustomed to say that he
purposed to dispense in charity an amount equal to his salary.
Many a poor widow has had dumped at her door a load of fuel,
without ever knowing who the donor was.   And many a poor,
sick child has received soothing delicacies without knowing
whence they came, and when able to return to his play-things
has wondered who brought the beautiful kaleidoscope, the Noah's
ark and picture-blocks.

Mr. Swett was a son of Col. Samuel Swett late of Boston,
whose wife was Lucia, the only daughter of William Gray, the
eminent merchant and Lieutenant Governor, and who was a
native of Lynn.   He, the Colonel, built for his son the house
on the rise of the hill, near Essex street, which afterwards became
the residence of Mayor George Hood.   But the good minister

did not live long to enjoy the place he so much admired. A year or two before his death he married Charlotte, a daughter of Col. Phinney, of Lexington, and by her had one child — a daughter.

TAYLOR, DAVID, for many years an extensive shoe-manufac turer; intelligent and enterprising. His residence was on South Common street corner of Commercial; and there he died, October 11, 1871, aged 68. See Annals, 1871.

THACHER, Rev. THOMAS, seventh minister of the First Parish. He preached the affecting sermon, in the Old Tunnel meeting-house, December 11, 1795, over the bodies of the eight drowned mariners, the only seaman who had escaped, standing in the aisle near the remains of his companions. Mr. Thacher died September 24, 1849, aged 78. See Annals, 1813.

TOMLINS, EDWARD — an early and prominent settler. His autograph appears on the Armitage Petition, page 106. See Annals, 1630, and other early dates.

TOMLINS, TIMOTHY, was a brother of Edward, just named. The extensive tract of forest and swamp land, in Lynn woods, known as Tomlins's Swamp, took its name from him. He seems to have been full of business, readily turning to some new enterprise when the old became unprofitable. In 1636 he added a "howse of intertainement" to his other industries. In the land distribution of 1638 the town granted him eighty acres; but that could not have been excessively liberal if he took it in land like that of the swamp now bearing his name. He was a Representative for several terms, and his autograph is among those appended to the Armitage Petition. See Annals, 1630.

TOWNSEND, THOMAS. This early settler at one time lived in the vicinity of the iron works, though it is probable that he owned lands in different quarters. He is supposed to have come from London, was a cousin of Governor Winthrop, and could trace his lineage to a Norman nobleman who flourished near the time of the Conquest. One of his ancestors, of the same baptismal name, had the honor of entertaining Queen Elizabeth in her progress through Norfolk, in August, 1578, and for loyalty and attention his wife afterwards received from Her Majesty a beautiful gilt bowl.

Mr. Townsend's five children were all born in Lynn, between 1636 and 1645 ; and his widow, Mary, died of camp fever, Feb. 28, 1692. The family has always maintained a good position in New England, some individuals becoming quite noted ; but within our own borders it has not been specially marked. Andrew Towsend of Lynn was wounded in the great swamp fight with the Narragansetts, December 19, 1675. And in the battle of Lexington, Daniel Townsend fell. See Annals, 1775. Charles Hervey Townsend of New Haven, Ct., a few years since published a limited Genealogy of the family, which cannot fail to interest those of the lineage. The autograph of Thomas Townsend is conspicuous among those on the Armitage Petition, page 106. And it is to the kindness of Charles Hervey Townsend, just named, that we are indebted for the use of the engraving of the autographs.

TREADWELL, Rev. JOHN — minister of the First Parish during the Revolution, and an ardent patriot. See Annals, 1782.

TREVETT, ROBERT W. — a lawyer of considerable acquirements, for many years in practice here. He died January 13, 1842, aged 53 years. He was a son of the noted Captain Trevett of the U. S. navy, a native of Marblehead. See Annals, 1842.

TUDOR, FREDERIC — projector of many improvements on Nahant, and father of the New England ice trade. He died Feb. 6, 1864, aged 80 years. See Annals, 1864.

TUFTS, Deacon RICHARD. Deacon Tufts was born in Lynn, and was a son of David Tufts, a corporal in the army of the Revolution, who, after the war was ended, took up the peaceful and multifarious employments of farmer, trader, and common carrier, all in a limited way. He owned and occupied a house that stood on the south-east corner of Federal street and Western avenue. The Deacon while still a young man became conspicuous for his zeal in the cause of temperance, and through life was characterized by rigidity of principle and persistency in labors for the moral reformation of the community. In religion he tenaciously adhered to the Calvinistic faith, and for many years held the office of deacon in the First Church, without reproach. And it was by the watchfulness and labors of such as he that that ancient shrine was preserved from the "liberalism" that has so changed the character of almost all the earlier churches planted by the Puritans. His son, Gardiner Tufts, was prominent in the civil war, for his efficient services in Washington and elsewhere in behalf of the Massachusetts soldiery. And since the close of the war he has acceptably filled several important public positions where skill and integrity were especially demanded. The Deacon died on the 29th of February, 1880, in the 83d year of his age.

TURNER, Capt. NATHANIEL—a brave and trustworthy colonial officer, and a public character of great merit. See Annals, 1630, and other early dates. The sword which he wielded against the Indians is still preserved by the Historical Society at Hartford, Ct. It has done efficient service, too, in other hands since the Captain's time; in the old French war and in the Revolution. A picture of this formidable weapon may be seen in Harper's Magazine, volume 17, page 3. He sailed for England in January, 1647, in hopes of promoting the interests of the New Haven Colony; but nothing was ever afterwards heard of the vessel or any one on board—unless the celebrated "Phantom Ship" which appeared off the harbor, some months after, and in a few minutes faded away, may be taken as a ghostly representative.

USHER, ROLAND G.—the eleventh Mayor of Lynn. For notice with portrait see Centennial Memorial. The following is a fac-simile of his autograph.

VINTON, JOHN—ancestor of the large and distinguished American family of Vintons. See Annals, 1650.

WALDEN, EDWIN — the thirteenth Mayor of Lynn. For notice with portrait see Centennial Memorial. A fac-simile of his signature is here given.

Edwin Walden

WALKER, RICHARD — a farmer, and military commander. See Annals, 1630 and other early dates. His autograph is on the Armitage Petition. He lived to the great age of 95 years.

WASHBURN, PETER T. — Governor of Vermont. Peter Thacher Washburn was born in Lynn on the seventh of September, 1814, and was a son of Reuben P. Washburn who settled here as a lawyer, in 1812, and married a daughter of Rev. Mr. Thacher, minister of the First Parish, her grandfather being the widely-known Dr. Peter Thacher, for many years minister of Brattle street Church, in Boston.

At an early age the subject of this sketch left Lynn, with his father, who removed to Chester, Vt., afterwards to Cavendish, and thence to Ludlow, where, in 1860, he died. Peter graduated at Dartmouth college, in 1835, and immediately engaged in the study of law, in his father's office. Afterwards, for a few months, he studied under United States Senator Upham, of Montpelier, and was admitted to the bar in 1838. The next year he began practice at Ludlow, where he gained a high reputation and a good business. In 1844 he removed to Woodstock, having formed a law partnership with Charles P. Marsh, which continued till his death. In the last named year he was elected by the Legislature Reporter of the Decisions of the Supreme Court of Vermont and continued in the office eight years. One excellent trait in any lawyer, or indeed in a man of any calling, it is said was possessed by Mr. Washburn in a marked degree ; and that is, a readiness to aid the oppressed. He is reputed to have been always zealous to do his utmost, without the expectation of reward, to protect the weak or poor when exposed to the machinations of the selfish and unscrupulous, who so often resort to the wearying intricacies of the law for the furtherance of their base purposes ; and who, unfortunately, can generally find enough in the profession to second their nefarious designs.

At the time of the breaking out of the civil war, he was in command of the Woodstock Light Infantry. And at the first call of the President for troops he volunteered, and soon raised a company of the full regulation standard. Early on the morning of May 1, 1861, with his little loyal band, he departed for the scene of war, marching from the armory to the stirring tune of Yankee Doodle. Arrived in Virginia, he soon became acting Colonel of the regiment of which his company formed a part. But in the fall of the same year he was called back for other important duties connected with the war. He was elected Adjutant and Inspector General of the State. And that position he continued to fill till the war ended. His labors in that office were so constant and exhaustive that many thought such inroads were made upon his health that it never again became fully established.

In September, 1869 he was elected Governor of the State, by a large majority. And though he was removed by death before he had held the office many months, he had made a remarkably favorable impression. His executive ability was freely acknowledged by all parties ; and there was every prospect of a more than ordinarily successful administration. At the time of his death, in addition to the Governorship he was a Trustee of the University of Vermont, a Trustee of the State Agricultural College, and President of the Woodstock Rail-road.

Governor Washburn died on the 7th of February, 1870, at the age of 55 years, leaving a widow and three children — a son and two daughters. His death was considered by the physicians to have proceeded from a general breaking down of the nervous system, from excessive labor, no evidence of disease, organic or functional, being discovered. He had been working almost unremittingly, when not engaged in public duties, on his Digest of the Supreme Court Decisions ; and literally went from that work to the bed from which he never arose. The funeral services took place at the Congregational church in Woodstock, the body being laid out in a full suit of black, with a military cloak, and amid profuse floral decorations. Highly eulogistic notices appeared in the newspapers, and there was every evidence of sincere mourning as for a great public loss. " He was," said the Vergennes Vermonter, " one of the few living illustrations of Phillips's positive men. They are rarely met with in public or private life. Vermont appreciated him, and he will be mourned as one of the few in public life whose sense of justice was stronger than personal preference or even the dictation of party." The Republican, of Springfield, Mass., remarked "It was in the office of Adjutant General that Governor Washburn's fitness for public service was first made known to the people. His accuracy of dealing was as certain and as rigid as mathematics. The discharge of a public duty was with him reckoned among the 'exact sciences.' If he had been less honest than he was, he would still have followed honesty from sheer devotion to its straightforwardness, its absolute correctness. We speak of this characteristic, not to elevate it above his unimpeachable integrity, but because it is what marks him among governors. Vermont has had honest executives before but it has been some time since she had a governor who governed, who picked up the loose ends in her administrative departments and set every thing in order. He was not only above jobbing and lobbying, rail-road or otherwise, but he forbade his private secretary to use so much as a two-cent stamp of the State's property, except for public purposes. With the same regard for the fitness of things, he introduced almost military formality in his intercourse with subordinates ; not that he was at all 'set up' by his position, but he would have order and system in every thing, insisting on every man's knowing his proper place and his responsibilities."

WASHBURN, REUBEN P., a learned lawyer, who settled in Lynn, in 1812. He removed to Vermont, and became a judge in a State court ; was father of Governor Washburn, just spoken of, and died in 1860, aged 79. See Annals, 1812.

WENEPOYKIN, an Indian Sagamore. See History of Lynn, 1865 edition, page 38.

WHEELER, THOMAS. Mr. Wheeler came to Lynn in 1635, and was made a freeman in 1642. He appears to have been a useful man, in an unostentatious way, while here ; was a mill owner, and a man of some property. His name figures in our Annals under dates 1633, 1653, and 1657. It was against him

that Captain Bridges issued the warrant for slander of Rev.
Mr. Cobbet. (See notice of Robert Bridges.) He remained till
1664, and then removed to Stonington, Ct., taking with him his
wife Mary, his son Isaac, and his daughters Elizabeth and Sarah.
He became the largest land-holder in Stonington, partly by
grants from the town and partly by purchase ; was an honored
member of the church ; held important public offices ; and died
there, in 1686, at the age of 84. His grandson Isaac, son of the
Isaac who went from Lynn, married a daughter of Rev. Jeremiah
Shepard, first minister of the Old Tunnel, December 9, 1697.
She was quite a business character, and amassed a handsome
property ; was accustomed to ride from Stonington to Boston to
purchase dry goods, and bought up all the spare beef and pork
in her neighborhood, for shipment to the latter place. She had
two children, Margaret and Thomas, and lived to a good old age.
Thomas was born in 1700, and died in 1750, the richest man in
the vicinity. See Annals, early dates.

WHITING, Rev. SAMUEL, a learned divine, for more than forty
years minister of the First Parish. See Annals, 1679 and earlier
dates. Of none of the New England fathers can a roll of nobler
descendants be presented. Some of them are named in our
pages of Annals, some in the Centennial Memorial, and some in
the book giving an account of the proceedings on the celebration
of the two hundred and fiftieth anniversary of the settlement. It
is not, however, recollected that we have heretofore named
Nathaniel Whiting, who was a Lieutenant in Pepperell's expedition, in 1745. He was born in 1724, and graduated at Yale, in
1743 ; was a Lieutenant Colonel in the Crown Point expedition,
and at the battle near lake George, succeeded to the command,
when Colonel Williams — from whom Williams College took its
name — fell. He was with Abercrombie at Ticonderoga, and
with Amherst in the reduction of Canada ; always acquitting
himself as a brave, prudent, and humane officer. All along,
through our whole history, we find examples of the heroic devotion of members of this noble family. We find them in all
departments, military, civil, and ecclesiastical, pursuing with
patriotic zeal and intelligent forecast, the highest interests of the
loved country of their birth. Who of this generation can forget

the devoted conduct of Hon. William Whiting, of Boston, during the civil war? Whiting school was named in memory of our early minister; also Whiting street; indeed the name of the town was adopted in courtesy to him. A fac-simile of a signature of his written at the age of eighty-two, follows. *Samuel Whiting S.*

WIDGER, THOMAS, a mariner and prisoner of war. He died January 21, 1871, aged 80 years. See Annals, 1871.

WILKINS, BRAY. This early settler was a husbandman by occupation, though like many others, at that period, he found it expedient to follow other callings at different times. See Annals, 1630. It is probable that he had something to do with the iron works, for when he and John Gingle purchased the Bellingham farm, they paid down £24 in bar iron, and £1 in money, mortgaging back for £225; this purchase being made after his return from Dorchester, whither he went from Lynn, and where he had been keeper of Neponset ferry. Gingle was a tailor by trade and lived in Lynn, but left no mark by which he can with any certainty be traced. In 1676 the mortgage was discharged, and Wilkins, having bought out Gingle's interest, became sole possessor of the farm, which originally comprised some hundreds of acres, and had been enlarged by other purchases. He had six sons, lusty and strong, some or all of whom settled around him, he remaining like a patriarch among them. He was stern and uncompromising in his religious views, and became conspicuous for his zeal in the witchcraft prosecutions, evidently having a sincere belief in the personality of the evil one and his vile attempts to harass and destroy the good people hereabout. John Willard, a grandson of his, was among the unfortunates who suffered death for the supposed crime, and the conclusion cannot be avoided that the course the grandfather took had no tendency to prevent the unhappy result. Hon. C. W. Upham, in his valuable work on the witchcraft outbreak, gives some touching details regarding Mr. Wilkins and his kindred as connected with the strange episode; but to many minds his narrations are more interesting than his conclusions satisfactory ; for it can hardly be possible that human nature, depraved as it is, could develop such examples of precocious cunning, lying, and dissembling, in mere children, as he supposes. No, no, the "delusion" must have arisen from some psychological condition different from that suggested by him.

Mr. Wilkins in a deposition says : "When John Willard [his grandson] was first complained of by the afflicted persons for afflicting them, he came to my house, greatly troubled, desiring me, with some other neighbors, to pray for him. I told him I was then going from home, and could not stay ; but if I could come home before night, I should not be unwilling. But it was near night before I came home, and so I did not answer his desire ; but I heard no more of him upon that account. Whether my not answering his desire did not offend him, I cannot tell ; but I was jealous, afterwards, that it did." And his jealousy appears to have gathered strength ; for, being seized by certain terrible pains, so that he " was like a man on a rack," he says, " I told my wife immediately that I was afraid that Willard had done me wrong ; my pain continuing, and finding no relief, my jealousy continued. Mr. Lawson and others there were all amazed, and knew not what to do for me. There was a woman accounted skillful came hoping to help me, and after she had used means, she asked me whether none of those evil persons had done me damage. I said I could not say they had, but I was sore afraid they had. She answered she did fear so too." We can only account for this cold way of estimating the conduct of a near relative who himself appears to have been intelligent and piously inclined, and who died upon the gallows like a Christian hero, through the prevailing hallucination. Whether Mr. Wilkins finally came to view the matter in its true light does not exactly appear ; but his minister, the Rev. Joseph Green, remarks : " He lived to a good old age, and saw his children's children and their children, and peace upon our little Israel." Many respectable families in various parts of the country claim descent from him.

WILLIS, THOMAS, the first resident of Tower Hill. He was a Representative from Lynn in the first General Court. See Annals, 1630, and other early dates.

WOOD, JOHN, was one of the first settlers, and from him Woodend took its name. See Annals, 1629. His autograph is among those on the Armitage Petition, page 106.

WOOD, WILLIAM, Lynn's earliest delineator. See Annals, 1629, and other early dates.

WORMSTEAD, JOHN B., A privateersman in the war of 1812. He died September 2, 1874, aged 85. See Annals, 1874.

YAWATA — an Indian princess. The name was much admired by Mr. Lewis. See History of Lynn, 1865 edition, page 40.

In closing our Chapter of Biographical Sketches, it is only necessary to remark that the aim has been to shadow forth the spirit of the people and the general condition of things here, at different periods of our history. For this end individuals living at different times and pursuing diverse walks of life have been introduced. Possibly some critical reader may think of other names that in his opinion should not have been omitted. But on reflection he may perceive a reason for the omission. There is something more to be considered than mere present popularity, as that may rest on a foundation that will soon crumble away. We are far from claiming that our judgment in these matters is perfect, or that we have been successful in carrying out a plan in itself good. But it is safe to say that no individual who has not done something for the benefit of a community has any claim to be remembered in that community, however he may have thirsted for posthumous fame or however his friends may desire his canonization. Yet it will be borne in mind, that our business has not generally been so much with the individuals themselves as with their external relations.

MISCELLANEOUS NOTES.

"Now will we gather up
Stray fragments that elucidate our story,
The breezy freedom of past years commingling
With these our busy times."

In the present Chapter will be presented a variety of what may, with propriety perhaps, be called detached matters relating to the History of beloved old Lynn ; but it will be the aim to select from the great number of topics that will naturally offer themselves, only such as best subserve the leading purpose of our volume. As to the arrangement of subjects, it can only be said that it will be somewhat arbitrary, as it would be difficult to adhere to any fixed rule ; but the endeavor will be to make it as convenient as possible for the reader, who, aided by the index, will not be at a loss to find any thing of importance that may come under notice.

FIRST PROJECTED RAIL-ROAD. In 1828 a proposition was made to construct a Rail-road from Boston to Salem ; and a circular was sent out from the House of Representatives, to various towns in the vicinity, seeking information from which a judgment could be formed as to the expediency of undertaking the formidable enterprise, either by individuals or the State. The circular sent to Lynn was addressed to the editor of the Mirror, and was responded to after evidently careful investigation and consideration. Without rehearsing the congratulations on the then existing prosperity, or the rosy predictions for the future of Lynn — which latter, by the way, have been fully real-

(221)

ized — we will present some of the statements touching the actual condition of certain matters of business here at that period. Swampscott and Nahant, it will be remembered, were then constituent parts of the town.

The principal manufacture of Lynn is shoes. Of these it appears that 1.038.189 pairs are annually made ; which at four shillings a pair will amount to $692.126. These, as they are usually packed, will fill 11.535 boxes ; the transportation of which, at one shilling a box, will cost $1.922.50. It is considered that about three fourths of the above amount returns to Lynn in sole leather and other articles for the manufacture of shoes, in English and West India goods, and other merchandize ; the transportation of which may be fairly estimated at $5.768. The article of flour alone — 2.500 barrels, at $6 a barrel — would amount to $15.000; the transportation of which would cost $750. The transportation of the same amount in shoes, would cost only $41.67. And many other heavy articles will bear an equal proportion. The transportation of a barrel of flour from Boston to Lynn, is 30 cents, about the same as the conveyance from Baltimore to Boston.

There have been about 1.000 tons of fresh fish, and 50 tons of cured fish, conveyed on the Turnpike, as far as Charlestown, during the past year ; the transportation of which, at twenty shillings a ton, amounts to $3.500. Fifty barrels of oil have also been extracted, the transportation of which, at two shillings a barrel, cost $16.66.

The other articles transported on the Boston route, are 60 tons of hay, 70 tons of chocolate, 26 tons of grain, 50 tons of cocoa, 20 tons of rice, 30 tons of ginger, 16 tons of neat hides, 12 tons of leather, 27 tons of goat and kid skins, 85 tons of sumac, 9 tons of iron, 36 tons of coal, 30 tons of barberry root, and 200 tons of marble — making in all 671 tons ; the transportation of which, at twenty shillings a ton, amounts to $2.236.67. Besides these a large amount of goods is annually conveyed to the dye house and [silk] printing establishment.

The average number of passengers is about eleven each day, for 300 days of the year ; the amount of whose conveyance, at $1.25 each, is $4.125. The amount paid by Lynn people, for tolls, is probably about $2.100.

By this statement it appears that the annual expense to the town of Lynn, on the Boston route, is $19.663.33.

The amount of property invested in baggage wagons, is about $4.000.

The small amount of coal brought hither at that time, which was when anthracite was just beginning to come into use in New England, shows how exclusively wood was still in use for fuel. And we are inclined to think that a large portion even of the thirty-six tons was bituminous, or such as blacksmiths use.

What will most surprise the reader, however, is the small number of passengers from Lynn to Boston — an average of *eleven* daily, and that when our population was 6.000. But such of us as remember those days can readily understand why it was so. Excepting here and there a prominent business man, few went to Boston more than once or twice a year ; many not more than once in five years ; and had it continued thus to this day there is little doubt that it would have been better for us, in many respects. Are we not too much on the wing ? " Shopping," what little there was, was done in town. A visit to the city ordinarily consumed a whole day and the expenses of the journey were very much greater than at present, to say nothing of the discomforts of the public conveyances. The few leading business men who went up once or twice a week usually had their own "teams," and often took in a neighbor, who would pay the tolls and horse-baiting. The anecdote related in our Annals, under date 1847, of a couple of business worthies, who rode to Charles-town bridge, when they got into a dispute over the payment of a toll, continuing to wrangle all day, and at night turning about and jogging home without going over, has reference to this custom as well as showing the obstinacy of the actors in the com-ical scene. Then there were others — some even of the smaller manufacturers — who were accustomed to go on foot, getting a lift, perhaps, part of the way, on some friendly baggage wagon.

In relation to steam transportation, it may be stated that up to 1828, no steam-propelled craft had ever stirred the waters of Lynn. The " Ousatonic," well remembered as a steamer of what would now be called diminutive size, was advertised to visit Lynn on Monday, the 8th of September, of that year, to take a party out on an excursion among the islands of Boston harbor. The announcement caused a real sensation, for hardly any one had seen a vessel moved by that mysterious motive power ; and before the appointed hour an eager multitude hast-ened to every point of observation, some even posting themselves on house-tops. But no steamer came on that day, and great was the disappointment, which manifested itself in various unsavory ways. And if we rightly remember, a boat did not come till the next year.

In connection with the above, and for the purpose of showing what great expectations were raised from the enlarged use of steam, the following paragraph which exultingly went the newspa-porial round of that propitious year, 1828, may be given :

" *Great Despatch.* The Benjamin Franklin, steamer, made her last trip from New York to Providence, in sixteen hours. She was seventeen minutes at Newport. The shortest passage ever made." The writer made a passage from Providence to New

York, in the "palatial" steamer President, in the summer of 1829, in what was then considered the very quick time of eighteen hours, the sea being calm and the weather beautiful.

RICHARD HAVEN, OR HART, HOUSE.

The above is a faithful picture of a very ancient house, which was owned by Richard Haven, who settled here as early as 1640. In later years it was known as the Hart house, the last occupant of the name being Joseph Hart, a farmer, who died in 1806. It was taken down, transported to Reservoir Hill, and there consumed in a sort of sacrifical bonfire on the morning of the Centennial Day of the Republic — July 4, 1876. It stood on the south-west corner of Boston and North Federal streets ; and it may be mentioned, in passing, was the birth-place of the writer — if that is a circumstance of interest to any one. The large tree in front was a buttonwood, and in the great gale of 1815, as the individual just alluded to well remembers, had its top blown off, while he was gazing from the lower window on the right. The singular out-branching of the new growth, as represented in the cut, followed the disaster of the gale. This venerable tree was cut down in 1881.

In the Lynn Reporter of July 8, 1876, appeared the following editorial account of the holocaust. There is a mistake as to the builder of the house, which is corrected in the foregoing paragraph, and it was older than the editor supposed, the western portion at least having been built before Mr. Hart's time.

THAT "BEACON LIGHT." Whatever points Lynn may have fallen behind in as to the celebration of the Fourth, she may fairly claim the honor of making the most remarkable bonfire in this section, in honor of its centennial opening. And thus it happened :

Samuel Hart was one of our early settlers, and built a house on Boston street, about 1670. His descendants always held and occupied the place down to Hon. James R. Newhall, who stands in the direct line on the mother's side. Now the house, so very old, was greatly dilapidated and not worth repairs. As it was then determined to remove it, it was sold at auction last week for a nominal sum, — ten or fifteen dollars, — and with the consent of Judge Newhall, given to the young men of West Lynn for a burnt-offering at the nation's jubilee. At it they went, at dusk on Saturday evening, and before morning every scrap and stick was torn down and teamed, load after load, to the tip-top of Pine Hill, two hundred feet high, and in plain sight of the country for miles away, in all directions. Before Monday night the whole was solidly packed in a great pyramid, near forty feet high, firmly stayed and bound, including several barrels of tar and kerosene, and one cask at least of benzine cement. During the evening, the pile was freely drenched with waterpots of kerosene, and as "the hour of midnight tolled," it was lighted on two or three sides at once, amid the wildest cheers of a great crowd, and the rapid reports of fire-arms, great and small. A more glorious blaze is rarely seen. Even under the clear moonlight the glare was most intense. The old timbers burned and burned, and at eight next morning were yet blazing. And such was the end of the homestead of two hundred years ; it flamed up to heaven at last to honor the celebration of American liberty and independence. Where else did they do any thing more significant than this?

The hill on which the bonfire took place, is the highest point back of the house, as shown in the picture, and the highest point in Lynn. It is two hundred and twenty-four feet in height, and distant about three fourths of a mile. Second Pine Hill was the name by which the range of which it forms a part was formerly known ; but after the construction of the City Reservoir, on the northern slope, this summit began to be called Reservoir Hill.

The "Old Indian," an enormous red cedar, stood within a few rods of the spot whereon the bonfire was kindled. This tree was a marked object for generations, as it towered above all its forest neighbors, its blanched limbs stretching out above their heads, in patriarchal dignity. Its age must have been very great ; and judging from its appearance, one might well accept

15

as true the assertion that long before the white settlers came
it was a guide for the Indian skiffs that skimmed about in the
offing. When it yielded to the ruthless woodsman's ax, which
was quite within the writer's recollection, it seemed as if one
of the few remaining links that bound our dispensation to that
of the red man, had been severed.

SLAVES. There were in Lynn, at the commencement of the
Revolution, twenty-six slaves. There had been a few from very
early times ; but they were most numerous throughout the
Province, in 1745. In 1754, there were four hundred and thirty-
nine in Essex County, and in all Massachusetts, four thousand,
four hundred and eighty-nine. In 1774 the General Court passed
a bill prohibiting the importation of Slaves, but Governor Gage
withheld his assent. The State Constitution was established
in 1780. The first article of the Declaration of Rights asserts
that all men are born free and equal ; and this was generally
supposed to have reference to slavery ; but it was a point on
which there was by no means unanimity of opinion. In 1781,
however, at a court in Worcester, an indictment was found against
a white man for assaulting, beating, and imprisoning a black.
The case finally, in 1783, went to the Supreme Court, and the
defense was that the black was a slave, and the beating, &c., the
necessary and lawful correction of the master. But the defense
was declared invalid. And this decision was the death-blow to
slavery in Massachusetts. In later years, when the resolute
movement for the extinction of slavery throughout the land,
commenced, Lynn manifested becoming zeal in the cause ; and
among the most efficient workers was Mr. Lewis ; whose zeal,
however, seemed somewhat to abate as age advanced. But yet,
for his efforts in the incipient stages of the noble cause, he was
worthy of greater praise than many of those who at the eleventh
hour and from less disinterested motives pushed noisily to the front.

JOHN DUNTON, the London bookseller, who visited Lynn in
1686, as mentioned in our Annals, under date 1635, was married,
at an early age, to Elizabeth Annesley ; and a sister of hers who
married Samuel Wesley, became mother of the celebrated John
Wesley. They were daughters of Dr. Samuel Annesley, a dis-

senting minister. Dunton seems not to have entertained the most friendly feelings toward his brother-in-law, as he says, "Sam Wesley has fouled his nest in hopes of a bishoprick." It might be interesting to know what connection, if any, the blasted hopes of the father, touching the bishopric, had with shaping the religious course of the son.

SPEAKER ONSLOW. On page 490 of the 1865 edition of the History of Lynn, mention is made of Governor Hutchinson's comparing Speaker John Burrill, of Lynn, with Speaker Onslow, of the British House of Commons. There were two Speakers of the House of Commons, named Onslow — Sir Richard, elected in the seventh year of Queen Anne, 1708, and Sir Arthur, in the first year of King George III., 1727. They were both eminent presiding officers, and extremely watchful of the dignity of the House. It is related that Col. Fitzroy, afterwards Lord Southampton, when on one occasion reprimanded for making a late appearance, excused himself by saying that he had been detained by attendance on the King. Speaker Onslow, in a loud voice and authoritative manner, replied, "Sir, do n't tell me of waiting; this is your place to attend in; here is your first duty."

LYNN, IN 1750 AND IN 1817. A New York merchant who travelled east, in 1750, says he put up at Mr. Ward's, in "Lyn, which is a small Country Town of ab⁺ 200 Houses, very pleasantly situated, & affords a Beautifull Rural Prospect." He arrived at about one o'clock, "and dynd on fryd Codd." After dinner, being refreshed by a glass of wine, he pursued his journey to Salem, "through a barren, rocky country," and the next day, after visiting Marblehead, returned to Boston, stopping again at Mr. Ward's, in Lynn, where he "dyned upon a fine mongrel goose."

In 1817, John Palmer, of King's Lynn, England, while on his travels in the United States and Canada, an account of which he afterwards published, in London, found occasion thus to speak of our vicinity: "After crossing [September 11] a bridge which joins Charlestown to Chelsea, another small suburb, we found the road very excellent, carried on for some miles through salt marshes where the hay stacks are all placed on frames to prevent

their being damaged by high tides, which sometimes overflow
the level. We passed through the town of Lynn, noted for its
extensive manufacture of elegant silk and cloth shoes. Morse
gives the number made in 1795 at 300.000 pairs, and in 1802
computes them to amount to 400.000 pairs. At present, I am
told, the trade is on the decline, the spirit of emigration having
seized many of the apprentices and journeymen. Lynn contains
four or five thousand inhabitants, but presents little appearance
of compactness. As is common in the United States, the houses
are spread over a wide tract of ground. Leaving Lynn [and
proceeding towards Salem] the remainder of the journey is
through a rocky country."

The barren aspect of the country between Lynn and Salem,
noticed by these travellers, though somewhat improved in our
day, yet furnishes evidence that they were observing chroniclers.
The pestiferous wood-wax is now an added annoyance.

———

First Corn from the West. It will be remembered that
the summer of 1816 is stated to have been remarkably cold, in
New England, that very little corn ripened, that there was a
frost in every month of the year, and that snow fell in June. In
connection with this it may be interesting to state that Captain
James Mudge, of Lynn, during the year, brought to Boston, from
Cincinnati, Ohio, in the brig Cincinnatus, a cargo of corn in the
ear. This was the first sea-going vessel ever built in Cincinnati,
and so lively was the interest felt, that many in different parts
of New England went to considerable pains to procure an ear
of the corn to preserve as a memento of the enterprise. The
vessel was built in 1814, by John Brooks, an emigrant from Maine.

———

Singular Record. The following remarkable entry appears
on the public records of Lynn: " Married, Daniel Gowing to
Mary Bowers, Dec. 25, 1764, by Rev. Mr. Adams. Said Gowing
took the s^d Mary naked, except a sheet & shift that she borrowed."
Rev. Mr. Adams was minister of the Lynnfield parish. Probably the bride appeared in that condition under the apprehension
that if she brought nothing to her husband he could not be
held responsible for any existing debt of hers. But why might
she not have borrowed a gown as well as the other articles?

RECORDS OF LYNN. In the preservation of her earliest records Lynn has been unfortunate. Yet it is probable that for many years they were kept in a manner so loose and imperfect as to have been hardly worth preserving, as a whole, though they undoubtedly contained some things that should have ensured their safe custody. The county records, however, supply, in the form of deeds, wills, inventories, depositions, and so forth, a great portion of the information the loss of which would be most seriously felt. For instance : among the county files may be found the copy made by Andrew Mansfield, of the land allotments of 1638.

The earliest regular town records now in existence commence in 1691. But there was an order passed in 1715 requiring that some of the previous records, then in a dilapidated condition, should be transcribed ; and the order was complied with to the extent of a few pages, it having been left to the selectmen to carry it out in such manner as they thought best. The copies relate to matters as far back as 1661.

The little volumes of records of " Marriages, Births and Deaths in the Town of Lynn," with the exception of the first, are yet in the custody of the city clerk ; and in the title-page of the second, is this note : " The first volume is lost. In 1820 I found this volume in ruins, bound it and furnished it with an index. Preserve it carefully. ALONZO LEWIS." These volumes contain quite a number of what are called " genealogies " of the old families, and are very useful, in many cases, in tracing pedigrees ; but they are not free from errors ; and the details are frequently so imperfect and involved as to occasion doubt and perplexity. Much difficulty arises from the identity of names, as middle ones were then seldom used. At one time, for instance there were eight persons here of the name James Newhall, not one having a middle name, but each relying for his identity upon some nickname benevolently bestowed by his neighbors ; marks of distinction, however, which could not appear on the public records. These " genealogical " records have been copied into a proper book, with an alphabetically arranged index, which adds greatly to the facility for examination ; but the copying afforded an opportunity, not altogether unimproved, to add to the errors of the originals.

It need not be added that ever since Lynn became a city, her records have been kept in the most careful manner; and indeed for many years before the adoption of the Charter, there was little reason to complain of the competency or faithfulness of our recording clerks.

The First Parish records extend back only to 1721–2; and they are the earliest church records that have been preserved.

MATRIMONIAL FINESSE. In our biographical sketch of Mr. Lewis, in the 1865 edition of the History of Lynn, an "intermediate" matrimonial companion is spoken of. The romantic affair of the supposed valid second marriage was the occasion of much comment among his friends. He unquestionably died without a doubt that she had, at the time of the separation, a former husband living, whatever his suspicions may have been as to some of her other and more equivocal declarations. About fourteen years after the death of Mr. Lewis, however, the writer was informed by a worthy priest of the Catholic church, that he had received a letter from the lady herself, who was then in London, informing him of her conversion to the Romish faith, and confessing that the story of her previous marriage was a fiction, framed by herself for the purpose of severing her connection with Mr. Lewis, under whose "gentle control" she had become restive. If this was true, she must have had a confederate in the person of a young man, for a marital claimant certainly did appear here in Lynn. Mr. Lewis himself, in considerable perturbation one morning informed the writer that he had just had an interview with such a one and requested some friendly interposition for the settlement of the unpleasant affair. A young literary flirt does not usually prove the most suitable conjugal companion for a staid citizen of advanced years. His age was fifty-six, and hers seventeen, at the time of the marriage, as the hymeneal notice in the newspapers stated.

SIAMESE TWINS. It was in 1831 that the famous Siamese twins, Chang and Eng, so mysteriously united in person, were first exhibited in this vicinity. During the warm season of that year they were for a short time rusticating in Lynnfield, and while out on a gunning excursion, one day, became so irritated by being followed and stared at, by men and boys, that they committed a breach of the peace, were taken before a magistrate's court, and put under bonds. It came near becoming a serious question how one could be punished by imprisonment, should it come to that, if the other were innocent. The difficulty vanished, however, when it appeared that both were guilty. They died in North Carolina, in the winter of 1873, within two hours of each other, aged 63 years.

FUNERAL EXPENSES. Much has been said, of late, and with justice, concerning the extravagance so commonly indulged in, on the burial of the dead. The expenditures for casket, floral decorations, carriages, and so forth, have become really burdensome to persons of limited income. Many seem to think it mean not to follow the fashion in these matters, and mean also to dispute any charge of those who furnish the appliances, however exorbitant such charge may be. But does not a sentiment very different from love for the departed or grief for one's own loss, rule here? Certainly it is not in ostentatious display that the grieved heart most naturally seeks relief. Of course we all realize that no good can come to the departed by glitter and parade, however costly they may be. Nor can they heal affection's deeper wounds. It would be truly lamentable if the time should ever come when heart-relieving ceremonials were dispensed with at the burial of the dead; but garish pomp is but fast fading drapery about a grave.

In early New England times the dead were committed to their last resting places with very little ceremony beyond the procession of mourning friends; the coffin was rude; and seldom was a prayer offered, an omission, however, that probably arose from anxiety to avoid any thing that approached the popish custom of praying for the dead. But before the beginning of the last century, new and strange customs began to appear, and expenditures were made for purposes more reprehensible than any extravagance of this day. Indeed funerals were sometimes made seasons of jollification. Especially when the deceased was a minister or other prominent personage, spirituous liquors were provided, and gloves and rings presented. And these customs prevailed to some extent even down to times within the memory of persons now living.   Here is a copy of the charges incurred at the burial of Rev. Mr. Brown, of Reading, in 1733 :

		£	s.	d.
To Thomas Eaton, for provisions,	. . . . . .	2	1	0
Nathaniel Eaton, for fetching up the wine,	. . . .	0	15	0
Lt. Nathaniel Parker, for 5 qts. Rhom [rum],	. . .	0	8	0
Samuel Poole, for digging Mr. Brown's grave,	. . .	0	8	0
Landlord Wesson, for Rhom [rum],	. . . .	0	10	6
Wm. Cowdry, for making the coffin,	. . . . .	0	15	0
Andrew Tyler, of Boston, 6 gold rings for funeral,	. .	10	18	0
Benj. Fitch, of Boston, Gloves, etc.,	. . . .	17	0	0
Mrs. Martha Brown, for wine furnished,	. . .	5	0	0
Eben Storer, of Boston, sundries,	. . . . . .	8	0	0
Total,	. . . . .	45	15	6

Until a comparatively recent period the burial places in the rural districts of New England were generally neglected spots, overgrown with rank weeds and all manner of unseemly vegetation.   And we cannot fail to rejoice that these unsightly enclosures are fast giving place to beautiful cemeteries, whose graceful adornments are a perpetual delight to the meditative mourner.   The simple monument that records the name and virtues of a dear departed one, however inexpensive or rude it may be, will long out-last the memory of any pomp or ceremonial that may have attended the committal of the body to the earth.

SPECIE TRANSPORTATION.   John Adams, afterwards President of the United States, but then a young lawyer, travelling his circuit, accompanied by his wife, mentions, under date Nov. 3, 1766, having "oated" at Martin's — the celebrated old Anchor Tavern, in what is now East Saugus — on his way to attend the court at Salem.   And returning, a few days after, he again "oated" at Martin's, "where we saw," he adds, "five boxes of dollars, containing, as we were told, about eighteen thousand of them, going in a horse-cart from Salem Custom House to Boston, in order to be shipped for England.   A guard of armed men, with swords, hangers, pistols and muskets attended."

VALUE OF A SHIRT, IN 1729.   There was a complaint made by Benjamin Newhall, of Lynn, before Theophilus Burrill, a Justice of the Peace, in behalf of His Majesty, the King, "That whereas some evil minded person, contrary to the peace of our

Sovereign Lord the King and the laws of his Majesty's Province of Massachusetts, did on or upon the 28th day of this Instant month of December, 1729, (being the Lord's day) steale, purloine, or Take and karry a way a new Shirtt of your Complainant's ffit for a Small Bodyed man, Either out of the new Dwelling hous where s^d complainantt Lives, or verry neare there to, which Shirt was made of cotton and Linning cloath, a middling sort of cloath, valued at about Twelve Shillings, and Doth Wehemently Suspect," &c. A search warrant was issued, but it does not appear whether the property was recovered. The "new Dwelling hous," it is presumed, was the two-story wooden house, known as the Hallowell house, still standing on North Common street, two or three rods east of the old Episcopal church.

FIRST DIRECTORY OF LYNN. Early in 1832 the writer purchased of Charles F. Lummus, the first Lynn printer, the little office which he had been running for about six years, and running to such disadvantage that he had run out the small means with which he commenced. It was the first printing office in Lynn, and very poorly supplied with material. By the sale, Mr. Lummus found himself out of employment ; and though not inclined to excessive industry, his circumstances required that he should not remain in idleness. He was about thirty years of age, a bachelor, and a boarder at Lynn Hotel, at that time perhaps the most genteel boarding place in the town. His habits were good, and his expenses small.

In casting about, under these circumstances, for something to turn his hand to, he conceived the project of compiling a Directory, the population then numbering about 6,200. A short season of pleasant work would by such means be afforded, as in collecting the information and procuring subscribers, he could travel about in pleasant weather, gossip with all sorts of people, and suspend labor when he felt inclined. He knew every body, every body knew him, and there were few who would not cordially greet him, and render such assistance as was in their power. So the work went on. When the information was gathered and the subscribers obtained the printing was to be done. There was no office in Lynn with sufficient type of a suitable kind, and he made an arrangement with an establishment in Boston. He did the type-setting himself, and as might have been expected the work did not proceed with remarkable vigor. However, it was a new thing, and the subscribers, not knowing exactly what they had a right to expect, did not manifest much impatience.

In the latter part of May the Directory made its appearance. It was in the shape of a duodecimo of seventy-two pages, was in paper covers, contained the variety of information usually found in works of the kind, was as accurate as it could well be made, and on the whole was quite creditable. But in a pecuniary way it was not much of a success, for Mr. Lummus afterwards told the writer that he realized only enough to make scanty day wages

Such is a history of the first Directory of Lynn, copies of which may yet occasionally be found in some of the older homes. As the first printer of Lynn, and the compiler of her first Directory, the name of Mr. Lummus will survive long after many who were more successful in " heaping up riches " are forgotten.

— — —

ELECTION DAY. To some of our elder people the mention of this now unnoticed anniversary will call up recollections of a peculiar character. The ancient Colony Charter ordained " That yearely, once in the yeare forever hereafter, namely, the last Wednesday in Easter tearme yeareley, the Governo^r, Deputy Governo^r, and Assistants of the said Company, and all other officers of the said Company shalbe, in the Generall Court or Assembly to be held for that day or tyme, newly chosen for the yeare ensueing by such greater part of the said Company for the tyme being then and there present."

Thus it was that the last Wednesday of May became the famous Election Day. During many of its latter years the period was more commonly called "'lection *time*," for the last four days of the week were embraced in the popular observance. And it was not till 1831, that the day so long noted above almost any other, was compelled, through a constitutional amendment, to fall back into the ranks of unnoted days. The worthy old legislators evidently considered this annually recurring election of their chief officers, a matter of very grave importance, fearing, no doubt, that their liberties might be endangered by such abuses as they had seen arise from longer official terms, and from modes of appointment in which the great body of the people were not allowed to participate. Their anxious watchfulness may be seen all along. At a General Court held in 1639, the matter was treated in this manner : " It is solemly & vnanimosly decreed & established, that henceforth vpon the day or dayes appointed by our patent to hold o' yearely Court for the election of our Governo', Deputy Governo', Assistants & other generall officers, being the last Wednesday of every Easter tearme, that the ffreemen of this iurisdiction shall either in person or by proxie, w^thout any sumons, attend & consumate the elections. . . As for the place of publike assembling, it shalbee wher the pceeding Court of Elections was held, vnlesse then & there some other place shalbee assigned. *This acte of o's wee conceive so nearely to concerne the good of this country that we earnestly intreate it may never be repealed by any future Courte.*"

This last sentence we put in *italic* for the purpose of emphasizing the admonition evidently intended. And it is agreeable to be able to remark that essentially the principle so urged by our sagacious forefathers became so interwoven with the very texture of our political economy that it has never yet ceased to work for good.

Why the popular observance of Election Day should have taken the turn it finally did, is a mystery. Our younger people can have little conception of the style of entertainment and diversion by which it was characterized. It was not like Fast, Decoration, Independence, or Thanksgiving day. Exactly how it was observed a hundred and fifty years ago, we cannot tell ; but how it was during the first quarter of the present century many now living can attest, and surely will agree that in view of its moral influence, it was not abolished any too soon.

It was pleasant to see the young men and maidens arrayed in their new "election suits," promenading with smiling faces, and joining in woodland pic-nics, or in merry household gatherings. And the decorations from the abundant floral provision of the season, were always to be admired. The "election cake," too, so spicy and so glossy, which was provided in every house, with the slightly stimulating but not inebriating diet-drink made glad the young hearts. But the egg-nog, the flip, the muddy ale, and other fight-inspiring drinks that freely flowed in the public dance houses, were the occasion of such irregularities, as happily have no match in these days. There were dance houses in various neighborhoods, notably one known as "Old Willis's," at North Bend, where dissipated men and lewd women assembled to spend the day and night in disgraceful revelry. It is hard to tell how such disreputable proceedings originated, for there was certainly nothing inherent in the original purpose to produce them.

For many of its latter years, the day was popularly known as "Nigger Election," which questionable appellation was given, as some have supposed, to distinguish it from Artillery Election, which occurred on the first Monday in June, and which still holds its place in the calendar. But the true reason for its having been so called no doubt was that so long as slavery existed in Massachusetts, our colored brethren — who were allowed by their masters an annual vacation of four days, beginning with the day on which the General Court made their elections — were accustomed then, in imitation of their masters, to assemble on Boston Common or in some other convenient place, and proceed to elect rulers from their own ranks ; or rather imitation rulers, rulers without authority and without subjects. They engaged in their sportive political ceremonies with a keen relish, the more so, perhaps from having no real interest to be anxious about, and wound up with scenes of unlimited jollity. And the whole of their vacation was marked by excesses such as might be expected from a class so ignorant and so excitable when freed from restraint ; for the masters did not interfere till the utmost verge of decency had been reached, good-naturedly submitting to the hard hits levelled against themselves, and possibly profiting a little by some shrewd allusion. Perhaps these excesses of the negroes gave rise to the vile manner in which the season was observed by the lower class of some of our own complexion ; and perhaps, also, "election time" extended to four days, in accordance with the limit of the vacation allowed the slaves. Pompey, a slave belonging to Daniel Mansfield, of Lynn, who is referred to on page 198 of this volume, and who is stated to have been a prince in his native land, appears to have had regal honors bestowed upon him, though destitute both of subjects and authority.

As has before appeared, the Court of Elections was abolished

in 1831 ; and then, of course, "election time" ceased to be
observed. We have seen what indulgences characterized its latter
days. And it may not be impertinent to ask if there are not
other seasons which are now observed in a manner quite as
inconsistent with the original purpose, if not in a manner quite
as reprehensible. How about our annual Fast ? Do we regard
it as a day of "fasting, humiliation and prayer," or as a day for
out-door sports and in-door games ? Some good Christian people, notably among them the late Rev. Dr. Cooke, have thought,
in view of the turn things have taken, that it would be wise to
discontinue altogether the appointment of such a day. But
would it not be better to reform than abolish ? It is rather
surprising that one of Dr. Cooke's spirit should counsel a course
that looks so much like a surrender. Then there is Independence
day, the day on which, in times past, in the public celebration,
the best orator and the best poet were called to spread their
wings in oration and ode, and patriotism and lofty sentiment
freely gushed in toast and banquet speech, with interludes of
trumpet notes and song. But now "Young America" rather
has the ascendancy hereabout ; and the "antique and horrible"
displays, the tub races and the bicycles take the leading part —
all well enough, perhaps, in their way, but seemingly not quite
up to the requirements of the dignity of so grand an occasion.

One word more about Artillery Election. It need not be
remarked that the name is derived from the fact that on that
day — the first Monday of June — the officers of the Ancient
and Honorable Artillery are elected. The company was organized as early as 1638, and quite a list of Lynn men have been
members. It continues in vigorous existence, but is, at this day,
not so much needed as a regulator in tactics, as it was in former
years ; in short it is now rather an organization of respectable
military citizens who meet in a semi-social way, than one adhering to the strict rules and requirements of martial life.

They have occasionally on parade days visited Lynn. Any
one in passing along Tremont street, in Boston, may observe
near the outer wall of the King's Chapel burying ground an
ancient gravestone bearing the name Hezekiah Usher. This
individual was one of the original members of the organization.
A son of his, of the same name, was an officer in the company, and

died in Lynn, though he was not a resident, in July 1697; and they marched hither to escort his remains to their last resting place beside those of his father. Our eleventh Mayor, Col. Roland G. Usher, is of the same ancestral line; and he became a member of the company in 1851.

SHAYS'S REBELLION. The following items appear in an account presented by the town of Lynn for reimbursement by the state for supplies furnished on the occasion of this memorable disturbance, which took place in 1786: "One thousand weight of Beef, at 2*d.* 1 farthing & 1-2 a pound; four hundred and thirty four pound of Bread, at 19*s.* pr Hundred; twenty two gallons of Rum, at 2*s.* 8*d.* pur gal.; a Barril to carry the Rum in, 4*s.*; one Bushel of salt, 2*s.* and a Bag 2*s.*; four Camp kittle at 5*s.* a peace, lost; the selectmen eleven days at 4*s.* pur Day for necessary time spent to collect s^d things," &c.

WOODWARD'S AWLS. The elder members of the shoe-making craft hereabout will remember the famous Woodward awls. Before shoes were made by machinery, they had a great sale in Lynn, as nothing could supply their place. They were manufactured in that part of Reading now known as Wakefield, by Thomas Woodward, who was a native of Lynn, or Lynnfield, as it now is, and was born in 1773. He was a very ingenious and dexterous mechanic, and has been credited with numbering among his other inventions that of the Emerson razor strap. Mr. Eaton, in his history of Reading, says of him: " He was an honest, industrious, and kind-hearted man, but possessed some peculiarities of character; he had an inquiring and rather credulous mind; any new idea, either in physic, physics or ethics, he was ever ready to adopt, and if he thought it valuable, he was disposed to pursue it with great sincerity and pertinacity of purpose; hence we find him ever trying some new experiment in manufacturing, using some newly invented pills or cordial, making a " Tincture," that becomes and still continues a popular medicine, becoming an anti-mason and abolitionist of the most approved patterns, and an honest and sincere believer in Millerism. He was, however, a very useful citizen. He lived to be aged, and his body outlived his mind." He died in 1860, aged 87 years.

RELIGIOUS DISCUSSIONS. In our Annals, under date 1702, an account is given of a characteristic discussion on religious topics, held in Lynn by Rev. George Keith, a Church of England missionary, and John Richardson a prominent Quaker preacher. There was at that period a wide-spread interest in such controversies, on both sides of the water, and the contestants often manifested most intemperate zeal. Soon after Mr. Keith's return to England the following appeared as an advertisement in the London Postman : " Whereas, the world has been told in public papers and otherwise, of numerous conversions of Quakers to the Church of England, by means of Mr. Keith and others, and whereas the Quakers give out in their late books and otherwise, that since Mr. Keith came out of America, there are not ten persons owned by them that have left their Society, Mr. Keith and others will very much oblige the world in publishing a true list of their proselytes."

PRESCOTT'S WALK. William H. Prescott, the eminent historian, was for some years a summer resident of Lynn, his estate being on Ocean street. There he composed a considerable portion of " Philip the Second," and did other writing. His physical infirmities were such that much air and exercise were absolutely necessary. The old cherry tree, alluded to in the following extract from the biography of the historian, by George Ticknor, stood in front of the mansion.

" One thing at his Lynn home, was, and still is, [1862] very touching. There was hardly a tree on the place except some young plantations, which were partly his own, but which he did not live to see grow up. But shade was important to him there as it was everywhere ; and none was to be found on his grounds except under the broad branches of an old cherry tree, which had come down from the days of Quaker shoemakers, who were so long the monarchs of the land there, and in all the neighborhood. Round the narrow circle of shade which this tree afforded him, he walked with his accustomed fidelity a certain length of time every day whenever the sun prevented him from going more freely abroad. There he soon wore a path in the green sward, and so deep did it at last become that now — four years since any foot has pressed it — the marks still remain as a sad memorial of his infirmity. I have not unfrequently watched him as he paced his wearisome rounds there, carrying a light umbrella, which, when he reached the sunny side of his circle, he raised for an instant to protect his eyes, and then shut it again, that the suffering organ might have the full benefit, not only of the exercise, but of the fresh air ; so exact and minute was he as to whatever could in the slightest degree affect its condition."

This same old cherry tree is referred to in the following impressive but slightly stilted sonnet, written after Mr. Prescott's death, by an esteemed poetess of New York :

No more, alas ! the soft returning spring
Shall greet thee, walking near thy favorite tree,
Marking with patient step the magic ring
Where pageants grand and monarchs move with thee,
Thou new Columbus ! bringing from old Spain
Her ancient wealth to this awaiting shore ;
Returning stamped with impress of thy brain,
Far richer treasures than her galleons bore.
Two worlds shall weep for thee — the Old, the New —
Now that the marble and the canvas wait
In vain to cheer the homes and hearts so true,
Thy immortality made desolate,
While angels on imperishable scroll
Record the wondrous beauty of thy soul.

THE SEA-SERPENT. In our Annals, under date 1819, is given a pretty full account of this wonderful marine monster who is yet regarded by many as a mere creature of the imagination. And under date 1875 may be found a few additional particulars. Till within a comparatively recent period leading scientists appeared to disdain even the discussion of the question of his existence. But new interest has, of late, from some cause, been awakened, and opinions more or less valuable are freely expressed by those who claim to be most learned in nature's mysteries. The speculations of scientists, however, are not always more satisfactory than the observation and experience of some who make no high claims ; for there are, even among the learned, wise and unwise, credulous and incredulous ones. In the present state of the question, it may be interesting to give a few items of testimony which are not to be found elsewhere in our history.

Nathan D. Chase, an aged and respectable citizen residing in the eastern section of the city, in a newspaper article published in June, 1881, referring to the appearance in 1819, says :

I had the pleasure of seeing his snakeship off Long Beach and Red Rock. He passed along within one hundred feet from where I stood, giving me a very good sight of him. At that time he carried his head out of water about two feet, and his speed was like that of an ordinary ocean steamer. What I saw of his length was from fifty to sixty feet. It was very difficult to count the bunches, or bony fins upon his back, as by his undulating motion they did not all appear at once. This accounts, in part, for the varied descriptions given of him by different parties. His appearance at the surface of the water was occasional and but for a short time. This is the best description I can give of him from my own observation, and I saw the monster as truly, though not quite so clearly, as I ever saw any thing.

There are honest neighbors of Mr. Chase, who, though they entertain not the slightest doubt of his veracity, yet believe that his eyes did not serve him with entire faithfulness ; or rather that imagination was unwittingly allowed to add a little of its illuminating power. The writer has conversed with several who were on the Beach at the time of the alleged appearance and found them to disagree considerably as to details, and in positiveness. One worthy man said, " Why, yes, I saw what they called the sea-serpent, but could not make out what some others present declared they saw." Yet none seemed to doubt that something wonderful was moving about there.

To this day, with here and there an exception, the Swampscott fishermen, the yachtsmen, and residents near the shore ridicule the idea of the existence of such a monster. Probably not three in ten of the old fishermen believe that any thing more like a serpent than a horse-mackerel ever sported in these waters. But all this is negative ; and the positive testimony of even three or four credible persons may reasonably be expected to outweigh it in most minds. Three persons might see a thing that forty others, did not see, though in a situation where they could hardly have avoided the sight ; but their not seeing it could not strike it out of existence.

A year or two before the alleged first appearance of the wonderful creature in these waters he was said to have been seen in the harbor of Gloucester, or about the waters of Cape Ann ; and the following description of him by Hon. Lonson Nash, a prominent and highly esteemed resident of that section, appears in a letter addressed to Hon. John Davis, and published in a pamphlet entitled " Report of a Committee of the Linnæan

16

Society of New England, relative to a large Marine Animal, supposed to be a Serpent, seen near Cape Ann, Massachusetts, August, 1817."

You request a detailed account of my observations relative to the serpent. I saw him on the fourteenth ultimo, [August 14, 1817] and when nearest I judged him to be about two hundred and fifty yards from me. At that distance I judged him in the larger part about the size of a half barrel, gradually tapering towards the two extremes. Twice I saw him with a glass, only for a short time, and at other times with the naked eye for nearly half an hour. His color appeared nearly black — his motion nearly vertical. When he moved on the surface of the water, the track in his rear was visible for at least half a mile.

His velocity, when moving on the surface of the water, I judged was at the rate of a mile in about four minutes. When immersed in the water, his speed was greater, moving, I should say, at the rate of a mile in two, or at most in three minutes. When moving under water, you could often trace him by the motion of the water on the surface, and from this circumstance I conclude he did not swim deep. He apparently went as straight through the water as you could draw a line. When he changed his course, it diminished his velocity but little — the two extremes that were visible appeared rapidly moving in opposite directions, and when they came parallel they appeared not more than a yard apart. With a glass I could not take in at one view the two extremes of the animal that were visible. I have looked at a vessel at about the same distance, and could distinctly see forty-five feet. If he should be taken, I have no doubt that his length would be found seventy feet, at least, and I should not be surprised if he should be found one hundred feet long. When I saw him I was standing on an eminence on the sea-shore, elevated about thirty feet above the surface of the water, and the sea was smooth. If I saw his head I could not distinguish it from his body, though there were sea-faring men near me who said they could distinctly see his head. I believe they spoke truth, but not having been much accustomed to look through a glass, I was not so fortunate.

I never saw more than seven or eight distinct portions of him above the water at any one time, and he appeared rough, though I suppose this appearance was produced by his motion. When he disappeared he apparently sank directly down like a rock. Capt. Beach has been in Boston for a week past, and I am informed that he is still there. An engraving from his drawing of the serpent has been or is now making in Boston, but I have not been able to ascertain how far his drawing is thought a correct representation.

It will be observed that Mr. Nash speaks as if there were no doubt as to the existence of the mysterious stranger. And a contemporaneous account, like his, is generally by far the most satisfactory ; because when one undertakes to describe what he saw many years before, the distance of time and the unconscious mingling of circumstances may, unless great care is exercised and the mind remains perfectly clear, however honest, give a false coloring. Very aged people, in looking back upon events of their childhood, are proverbially prone to take up the magnifying glass ; and being less liable than contemporaneous narrators to be confronted by living witnesses, if they err, are free from some of the restraints that lie outside of conscience.

It is not improbable that this supposed representative of a tribe that existed in ages long past, if he has the temerity to continue his visits to our coast, may yet be captured, and the agitating questions concerning him settled.

MAJOR GENERAL WHITING. Rev. Mr. Whiting, the second minister of the first church of Lynn, and his descendants have been under notice several times in our pages. And it is perhaps well to add that Major General Whiting, of the Confederate army, in the great civil war, who was considered, next to Beauregard, the ablest officer in their engineer department, was a son of Col. John Whiting, and a lineal descendant from our venerated minister. In 1839 he graduated from the Public Latin School at Boston, and at West Point took the foremost rank in the engineer corps. He was in charge of the fortifications near Savannah, about the time the war broke out, was taken prisoner while in command of the Confederate forces at the mouth of Cape Fear river, and died while a prisoner in New York harbor. He is represented to have been a man of rare accomplishments.

It is not to be doubted that many of those who espoused the Confederate cause, sincerely believed they were acting the part of true patriots, though it is difficult to understand how some of the intelligent and humane leaders could have brought their minds to approve of a part at least of the principles contended for — especially those relating to slavery. They must have been laboring under a sort of self-delusion, as it cannot be supposed they acted without any systematic view of duty or right. Such a man as General Whiting is represented to have been, so undisturbed by ambition or selfish aspiration, appears entirely out of place among those companions in the finally "lost cause," who, destitute of the higher principles that should regulate human conduct, were governed by insatiable thirst for political advancement or self-aggrandizement.

If it were desirable to present a character in set-off to the individual who is the subject of this notice, we should refer to his no less prominent kinsman, the Hon. William Whiting, late of Boston, by whom the Whiting shaft in our Old Burying Ground was erected. He was as ardent a supporter of the Union cause as the other was of the Confederate ; wa$ Solicitor of the War Department, at Washington, from 1862 to 1865, performing the arduous duties with a zeal and fidelity that elicited the highest commendation, and by his writings — particularly those on the " War Powers under the Constitution of the United States," — materially strengthening the hands of the government. He was a descendant, of the seventh generation, from our beloved old minister, was born in 1813, graduated at Harvard, in 1833, was admitted to the bar of Massachusetts and the United States Courts in 1838, was a Presidential Elector in 1868, and Representative of the Boston District in the Forty-third Congress. He took great interest in historical studies, was President of the New England Historic-Genealogical Society, and author of the highly-appreciated " Memoir of Rev. Samuel Whiting, D. D., and of his wife Elizabeth St. John," a beautiful volume of 334 pages, a copy of which the writer procured for our Public Library. He died a few years since.

POINT OF PINES — or Pines Point, or simply The Pines, as the former and familiar names were — is the easterly section, without any definitely marked boundaries, of old Chelsea (now Revere) Beach. Though in the adjoining county of Suffolk, it seems rather to be a mere territorial outpost of ancient Lynn. This beach was always beautiful, but in former years not much visited excepting by those who went with rickety cart and stumbling dobbin to gather of the abundant up-castings of the sea, to enrich their farm lands ; and excepting, also, that in the warm season a rough sort of pic-nic party sometimes went over in boats or down in wagons to have a jolly time over their fish chowder, fried clams, and boiled lobster, washed down by the exhilarating drinks of the day.

The land hereabout was of little value, for it could be turned to few profitable uses. A friend of the writer once refused to purchase a tract of several acres when the whole was offered for a hundred and fifty dollars. There was, however, many years ago a sort of public house, where scant accommodations could be had ; a house not sustaining the most unblemished reputation, but perhaps quite as good as is usually found in retired places near

large cities ; but even that induced the visits of some who could
appreciate the beauties of the place and perhaps see that in the
future it would become of note.   In later years one or two houses
of greater pretension and better reputation appeared ; but the
patronage was limited and the appointments not of the most
genteel order.   The road that led to the Point was round-about
and in some places rough and exposed.   There was little to
attract the sportsman, or the shore fisherman ; neither was there
much to be found among the sands and pebbles to interest
the naturalist or curiosity seeker.   Yet there seemed a tendency
by degrees to recognise the Beach as a place for summer resort.

But when the "Boston, Revere Beach and Lynn Rail-road" was
built, in 1875, the whole region was opened up at once, as it were,
to the light of day — the day of speculation, most certainly — and to
the notice of people of refinement, as well as to fashionable pleasure
seekers.   Very rapid was the increase in the price of lands ;
for which there can be little wonder, as the whole vicinity — the
Revere and Chelsea hills, and the lawn-like levels — furnish some
of the most charming views and salubrious airs that are to be
found on the New England coast.   And it can hardly be doubted
that this well-favored region, with its wholesome breezes, bathing
facilities, ease of access and befitting accommodations for all
classes of visitors, will soon take rank as a most popular watering place.

The Point of Pines, with its groves and its spacious and
tasty architectural erections, now presents a remarkably picturesque appearance as viewed from the heights of Lynn.   And
when at evening the grounds are aglow with the brilliant electric
lights, sharply defining the swaying branches and lightly gilding
the ocean swells, and the capacious houses are illuminated, story
above story, the scene is very striking — almost fairy like when
is added the softened music of the band floating over the intervening waters.

And in this we see what wonderful changes may suddenly,
and as it were incidentally, take place by the accomplishment
of some shrewdly conceived "public improvement," like the
building of a small piece of road.   And there are other places in
our favored neighborhood fully as capable as that in question, of
being brought into similar notice and made equally remunerative.

HISTORIC TEA. In our Annals, under date 1773, the destruction of the tea, in Boston harbor, is spoken of. And in connection it may be stated that at the National Sailors' Fair, held in Boston, in November, 1864, Mrs. E. N. Cheever contributed some of the tea from one of the fated chests. It was taken from the shoe of Ezekiel Cheever, of Saugus, one of the persons engaged in the destruction of the cargoes. He had stopped on his way home, at the house of Col. Abijah Cheever, in Saugus, where it was emptied from his shoe, and preserved.

RESOURCES AND SUPPLIES. The ocean has always proved a hospitable friend to the people of Lynn, and they may well praise the sagacity of the shrewd forefathers who cast their destinies here upon its pleasant borders. It has yielded a great variety of fish, and a store of rich dressing for the arable lands. To the indigent settler it was a never failing source of supply in the days of greatest need ; and to this day there has never been a time when the destitute could not resort to the lobster-rocks, the eel-beds, or the clam-banks, for a wholesome repast ; to say nothing of the cod, haddock, mackerel, and other finny varieties that abound upon our coast, nor of the shoals of alewives that occasionally appear in the streams that flow by some of our very doors. When we read of the destitution that season after season prevailed in some of the more inland settlements, of their sometimes reaching the very verge of starvation, we are led most fully to realize the benefits of our position.

At no period, during her whole history, has Lynn been compelled to call on her neighbors for assistance, though she has many times extended a helping hand to calls from others. It has often been a matter of wonder, that the early settlers in various parts of the old colony, should ever have found themselves in such straits for food as we read of their occasionally having been, for none of them were very far from the sea. It seems as if there must have been some sort of improvidence or lack of skillful management somewhere. But we are not to judge them, and probably do not fully understand the difficulties by which they were encompassed.

The extraordinary fecundity of some of the smaller kinds of fish is well attested. That the milt of a single cod "contains more animals than there are men on the earth," we are not prepared to dispute — certainly not from any actual enumeration ; nor would we undertake to deny that were it not for the gormandising propensities of the larger corsairs of the deep the smaller would so increase that ships would be obstructed in their movements ; yet we are prepared to say that some kinds, once abundant hereabout have almost entirely disappeared — salmon, shad, and bass, for instance. As to shell-fish : the clam is yet measurably abundant, though the population is so rapidly increasing that his admirers are already beginning to fear great scarcity ; sixty years ago ten or twelve cents was a fair price for half a bushel. And as to lobsters, though large numbers are yet every year taken, about the rocks of Nahant and Swampscott, and out in deeper water, their haunts are so unceasingly invaded that even their graceful forms and sunny tempers, without the intervention of the strong arm of the law could not save them from apprehended extinction. Our present laws, with their rather severe penalties may succeed in affording future generations a taste of the delicate meat.

Eels do not seem to elicit the tender sympathies of people, as do some of their companions of the shoals ; perhaps because they have the misfortune to so resemble snakes. They yet bed, in large numbers, in Saugus river and other places where soft, muddy bottoms are found, and in winter especially furnish to their captors many a savory meal. Tons of them were formerly taken, every winter, in the river alone. And the grim old iron workers had there a well-improved harvest field.

The sportive little "nippers," are much less abundant about the rocks of Nahant, than formerly, if the testimony of the pretty amateur fishers who so unskillfully cast their lines is to be taken as conclusive.

But we thankfully reiterate that the yielding sea has always proved a liberal friend to Lynn. Lynn, however, has likewise proved a friend to herself. Our people have never been given to moroseness, or complaining. In the outset there was no aspiraration for things too high ; and we have ever remained an industrious, working people — a people not unduly prone to speculative and haphazard enterprises. These habits, early established, have stood us in good stead, through the mutations of all our country's history, often saving from the disasters which ever attend fast living, whether in the individual or the community.

Not having devoted her energies to employments such as sometimes result in the accumulation of great individual wealth, thereby creating withering social distinctions, Lynn has been remarkably free from the mischiefs, annoyances, and discomforts which always, in small communities, arise from class distinctions. What care we, if in former years some of our amiable neighbors affected to look down upon us as a community of humble plod-ders — what care we, now that we have, by our small gains, our industry and frugal habits, left them in the rear? We would not, however, assume a boastful tone, though it somehow does seem as if good example should not always be veiled.

Our esteemed neighbors, Salem and Marblehead, for instance, have hitherto directed their attention to pursuits widely differing from our own, and the results have differed accordingly. The commerce of the one and the fisheries of the other, with the attendant West India trade, have decayed, and they have already resorted to other employments more likely to ensure the perma-nence of the thrift they so well deserve ; some of which employ-ments are akin to the once disdained business of Lynn — shoe manufacturing. But the good they have done the nation is not to be counterbalanced by any local hindrances. They long since opened sources of traffic which have added immensely to the prosperity of the country, and raised her name abroad. In this, it must be admitted, they are entitled to rank above ourselves.

The New England fisheries, especially, were early looked upon by the British government with favor, though the later Naviga-tion Laws of the kingdom greatly interfered with their success. They were really important training schools for the supply of the commercial and naval marine of the father land. And finally, when the exigencies of the Revolution demanded the most hardy, skillful, and brave, for the manning of her little navy, the eye of the nation was confidently turned, and turned with eminent success, to those robust wayfarers of the sea.

Such differences in the early economy of neighboring settle-ments should be kept in mind, if one is curious to trace the causes of social distinctions, and the cause of the high or low name a given place may receive. And they furnish, too, abun-

dant reason for the repression of any feeling of sectional pride.
Yet we must maintain that old Lynn has been a favored place,
favored in the high scriptural sense of being oppressed neither
by poverty nor riches.

ANCIENT DOCUMENTS. Two or three years ago, Mr. James
W. Webber, of Lowell street, in repairing a piece of old furniture,
found, pressed in back of a drawer from which they had evidently
fallen, two or three old, time-stained papers. Instead of burning
them, as many would have done, he kindly handed them to the
writer, to whom one at least proved of much interest, as it was a
receipt written by an ancestor, a specimen of whose handwriting
he had long desired to possess.

Another, was the quaint public document that follows in which
many who are interested in our local history, will recognize some
old, familiar names :

ESSEX, ss.   To Joseph Newhall, Constable, In Lynn, March 3d, 1755,
GREETING :
In his majesties name you are Required to warn the Several Persons here
after named, to attend att the house of Benjamin Bowdens on friday next, at two
of the Clock in the afternoon, in order to take the oath to there office thay wair
Chose to Serve in, this Day, and make Return of this your Doings.   fail not.
By order of the Select Men.
JOSEPH FULLER, town Clerk.

Nathaniel Bancroft,
    Survar of high ways, Tithen man also.
Amos & Joseph newhalls,
    fence viuer.
David Gowan, Jur. & } hog reeves.
Abraham welman   }

The document is labelled, " 1755. A warrant to warn Town
officers." And on the back, besides the imperfect return, appears this record : "At a meeting of the Select men, April 7,
1755, apinted Locker newhall, hog Reeve and Joseph Skinner,
hog Reeve." This "Locker newhall," was the father of the
noted Landlord Jacob Newhall, who, during the Revolution, kept
the famous old Anchor Tavern — at that time under another
name — on the Boston road, in what is now East Saugus. The
Joseph Fuller, who was Town Clerk, was chosen to the office
that year, 1755, succeeding his kinsman John Fuller. The
Fullers were farmers, and the family seat was at the westerly
end of Waterhill, the present Cottage street running through

a part of what was their noble orchard. It was here, too, that an ancient Indian encampment is supposed to have existed, as arrow-heads and implements used by the red men have been found. Hon. Joseph Fuller, the first State Senator from Lynn, [1812] and a Representative for six years, likewise [1814] first President of the Mechanics — now the First National — Bank, was of the old Fuller line, and born on that salubrious spot. Maria Augusta Fuller, the poetess, was a daughter of his.

Speaking of the old document here copied, which is not of value excepting as a mere curiosity, leads to the remark that such chance-findings sometimes prove of exceeding importance. And if those who come across them, and to whom they are of no interest, would take the trouble to hand them to some one who is in the way to understand their worth, a good end might often be subserved.

FIRST SERMON. It has been stated in various publications that Rev. Mr. Phillips, of Lynn, preached the first sermon ever delivered in Waldo county, Maine. The Phillips family was early known in Lynn ; but there was no settled minister of the name. They appear to have at first located in Swampscott, where descendants yet remain, though they were soon found in various parts of the town. They were generally a thrifty, enterprising people. The reverend gentleman referred to may have been a resident minister though not parochially settled.

The sermon alluded to was a funeral discourse on the death of General Samuel Waldo, who died on the 23d of May, 1759, at the age of 63. He was a distinguished officer, and a native of Boston, though a resident of Maine ; was a Brigadier General at the capture of Louisburg, in 1745, owned extensive tracts on the Penobscot, and had made several voyages to the old country. In Drake's Biographical Dictionary, it is said : "There were remarkable coincidences between his life and that of his friend Sir William Pepperell. They lived in Maine, and were rich bachelors ; they were councillors together ; they commanded regiments, and were together at Louisburg ; they passed a year together in England ; were born the same year ; and died nearly at the same time." Mr. Phillips certainly had a good subject for an eloquent and pathetic discourse.

THE HILLS OF LYNN. Whoever has had an opportunity to range about the woody, rock-bound hills that skirt along our northern border, cannot have failed to perceive that we are surrounded by some of nature's most charming scenery. And the hills themselves, when viewed from the town, present features of romantic interest. Some slight idea of their appearance may be obtained from the little picture on page 224, of the present volume. Yet they appear, when seen from the water or from the shore-ward levels, of greater height than actual measurement determines. In the picture, the highest point, Reservoir Hill, is shown. And the following table gives the height of that and several other points within the old town limits, in feet:

Reservoir Hill,	224	Lover's Leap,	133
Dungeon Hills,	200	Egg Rock,	86
High Rock,	170	Sagamore Hill,	66
Sadler's Rock,	166	Bailey's Hill, (Nahant)	63

HISTORY OF LYNN. The first edition of the History of Lynn appeared in four numbers, in 1829. The next edition was issued in 1844, in the form of an octavo of 278 pages. These were by Mr. Lewis, who died on the twenty-first of January, 1861. In 1865 appeared the edition bearing the imprint of that year. This was a volume of 620 octavo pages, and is the one so many times referred to in the present work as the " 1865 edition of the History of Lynn," and which contains the "Annals," from the time the settlement commenced, in 1629 down to the close of 1864. It embraced the whole of Mr. Lewis's work, with additions and a continuation down to the time of its publication, by James R. Newhall. The volume now in the reader's hands, and which is by the individual last named, takes up the "Annals" where the 1865 edition left them, and continues on to 1882, with the addition of many pages of historical matter relating to detached topics.

It will be perceived that Mr. Lewis's contribution was not very great, if only the number of pages is taken into view. But when his arduous labors in collecting in so new a field, his carefulness, and the rich suggestiveness of his pages are considered, all wonder at the high praise bestowed on him ceases. And it is a matter of keen regret that his labors were confined to so limited a sphere as a single town. He did, indeed, many years ago, propose preparing a history of Boston, which would in some sense have been a history of the whole State, or indeed of all New England. And why he failed to execute his purpose is not known. Some very worthy people manifested a deep interest in his plan ; but perhaps the pecuniary aid was lacking, for it is as generally true that those whose energies are devoted to nourishing the purse have little regard for the nourishment of the mind, as that those who minister to the mind neglect the purse. Mr. Drake, in the preface to his History of Boston, published in 1856, very kindly says that if Mr. Lewis had written a history of that city, there would have been no need of his own work.

DISCOMFORTS OF TRAVEL. It is well known that along in the latter part of the last century and the early part of the present, the few shoe-manufacturers whose trade extended beyond Boston, were subjected to hardships and discomforts of which the manufacturers of this day know nothing ; not the least of which were their tedious journeys to New York and places farther south, to dispose of their shoes and collect, or try to collect, their dues. The writer has heard good old Col. Brimblecom, whose manufactory and dwelling were on the lonely Turnpike near the Franklin street crossing, and who died in 1850, describe some of his expeditions in a manner to which it was doubtful whether laughter or tears were most appropriate.

In the early part of this century President Quincy, who was wooing the fair lady of New York who afterwards became his wife, speaks thus feelingly of the difficulties that beset his way : " The carriages were old and the shackling and much of the harness made of ropes. One pair of horses carried us eighteen miles. We generally reached our resting place for the night, if no accident intervened, at ten o'clock, and after a frugal supper, went to bed with a notice that we should be called at three, next morning — which generally proved to be half past two. Then, whether it snowed or rained, the traveller must rise and make ready by the help of a horn lantern and a farthing candle, and proceed on his way, over bad roads, sometimes with a driver showing no doubtful symptoms of drunkenness, which good hearted passengers never failed to improve at every stopping place, by urging upon him the comfort of another glass of toddy.

Thus we travelled eighteen miles a stage, sometimes obliged to get out and help the coachman lift the coach out of a quagmire or rut, and arriving in New York after a week's hard travelling, [from Boston] wondering at the ease as well as the expedition with which our journey was effected." Of course all the difficulties and disasters of the way were compensated for by the happy termination of the wooing. But the poor shoe-manufacturer was too often compelled to travel the route with misgivings that were not to be thus satisfactorily relieved.

PERPLEXITIES AND DUTIES OF AUTHORSHIP. In the Preface to the 1865 editon of our History, a word is said about the labor and perplexity attending the preparation of a work for the press, especially one in which a multitude of dates and facts appear. Dr. Livingstone, in the preface to his South African Researches says: " Those who have never carried a book through the press can form no idea of the amount of toil it involves." The toil, however, is not so great as the anxiety a careful author must feel to have his statements correct. Dates and facts are not always so readily obtained as the inexperienced may imagine. We remember that once, after a fruitless search for a certain date the thought occurred that it might be found on a grave-stone in the Old Burying Ground. The printer's call for "copy" was imperative; and so, on a dreary winter night, borrowing a lantern of the undertaker and receiving his comforting caution to beware lest a bullet, intended by some wary watchman for a body-snatcher, should suddenly put a period to the search, we entered the ground, found the stone, and after scraping away the snow, were rewarded by finding the object searched for. This is given only as an illustration of what is often necessary to ensure accuracy, and to bespeak indulgence for trifling errors.

In the Preface first mentioned, too, a word is said about the redundant, inappropriate, and often ridiculous use of titles in which we Americans indulge. The writer has been somewhat sparing in the use of the titular pepper-box, believing that such free application of nominal distinctions seldom adds to the dignity of a name, though sometimes useful for identification. Horace Smith defines "Esquire" as "a title very much in use by vulgar people." But on this subject nothing further need be said here.

FREE PUBLIC FOREST. GLEN LEWIS. On page 90 of the present volume the reader may find a brief account of a "Camp Day" of the "Exploring Circle." And to the few remarks there made a little something should be added, as the movement has now assumed a rather more definite shape.

The intelligent and public-spirited gentlemen who enlisted in the praise-worthy "Free Public Forest" enterprise, soon formed themselves into a voluntary association, having in view, briefly, the preservation, as far as possible, of the extensive range of forest that traverses our northern border, and its devotion to the free use of the public, forever — a noble purpose, most surely.

The association is not a legally incorporated body, but an entirely voluntary one, and dependent for its success upon the good-will and contributions of the people. Of course, as responsibilities increase and perplexing questions arise, it may become necessary to introduce new features into the organization ; but for the present nothing further seems required, as the trustees, in whose hands the general management now rests, are of a character that cannot fail to command the confidence of their fellow-citizens. In time, others, of a different order, may be called to occupy their places, and further safeguards become necessary. Yet, should any rights be invaded, protection may always be found in the courts, for they cannot, if they would, put themselves beyond the jurisdiction of at least a court of equity ; and as to the present officers, we are sure they would not plant themselves outside of the law, if they could, however strong a temptation might arise.

On the thirtieth of May — Memorial Day — 1882, another Camp Day was held, far back in the woods, at which the principal ceremony was the consecration of GLEN LEWIS — a wild and secluded spot in the extensive tract known as Blood Swamp. The ceremonies were of a character similar to those spoken of on page 90, before referred to, with the addition of certain features appropriate to the leading purpose. The day was pleasant, and there, surrounded by the budding beauties of the season, the large company of ladies and gentlemen, youthful and mature, passed some very enjoyable hours in witnessing ceremonials induced by a warm desire to duly honor the memory of Lynn's esteemed historian and bard.

Whether any present were actuated by awakened consciences, and desired to atone for former neglects, or had any to atone for, may not be inquired into here. But it is not to be denied that Mr. Lewis, during his life, did not receive from the great body of his fellow-citizens the consideration which his talents and services merited. His literary efforts, perhaps we should say aside from his history, were not duly appreciated; and the pecuniary returns were meagre. He was keenly alive to the opinions of others, and delighted with expressions of approval, especially when those expressions appeared in print. And his life would have been rendered vastly more happy, if he had received, while among us, but a small portion of the praise that has been awarded since his decease, and which was justly his due. Posthumous acknowledgments are pleasant to the friends of departed ones; but it is doubtful if the departed themselves can be much moved by them.

The writer is not unmindful of his own short-comings, and in the biographical sketch in the 1865 edition of the History of Lynn, has endeavored to present some of the points of character wherein our friend was clearly misunderstood and consequently misjudged. That Mr. Lewis, especially in the earlier stages of his literary career, was extremely sensitive in matters touching his growing fame, and a little jealous of the aspirations of others, may not be disputed; nor can it be disputed that occasionally, by some singularly unfortunate assumption, he exposed himself as a conspicuous mark for the shafts of criticism. But his appeals usually had in them such a measure of good sense and such a worthy purpose, that they could be counted as good seed, a little unwisely scattered.

Among other things, with now and then a needlessly tart expression, he deprecated the disposition to undervalue the efforts of natives. In an "open letter" to the writer, dated October 1, 1833, and addressed through the columns of a Boston paper, he says: "I have long observed the disposition prevalent in this town, to put down every individual, that was a native of it, who possessed any unfortunate tendency to rising. It is a disposition that appears to prevail in this town more than in any other, with which I am acquainted. Other towns know that the honor of their sons is their own, and they conduct accordingly. If they can

promote the welfare or advancement of an individual, they consider that an equal amount is added to their own. But it would
seem as if we acted on a principle exactly different ; for it too
often happens that they who manifest the greatest degree of
public spirit, and do the most for the town, fare the worst."

The foregoing somewhat acidulous sentences it will be noticed, were written about fifty years ago. And it may not be
improper to ask if there has been much improvement since.
The letter was elicited by the only occasion where a disagreement between Mr. Lewis and the writer culminated in a newspaper controversy ; and it is believed the result was in no small
degree beneficial ; it certainly was to one of us, and perhaps
to both. The true theory, undoubtedly is, that every community
should make use of the best talent it possesses, whatever the
origin ; but a native should not be denied an equal chance, as
Mr. Lewis seemed to think he often was. And it certainly does,
in some instances, look as if one native thought there never
could be a fellow-native equal to a transplanted resident.

It is not easy to determine whether Mr. Lewis preferred fame
as a poet or historian. His writings were about as voluminous
in one department as the other, though it was apparent that
certain critics did not consider him equally successful in both.

Many a time have we looked back to the cheerless day on
which the remains of our friend were conveyed to their last
resting place, with feelings of deep sadness. The funeral service
took place on the twenty-third of January, 1861, in the Central
Congregational Meeting-house, on Silsbee street. It was a
dreary day, without, though no storm was actually raging ; and
within, there was little to relieve the dreariness. The house
was cold, and the sombre exercises quite brief. No remarks
touching the ability, character, or merits of the departed, were
made ; indeed there was nothing beyond the reading of some
passages of Scripture, a prayer, and a few strains of sacred music — such an apparently empty service being very uncommon
in a Congregational place of worship, hereabout, on the occasion
of a burial, at that period. But the saddest part of the whole
was the singularly small attendance. And as, in passing out,
we paused in the porch, almost alone, to take a last look upon
that manly face, upturned in the casket, we almost fancied that

the pallid lips would part, and the well-known voice in sorrow
ask, "Where, now, are all my worthy friends?" And what
answer could there be, but the chilling echo, "Where?"

That Mr. Lewis's poetic conceptions led him to admire the
picturesque and beautiful in every department of nature, is true ;
but it is likewise true that he had his preferences. The drowsy
silence of the woody glen had its attractions ; but as a retreat in
which to meditate, he would rather have sought some rocky
niche by the sea, where the lulling melody of the peaceful, or the
stern harmony of the storm-tossed, waves, was ceaselessly heard.
His loved home, against whose very walls the sea murmured its
matins and vespers, sufficiently evinces this. And by the sea
would he have had his last resting place, pleading therefor in
these imploring strains :

> O bury me not in the dark old woods,
> Where the sunbeams never shine ;
> Where mingles the mist of the mountain floods
> With the dew of the dismal pine !
> But bury me deep by the bright blue sea,
> I have loved in life so well ;
> Where the winds may come to my spirit free,
> And the sound of the ocean shell.

It is hoped that none of the foregoing remarks will be regarded
as made without a purpose, or in a captious spirit. The occasion
of the consecration of the Glen was a highly interesting one, and
forced upon the writer reflections, some of which, thus expressed,
may awaken in other minds considerations leading to results
beneficial to all of us.

THE MAYFLOWER. In the Calendar of British State Papers,
under date April 12, 1588, is found the following : " Thos. San-
dyll, Mayor, and Aldermen of King's Lynn, to the Council :
Pray them to direct letters to the town of Blakeney and other
members of the port which refused to contribute their share
towards the furnishing of the ships required. They are willing
to furnish the Mayflower, of Lynn, of 150 tons, and a fine pinnace,
to join her majesty's fleet." It would probably be esteemed an
honor, by some of us, to discover a connection, however remote,
between Lynn and the famed Mayflower ; and hence it may be
gratifying to have it appear that the vessel here named, was

17

the renowned little rover the seas that afterwards brought the pilgrims, with their thousands of tons of trumpery to "wild New England's shore." King's Lynn, from which our own city derived its name, was not, indeed, noted for its puritanical proclivities, but as "business is business," would no doubt have been ready, for a consideration, to enter into negotiations touching the emigration had they still owned the favored craft. The stated tonnage, though it does not exactly tally, yet comes so near that it may well be taken as some evidence of identity.

FIRST CHURCH CELEBRATION. On the eighth of June, 1882, a very interesting celebration took place — the celebration of the two hundred and fiftieth anniversary of the founding of the "First Church of Christ in Lynn" — one of the very few churches that have remained steadfast in the faith of the New England fathers. It was something more than a mere society or denominational observance, being one well calculated to enlist the sympathies and stir the feelings of all natives of the town, and to interest all who have a regard for her prosperity and good name.

Yet it must be admitted that the attendance on the various exercises was not so large as might have been expected, the weather, in particular, being propitious. No doubt many forbore to suspend their ordinary avocations, in the belief that the good things to be said would immediately be published in a form that could be perused at any leisure hour. But the absentees lost much in failing to witness features that lay beyond the reporter's skill. They would have been especially pleased with the air of cordiality and Christian fervor that pervaded all the proceedings. There was, however, a very fair attendance, and that by no means confined to members of the society. Among the visitors from abroad was the Rev. Dr. Henry M. Dexter, one of the most prominent of our New England scholars and divines; an accomplished antiquary and author of various works, among which is the highly-commended "History of Congregationalism." He is a lineal descendant from farmer Thomas Dexter, who conspicuously figured in our early history, and for a long time kept the town authorities in a disturbed state by persistently urging his claim to the whole territory of Nahant, under a purchase from the Indian sagamore Poquanum — otherwise called

Duke William, or Black Will — for a suit of clothes, in 1630. As editor of a leading religious paper, Dr. Dexter has done much to defend the ancient "orthodox" faith, against the inroads of modern "liberalism." There were also present other conspicuous individuals from abroad, some of whom took part in the proceedings.

The exercises consisted of addresses appropriate to the occasion, interspersed with sacred music ; the principal address being an historical one by the pastor, Rev. Walter Barton. And at noon an excellent collation was provided, sufficient for the abundant supply of all present, who desired to partake. The decorations, floral and otherwise, were in good taste, and everything conspired to make the occasion one most enjoyable and pleasant to be remembered.

The following is a list of the ministers of this venerable parish from the commencement of worship here to the present time. 1632, Stephen Bachiler. 1636, Samuel Whiting. 1637, Thomas Cobbet, (colleague.) 1680, Jeremiah Shepard. 1680, Joseph Whiting, (colleague.) 1720, Nathaniel Henchman. 1763, John Treadwell. 1784, Obadiah Parsons. 1794, Thomas Cushing Thacher. 1813, Isaac Hurd. 1818, Otis Rockwood. 1832, David Peabody. 1836, Parsons Cooke. 1865, James M. Whiton. 1872, Stephen R. Dennen. 1876, Walter Barton. Rev. Joseph Cook, who afterwards became noted here and in Europe as a lecturer on ethical subjects, was stated minister for some months preceding the settlement of Mr. Dennen.

PROTESTANT EPISCOPAL WORSHIP. There was no Protestant Episcopal Church edifice in Lynn, for more than two centuries after the settlement began. It was in 1819 that the first attempt to form a Parish was made ; but nothing permanent was effected. In 1836, Christ Church Parish was organized, and during the following year the modest house of worship on North Common street, between Franklin avenue and Hanover street, was consecrated. It is a wooden structure, faithfully represented by the engraving appended to this notice. But Christ Church Parish did not long sustain itself. In 1844, the now flourishing St. Stephen's Parish was organized, and continued to worship in the old edifice till November, 1881, when the elegant Memorial

Church, on South Common street, was consecrated, and immediately occupied. This church, the most costly public building yet erected in Lynn, with the exception of the City Hall, was the gift of Hon. Enoch Redington Mudge, of whom a notice may be found in our Annals, under date 1881 ; and under the same date an account of the consecration services appears.

FIRST PROTESTANT EPISCOPAL CHURCH IN LYNN.
CONSECRATED IN 1837.

The following is a complete list of the ministers who served in this first Episcopal Church in Lynn. 1836, Milton Ward. 1837, George Waters. 1839, Frederic J. W. Pollard. 1841, William A. White, (Lay Reader.) 1844, George D. Wildes. 1846, Isaac W. Hallam. 1860, Edward H. True. 1863, George S. Paine. 1865, Gordon M. Bradley. 1868, Benjamin W. Attwell. 1870, Edward L. Drown. 1876, Louis DeCormis.

ECCLESIASTICAL PROCEEDINGS. In connection with the two next preceding Notes, a few remarks may be made, though it can hardly be required to go much into detail, especially in the matter of statistics, for the carefully prepared works that have of late from time to time appeared, give all the necessary information. Yet this is perhaps as suitable a place as any for an observation or two of a historical nature, designed, so far as they go, to supplement those in our former edition. Lynn, as has already appeared, had her share in the ecclesiastical agitations of the olden time; but she came forth from her trials as bright as any.

Whoever takes pains to examine the court files, will be satisfied that there always existed an under-tide of free thought which could not be suppressed, however it might be driven to conceal-ment by stormy malediction or by the strong arm of the law. Enough has been said touching the persecutions of the Quakers and Baptists — to say nothing of the antinomian come-outers — for their alleged heresies of opinion; heresies that were the natural result of the admitted right of individual interpretation of Scripture. " Read your Bible," said the good old father, " and whatsoever doctrine you there find, that follow." " I do, by God's help, honestly and prayerfully," replies the recusant. " O, but you understand and interpret amiss, and cannot be permitted to promulgate your poisonous errors," is the rejoinder. The jurisdictions of church and state were very closely interwoven in the legislative proceedings of our early times; and hence it has been said, the persecutions for deviation in doctrine were simply punishments by the civil authorities for breaches of positive law. It was, indeed, a time when errors of faith were regarded, all over the Christian world, as offences against the state. The Inquisition itself turned over to the secular authorities subjects for the auto-da-fe. But many of our New England fathers had a more rational conception of human rights, and the true princi-ples of human government, and might reasonably have been ex-pected to avoid those grosser fallacies that elsewhere held sway.

Most of the present shades of belief can easily be traced. And the following instance of the out-cropping of Universalism, that singularly enough seems to have passed on to atheism, which took place as early as 1684, is a case in point, and is found in detail in the county court proceedings: Joseph Gatchell, of Marblehead, "not hauing the feare of God before his eyes, being instigated by the devill, at the house of Jeremiah Gatchell, in discourse ab^t generall Salvation (wch he s^d was his beleife) & that all men should be saved, being answered that our Saviour christ sent forth his disiples and gave them comission to preach the Gospell, and that whosoever Repents and believes shall be

saued ; to which Joseph Gatchell Answered if it be so he was
an Imperfect saviour and a foole. And this was a yeare agoe
and somewhat more, as p' the evidences of Elizabeth Gatchell
and since in the moneth of March last past and at other times
and places hath uttered seuirall horrid blasphemous speeches
saying ther was no God devill or hell as in and by their evidences
may appeare, contrary to the peace of our Souiraigne Lord the
King his croune and dignity the law of God & of this Jurisdiction."

For his utterances Mr. Gatchell was " sentenced to be returned
from this place to the pillory, to have his head and hand put in,
have his toung drawn forth out of his mouth and peirct through
wth a hott Iron then to be returned to the prison there to
Remayne until he sattisfye and pay all ye charges of his tryall
and ffees of Court wch came to seuen pounds."

The remark is now often heard that the differences between
religious denominations are rapidly lessening ; that the old walls
of partition are crumbling. There can be no doubt that this is,
in general, quite true. We frequently see Baptists, Methodists,
Trinitarian and Unitarian Congregationalists, and others, meeting
on the same platform, shaking hands, and congratulating each
other on their fraternal nearness. This, though it sometimes
seems to arise rather from indifference to any religion at all,
than from true spirituality, is, at least in a social view, an improvement on the old, inflexible ways.

There are at present in Lynn twenty-five religious societies,
standing denominationally as follows :

Methodist, (1 African)	 7	Protestant Episcopal,	 1
Baptist, ...	5	Congregational, (Unitarian)	. . 1
Congregational, (Trinitarian)	. . 4	Friends'	. . . , ... 1
Roman Catholic,	 2	Second Advent,	 1
Universalist, ...	2	Christian,	 1

REV. SAMUEL KERTLAND, who, by request of the Provincial
Congress, labored with the Indians of the Six Nations, at the
opening of the Revolution, to induce them to espouse the American cause, and was to a considerable extent successful, especially with the Oneidas, was a direct descendant from Philip
Kertland, the first Lynn shoemaker. Kertland street, has the
honor of perpetuating the name.

IMMIGRATION OF RODENTS. In our Annals, under date 1861, appears some account of the famous Nahant Hotel, a huge structure, which, after an unsuccessful career of some years, as a watering-place hotel, was destroyed by fire on the night of September 12, of that year. Romantic stories were long current about the annual emigration of rats from Lynn, to its hospitable precincts. An old resident solemnly affirmed that he had seen troops of the gluttonous animals wending their way over the beaches towards those luxurious quarters on the opening of the season ; asserting, with a positiveness that he seemed to think ought to insure belief, that on one occasion he had seen an old blind rat with a long straw in his mouth, by which some of the younger ones piloted him along. Rats are known to be remarkably sagacious animals, and of extraordinary acuteness of scent. Some may have been toled up from their hiding places among the rocks ; but travelling over the beaches is quite another thing. The story, however, is not more wonderful than some other stories told of transactions about that celebrated house.

The oldest portion of this Hotel was built in 1819 ; and by a marvelous coincidence — perhaps we should say gracious providence — it was hardly finished when the astounding news of the first appearance of the sea-serpent in the offing, took the country by surprise.

In the first edition [1829] of the History of Lynn appeared a fine engraving of the house as it then stood — picturesque and beautiful — with its airy piazzas and sunny surroundings. And in the 1865 edition there was an engraving of it as it appeared at the time of its destruction, in 1861. The history of this noted establishment furnishes some weighty lessons for enterprising landlords to ponder over.

———

DEFENSE OF BOSTON. At the building of the fort in Boston harbor, in 1813, some eighty-five of the patriotic men of Lynn volunteered to labor on the works, one day. Early in the morning they left town, with drum and fife, rode to Winnesimmet ferry, and were thence taken by boats to the fortification, where they industriously worked during the day, and marched home about nine o'clock in the evening, in jolly trim, as might have been expected from such an expedition.

LYNN POST-OFFICE.   The Post-office was established in 1793,
the population being then about 2.500 — including Lynnfield,
Saugus, Swampscott, and Nahant.   Ebenezer Breed, a native
of the section now known as West Lynn, and who was at that
time a prominent business man in Philadelphia, but who became
reduced, and died in our alms-house, on the 23d of December,
1839, at the age of 74, was chiefly instrumental in securing its
establishment.   Previously to that time the Lynn people received
their mail matter at Boston.   It was ten years before the Turnpike was opened, and forty-five before the Rail-road was built,
Boston street still being the chief avenue of travel and business.
A biographical notice of Mr. Breed may be found in the 1865
edition of our History.

Col. James Robinson was the first post-master.   He lived in
the ancient house, built in or about the year 1700, still standing
on Boston street at the south-east corner of North Federal, and
kept the office in a small building near the house.   A large
family of sons and daughters were there born to him, and the
writer holds occasional correspondence with descendants of his
now dwelling in widely separated and distant parts of the country,
where they maintain honorable positions.   Like many others
who in active manhood did much to advance the interests
of Lynn, he died in indigence and comparative obscurity.

Col. Robinson was succeeded in the office, in 1802, by his
brother-in-law, Major Ezra Hitchings, a biographical notice of
whom the reader may find by turning to page 154 of the present
volume.   He continued the office in its first location, in connection with his West India goods and grocery store, for the few
months he held the position.

In 1803, Samuel Mulliken became post-master.   And the
Turnpike being opened that year and diverting the travel and
business from Boston street, he removed the office to the south
end of Federal street, where, and in the vicinity, it remained till
the Rail-road was built, at which time it began to move towards
its present location on Market street, halting for a brief space
on South Common street, corner of Pleasant.   Mr. Mulliken was
a man of worth, and at one time did a large business in tanning
and the morocco line.   He possessed some occasionally uncomfortable gifts, among which was a notably uncompromising will,

which sometimes led to untoward consequences. A whimsical instance is given in our Annals, under date 1847, where a brief notice of him appears.

The entire line of post-masters is as follows: 1793, James Robinson. 1802, Ezra Hitchings. 1803, Samuel Mulliken. 1807, Elijah Downing. 1808, Jonathan Bacheller. 1829, Jeremiah C. Stickney. 1839, Thomas J. Marsh. 1841, Stephen Oliver. 1842, Thomas B. Newhall. 1843, Benjamin Mudge. 1849, Abner Austin. 1853, Jeremiah C. Stickney. 1858, Leonard B. Usher. 1861, George H. Chase. 1869, John Batchelder. 1877, John G. B. Adams.

———

LYNN FIRE DEPARTMENT. The means supplied for protection against fire have long been the boast of our people. We have hitherto been singularly favored in freedom from such great losses by fire as most places of so extended a history as ours have suffered ; and well may we fervently pray for a continuance of our good fortune. But security will be most certain to result from unrelaxed preparation.

The Department is now well provided with discreet officers and alert men, trained horses and approved " machines." There are five engines, worked by steam, and a number of chemical extinguishers ; several thousand feet of hose, ladders, hooks, and all other things necessary for an efficient contest with the fiery element. Then we have about the streets 453 hydrants, 19 reservoirs, and numerous wells, to say nothing of our brooks and ponds, Saugus river, and the Atlantic ocean.

The number of fire alarms during 1881, was 122. And the total loss was $199.544.50 ; of which $161.877.50 were returned by way of insurance.

As the city year by year becomes more compact, and taller buildings and those less isolated are erected in the different neighborhoods, it is evident that tireless vigilance will be required to preserve our traditional immunity. As to the past, we can only speak favorably ; and there seems no reason to apprehend that in the future we may not have as good a record. There is, indeed, an old insurance maxim, declaring that all " wooden " towns, and all large towns, must sooner or later have a sweeping conflagration ; but let no one be disturbed by it, though all of us have some tincture of fatalism; let us rather endeavor to show that there may be at least one exception.

Our authorities have all along been prompt in adopting such new measures and procuring such new appliances as promised most favorably; and a policy of that order, in municipal affairs, is, notwithstanding all murmuring and discontent, the most approved and satisfactory, whatever the result. Why, supposing the authorities had refused to procure steamers, or to establish the electric alarm, or furnish hydrants — what would have been the effect, in many conceivable ways; on insurance rates, for in stance; to say nothing of comfort and safety? Even Boston worked the old hand "machines" till within a few years; but it was because nothing better was known. Possibly somewhere in the future an invention will be made to supersede the best we now have; and when it comes, undoubtedly it will be welcomed by all who are most faithful to our municipal interests.

———

LYNN SCHOOLS. So many allusions have been all along made in our History, in relation to the Schools, their grades and condition, that nothing more than a remark or two and a brief summary can now be desirable. The boast that these primary seats of learning, in our day, are far superior to anything known in former years, is often heard. But is it exactly so? They are unquestionably superior in costliness, elegance of appointment and variety of studies. But are they superior in adaptation to existing wants?

In former years, such studies were pursued as best prepared the pupil to meet the requirements of the position he was in homely honesty expected to occupy in after life; not such a position as imaginative parental affection might picture. There is so much knowledge, the possession of which is sure to add to our well-being, that it seems unwise to occupy ourselves in efforts to gain that which is of doubtful utility. It has been said that all knowledge is useful; but that must be understood in a limited sense; most certainly all knowledge is not equally useful. No one can learn everything, as life is not long enough for that; and hence, is it not the part of wisdom to learn as thoroughly as may be, that which is indispensable, or sure to be most useful? There is a gray-headed aphorism that speaks of the jack-at-all-trades being good at none; and why not apply the suggestion to the departments of learning?

Our venerated fathers, practical and shrewd, kept these things in view. We their children are more prone to theorise; more charmed with the ideal; perhaps a little more under fancy's lead. But it may be asked, Is not the mind more fully developed and strengthened, better disciplined and polished, through these modern requirements — are not more extensive, beautiful, and ennobling avenues of thought opened through such means? This is a point for the wisest to discuss. And some philosophical "exploring circle" may yet discover a way out of the difficulties that beset the great educational interest. Every true philanthropist will pray for the adoption of any course that will make men better and happier; for there yet linger in the world vice and misery enough to call for determined warfare with the best weapons we can find.

The studies in our common schools, are however, apparently to an injudicious extent, prescribed by statute; and hence to the local supervisors entire freedom of action is not allowed; but there are so many details to be observed, so much care and oversight to be exercised, that their sphere of duty is large and their labors great. The School Committee is wisely made by law, to a considerable extent, an independent board, a board not to be controlled by the caprices of any other body, whose line of duty may not be expected to embrace special qualifications.

The full and perspicuous reports made annually by the Committee furnish all the information that can be needed by our fellow-citizens to understand the condition and requirements of the entire educational interest. And a few statistical items only need be added here. It is easier for lookers-on to make suggestions, perhaps very good in themselves, than to show how they can be properly dove-tailed into a system; but it is yet true that useful suggestions may sometimes come from minds hardly expected to bear ripened fruit. There seems no reason to doubt, that with here and there an exception, those selected to supervise our schools are actuated by a sincere desire faithfully to perform their responsible duties, and endeavor to adopt the best means to accomplish the best ends.

Number of Schools. The whole number of our Public Schools, in 1881, was 64: namely, 1 High School; 7 Grammar Schools; 55 Primary Schools; 1 Evening Drawing School.

School Houses: These are in number as follows: for High School, 1; for Grammar Schools, 7; for Primary Schools, 21; and there are 7 Primary Schools in Grammar School-houses.

Teachers. Whole number in day Schools, 118; in evening Drawing School, 3.

Pupils. Number belonging to all the day Schools, between the ages of 5 and 15 years, 5,516; of the age of 15, and upwards, 400; making the pupils in the day Schools, 5,916.

High School Graduates, June 1, 1881, 30.

Cost of Support. The following extract from the Report of the Committee for 1881, sufficiently exhibits the items of expenditure:

The charge upon the city for the maintenance of its system of public schools has been $93,677 17, divided into the following items of expenditure:

Teachers' salaries,	$65,823 79
School-houses and repairs,	6,042 65
Apparatus and furniture,	2,058 69
Care of school-houses,	6,438 78
Fuel,	5,030 86
Books and stationery,	5,452 45
Printing,	1,285 63
Incidentals,	1,544 32
Total,	$93,677 17

To gain some knowledge of the increase in our school system, the reader can refer to the brief summary on page 586 of our 1865 edition. The number of schools at that time was 48; teachers, 59; pupils. 4,332.

———

LYNN NEWSPAPERS. The proximity of Lynn to Boston and Salem, may be sufficient to account for our not having had a local newspaper before the year 1825. And for forty years after that date it can hardly be claimed that we had a permanently successful publication, in a pecuniary way, though there were three or four that by their ability and usefulness well deserved success. But within the last few years a great advance has been made. The papers are now much better, as a general thing, and much cheaper; and they have greatly improved in the quality of the paper, the printing, and in the mechanical aspect generally; excepting that just now it is the fashion to make such displays in the advertising columns that some have the appearance of tradesmen's handbills.

The relative number of readers has increased quite as rapidly as anything connected with the business. At the time Mr. Lummus published the Mirror, four hundred subscribers were thought a goodly number for a country weekly ; and thus it was, with here and there an exception, for many years. Indeed the great bulk of working people thought they could not afford to take a paper ; and it was not difficult after a little experience, for a publisher to know on just what individuals to call, with any prospect of success, when he set out on his soliciting tours. The writer well remembers a conversation with Mr. Lummus, during which, in his hyperbolical way, he remarked after this sort : Why, I know just who will take a paper ; I can get four hundred subscribers for anything I will print ; but I can't get four hundred and one — without I will accept a Woodender ; and do you suppose I would do that ? His antipathy to the people of Woodend would often crop out in that brusk way. Yet it is doubtful whether the feeling was not rather feigned than real, for some of his best friends and correspondents lived in that section — Mr. Lewis and Enoch Curtin, for instance. But his tart declaration that if certain persons wanted his paper they would have to move out of Woodend to get it, was made while he was actually crossing their names from the carrier's list.

The papers were then published strictly on the subscription plan, the purchase of single copies being almost unknown.

We now [1882] have in Lynn two dailies and four weeklies, that circulate their thousands ; and by the ability and industry of their conductors deserve the success they enjoy. In addition to this home supply, thousands of papers from Boston and other places are every day sold in our streets. The Lynn papers are at this time as follows :

Daily Evening Item, established in 1877.

The Lynn Bee, (daily) established in 1880.

The Lynn Reporter, (weekly) established in 1854.

The Lynn Transcript, (weekly) established in 1867.

The Lynn City Item, (weekly) established in 1876.

The Lynn Union, (weekly) established as *The Lynn Record*, in 1872 — adopting the name of the old Record, of 1830.

LYNN HOSPITAL. This beneficent institution was incorporated in 1880, and after a thorough examination into the merits of several proposed locations, early in 1882 the Hathorne estate, so called, on Boston street, was purchased as a site for the necessary buildings. It is on the southerly side of the street, a few rods east of Franklin. The brook which runs from Flax Pond flows in front, and in the vicinity rise abrupt woody hills, with here and there a towering porphyry cliff; the whole surrounding being strikingly picturesque. It is in the quarter known from early times as Mansfield's End. Deacon Mansfield's house stood on the hospital grounds ; and there, also, one or two other conspicuous individuals of the name resided. And being on the principal thoroughfare, some of the most prominent people of the town lived in the vicinity. The old mansion standing at the time the hospital corporation purchased, was long known as the Deacon Farrington house, that dignitary having lived there for some years. Long afterwards it was occupied by Capt. John White, of the United States navy, who, in addition to his fame as a naval commander, gained some reputation as an author. Subsequently it was occupied by Rev. Mr. Barlow, second minister of the Unitarian society, and later still by William Hathorne, from whom it took the name of Hathorne house. The estate formerly embraced many acres ; and Washington street was extended over a portion.

In our Annals, under date 1875, a " Lynn Hospital" is spoken of as having been formally opened on the 31st of March, in the Phillips mansion, on Water Hill. The site was airy and pleasant, and the institution seemed to be doing much good. But the contributions for its support were not sufficient, and its doors were soon closed, much to the regret of worthy but not wealthy friends.

Several liberal donations in aid of the funds of the present hospital have already been made, the largest of which was by John B. Alley — $10.000. John B. Tolman, an old Lynn printer, gave $2.500, in respect of his craftship. And numerous other generous contributions have been made, some of hundreds of dollars, and thence down even to a few cents. Little tin receptacles were deposited all about the city, in convenient places, to receive the sanctified mite that even a poor widow might give.

POPULATION OF LYNN. At this time [1882] the population no doubt is a very little above 40.000. The last numbering related to June 1, 1880; and at that time we had 38.284; — males, 18.255; females, 20.029. From the first, there has been a steady, but not rapid accession. The first recorded census, [1765] gave the number of inhabitants as 2.198. In 1800, it was 2.837. In 1820, 4.515. And for each ten years thereafter, the enumeration has stood as follows — Swampscott having been set off in 1852, and Nahant in 1853:

Years : : : :	1830	1840	1850	1860	1870	1880
Population : :	6.138	9.367	14.257	19.083	28.233	38.284

STREETS OF LYNN. The number of streets, the present year, [1882] is 509, and the lighting is by 313 gas burners and 253 kerosene lamps. The first paved street was Munroe; and the paving was done during the summer of the year just named, the material being dimension granite blocks. It has hitherto been an expensive and laborious charge to keep our streets in a proper condition, for they are extensive and not in all cases laid upon the best bottoms. But yet they have been kept in remarkably good repair, for we have had at hand a supply of serviceable material. Our many beautiful drives have long been a source of boasting for ourselves and of pleasure for visitors. When however, a place has attained a population of forty thousands, something more than crushed stone and gravel is needed on the constantly used avenues.

POLICE BUSINESS — POLICE COURT. The number of arrests for criminal offences, in 1881, was 1.289; among them, for drunkenness, 771; assault and battery, 156; larceny, 89; truancy, 30; profanity, 27; vagrancy, 21; breaking and entering, 20; stubbornness, 16; malicious mischief, 13; violation of liquor law, 12; and one or more for almost every other offence known in the catalogue of crime. A large portion of the persons arrested were examined in the Police Court.

Down to 1849, all justices of the peace here, had authority to try minor cases, civil or criminal. But population having then become considerable, it was thought best to have some more centralized and regular jurisdiction. In pursuance of this view the writer headed a petition to the town asking their intercession with the legislature for the establishment of a Police Court. The matter was favorably acted on, and the Court went into operation during that year. It was made a court of record, in 1862. And before it are tried the "small cawses," as they were called in colonial times, civil and criminal. It has a Standing Justice, two Special Justices, and a Clerk. See Annals, 1879.

CHILDREN'S HOME. In 1881 a two-story wooden building was erected on Tower Hill, and called by the above name—the purpose being to provide suitable nurture and education for exposed young children, to save them from the stigma of work-house life and from the sometimes worse consequences of vicious and degraded homes. The house occupies one of the most healthy and beautiful sites in all Lynn—airy, and commanding charming views. This unpretending institution can hardly fail to do a meritorious work, and may be the means not only of saving many from lives of degradation and misery, but of developing characters that will in a ten-fold degree repay all the cost and care that the benevolent enterprise will involve. At the opening of the Home, in 1882, some twenty-five children were received from the alms-house.

STATISTICAL ITEMS. As elsewhere remarked, it can hardly be necessary to occupy much space with statistical details, as the information that is given year by year in our Annals, supplies all that will in most cases be desirable. And then, as to the management of our municipal affairs : the annual reports from the various departments are so full and so accessible, that nothing beyond here and there a brief summary can now be needed. Yet, in a work of this kind, which in years hence may be looked to for information of almost every kind there is scarcely any topic that should be passed by in entire silence. The few items that follow relate to the year 1881, excepting where otherwise stated.

Valuation and Taxation. The total valuation of the city was $24.992.084, viz: Real Estate, $19.036.008 ; Personal Estate, $5.956.076. Rate of taxation, $17.40 on $1.000. [In 1882 the valuation was a little lower, and the rate of taxation $21.00 on $1.000.]

City Debt. Whole debt, $2.208.000.00 ; but by certain assets, usual in municipal reckoning, the net amount of the debt was $1.646.633.94.

Appropriations and Expenditures. Whole amount of appropriations, including certain receipts, $706.591.15. Expenditures, $686.571.45.

New Buildings. Two hundred and sixty-five buildings were erected during the year — 253 of wood, 11 of brick, and one of stone. 153 were dwellings. That the frequent removal of buildings, for which Lynn has been long noted, is a custom still in practice, is shown by the fact that during the year sixty-two were started on their travels.

Number of Polls — 10.990. [In 1882, 11.465.]

The number of *Houses* in Lynn, in 1882, was 6.309. The number of *Horses*, 1.962. The number of *Cows*, 438.

Free Public Library. There is, and always has been, a steady accession to the number of volumes in this institution, from month to month, and, it is believed, a corresponding increase in its usefulness. The number of volumes at the close of 1881 was 30.500 — a very satisfactory growth from the 4000 of 1862. Number delivered during the year, 95.927. The largest number taken out in one day was on Saturday, March 5, when 972 were delivered.

Pine Grove Cemetery. The number of interments in this beautiful burial place, during the year, was 418, which was a little more than half of the whole number who died, the other burial places receiving the remains of the others. The first interment in this cemetery was on Sunday, October 13, 1850, when the remains of Harriet Newell, wife of George W. Stocker, were laid there. And the whole number of burials there has now reached 7.801.

Vital Statistics. There were 799 deaths in Lynn, during 1881, of which 153 were by consumption, 59 by pneumonia, 50 by diphtheria, 39 by cholera infantum, 24 by typhoid fever, and 6 by scarlet fever. Two hundred and seventy-two of the deceased were under the age of five years.

Marriages. The number of marriages during 1881, was 513.

Banks — of discount and circulation, 4, with an aggregate capital of $1.000.000. Savings banks, 2.

18

CITY CLERKS. In our 1865 edition may be found a list of *Clerks of the Writs* and *Town Clerks*, extending back to the earliest days. It is unnecessary to repeat the list here. But it may be convenient for the reader to have by him the names of the *City Clerks*, in the order in which they served. And having at hand engraved fac-similes of their autographs it may not be amiss to use them, as they will not require much space, although one or two appear in other connections in the present volume.

Wm. Bassett.

WILLIAM BASSETT — Served in 1850, '51 and '52.

Chas. Merritt.

CHARLES MERRITT — Served in 1853, '54, '56, '57 and '58.

John Batchelder.

JOHN BATCHELDER — Served in 1855.

E. A. Ingalls.

EPHRAIM A. INGALLS — Served in 1859 and '60.

Benj. H. Jones.

BENJAMIN H. JONES — Served from 1861 to 1875, both inclusive.

Chas. E. Parsons.

CHARLES E. PARSONS — Elected in 1876, and yet [1882] in office.

It need not be remarked that the Clerks are elected annually by the City Council. And the neatness and accuracy of the multifarious records are the best evidence that thus far no mistake in the choice has occurred.

CHRONOLOGICAL TABLE.

A GOOD Chronological Table is, of itself, a succinct history. And the following is inserted without hesitation, on account of its unquestionable usefulness, though it was prepared by the writer for the Centennial Memorial, in which and in the book giving an account of the proceedings on the celebration of our Two Hundred and Fiftieth Anniversary, it substantially appeared. Additions, however, have been made, and occurrences down to 1882, noted.

1629.   Five families, chief among them Edmund Ingalls and his brother Francis, arrive and commence the settlement.
1630.   Thomas Newhall born — the first person of European parentage born here.
        Wolves kill several swine belonging to the settlers, September 30.
        Fifty settlers, chiefly farmers, and many of them with families, arrive and locate in different parts of the territory.
1631.   Governor Winthrop passed through the settlement, October 28, and noted that the crops were plentiful.
1632.   First Church — fifth in the colony — formed ; Stephen Bachelor, minister.
1633.   A corn mill, the first in the settlement, built on Strawberry brook.
1634.   John Humfrey arrives and settles near Nahant street.
        The settlement sends her first Representative — Capt. Nathaniel Turner — to the General Court.
        William Wood, one of the first comers, publishes " Nevv Englands Prospect.'
1635.   Philip Kertland, the first shoemaker, arrives.
1637.   Name of the settlement changed from Saugus to Lynn.
        At this time there were thirty-seven plows in the colony, most of them in Lynn.
        Settlement of Sandwich commenced by emigrants from Lynn.
1638.   First division of lands among the inhabitants.
1639.   Ferry established across Saugus river.
        First bridge over Saugus river at Boston street crossing built.
1643.   Iron works established near Saugus river ; the first in America.
1644.   Hugh Bert and Samuel Bennett, of Lynn, presented to the grand jury as " common sleepers in time of exercise." Both were convicted and fined.
1646.   Lynn made a market town — Tuesday, the lecture day, being market day.
1658.   Dungeon rock alleged to have been rent by an earthquake, entombing alive Thomas Veal, the pirate, with treasure.

(275)

1666. A year of disasters. Several die of small pox. "Divers are slain by lightning." Grasshoppers and caterpillars do much mischief.

1669. Boniface Burton dies, aged 113 years.

1671. A year remarkable for storms. A violent snow storm, Jan. 18, with much thunder and lightning.

1680. Dr. Philip Read, the first physician here, complains to the Court of Mrs. Margaret Gifford, as a witch.
The great Newtonian comet appears in November, exciting much alarm.

1681. The Court allows Lynn to have two licensed public houses.

1682. Old Tunnel Meeting-house built.

1686. Indian deed of Lynn given, September 4.

1687. Thomas Newhall, the first white person born here, dies, in March, aged 57.

1688. Excitement about Edward Randolph's petition for a grant of all Nahant.

1692. Great witchcraft excitement.

1694. A church fast appointed by Rev. Mr. Shepard, July 19, for the arrest of the "spiritual plague" of Quakerism.

1696. Severe winter ; coldest since the settlement commenced ; much suffering.

1697. Great alarm on account of small pox.

1706. Second division of lands among the inhabitants.

1708. A public fast held on account of the ravages of caterpillars and canker worms.

1716. Extraordinary darkness at noonday, Oct. 21 ; dinner tables lighted.

1717. Memorable snow storms, Feb. 20 and 24 ; one-story houses buried.

1719. Northern lights observed for the first time, Dec. 17 ; an alarming display.

1723. Terrific storm, Feb. 24. The sea came in raging and roaring fearfully.
First mill on Saugus river, at Boston street crossing, built.

1726. £13.15 awarded to Nathaniel Potter, for linen manufactured in Lynn.

1745. Rev. Mr. Whitefield preaches on Lynn Common, creating much excitement.

1749. Great drought, hot summer, and immense multitudes of grasshoppers.

1750. John Adam Dagyr, an accomplished shoemaker, arrives.

1755. Greatest earthquake ever known in New England, occurs Nov. 18.
A whale, seventy-five feet in length, landed on King's Beach, Dec. 9.

1759. A bear, weighing 400 pounds, killed in Lynn woods.

1768. A catamount killed in Lynn woods, by Joseph Williams.

1770. Potato rot prevails, and canker worms commit great ravages.

1775, Battle of Lexington, April 19 — five Lynn men killed.

1776. Twenty-six negro slaves owned in Lynn.

1780. Memorable dark day, May 19 ; houses lighted as at night.

1782. Whole number of votes given in Lynn, for governor, 57 ; all but 5 for Hancock.

1784. Gen. Lafayette passed through Lynn, Oct. 28, receiving enthusiastic plaudits.

1788. Gen. Washington passed through town, in October, and was affectionately greeted by old and young.

1793. Lynn post-office established, and first kept on Boston street, near Federal.

1794. On Christmas day, at noon, in the open air, the thermometer stood at 80 deg.

1795. Brig Peggy wrecked on Long Beach, Dec. 9, and eleven lives lost.

1796. The first fire engine for public use purchased.

1800. Memory of Washington honored ; procession and eulogy, January 13.
An elephant first exhibited in Lynn. First dancing school opened.
Manufacture of morocco introduced.

1803. Boston and Salem Turnpike opened, and Lynn Hotel built.
A snow storm occurred in May, the fruit trees being then in bloom.
Miles Shorey and his wife killed by lightning, July 10.

1804. Independence day first celebrated in Lynn. Snow fell in July.
1805. First Masonic Lodge — Mount Carmel — constituted June 10.
1808. First law office in Lynn, opened by Benjamin Merrill.
Great bull fight at Half Way House. Bulls and bull dogs engaged.
Lynn Artillery chartered, November 18, and allowed two brass field pieces.
Trapping Lobsters first practised at Swampscott.
1812. Lynn Light Infantry chartered, June 30.
1813. Moll Pitcher, the celebrated fortune-teller, dies, April 9, aged 75.
1814. Lynnfield incorporated as a separate town.
First Town House built.
First Bank established.
1815. Saugus incorporated as a separate town.
Terrific southeasterly gale, Sept. 23; ocean spray driven several miles inland; fruit on the trees impregnated with salt.
1816. Great horse trot on the Turnpike, in Lynn, Sept. 1; said to be the first in New England. Major Stackpole's "Old Blue" trotted three miles in eight minutes and forty-two seconds.
1817. President Munroe passed through town.
1819. The great sea-serpent appears off Long Beach. Nahant Hotel built. Alms-house at Tower Hill built.
1824. Gen. Lafayette visits Lynn, Aug. 31, and is enthusiastically welcomed.
1825. First Lynn newspaper — the Weekly Mirror — issued September 3.
1826. First Savings Bank incorporated.
1827. Broad and brilliant night arch, Aug. 28.
1828. A whale, sixty feet long, cast ashore on Whale Beach, May 2.
1829. Splendid display of frosted trees, Jan. 10.
1830. Donald McDonald, a Scotchman, dies in Lynn alms-house, Oct. 4, aged 108. He was at the battle of Quebec when Wolfe fell, and at Braddock's defeat.
1832. First Lynn Directory published by Charles F. Lummus.
1833. Extraordinary shower of meteors, Nov. 13.
1837. Surplus United States revenue distributed. Lynn received $14.879, and applied it to the payment of the town debt. Saugus received $3.500, and appropriated it to the building of a Town Hall. Lynnfield received $1.328 29, and applied it to the town debt.
1838. Eastern Rail-road opened for travel from Boston to Salem, Aug. 28.
1841. The first picture by the new art known as Daguerreotype, or Photography, ever taken in Lynn, was a landscape, taken this year, by James R. Newhall, by apparatus imported from France.
1843. A splended comet; first appeared at noonday, Feb. 1.
Schooner Thomas wrecked on Long Beach, March 17, five men perishing.
Breed's Pond formed. Theophilus N. Breed built a dam across the valley, on the northeast of Oak street, flowing some fifty acres, thus forming the pond and securing water power for his iron works.
1846. Mexican war commenced. Lynn furnished twenty volunteers.
Congress boots began to be manufactured.
Destructive fire on Water Hill, Aug. 9. Large brick silk-printing establishment, spice and coffee mill, and two or three smaller buildings destroyed.
1847. President Polk made a short visit to Lynn, July 5.
1848. Carriage road over harbor side of Long Beach built.
Lynn Common fenced.
George Gray, the hermit, dies, Feb. 28, aged 78.

1849. Lynn Police Court established.
Large emigration to California.

1850. Lynn adopts the city form of government.
Pine Grove Cemetery consecrated, July 24.
Thirteen persons of a pic-nic party from Lynn, drowned in Lynnfield Pond, August 15.
Ten hour system — that is, ten hours to constitute a day's work — generall adopted. Previously the time was indefinite. Bells were rung at 6 p. m.

1851. On March 18, and April 15, the tide, during violent storms, swept entirely over Long Beach.
Hiram Marble commences the excavation of Dungeon Rock.

1852. Swampscott incorporated as a separate town.
Louis Kossuth, the Hungarian exile, is enthusiastically received here, May 6.
Henry Clay's death noticed ; flags raised at half-mast and bells tolled, July 3
Funeral services in memory of Daniel Webster, in First Congregational meeting-house, Oct. 29, the day of the statesman's burial at Marshfield.

1853. Nahant incorporated as a separate town, March 29.
Prize fight on Lynnfield road, Jan 3 ; parties arrested.
Illuminating gas first lighted in Lynn, Jan. 13.
Cars commence running over Saugus Branch Rail-road, Feb. 1.

1855. City Charter so amended as to have the municipal year commence on the first Monday of January instead of the first Monday of April.

1856. Two bald eagles appear on the ice in Lynn harbor, Jan. 17.
Ezra R. Tebbetts, of Lynn, killed by a snow-slide from a house in Bromfield street, Boston, Feb. 12.
Egg Rock light shown for the first time, Sept. 15.

1857. Bark Tedesco wrecked at Swampscott, all on board, twelve in number, perishing, Jan. 18.
Many small pearls found in muscles at Floating Bridge and Flax ponds.
Trawl fishing began to be practised this year.

1858. Telegraphic communication between Lynn and other places established.
Impromptu Atlantic cable celebration, Aug. 17, on the arrival of Queen Victoria's message to President Buchanan.
Blue fish appear in the offing, in large numbers, in early autumn, and are supposed to have carried on a successful war against the menhaden, as bushels of the latter were picked up dead on the shore.
Magnificent comet, Donati's, visible in the north-west, in the autumn.
Catholic Cemetery, St. Mary's, consecrated, Nov. 4.

1859. British bark Vernon, from Messina, driven ashore on Long Beach, Feb. 2. crew saved by life-boat.
Roman Catholic church, St. Mary's, Ash street, burned, May 28.
Brilliant display of northern lights ; whole heavens covered, Aug. 28.
Union street Methodist meeting-house destroyed by fire, Nov. 20.
Church bells tolled at sunrise, noon and sunset, Dec. 2, in observance of the execution of John Brown, at Charlestown, Va.

1860. Harbor so frozen in January, that persons walked across to Bass Point.
Shoemakers' great strike commenced in February.
Prince of Wales passed through Lynn, Oct. 20.
First horse rail-road cars commence running, Nov. 29.
Market street first lighted by gas, Dec. 7.

1861. Alonzo Lewis, historian and poet, dies, Jan. 21, aged 66.

1861. A splendid comet suddenly appears, July 2, the tail having actually swept the earth, three days before, producing no disturbance, and only a slight apparently auroral light in the atmosphere.

The extensive edifice known as Nahant Hotel, destroyed by fire, Sept. 12.

Lynn Light Infantry and Lynn City Guards, two full companies, start for the seat of the Southern Rebellion, April 16, only four days after the attack on Fort Sumter, and but five hours after the arrival of President Lincoln's call for troops.

1862. Lynn Free Public Library opened.

Enthusiastic war meeting on the Common, on Sunday, Aug. 31 ; church services omitted.

Soldiers' Burial Lot, in Pine Grove Cemetery, laid out. .

Nathan Breed, jr., murdered in his store, Summer street, Dec. 23.

1863. Extraordinary ravages of caterpillars and canker worms.

1864. The thermometer rose to 104 degrees in shady places, in Lynn, June 25 ; indicating the warmest day, here, of which there had been any record.

Free delivery of post-office matter begins.

Great drought and extensive fires in the woods, during the summer.

First steam fire engine owned by the city, arrives, Aug. 11.

The Town House burned, Oct. 6, and Joseph Bond, confined in the lockup, burned to death.

Schooner Lion, from Rockland, Me., wrecked on Long Beach, Dec. 10, and all on board, six in number, perish. Their cries were heard above the roaring of the wind and sea, but they could not be rescued.

1865. News of the fall of Richmond received, April 3. Great rejoicing—church bells rung, buildings illuminated, bonfires kindled.

News of the assassination of President Lincoln received, April 15. Mourning insignia displayed in public buildings and churches.

Corner stone of City Hall laid, Nov. 28.

1866. Gen. Sherman passes through Lynn, July 16, and is cordially greeted.

A meteoric stone falls in Ocean street, in September.

1867. Terrific snow storm, Jan. 17.

City Hall dedicated, Nov. 30.

1868. Memorial Day—called also Decoration Day—observed, May 30. Soldiers' graves strewed with flowers. [In 1881 the day was made a legal holiday.]

Hiram Marble, excavator of Dungeon Rock, dies, Nov. 10, aged 65, having pursued his arduous and fruitless labors about 17 years. [His son Edwin succeeded him in the work and died at the Rock, Jan. 16, 1880, aged 48, without having reached the supposed deposit of gold and jewels.]

Destructive fire on Market street, Dec. 25. Lyceum Building, Frazier's and Bubier's brick blocks destroyed. Whole loss about $300.000.

1869. Mary J. Hood, a colored woman, dies Jan. 8, aged 104 years and 7 months.

Another destructive fire on the night of Jan. 25, commencing in the brick shoe manufactory of Edwin H. Johnson, in Munroe street, and destroying property to the amount of some $170.000.

On the evening of April 15, there was a magnificent display of beautifully tinted aurora borealis, during which a meteor of great brilliancy shot across the eastern sky.

Severe gale on Wednesday afternoon, Sept. 8 ; next in violence to that of Sept. 23, 1815. Several small buildings destroyed, and a multitude of trees uprooted. More than 400 shade trees prostrated in Lynn.

1869. The old Turnpike from Salem to Boston becomes a public highway this year. Sidney B. Pratt dies, Jan. 29, aged 54, leaving by will $10.000 for the benefit of the Free Public Library.

1870. Young Men's Christian Association incorporated, March 31.

First regatta of Lynn Yacht Club, June 17.

Land near Central rail-road station sold at $5 per square foot; the highest rate known in Lynn up to this time.

1871. Rev. Joseph Cook, at the time minister of the First Church, gives a series of Sunday evening lectures, in Music Hall, early this year, creating considerable excitement by his rather sensational denunciations. [He afterwards became famous in this country, in Europe, and in other parts of the world, by his ethical discourses.]

Terrible rail-road disaster at Revere, Aug. 26; eleven Lynn persons killed. Whole number of lives lost, 33; number of wounded, about 60.

Electric fire alarm established.

President Grant passed through Lynn, Oct. 16.

William Vennar, alias Brown, murders Mrs. Jones, is pursued, and in his further desperate attempts is shot dead, Dec. 16.

1872. City Hall bell raised to its position in the tower, March 2.

Meeting of the City Council commemorative of the recent death of Professor Morse, inventor of the electric telegraph, April 16.

S. O. Breed's box factory, at the south end of Commercial street, struck by lightning and consumed, Aug. 13. [The summer of this year was remarkable for the frequency and severity of its thunder storms.]

Brick house of worship of First Church, South Common street, dedicated Aug. 29.

Ingalls and Cobbet school houses dedicated.

Odd Fellows' Hall, Market street, dedicated, Oct. 7.

Brick and iron station of Eastern Rail-road, Central square, built.

Singular disease, called epizootic, prevailed among horses during the latter part of the autumn. Wheel carriages almost entirely ceased to run, excepting as drawn by oxen, dogs, or goats, and sometimes by men.

Much speculation in real estate; prices high, and business active.

Pine Hill Reservoir built.

1873. Pumping engine at Public Water Works, Walnut street, first put in operation Jan. 14.

English sparrows make their appearance in Lynn — no doubt the progeny of those imported into Boston. [Soon declared a nuisance.]

Soldiers' Monument, Park square, dedicated Sept. 17.

Grand Masonic parade, Oct. 22.

Friends' Biennial Conference held here, Nov. 19.

Birch Pond formed, by running a dam across Birch Brook valley, on the east of Walnut street, near Saugus line.

874. "Lynn Home for Aged Women" incorporated, Feb. 6.

Grand celebration of St. Patrick's day, in Lynn, March 17, by the Irish organizations of Essex county.

1875. Boston, Revere Beach and Lynn Rail-road opened for travel, July 22.

Sea-serpent alleged to have been seen off Egg Rock, in August.

The General Convention of Universalists meet in Lynn, Oct. 20.

Great depression in business affairs succeed the days of unhealthy prosperity. Many tradesmen and merchants fail, and real estate falls greatly in price.

1875. An unusual number of Tramps—that is, homeless wanderers from place to place—appear in Lynn, and receive temporary relief.

1876. The great World's Exposition, at Philadelphia, marking the centennial year of the Republic. Lynn makes a good show of her manufactures, and a large number of her people attend the exhibition.

A fire occurred in Market street, July 26 destroying some $10.000 worth of property.

The destructive Colarado beetle, or potato bug, first appears in Lynn, this year.

Appropriate observance of the centennial year, July 4. "Centennial Memorial" published.

Brick engine house, Federal street, built.

Benjamin F. Doak dies, Nov. 8, aged 50 years, bequeathing $10.000 for the poor of the city. [This legacy is now known as the "Doak Fund."]

A splendid meteor passed over the city on the evening of Dec. 20.

1877. Sweetser's four story brick building, Central avenue, with an adjacent building, burned, April 7 ; loss about $115.000.

Extraordinary phosphorescent glow along the shores, in September.

1878. Successful balloon ascension, July 4, Alderman Aza A. Breed, City Marshal Fry, and Mr. Fred Smith, journalist, accompanying the æronaut.

Dennis Kearney, radical agitator and California "sand lot orator," addresses a large crowd on the Common, on the evening of Aug. 12.

Brick fire engine house, Broad street, built.

Higher temperature in Lynn and vicinity, at midnight, Dec. 2, than in any other part of the United States—six degrees higher than in New Orleans, La., seven higher than in Savannah, Geo., nine higher than in Charleston, S. C., and ten higher than in Jacksonville, Florida.

Gold held at par, Dec. 17, for the first time in sixteen years ; that is $100 in gold were worth just $100 in greenback government notes. The extreme of variation was in July, 1864, when $100 in gold were worth $285 in notes.

1879. The brick house of worship of the First Methodist Society, Park square, dedicated, Feb. 27.

The newly-invented telephone, comes into use in Lynn, this year.

Two hundred and fiftieth anniversary of the settlement of Lynn, celebrated, June 17. [A volume embracing a full account of the proceedings was published by order of the City Council.]

Business begins to become decidedly active after seven years of depression.

John A. Jackson, designer of the Soldiers' Monument, Park square, died in Florence, Italy, in August, aged 54.

St. Joseph's Cemetery (Catholic) consecrated, Oct. 16.

Extraordinary occurrence of a perfectly clear sky, all over the United States, from the Atlantic to the Pacific, Nov. 4, as reported by the United States Signal Corps.

1880. Hawkes family gathering, July 28 and 29.

Tubular Wells, Boston street, sunk by the city authorities to gain additional water supply ; first pumping from them, Sept. 4.

The notorious "Morey Letter" appears in the autumn, creating much sensation throughout the country.

Beautiful mirage in the bay, Nov. 22.

1881. Young Men's Christian Association Building, Market street, dedicated, Jan. 17.

Government weather signals, on High Rock, first shown, Feb. 23.

Lynn Hospital incorporated.

1881.   The "yellow day," so called, occurred Sept. 6.
Beautiful celestial phenomena, Sept. 12.
President Garfield's death announced by the tolling of the church bells at
midnight, Sept. 19.   Memorial services held, Sept. 26.
Free Public Forest Association, or Exploring Circle, formed.
Hon. Enoch Redington Mudge, donor of St. Stephen's Memorial Church,
dies, Oct. 1.
St. Stephen's Memorial Church consecrated, Nov. 2.

———

[As our chapter of Annals closes with 1881, and it seems desirable to take some
notice of events down as near as possible to the time of publication, the following
additions are inserted.]

1882.

The winter of 1881 and '82 was rather remarkable for the quantity of snow, and
the long time the earth remained covered.   A storm began on the afternoon of January 31, during which some eighteen inches fell.   And on the next Sunday, Feb. 5, a
snow storm occurred that was not for many years before exceeded in violence.   The
drifts in some places were for a time insurmountable ; and services at several of the
principal churches were omitted.

On the night of Feb. 15, a building on Munroe street, owned by Charles G. Clark,
together with one or two others, was burned, causing a loss of some $20.000.

The Grand Army Coliseum, on Summer street, was dedicated March 15, with
appropriate ceremonies.   Its seating capacity is much greater than any other place
of assembly hitherto erected here.

On the morning of the 15th of March, just before the time for workmen to assemble, a terrific steam boiler explosion took place in the rear of the Goodwin last factory,
in Spring street.   The engineer was killed, and several others badly wounded.   One
or two adjacent buildings were much damaged, and a piece of the boiler, weighing
about 1.500 pounds, was thrown two hundred feet up into the air, and fell in Newhall
street, seven hundred feet distant.

A fire occurred on the morning of April 22, at Houghton, Godfrey and Dean's
paper warehouse, Central avenue, destroying property to the amount of $3.000.

Electric lights made their appearance here, in the spring.

At midnight, May 12, according to the weather reports, the thermometer, in Lynn
and vicinity, reached a lower degree than in any other part of the United States ; yet
it was not so low as to be particularly noticeable.

Memorial Day, May 30, was observed as usual ; address by Comrade James M.
Tanner, of Brooklyn, N. Y.

Glen Lewis was consecrated, May 30.

Barnum's "greatest show on earth," visited Lynn, July 22.   Some half a score
of elephants appeared in the street parade.   The giant elephant Jumbo and the nursing
baby elephant were both members of the caravan.   Some 25.000 persons attended the
exhibition, and the amount of money received for admission, reached nearly $11.000.
The show consisted of a large collection of animals, equestrian, acrobatic, and other
circus and semi-dramatic performances.   It was, no doubt, the grandest and most
costly show ever in Lynn.

An explosion of a part of the underground equipment of the Citizens' Steam Heating Company, at the corner of Washington and Munroe streets, took place, July 27,
injuring the street somewhat, and throwing up stones and gravel to the danger

and fright of persons in the vicinity. And subsequently other explosions took place inducing an appeal to the city authorities for protection.

Nickerson's oil clothing factory, in Swampscott, was burned, August 4. Miss Emma Stone, employed in the establishment, lost her life, and the loss of property amounted to about $9,000.

An extraordinary drought prevailed during the latter part of the summer. Most of the crops about Lynn were absolutely ruined, the unripe fruit dropped from the trees, and much of the shrubbery and many of the trees had the appearance of having been exposed to fire blasts. Yet the springs and wells did not indicate any very marked deficiency of moisture somewhat below the surface. We had an uncommonly long succession of very warm days, with westerly winds and clear skies. And the peculiar effect on vegetation was, no doubt, attributable rather to the burning sun than the lack of moisture. The spring was backward by full two weeks, and the weather was on the whole anomalous, most of the year.

The Ocean House, in Swampscott, a summer hotel of considerable note, was destroyed by fire, on the evening of September 6. It was a large wooden building, six stories in front and five in the rear. The loss was about $65,000.

In October, the fare to or from Boston was reduced to five cents on all the trains of the Narrow-gauge Rail-road, and on a part of those of the Eastern.

Mayor Lovering was, on the 7th of November, elected a member of the U. S. Congress — the second Lynn man ever chosen for that honorable position.

The morning sky for several weeks in October and November was adorned by a splendid comet which rose two or three hours before the sun, in the south-east. A very good representation of it, as seen from High Rock is here given. The steeple of the Central church, in Silsbee street, is seen on the right of the picture, and Phillips's Point, Swampscott, on the left. Astronomers had wonderful stories to tell of this comet — its inconceivable speed and partial disruption as if by some collision.

COMET OF 1882,
As seen from High Rock, Lynn.

The foregoing Chronological Table, as elsewhere remarked, it is thought will be sufficient for a glimpse at our whole history; and in the present volume nothing more than a mere glance at the times anterior to the point at which the 1865 edition record closes, could be expected or desired, at least by those possessed of a copy of that issue.

Near the close of that volume are various tables, among which are: lists of the surnames of all residents of Lynn from 1629 to 1700 — of Assistants and Counsellors — of early Representatives — of members of the Ancient and Honorable Artillery — of soldiers of the Revolution — of members of important Conventions — of Senators — of Newspapers and Editors — of the successions of Ministers of the various religious societies, &c. These, for the most part, are of course omitted here, as the great accumulation of names would have required space that could perhaps be filled with more interesting matter, inasmuch as they can be readily found elsewhere. A few, however, of those most commonly useful for reference, will be found in their proper connections in these pages; all of which the reader can easily find by referring to the Index.

PRESIDENTS OF THE COMMON COUNCIL.

1850. Daniel C. Baker.	1867. Theodore Attwill.
1851. James R. Newhall.	1868. Theodore Attwill.
1852. Edward S. Davis.	1869. Nathan M. Hawkes.
1853. Edward S. Davis.	1870. Nathan M. Hawkes.
1854. Gustavus Attwill.	1871. Bowman B. Breed.
1855. Gilbert Hawkes.	1872. Nathan M. Hawkes.
1856. Edward S. Davis.	1873. Bowman B. Breed, [died.]
1857. Edward S. Davis.	1873. Ezra Baker, [part of the year.]
1858. Edwin Q. Bacheller.	1874. William C. Holder.
1859. Nathan Clark.	1875. George D. Whittle.
1860. Noah Robinson.	1876. George T. Newhall.
1861. George H. Chase.	1877. George T. Newhall.
1862. George H. Chase.	1878. George T. Newhall.
1863. Jesse L. Attwill.	1879. Charles E. Kimball.
1864. Jesse L. Attwill.	1880. George C. Neal.
1865. Jesse L. Attwill.	1881. Edward C. Neal.
1866. Jesse L. Attwill.	1882. Charles D. Hollis.

CONCLUSION.

A GREAT many individuals who have figured in different periods of the history of Lynn have in the present volume been introduced to the reader ; some of them of characters altogether worthy of imitation ; others, perhaps, useful as examples to be avoided. It is not unfrequently difficult to determine the ground of action in a fellow being — whether it be principle, habit, or natural disposition. And many appear to act as if they considered this or that virtue or vice theirs by prescription or inheritance. A prominent fellow-citizen some time ago, when checked for his profanity, replied, with perfect coolness, and an air that indicated his full belief in the sufficiency of the plea, "Why, my grandfather used to swear ; my father used to swear ; and I mean to swear." Parental example, certainly, had influence here. However, our chief means for judging of men in common life, are found in their daily walk ; and if we can discover the tenor of the holding there, a reasonably fair estimate can be made. It is ardently hoped that in the foregoing pages the attempts to elucidate traits, have not been altogether unsuccessful, nor the lessons attempted to be enforced, entire failures. The reply of Rev. Mr. Mottey, the old Lynnfield minister, to one of his complaining parishioners, who called him "odd" was shrewd as well as witty : "Yes," said he, "I set out to be a very good man, and soon found that I could not be without being very odd."

> "God gives to every man,
> The virtue, temper, understanding, taste,
> That lifts him into life, and lets him fall
> Just in the niche he was designed to fill."

So says the poet ; but observation would pronounce this predestinarian sentiment more poetic than true ; at least, if it be taken in the broad sense that the adjoining lines represent :

(285)

> " To the deliverer of an injured land,
> He gives a tongue to enlarge upon, a heart
> To feel, and courage to redress her wrongs.
> To monarchs dignity, to judges sense,
> To artists ingenuity and skill."

The great body of mankind fall into niches but poorly fitted for them, and become entangled among cares and vexations that cramp and enervate their very souls

It is believed that in the foregoing pages, abundant evidence will be found that Lynn has produced her full share of worthies in the different walks of life. True, perhaps, she is not able to number among her children any specially illustrious examples in statesmanship, philosophy, or literature; but on a slightly lower level she can firmly stand. The writer has much enjoyed the companionship of the genial ones with whom he has trudged along the historic way; and will feel disappointed if the reader has not likewise been pleased. It is always a pleasant road that is travelled with agreeable companions.

Here and there suggestions have been made, not always in the direct line of narrative, which it is hoped will not appear obtrusive; at all events, devotion to supposed duty, and innocency of purpose, will be the excuse if one seems necessary. Any kind of a history ought to embrace something more than a mere narration of past events. And when treating of individuals, an author's preferences, sympathies, or prejudices, should never lead to invidious condemnation nor to such a tender veiling of imperfections as to conceal true characteristics.

Perhaps the reader may have occasionally noticed in the foregoing pages an item which appeared to him to relate in no special manner to the history of Lynn. But he will find such subservient to the general purpose. It may be asked, What has the appearance of a comet, a dark day, or any similar natural phenomenon to do with the history of a town? — a question rather cavilling than comprehensive; for is it not true, for instance, that the last comet or eclipse visible here, or the "yellow day," belonged as much to Lynn as any other place? It is often as impossible to clearly set forth a matter or elucidate a principle, without a seeming divergence for illustration or comparison, as it is to gather the rarest flowers without an occasional detour.

Nearly fifty years ago, as will be perceived by the date of the appended Prospectus, Mr. Lewis and the writer proposed issuing a volume of selections from Lynn writers ; and the reason why the project was not consummated is not now clearly recollected. Attention, however, is here called to the matter, in the hope that the "labor of love" will yet be accomplished. If some one of the gifted coterie now among us, whose literary electric lights are trimmed and burning, would pursue the plan, they would perform a work to which in after years they might recur with much satisfaction, and for which future generations would be thankful — even if they did not receive a commensurate pecuniary return. The design was to have nothing appear that was not the production of a native ; but that might, of course, be modified if deemed expedient. Our prospectus had not been long before the public, when the "Boston Book" was announced ; and in that, very little discrimination as to natives was observed ; indeed it almost seemed as if merely passing through the city entitled a writer to a place. The Prospectus alluded to, tells its own story, and is as follows :

WILD FLOWERS AND SEA-SHELLS : *Being a Selection from the Writings, Poetical and Prosaic, of Natives of Lynn : embracing the whole period of its History.* Edited by ALONZO LEWIS and JAMES R. NEWHALL.

During the period embracing the history of this town, there have from time to time appeared among us, our fellow-citizens are all aware, those of either sex, who were justly looked upon as endowed with mental qualities far above the ordinary standard — those who have shone as stars of the first magnitude in our little commu- nity, and who, haply, under more auspicious circumstances, would have been hailed as brighter lights to a more extended sphere ; — but who have yet passed from among us, leaving a few gems only scattered in their path to the tomb, as memorials of the peculiar favor of their God ; — leaving here a few *Flowers* gathered from the dark glen or the sunny height, and there a little glittering cabinet of *Sea-Shells* gleaned from the romantic shores of their own loved home.

. It is the object of the editors to gather up these fragments and select from among them such as they esteem most worthy of preservation ; adding a series of articles, original and select, from the writers of the present day. It is not their aim to gain any thing in a pecuniary point of view ; they ask only remuneration for their actual expenses, deeming the pleasure of presenting the little volume to their fellow-citizens sufficient reward for all their toil. It is believed that the work will also be interesting beyond the immediate sphere of its publication, as the interests and sympathies of this town and those around her have ever been most strongly united ; — together have they toiled through the darkness of by-gone years, and together have they arrived upon the sunny lands of prosperity.

The Prospectus was dated July 15, 1835 ; and the work was to have been an 18mo of about 250 pages, at $1 per copy.

The facilities for travel have now become so great that almost every one, high or low, must have an annual vacation tour. The vacation itself, which a few years ago was hardly thought of by any save a few of those in the so called upper walks of life, the more wealthy and unoccupied, is now deemed almost indispensable by every one above the rank of day laborer, who of all others would seem most in need of an occasional temporary intermission. None will deny that one of the best purposes to which spare pecuniary means can be devoted, is travel for the improvement of mind or body ; and for reasonable self-gratification, too ; but when undertaken for the inferior object of genteel show or vain boasting, its usefulness is not apparent. What are balls, and banquets, and all such entertainments and revels in comparison with right-purposed travel ? And thanks be to those who invented these modern ways and means which enable us at so little expense of time and money to secure the benefit.

There is the "bridal tour," which every young couple must take on being joined by the silken bonds ; and fortunate it may be if the first disagreement doesnotarise on the question of where and how long it shall be. There is the clergyman's vacation tour which the poor parish as well as the rich is expected without a murmur to accord and further ; for he must have rest and change of scene, although it may happen that the new scene be a niche wherein he is providentially detained to preach a few sermons at extra pay, or, haply, under the same mysterious ordering, become the unforewarned recipient of a call to an improved settlement. There, too, is the schoolmaster's vacation and tour. Well, the faithful teacher is worthy of consideration and esteem though it may be that more hearts swell with joy at his departure than at his return. But we need not further particularize.

Towards Europe the faces of many excursionists are set ; the land where, amid the historic scenes, the depositories of art and learning, and under the stimulation of buoyant inquietude, and renovating airs, the vigor and elasticity of body and mind, diminished by the onerous duties of home, may be restored. In our Annals under date 1871, it will be found stated that four of the Lynn clergymen were then travelling in Europe. But the vacation excursion to the old countries is by no means confined to professional persons or to the wealthy. Lynn every season is largely, and we trust not unfavorably, represented abroad by numbers of her comely daughters and manly sons, who return refreshed, with sunburnt countenances, rosy descriptions, and declarations of unbounded satisfaction.

We have here in Lynn a full share of mutual benefit, benevolent, sanitary, and temperance organizations, as well as masonic, odd fellow and military. Various companies for the supply of material wants, we also have, working for the good of the people and profit of themselves. Then there are various clubs and associations for discussion and social entertainment, of a character deserving well of an intelligent and hospitable community. In them assemble the city statists and savants who put to rights the great matters of public concern and the smaller interest of private life. But whether, if the ghost of Johnson should swagger in at a formal club meeting, he would imagine himself again in the company of his friends and compeers — of Burke, Reynolds, Garrick, Sheridan, "Goldy" the favorite, and those other glowing lights of the time, who shed such lustre upon statesmanship, legal erudition, literary and art criticism — he would be inspired anew, astonished, or diverted, no lesser mind than his is competent to determine.

But after all our boasted privileges, inventions, progress, and attainment — after all the revelations in philosophy, science, and mechanics — after all our rail-roads, steam-driven machinery, telegraphs, and electric lights — are there better, wiser, or nobler men and women — better rulers, statesmen, or philanthropists — better fathers, mothers, or children — than there were in the days of yore? Why, no, probably not. Mankind preserves about the same old average and very likely always will. Yet, to come down to our own limited case, there appears reason for congratulation in that the great rank and file of the community are at this day in a physically better condition than at any former period; better fed, clothed, and sheltered; better provided with the necessaries and conveniences of life. And would it were possible to say the same of all civilized humanity; yes, and likewise of all benighted, barbarous, and savage.

The ancient history of the land we occupy is a sealed book, never probably to be opened; no research has given any satisfactory account of what transpired here, in ages past. The sacred beams

19

that lighted up the Holy Land — the sombre twilight that glimmered through old Egypt's gloom — the dreamy scintillations of the pagan realms — the lustre of the old mythology that so adorned the classic lands — shed no radiance here; no, not even the rugged surges of an Ossian's song tell of the achievements of the unknown people. The red 'men had some characteristics now found among no other people; but the race was not one to make an impression on the world's destiny; and so they have passed away, leaving scarcely a footprint behind.

What civilized nation has so little of a past history as ours? We have none of the stirring episodes that so enliven the old world chronicles; no crusaders with their romantic and sentimental bravery; no knight-errants with their decorative justice and ideal honor; no troubadours with their songs of valor and love's enchantments. No, none of these; our knowledge thus far is of stern and hard realities. And are we not still a nation without a name — a family of near forty, each separately called, but collectively with no name indicating consolidated nationality? In view of the great centralizing achievement of the civil war ought we so to remain? O, give the nation a name.

The changes that have been steadily going on since the day when the Ingalls brothers and their sturdy companions struck the first blows for civilization within these borders, have attained to what we now behold — a fair city, with a population we would fain believe, as virtuous and as happy as is any where to be found. And could those old worthies return to re-traverse the hills and plains over which they once trod, haply with misgiving hearts, what would be their feelings. And could the few Indians they found here return in their company, what mad antics would they display, and what frenzied ejaculations and resounding whoops would they utter, as they beheld their old trapping thickets and open hunting grounds occupied by stately buildings and the flaunting insignia of a life never conceived of in their wildest dreams.

But there are some things that in the great cycle of ages do not change. The sun, the moon, and the bright retinue of stars which looked complacently down upon the land in the far-off days of forest silence and shadows, now look down with the same complacency upon our own thronged streets rife with the glittering appointments of trade, and flanked by shrines for ghostly worship, and the worship of mammon as well. And the restless ocean, too, rolls up its storm-driven billows against the rocky battlements with the same wild rhythm that it did when the lonely skin-clad red man stood upon the trembling cliff and beheld advancing with the coming blasts the misty giants of the spirit land. . . . Here we must pause.

Whether the writer will ever again travel along the historic way in the goodly company he has so much enjoyed, cannot now be known. The generations have passed on in their silent march to the bourn whence none return ; and in the common course of events he must soon join them — soon bid an everlasting adieu to all here, and lie down with the great company now at rest :

> "That silent company
> Which far outnumbers all upon earth's face."

FIRST BURYING-GROUND IN LYNN.

MAYORS OF LYNN.

In the Chapter of Biographical Sketches, appear the names of all the Mayors of Lynn, from the adoption of the City Charter, to 1882, with fac-similes of their signatures. But it is so convenient for reference to have them all arranged together, with a statement of their terms of office, that they will be here given in chronological order. The autographs, too, will be re-inserted, as it is believed that the little space required cannot be filled in any way more acceptable.

By the original Charter the municipal year was made to commence on the first Monday of April; but by an amendment which took effect in 1855, it was changed to the first Monday of January.

1850 and 1851, GEORGE HOOD.

1852, BENJAMIN F. MUDGE.

1853, DANIEL C. BAKER.

1854, THOMAS P. RICHARDSON.

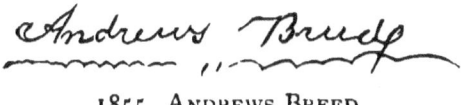

1855, ANDREWS BREED.

1856 and 1857, EZRA W. MUDGE.

1858, WILLIAM F. JOHNSON.

1859 and 1860, EDWARD S. DAVIS.

1861, HIRAM N. BREED.

1862, '63, '64, and '65, PETER M. NEAL.

1866, '67, and '68, ROLAND G. USHER.

1869 and 1872, JAMES N. BUFFUM.

1870 and 1871, EDWIN WALDEN.

1873, '74, '75, and '76, JACOB M. LEWIS.

1877 and 1878, SAMUEL M. BUBIER.

1879 and 1880, GEORGE P. SANDERSON.

1881 and 1882, HENRY B. LOVERING.

INDEX.

(295)

WITT'S ROCK.
(Now called Lover's Leap.)

INDEX TO PICTORIAL ADDENDA.

OLD TIME SHOEMAKERS AT WORK.   [*See Page* 316.]

PICTORIAL ADDENDA.

A few closing pages may, without doubt to the acceptance of the reader, be devoted to a limited number of pictorial illustrations, such as cannot fail, in a manner clearer than words, to elucidate certain matters pertaining to our history, which it is well not to overlook. It is interesting to compare one period with another; and not only interesting but highly useful; for by such means we are enabled to discern what progress has been made — upward or downward. We need no Shakspeare or Hogarth to demonstrate that "Progress" may be pictorially represented. The intelligent reader will not be at a loss to perceive our purpose in the character and arrangement of the engravings. Most of the subjects have at least been alluded to in the foregoing pages; and each cut will be accompanied by such remarks or catch-lines as may seem necessary for a full understanding.

THE FIRST MEETING-HOUSE.

This graphic little illustration was in fact drawn for the first meeting-house in Boston; but it can hardly fail to answer as well for the first in Lynn — that in which the venerated Whiting so long ministered, and that, too, in which the stirring voice of Cobbet so frequently resounded. The fiery Hugh Peters, also, though minister of the church in the neighboring settlement of Salem, no doubt often appeared within those unadorned walls, and by his rugged eloquence and undaunted zeal in confronting every approach of tyranny towards these shores, did much to inflame

(311)

the patriotism of the little flock of toilers who gathered there ;
little dreaming that that generation would not pass away ere his
own severed head would be mounted on London bridge as a
ghastly warning to all who dared to labor for the subordination
of regal claims to human rights. We do not know the precise
date at which this humble house was reared. The first minister,
Rev. Stephen Bachelor, came in 1632 ; but meetings had been
somewhere held before his arrival. The forlorn little structure stood in a hollow, on the east side of Shepard street, near
the present Summer street crossing ; and for protection against
the wintry blasts was placed partly under ground. Even dwellings were at first sometimes so placed, for the same reason.

The famous edifice so long known by the expressive though
rather inelegant sobriquet of " Old Tunnel," succeeded this
primitive structure. It stood on the latitudinal centre of the
bleak, unfenced Common, about opposite the entrance of the
present Whiting street, and its graceful proportions are here
faithfully delineated.

OLD TUNNEL MEETING-HOUSE. 1682 — 1827.

The Old Tunnel was built in 1682, and within its walls the ardent, almost ferocious patriot, Shepard, ministered for nearly forty years. There, too, Henchman, Treadwell, Parsons, Thacher, Hurd, and Rockwood, exercised their gifts. About it the military were wont to assemble, and the effect of the unrestrained flow of "strong water," at the booths erected against the very walls, was apparent in bloody noses and torn garments. After the removal of the house, the unique belfry was transformed into a cozy little shoemakers' shop, and remained a picturesque object, near High Rock, till destroyed by fire, on the 25th of March, 1849.

In 1837, the house of worship shown in the following engraving, was erected on South Common street, corner of Vine.

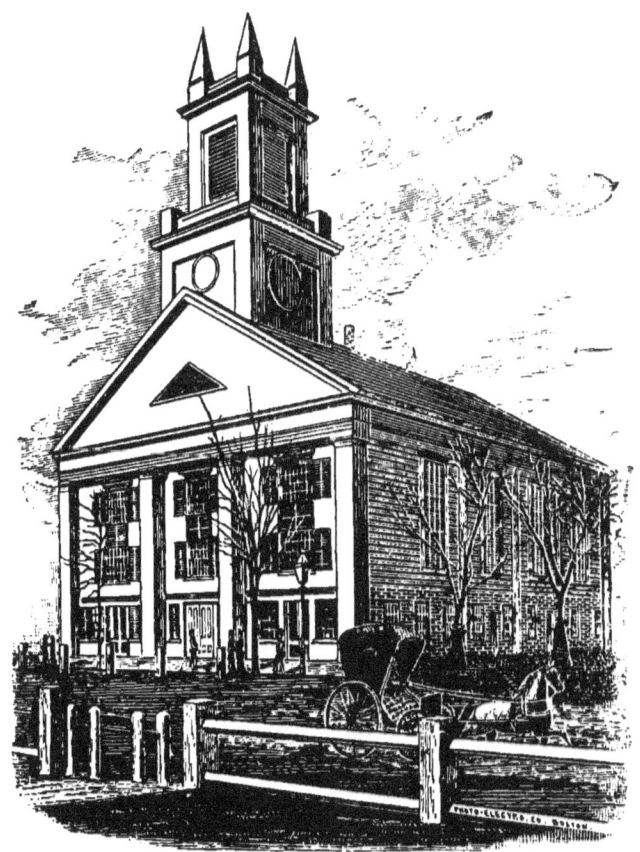

FIRST PARISH MEETING-HOUSE. 1837 — 1870.

This was the house in which the redoubtable Dr. Parsons
Cooke for about a quarter of a century exercised his high-keyed
elocution in fervid warning to his own flock, and his keen
power of vituperation in illustrating the blemishes in other Christian bodies. It was entirely destroyed by fire on the evening
of Christmas day, 1870. The site was soon occupied by the
much more stately brick edifice which is now the spiritual
anchorage of this ancient parish. And all will agree that if the
spiritual growth of this our elder worshiping body has been
commensurate with the architectural progress, its heavenward
advancement has not been inconsiderable.

The foregoing, in connection with the others referred to, are
sufficient to give a pretty good idea of the improvement in ecclesiastical architecture here. There are now several very fine
and costly churches in Lynn — St. Stephen's Memorial Church,
a picture of which may be found on a leaf preceding the title-
page being the most costly and in its features and appointments, perhaps the most perfect and beautiful. It was erected
by the late Enoch Redington Mudge at an expense of about
$250,000. By turning to page 260 the reader will find a view
of old St. Stephen's, the first Protestant Episcopal Church ever
built here.

Methodism took root in Lynn at an early period of its propa-
gation, and has continued to flourish, in what appears to be a
genial soil. The first service was held by Rev. Jesse Lee, in
December, 1790. It was commenced in the house of Joseph
Johnson, which stood on the north-east side of Market street, a
few rods from Essex, but for lack of room was adjourned to a
neighboring barn. This Johnson house was the same that many
of our elder people will remember as that in which "Old Gates,"
as he was called, had his law office for some time, and in which
Hilton and Newcomb subsequently kept their furniture store.

The first Methodist society was organized in February, 1791 —
about two months after Mr. Lee's coming ; and in about four
months after the organization, they erected a house of worship,
which is said to have been the first of the order in Massachusetts. This was succeeded, in 1813, by the one which now
makes a part of Lee Hall building, on Park square. The fine
brick structure on the other side of the same square, is the So-

ciety's present place of worship. The "Cradle of Methodism," as the old Johnson house has been called, is here depicted.

OLD JOHNSON HOUSE, MARKET STREET, LYNN.
The "Cradle of Methodism."

The buildings erected in Lynn, for municipal uses, till within a few years, were of a character almost deserving the epithet bestowed by some of our amiable neighbors — shabby. But we have now some of the finest and most costly in the state. Our present City Hall is the admiration of every citizen — excepting, perhaps, a few jejune tax-payers — and so are our school and engine houses. The City Hall appears on a page before the title, and here we place the old Town House, as in blushing contrast.

OLD TOWN HOUSE, LYNN.
Built in 1814 — Destroyed by fire in 1864.

Next we present an engraving of the first rail-road depot in
Lynn ; and a poor little one it was, as will be seen. It was
erected by the Eastern Rail-road Company as soon as they were
ready for travel, in 1838, and stood on the north-west side of the
track, occupying as much of the site of the present brick and
iron station, in Central Square, as its diminutive proportions
required. Half a dozen trains or so of small cars, not much
larger than old-fashion stage-coaches, and like them opening
only at the sides, passed up and down daily ; and the freight
transportation was but a fraction of what it now is. After ten
years' service it was in 1848 succeeded by the more capacious
and convenient but hardly more tasteful brick station, of which
a picture may be seen on page 40 ; and this latter, in 1872, gave
place to the well-appointed station that now adorns the Square.

FIRST RAIL-ROAD STATION IN LYNN.
Central Square, 1838.

For a hundred and fifty years shoe-manufacturing has been the
leading mechanical industry of Lynn, and till within a few years,
the work was done by hand ; the buildings required were small
and very common in their appointments ; but when ponderous
machinery was introduced substantial and capacious structures
began to appear. While the work was done by hand, the shoes
were cut out in small buildings occupied by the "bosses," and
thence taken by the "jours" to their own little shops, made
up and returned. These shops were to be seen in all quarters,
for they rather affected positions whence the incomings and
outgoings of neighbors could be observed ; and the sprightly
music of the lapstone and hammer was well-nigh ceaseless.
In the picture of Market street, which precedes the title-

page of this volume, several which adorned that thoroughfare are seen. But hardly any of these interesting historical
dots now remain. The great brick factories loom up triumphantly and the hoarse voice of the steam-driven machinery pro-
claims invention's conquest. The two following are fair specimens of our modern manufactories.

MODERN SHOE-MANUFACTORY, LYNN.
Exchange Street Block.

MODERN SHOE-MANUFACTORY, LYNN.
Sweetser Building, corner of Washington and Oxford Streets.

Allusions have been made in former pages to the style of dwellings common in earlier times. Of course the taste, means, and ambition of individuals had a controlling influence in given cases ; but yet there were certain characteristics marking the ordinary erections. In some instances the habitations, of the poorer classes especially, were placed partially under ground, for shelter from the cold ; while others, more desirous of the cheering sunlight, dotted the clearings and enlivened the acclivities ; but in most cases they were rude and unadorned ; not indeed more elegant than the one here represented.

AN EARLY DWELLING-HOUSE.

A little later on, we find the style of building adopted by many of the well-to-do folk like that represented by the following cut of the well-known Rebecca Nurse house.

REBECCA NURSE'S HOUSE.

In various parts of Lynn, now dilapidated specimens of the foregoing style are to be seen, and many have disappeared within the recollection of the writer. In our view of Market street, preceding the title-page, one or two may be observed. The Nurse house is famous in our county annals, and has a deeply touching history. Mrs. Nurse was a woman of many virtues and much beloved by her neighbors ; yet she fell a victim to the witchcraft infatuation, and was executed for the supposed crime, meeting her ignominious death like a true Christian heroine.

The gambrel-roof house soon appeared, though it is hard to see what special recommendation it had. Perhaps it was thought picturesque ; and it was somewhat so, when amid surroundings like those represented in the engraving here given, which was drawn from an ancient house in Norfolk county.

AN ANCIENT GAMBREL-ROOF HOUSE.

A neat example of this style may be seen on Marion street, in the historic Dr. Flagg or William Gray house. It was there that Dr. Flagg, a learned man as well as skillful physician and ardent revolutionary patriot lived ; and there, too, Lieutenant

Governor Gray, famed in his day as the most wealthy man in New England, was born. He was grandfather of Judge Horace Gray, at present an associate justice on the bench of the Supreme Court of the United States, and late chief justice of the Supreme Court of Massachusetts. Another and rougher example of this style of building is the "Uncle Jed" house, as it was called sixty or seventy years ago — on Boston street, corner of Kirtland. Our Market street view also exhibits a specimen.

As has been intimated, there was, in early times, here and there a residence widely differing from the generality, in costliness and elegance. One of the most notable, of whatever degree, in this vicinity, is the "old witch house," so called, still standing in Essex street, Salem, at the corner of North. There was, as builders say, "a good deal of work in it;" a fact made evident by the picture here given.

OLD WITCH HOUSE.

This is also sometimes called the Roger Williams house, and has an uncommonly interesting history, having been the residence, as early as 1636, of the persecuted divine just named — Roger Williams — who for his invading religious opinions and progressive political principles was compelled, during the dark days of winter, to flee for rest to the savage but yet more hospitable Narragansett country, beyond the colonial jurisdiction, where he founded the plantation that finally became the state of Rhode Island. The name "witch house," arose from the circumstance that beneath its roof some of the witchcraft examinations, in 1692, are alleged to have taken place.

But it is not expedient to travel much into places beyond our own borders for illustrative examples.

For a period reaching back far beyond the time to which any man's memory extends, the cheap, unadorned cottage, or plain, one-story dwelling, has been common in Lynn, with those of limited means. And since that poor man's godsend, the street rail-road, has been extended to the out-lying neighborhoods, such have sprung up in increased numbers. It is a grand thing for a man to own his home, be it ever so humble. It makes him a better citizen — more fixed in his habits, more contented, and more ambitious to maintain a creditable position. An example of this kind of habitation may be seen on page 166. But Lynn has homes of all grades, and is not deficient in the sumptuous class concomitant to wealth and gentility.

ELMWOOD.
Country Residence of the late Hon. E. R. Mudge.

The above is a picture of the beautiful summer home of the late eminent merchant and highly respected citizen, Hon. E. R. Mudge, and that in which he died, with such startling suddenness, on the first day of October, 1881. There are residences in Lynn

21

of probably greater cost, but none, it is believed, that indicate more refined taste or are more attractive in surroundings.

But our illustrated "annex" must not exceed due limits.

———

The rapidity with which the vacant territory of Lynn is being occupied, warns us that few years will elapse before most of the beauty and romance of her surroundings will be extinguished. There are competent artists among us who would be glad to apply their skill to the preservation of scenes which to us of this day are sources of so much enjoyment, and which by those of future generations would be viewed with ten-fold delight. But artists, as a rule, are not overburdened with this world's goods, and are seldom able to labor without the cheering hope of some pecuniary reward. And it may well be lamented that so few of those who would fain be reckoned among the wealthy and cultured have little taste for rich adornments of the character here alluded to, or any thought of employing a small amount of their substance for the gratification of those who in future years may occupy this goodly heritage.

On the three following leaves are re-produced — for they appear in our 1865 edition — illustrations which preserve at least a glimpse of what has been. They are from faithful sketches made for the writer, in 1864.

"Forest Place" has already been shorn of its most attractive features — groves and shady walks have disappeared, and high-ways and by-ways, with ambitious habitations, intruded. See page 33. And even the Point of Pines — recognizable by the house and flag-staff in the distance — has yielded to the march of improvement, and become an alluring resort. See page 244.

"Lynnmere" retains many of her old-time charms ; and when shorn of her natural beauties her interesting history will survive.

The view represented by the other picture, and our last, has undergone but comparatively little change. The point from which it was taken being a sort of rocky fastness has withstood the invading march of the destroyer. But the vacant lands in front are already penetrated by streets ; house-lots are staked out and dwellings appearing. The rear lands, however, remain almost unchanged ; and old ocean still perfects the view — old ocean, ever changing, ever grand, in sunshine and in storm.

VIEW IN LYNN—Forest Place, Residence of the late J. C. STICKNEY, Esq.

LYNNMERE.

BROWN & RUSSELL SC BOSTON

VIEW IN LYNN.—From Residence of James R. Newhall, Walnut Street.

SUPPLEMENT.

ANNALS.

1882.

The winter of 1881 and '82 was rather remarkable for the quantity of snow, and the long time the earth remained covered. A storm began on the afternoon of January 31, during which some eighteen inches fell. And on the next Sunday, Feb. 5, a snow storm occurred that was not for many years before exceeded in violence. The drifts in some places were for a time insurmountable; and services at several of the principal churches were omitted.

On the night of Feb. 15, a building on Munroe street, owned by Charles G. Clark, together with one or two others, was burned, causing a loss of some $20,000.

The Grand Army Coliseum, on Summer street, was dedicated March 15, with appropriate ceremonies. Its seating capacity is much greater than any other place of assembly hitherto erected here.

On the morning of the 15th of March, just before the time for workmen to assemble, a terrific steam boiler explosion took place in the rear of the Goodwin last factory, in Spring street. The engineer was killed, and several others badly wounded. One or two adjacent buildings were much damaged, and a piece of the boiler, weighing about 1,500 pounds, was thrown two hundred feet up into the air, and fell in Newhall street, seven hundred feet distant.

A fire occurred on the morning of April 22, at Houghton, Godfrey & Dean's paper warehouse, Central avenue, destroying property to the amount of $3,000.

Electric lights made their appearance here, in the spring.

At midnight, May 12, according to the weather reports, the thermometer, in Lynn and vicinity, reached a lower degree than in any other part of the United States; yet it was not so low as to be particularly noticeable.

Memorial Day, May 30, was observed as usual; address by Comrade James M. Tanner, of Brooklyn, N.Y.

Glen Lewis was consecrated, May 30.

Barnum's "greatest show on earth" visited Lynn, July 22. Some half a score of elephants appeared in the street parade. The giant elephant Jumbo and the nursing baby elephant were both members of the caravan. Some 25,000 persons attended the exhibition, and the amount of money received for admission reached nearly $11,000. The show consisted of a large collecton of animals, equestrian, acrobatic, and other circus and semi-dramatic performances. It was, no doubt, the grandest and most costly show ever in Lynn.

An explosion of a part of the underground equipment of the Citizens' Steam Heating Company, at the corner of Washington and Munroe streets, took place, July 27, injuring the street somewhat, and throwing up stones and gravel to the danger and fright of persons in the vicinity. And subsequently other explosions took place inducing an appeal to the city authorities for protection.

Nickerson's oil-clothing factory, in Swampscott, was burned August 4. Miss Emma Stone, employed in the establishment, lost her life, and the loss of property amounted to about $9,000.

An extraordinary drought prevailed during the latter part of the summer. Most of the crops about Lynn were absolutely ruined, the unripe fruit dropped from the trees, and much of the shrubbery and many of the trees had the appearance of having been exposed to fire blasts. Yet the springs and wells did not indicate any very marked deficiency of moisture somewhat below the surface. We had an uncommonly long succession of very warm days, with westerly winds and clear skies. And the peculiar effect on vegetation was, no doubt, attributable rather to the burning sun than the lack of moisture. The spring was backward by full two weeks, and the weather was on the whole anomalous, most of the year.

The Ocean House, in Swampscott, a summer hotel of considerable note, was destroyed by fire on the evening of September 6. It was a large wooden building, six stories in front and five in the rear. The loss was about $65,000.

In October, the fare to or from Boston was reduced to five cents on all the trains of the Narrow-gauge Rail-road, and on a part of those of the Eastern.

Mayor Lovering was, on the 7th of November, elected a member of the U.S. Congress — the second Lynn man ever chosen for that honorable position.

The morning sky for several weeks in October and November was adorned by a splendid comet which rose two or three hours before the sun, in the south-east. A very good representation of it, as seen from High Rock, is here given. The steeple of the Central Church, in Silsbee street, is seen on the right of the picture, and Phillips's Point, Swampscott, on the left Astronomers had wonderful stories to tell of this comet — its inconceivable speed and partial disruption as if by some collision.

COMET OF 1882.

1883.

Electric works established in Lynn. They rapidly developed into a very large business, the factory buildings occupying a good part of Centre and Federal streets. Lynn capitalists invested largely. A visible impulse was soon felt in real estate movements, and all the westerly part of the city, even to the woody highlands, was presently booming, to use a current expression of the time. The company was chartered in Connecticut, but soon became practically a Lynn enterprise, the plant being brought hither. Professor Elihu Thomson, an experienced electrician, was prominent in the business, and by persevering studies concerning the nature and application of electricity was able to add much to the substantial character and success of the business. Something more will be said of these works, in the proper place, further on.

The Sweetser building, corner of Central avenue and Oxford street, was burned Jan. 26. Loss, $81,000.

The Lynn Hospital, incorporated in 1880, was opened for the reception of patients, March 12. Facts concerning this beneficent institution appear elsewhere in these pages.

Col. Gardiner Tufts publishes, in the Lynn Transcript, during this year, a series of articles on the "Old Choirs of Lynn," embodying many interesting facts concerning the history of music here, anecdotes of early musicians, and well-timed suggestions.

Fales Henry Newhall, D. D., a minister of the Methodist denomination, of more than ordinary ability and scholarship, died at the Asylum for the Insane at Worcester, April 6. He was born in Saugus, June 19, 1827, graduated at the Wesleyan University, with the 1846 class, soon prepared for the ministry, and held prominent appointments, till overtaken by mental disorder from which he never entirely recovered.

The semi-centennial anniversary of the First Universalist Society was celebrated in the Nahant street church, April 29. A free banquet was served on the following evening.

The street railway to Peabody was opened for travel, May 15. Died in Lynn, May 17, Mrs. Lydia E. Pinkham, aged 64. She was known throughout the country and to some extent throughout the civilized world, as proprietor of a popular patent medicine. Her portrait adorned numerous publications in connection with advertisements of her specific. She was a woman of intelligence and excellent character.

May 30. The Memorial Day address, delivered in the Coliseum, was by George H. Patch, of Framingham.

The Soldiers' Monument, Swampscott, was dedicated June 16.

The Boscobel, probably the best appointed hotel ever established in Lynn up to this time, was opened in October. It was a part of the fine brick structure near the west end of the Common, known as the Arcade. But it was not successful in the intended line, and in four or five years ceased to rank as a hotel. The name was from Shakspeare.

1884.

John W. Skinner, for many years prominent in musical circles, died very suddenly, Jan. 4, aged 73. He rendered efficient service in church choirs, before the introduction of organs, by skill on the double-bass viol, trombone and other instruments.

A Grand Army fair closed, March 19. 29,550 tickets were sold.

Theophilus N. Breed died March 21, aged 78. He was for many years an active business man, chiefly in the line of hardware and shoemakers' tools. He was perseveringly inclined to making "improvements," sometimes much to his pecuniary detriment. His name will long survive in the picturesque and useful lakelet known as Breed's Pond, which he formed by building a dam across the valley at Oak street.

The annual session of the New England Methodist Conference began in the First Methodist Church, April 2.

A Lasters' fair closed March 25. 30,272 tickets were sold.

Miss Maria Monds died at the Home for Aged Women, April 4, aged 81. She was a native of London, Eng., but came to Lynn in 1836, and was the first teacher on the piano here, was an accomplished organist and at different times did duty in two or three of our churches. She also taught drawing and painting, and on the whole did much to advance those fine arts in Lynn. At the time she came there were but three pianos in the town.

John B. Tolman gives to the Young Men's Christian Association, in trust, an estate on Market street, valued at $30,000, the income to be expended for the suppression of the sale of intoxicating liquors. The trust was accepted, April 26.

May 30, Memorial Day. The address was by W.A.Simmons.

The new organization known as the Salvation Army appeared in our streets, June 4, marching to the music of tambourines and other instruments. This new order of religious enthusiasts, zealous as they were, made but few converts in Lynn.

Lightning struck in Chatham street, June 5, killing a lad of 12 years, named John Tyler, and considerably injuring two of his companions.

The city was divided into voting precincts in June.

The street railway to Marblehead was opened June 25.

Government commenced dredging Lynn harbor this summer.

Died, Oct, 23, at the great age of 99 years, Francis Johnson, a native of Ireland, but for many years a resident of Lynn.

Home for Inebriates, New Ocean street, established, Oct. 27.

The ladies open a grand fair for the benefit of Lynn Hospital, Dec. 2.

1885.

James M. Sargent died, Jan. 5. He was born in Haverhill, Jan. 20, 1810, and came to Lynn in 1829. Here he soon acquired a knowledge of shoemaking and for many years was a member of the craft. He held various offices of public trust and in all of them acquitted himself with marked fidelity. He was a member of the First Universalist Society, from its foundation, in 1833 ; was elected clerk at the time of the organization, and for more than fifty years, till the time of his death, continued in the office.

The Lynn National Bank was organized this year.

Several destructive fires occurred in the early part of this year. Jan. 11, by a fire in Henry A. Pevear's building, Washington street, there was a loss amounting to $3,337. By the burning of

Lucian Newhall's wooden building, on Central avenue, Feb. 17, there was a loss of $56,600. By a fire in C. B. Tebbetts's brick building on Willow street, Feb. 17, the loss was $3,760.

March 20. Lynn Associated Charities organized.

Rev. Dr. Pullman, as minister of the First Universalist Church, occupied the pulpit for the first time, April 12.

Col. Carroll D. Wright delivered the Memorial Day Address.

Trinity (Methodist) Church, Tower Hill, dedicated June 4. Church of the Incarnation (Episcopal) formally organized, June 9. St. Joseph's (Roman Catholic) Church consecrated, June 21.

Church bells tolled, July 23, in observance of the death of President Grant, and a special meeting of the City Council was held, at which resolutions of respect were passed. On the 8th of August commemorative services were held in the Coliseum, business being generally suspended and insignia of mourning displayed in many places.

Hon. John Batchelder died, Aug. 6, aged 80. He was born in Topsfield, but came to Lynn when about twenty-five years of age, and took the position of teacher of the fifth ward grammar school, which position he held till 1854. He was then elected to the State Senate, and by re-elections remained in that body for two other terms. He also held positions in our municipal government, and in every place performed the duties with promptness and fidelity. In 1857 he was again in harness as a teacher; but in 1869 he bade a final adieu to the profession, being then appointed postmaster. The latter office he held till 1877. The incipient moulding of many a worthy character may justly be attributed to him.

Died in London, Eng., Aug 17, Minot Tirrell, aged 55. He was for many years a well-known resident of Lynn, though not a native. To his enterprise and wealth the westerly section of the town especially was greatly indebted for substantial improvements. The first building of the electric works, the Boscobel, the Mildred Range, and a large number of other structures are examples of his liberal expenditure and enterprise. Indeed he gave an impetus to the business of our western section, that cannot fail to be long felt. He studied law and was admitted as a regular practitioner, but did not entirely or for any long time apply himself to the duties of a profession that was not probably congenial. He had generous and kindly traits, and considerable literary taste, but unfortunately possessed a temper that was at times almost uncontrollable, a circumstance that detracted from his social popularity. His remains were embalmed and reached Lynn, Sept. 8.

The large brick building, owned by Lucius Beebe and Son, Western avenue, corner of Federal street, occupied as a glove-kid and morocco factory, was burned Sept. 3. Loss, $75,500.

Corner stone of the Church of the Incarnation laid, Sept. 25, Bishop Paddock delivering an appropriate address.

A heavy thunder storm, Oct. 3, flooded several business places in and near Munroe street, and delayed railroad trains.

Lynn Shoe and Leather Association organized, Oct. 9.

Horse car line through Washington street opened, Nov. 30.

1886.

Died in Lynnfield, Jan. 17, Rev. Jacob Hood, aged 94. He was a school teacher in early life, of a thoughtful, serious turn of mind and always much respected. He belonged to the old Hood family of Lynn and Nahant.

Benjamin A. Ward, a well-known citizen, was, on the night of Feb. 1, attacked by three highwaymen, who severely assaulted him and robbed him of eighty dollars and a gold watch. He was on his way home from his office in Central square, and the attack was made on Chestnut street. One of the robbers, named Timmins, was soon arrested, and in due course of law sentenced to the state prison for fifteen years, where, in about two years, he died. The two others were convicted in New York of prior offences and sent to Sing-Sing prison, each for fifteen years.

An unusual overflow of the water courses took place in and about Lynn during February, caused by the falling of abundant rains on the frozen ground. Meadows were changed to lakes and in some localities basements were abandoned and boats called into use. The Sluice pond gate was opened, February 13, to save the dam.

The Lynn Daily Item and the Daily Bee, newspapers that had before been published at one cent per copy, raised the price to two cents, March 1.

Mechanics' Exchange formally opened, April 1.

Grand Army building, Andrew street, dedicated, April 21.

St. Stephen's chimes rang for the first time, April 25, Easter day. This was the first set of bells Lynn ever had.

Hon. Josiah C. Bennett gives to the Lynn Hospital the entire amount of his year's salary as Senator — $652.

Rev. George A. Crawford delivered the Memorial Day address, in the Coliseum, May 31.

There was a rowing regatta in Lynn harbor, June 19.

Lynn contributed $2,060 for relief of the sufferers by the destructive earthquake at Charleston, S. C., Aug. 31. And St. Stephen's Church sent a separate donation of $77 towards repairing the shattered tower of the venerable St. Michael's.

On the 25th of September Capt. Martin V. B. Stone of Swampscott received an ovation in consideration of his triumph in the race for the America's prize cup between the yacht Mayflower under his command, and the English yacht Galatea, under command of Lieut. Henn. A gold watch, bearing an engraved representation of the yacht, was presented.

Nov. 22, the day on which ex-President Arthur was buried, marks of respect were shown in Lynn by the closing of public offices, raising flags at half-mast, and the execution of a dirge on St. Stephen's bells.

The religious Society of the New Jerusalem (Swedenborgian) was formed this year. The French Catholic Church was also organized.

1887.

On Thursday evening, Jan. 13, Washington Irving Bishop gave an exhibition of his power of "mind reading," in Music Hall, to an intelligent though rather small audience. A somewhat pretentious circular had heralded his coming, giving accounts of his marvelous success before sovereigns and nobles in Europe. But it did not appear that his feats were more astonishing than those of some others of humbler pretension who had from time to time appeared here as illustrators of "mental science."

A successful fair was held by Post 5 of the Grand Army, commencing Feb. 15. The net proceeds amounted to $8,623.48.

On the 25th of February, President Cleveland sent to the U. S. Senate a message vetoing the bill passed by Congress appropriating $100,000 for the erection of a public building in Lynn, chiefly for postoffice accommodation. The President's reasons were generally viewed with candor though considerable disappointment was felt.

On the 28th of Feb. the enthusiastic revivalist, "Sam Small," commenced a series of meetings in the First Methodist Church. They were well attended, and closed March 6. Honest seekers after good, and others from idle curiosity were there.

Henry A. Breed, a well-known citizen, died April 15, aged 86. He was a descendant from the early Lynn settler, Allen Breed, and a son of Thomas A. Breed, for many years onward from 1813, landlord of Lynn Hotel, which, under his management, attained an enviable reputation. Henry A. commenced his active business life about 1819, did a great deal in the building line, and was zealous in forwarding improvements of almost every kind. Being of a sanguine and somewhat credulous turn, and withal attracted by projects of a speculative character, he had serious business ups and downs ; the finality being of the latter sort. But he always maintained the respect and good-will of his fellow citizens by his genial manners, readiness to aid the unfortunate, and other good qualities. His business prostrations were undoubtedly sometimes attributable to over-confidence in his own ability to "read" those with whom he dealt ; but more

often in the ability of those others, not half as honest as he, to
" read " him. He was one of the founders of the Second Congregational (Unitarian) Society, and was a devoted member till
his death.   He was for many years a member of Mount Carmel
Lodge of Freemasons, and likewise an accredited member of the
fraternity of Odd Fellows.

The Memorial Day address was delivered by Rev. Henry E.
Mott, of Newburyport, May 30.

Hon. James N. Buffum died June 12.   He was for many
years a marked character among us ; bright, busy, of positive
opinions, readiness of expression, great perseverance and withal
of kindly sympathies and benevolent instincts.   He was born in
North Berwick, Me., May 16, 1807, and was what is usually called
a self-made man.   And it would be doing violence to the general
sentiment of the community to intimate that he was not well
made.   He married, April 20, 1831, a daughter of Dr. John
Lummus, and by her had three daughters, two of whom survive
him.   He was twice Mayor — 1869 and 1872 ; and likewise
served a term in the Legislature.

The Robert E. Lee Camp of Confederate Veterans, of Richmond,Va., visited Post 5 of the Grand Army, Lynn, June 18.   A
banquet was held in a capacious tent on the Common, and the
most fraternal feeling was manifested among those who had
met as antagonists on the battle field.   It was an occasion of
much more than ordinary interest.   Col. Allen G. Shepherd
acted as Chief Marshal.   A delegation of Post 5, 160 in number,
left Lynn, July 1, on a return visit to the Confederate Veterans,
and after an absence of eight days reached home, on the whole
well pleased with their excursion.

On the 8th of July, the old mill on Saugus river, at the Boston
street crossing, was burned.   This was a famous mill, for generations, and did faithful service as a grist, snuff, and spice mill.
More especially did its product in the shape of Childs's chocolate
become an admired article the world over.

On the 3d of August the Mayors of several Massachusetts cities
visited Lynn by invitation of Mayor Hart.   The Mayors of Boston, Brockton, Chelsea, Fitchburg, Gloucester, Haverhill, Lawrence, Lowell, Newburyport, Northampton, Somerville, Waltham
and Worcester came.   The conclusion of the day's entertainment
was a drive to Nahant, and a banquet at the Bass Point House.

Died, Aug. 7, at his home in Summer street, Hon. Edward S.
Davis, aged 79.   He was a native of Lynn, and a descendant
of Rev. Stephen Bachelor, the first minister.   There was a
marked difference between Mr. Buffum, just spoken of, and Mr.
Davis, the one being bold, aggressive and sometimes even defiant ; while the other was quiet and unassuming, possessing
indeed those amiable characteristics that are often mistaken for

timidity. But each had the respect of his fellow-citizens in a large degree, and each in his own sphere did much that was highly appreciated. Mr. Davis had a discriminating literary taste and accumulated a large library. He was considerably in public life ; was four years President of the Common Council, and two years Mayor. He likewise for a term represented the town in the Legislature. In religious sentiment he was long and firmly attached to the Episcopal Church, and probably did more than any other to plant the Church in the once rather uncongenial soil of Lynn. The resolutions of respect passed by the various bodies, literary, benevolent and religious, with which he was connected, fully attested to the high esteem in which he was held. Mr. Davis was happy in his domestic relations. On the 26th of March, 1835, he was united in marriage with Elvira, daughter of Capt. Nathaniel Newhall, and she survives him. They had no children.

The newly-established " Labor Day " was first celebrated here, September 5.

By a fire on Lamper's wharf, Sept. 11, nineteen horses perished.

A notable ceremony took place in St. Mary's (Roman Catholic) Church, Oct. 18, namely, the investment of Rev. Patrick Strain with the title and insignia of Monsignor. He had been a faithful and laborious minister of the Church here, for nearly forty years, having commenced in January, 1851. His labors had been wonderfully successful and well deserving the honor conferred. An approved writer, in giving an account of the ceremony, said : " At the present time, in the very townships where Mgr. Strain labored for years without a coadjutor ten hard worked priests administer to the wants of the faithful. And now this priest of 65 autumns and 37 years of relentless struggle, begins to reap the golden harvest of his arduous labors. He is made a Permanent Rector, by order of the late Council of Baltimore, with the approbation of his venerable Archbishop. Again we find him raised to the dignity of Missionary Apostolic of the Holy See, and to-day he has received officially the purple of a Roman prelate with the title of Very Reverend Monsignor, the first resident priest of New England thus honored."

The French Catholic Church — St. Jean Baptiste — on Franklin street, was consecrated Dec. 4. The edifice cost $26,500.

1888.

The Camera Club was formed early this year. They soon began to exhibit marked progress in the fascinating art of photography, and their exhibitions were largely attended by highly gratified audiences.

The factory of Thomas Green and Company, Summer street, was burned May 15. Loss, $21,000.

Died, in East Walpole, Mass., May 22, Rev. Edwin Thompson, aged 78. He was a native of Lynn, and well-known, from early life, as an ardent advocate of temperance and an inflexible opponent of slavery. He was intelligent, affable in manners, candid in discussion, and impressed every one with a conviction of his entire sincerity. His parents belonged to the Society of Friends, but he swerved from the faith of his fathers, and was one of the first and most efficient workers in the foundation of the First Universalist Church, and became a minister of the order. His zealous advocacy of reformatory principles led to association with many of the leading philanthropists of the time, and the expressions of deep regard from such men as Wendell Phillips and the poet Whittier, were sufficiently indicative of the high place he held in the respect of the community.

Gen. Devens was orator on Memorial Day. 572 soldiers' graves were decorated.

John T. Moulton and Isaac O. Guild, two well-known citizens, erected this year, in the old burying ground, a stone to mark the grave of "Moll Pitcher," the renowned fortune teller. She died in 1813, and her grave had remained unmarked and almost unknown for seventy-five years. They ascertained the burial spot by one who was present at her funeral.

The Lynn Belt Line Street Railway Company was organized August 22.

The new armory of the military companies I and D, on Franklin street, was informally opened, on the evening of Aug. 24. The grand dedication ball took place Oct. 26.

The Lynn Theatre, Summer street, was opened Sept. 6, with the play "Lights of London."

The Highland Circuit Street Railway was opened Sept 4. Electricity was applied as propelling power, Nov. 19.

George Hussey Chase died at his residence, Newhall street, Sept. 5, aged 62. His natural abilities were above the average, and receiving a good education his mind became rapidly stored with varied and available information. He became an accomplished public speaker, and his stirring addresses were replete with good common sense and well-rounded periods. Indeed he was for many years known as "the orator of Lynn." By President Lincoln he was appointed postmaster, and held the office eight years. For years he was a participant in the management of our municipal affairs ; was a member of the Legislature ; and in 1880 was appointed deputy collector of customs, in which position he remained till his death. In social life he was attractive ; and in his latter years, having visited other lands, was able to give descriptions that were keenly relished by those who had an opportunity to listen to his graphic details and shrewd deductions.

St. Luke's (Methodist) Church was dedicated October 28.
Hon. William F. Johnson died at Nahant, Nov. 24. He
was born on Nahant, then a part of Lynn, July 30, 1819, and
was a son of the peninsular patriarch, Caleb Johnson, who
was also born there and lived to about the age of ninety.
The early education of Mr. Johnson was somewhat limited,
so far as book instruction was concerned, but his quick apprehension and taste for reading, his penetrating examination
of current subjects, and patient inquiry into the wherefore of
things, soon placed him among the most intelligent. For the
wear and tear of mercantile life he soon seemed to discover
that he was not well adapted, and hence, as soon as circumstances permitted, accepted more quiet and congenial employment. For many years he was Secretary of the Lynn Mutual
Fire Insurance Company, and during his official period that
institution lost nothing of its high reputation. But his daily
duties at the desk did not prevent his cordial participation in
the benevolent, reformatory and social movements of the day.
The Hospital and the Home for Aged Women, especially,
had his sympathy, his labors, and his contributions. In municipal affairs Mr. Johnson bore a conspicuous part for many
years, always doing faithful service. He held the office of
Mayor in 1858, fulfilling the duties with credit and ability.
He was genial in manners, a faithful friend and the enemy
of none; and one of the attractive few who are welcome
every where. In religious affiliation he was for some time a
member of the Baptist connection, but in middle life became
a member of the Episcopal church, and remained steadfast in
that communion to the end of his life. For a number of years
he was a warden of St. Stephen's, and on the organization
of the Church of the Incarnation, was elected to the same
office in that body. He did much to promote the growth of
his beloved church in Lynn. Mr. Johnson was thrice married, and left a widow and four children. His funeral took
place on the afternoon of Nov. 27, from the Church of the
Incarnation.

Lennox's brick factory, Market street, with other buildings,
was burned, Dec. 22. Loss, $136,000.

J. W. Lewis & Co. of Philadelphia, publish their History
of Essex County, 2129 pages, large quarto. The Lynn
chapters occupy 127 pages. The first volume contains some
thirty fine portraits of business and professional citizens, accompanied by biographical sketches.

1889.

John W. Berry was appointed Judge of Lynn Police Court, Jan. 23, succeeding Rollin E. Harmon who had resigned to take the office of Judge of Probate for Essex County.

Philip Pitts, a police officer of Saugus, died in Lynn Hospital, Jan. 26. He was on duty in Cliftondale on the night of Jan. 23, when he was shot by a burglar, the wound proving fatal.

On the evening of Jan. 30, the planing mill near the southerly end of Commercial street was burned, with one or two smaller buildings. Loss about $25,000.

Josiah F. Kimball died in Boston, Feb. 3, aged 68. He was a native of Ipswich, but came to Lynn in early life and learned the printing business in the *Freeman* office, which business he followed many years, as printer, publisher, and editor. Few men were better known or more highly respected. He was careful that any paper issued by him should be what is known as a "clean paper" — free from sensationalism, unkind personalities or erroneous statements of any kind. His literary taste was far above mediocrity, and he wrote many poems, largely of a humorous character, that were widely circulated and deservedly praised. He held various public offices; served in the Legislature; and for several years held a position in the Boston Custom House. He was nurtured in the old New England orthodox faith, but in manhood became a devoted member of the Episcopal Church. His funeral took place from St. Stephen's, which had long been his spiritual home. His first wife was a daughter of County Treasurer Wade; and his second, who survived him, was a lady from Portsmouth, N.H. He had no issue.

The Light Infantry and Wooldredge Guards left Lynn for Washington, March 2, to take part in the ceremonies of the inauguration of President Harrison, and returned, March 7, much pleased by their trip and reception.

Died in Tyson, Vt., March 2, Lewis Josselyn, aged 83. Mr. Josselyn was a prominent figure in Lynn for a number of years. Editors are usually conspicuous members of the community; especially such editors as Mr. Josselyn — so alert, so ubiquitous. He was editor, proprietor and publisher of the "Lynn Bay State," a large and handsome weekly sheet, of pronounced Democratic principles. He was a vigorous writer and occupied a prominent place in the editorial fraternity of New England. Few persons connected with the newspaper press had a more just conception of the duties and responsibilities of an editor; and the spirit of fairness that characterised the trenchant emanations from his pen was worthy of imitation. He made an attempt, in connection with his son, to establish a daily "Bay State," but the golden day evidently had not arrived when every town, village and hamlet could rejoice in its daily service of news from every quarter of the globe, seasoned, in too many instances, with neighborhood gossip and social scandal — and so the attempt was given over. Mr. Josselyn was a native of Pembroke, Plymouth county. During his career he held various offices ; was at one time Clerk of the House of Representatives, and held positions in the Boston and Salem Custom Houses. He was what was known as a war democrat during the civil war, and fought vigorously with pen and tongue in the Union cause. The most daring partisan did not venture to call him a "copper head."

Hon. Edwin Walden died, March 12, aged 70. He was born here and educated in the public schools of Ward 6, of which Ward he was a native. For many years he was connected with the shoe business ; but in mature life was more especially known for his excellent management in public affairs. Though at times exhibiting strong party feeling, he always acted from settled principle and well-considered convictions. One so qualified, with such utilitarian views and forecast, could not fail of being closely identified with public affairs. In municipal matters, after serving in both branches of the Council, he found himself, in 1870, in the Mayor's chair, where he remained for two terms, doing the duties fearlessly and with the unfeigned applause of the most considerate and unprejudiced. But perhaps he was best known by his persevering and judicious labors as one of the moving spirits in the attainment of our now generous supply of pure water. The series of plans which have so favorably resulted are in a large degree attributable to his foresight, sagacity and perseverance. And it seems most fitting that the last-formed and most beautiful lakelet — Walden pond — should bear his name. He served in several State offices, with increasing reputation for devotion to duty and for promptness and vigor of action ; was a Representative and a Senator, and a commissioner in two or three important State projects. As President of the Boston, Revere Beach and Lynn Railroad, his services were apparent in the unvarying success of the corporation, notwithstanding the grave doubts and surmises that attended its inauguration. Mrs. Walden and five children survived the husband and father.

General Joshua L. Chamberlain delivered the Memorial Day address, May 30.

Lynn contributed something rising $5,000 for the sufferers

by the terrible disaster at Johnstown, Pa., that occurred May 31, by the breaking of the dam of the great reservoir 450 feet above the town and some 12 miles distant, at the upper end of the valley. The dam held a body of water covering 750 acres and of an average depth of 30 feet. From 4,000 to 5,000 lives appear to have been lost, and 2,500 houses destroyed. Estimates as to the loss of lives however, varied, some placing the number higher than 5,000. The place was substantially destroyed.

Died in Lynn, June 28, Maria Mitchell, for many years professor of astronomy in Vassar College, aged 70. She was known throughout the scientific world for her attainments, especially in astronomy. She was a native of Nantucket, and inherited from her father a love for scientific pursuits and power of application.

A sudden tempest arose about noon, July 23d, with vivid lightning and heavy thunder. Damage was done in some parts of the city by the heavy rainfall, and the lightning struck in several places. One of the electric cars was stopped by the melting of a wire.

The annual parade of the Essex County Odd Fellows took place in Lynn, Sept. 24. The weather was fine, and about 1,200 members marched in line. Many buildings were decorated.

A notable military parade took place in Lynn, Oct. 3d. The Fifth, Eighth and Ninth Regiments of Infantry, the First and Second Battalions of Artillery, the Second Battalion of Cavalry, Signal and Ambulance Corps, appeared and made an extended march through a number of our principal streets with several bands of music. The day was beautiful, and there was a large gathering of spectators. A barricade was thrown across Market street, near Liberty, and a feigned mob assembled to intercept the march of the troops. Four lines of skirmishers approached the barricade, and a gatling gun being brought to bear, the mob dispersed and the victors, clearing away the debris, marched on triumphantly. Evidently General Peach, the commander of the victorious forces, had a good conception of the manner in which a mob should be met.

The Walnut and Washington streets electric line of cars from the Myrtle street stable to Central square was opened October 3.

The U.S. General Convention of Universalists was held in Lynn, Oct. 22, and continued four days. More than a thousand delegates and friends attended.

American flags were raised on several of the public school buildings during November — on the Burrill, Nov. 4; on the Ingalls, Nov. 9; on the Shepard, Nov. 12. On the 15th, Post 5 of the Grand Army presented a flag to the Classical High School. By such means it was thought the youth would be more thoroughly imbued with patriotic sentiments.

At the State election, Nov. 5, our citizens for the first time had an opportunity to vote under what has been called the Australian system, a system which seems substantially to have been evolved by the genius of the Australians, and which enables the voter to ballot with the utmost privacy. It had marked success and was highly praised for its convenience, its secrecy, and its avoidance of confusion and excitement at the polls. To Elihu B. Hayes, a Lynn Representative in the Legislature, much of the honor of introducing the system was attributed; indeed he was called by his fellow legislators the father of the system in Massachusetts.

James R. Newhall was tendered a reception, at the City Hall, on Christmas, that being the day on which he completed his four score years. The Mayor presided.

A somewhat singular disease, under the French name *la grippe*, prevailed here, and indeed over nearly the whole world, during the latter part of the year. It seemed to operate differently in different constitutions. In some cases there was a loss of appetite, and a tired, languid feeling. In other cases it suddenly seized with severe pains in the head or back, with slight nausea. Very few escaped its attack in some way and to some extent. In many instances it proved to be the precursor of other diseases and not unfrequently terminated fatally.

The Great Fire. The greatest calamity that ever overtook Lynn in her whole history occurred on the 26th of November, of this year, 1889; that is, so far as loss of property was involved, though she was singularly fortunate in escaping loss of life or serious personal injury. We allude to what will hereafter be known as the Great Fire.

It was about noon, of a sunny day, that the fire broke out in the large wooden building on Almont street known as Mower's block. There was a pretty high wind, and in an exceedingly short space of time several of the adjacent buildings were in flames. It soon became apparent that our own fire department, single handed, would be powerless to control the conflagration; and therefore telegraphic despatches, asking aid, were hastily forwarded to Boston, Chelsea, Salem, Gloucester, Newburyport, and a number of other places.

CENTRAL SQUARE, LYNN — *Before the great Fire of Nov. 26, 1889.*
[Every building represented in the cut was destroyed.]

MOUNT VERNON STREET, LYNN — *Before the great Fire of Nov. 26, 1889.*
[The entire length of this fine street was burned.]

The despatches were responded to with the utmost alacrity, and the assistance thus promptly rendered added much to the ardor of our own firemen, as well as in itself being of great value. Within an hour or two several of the finest four or five-story brick business buildings were destroyed, together with many of inferior kind ; and still the flames raged. Four banks, namely, the First National, the Central National, the National Security, and the Lynn Institution for Savings, were soon out of doors ; so likewise were the three daily newspapers — the *Bee*, the *Item*, and the *Press*.

The area of ground burned over, including streets and squares, was thirty-one acres, and it was in the most central business part of the city. The total loss, according to the Chief Engineer's report, was $4,959,989.08, though the State Commissioner's report made the loss about $2,000 less. The insurance was stated at $4,133,516.67.

During the fire very commendable order was maintained, for the authorities, as a safeguard, promptly called out the military companies I and D of Lynn, and to these was added company H of Salem. A squad of twenty-five of the Boston police also appeared for duty.

The number of buildings destroyed was 334, some of them massive brick business structures, some wooden factories and some wooden dwellings. The various streets suffered in the loss of buildings as follows :

Almont street	11	Munroe street	4
Amity street	16	Sagamore street	25
Beach street	48	Silsbee street	6
Broad street	58	Spring street	18
Central square	17	Suffolk street	18
Exchange street	24	Suffolk street place	8
Farrar street	11	Union street	45
Mt. Vernon street	4	Washington street	21

Our active and efficient Mayor, Hon. Asa T. Newhall, was unwearied in his endeavors to mitigate the sufferings of those most severely affected personally by the calamity ; and all others of his official coadjutors worked with a will for the common good. The result was that immediate wants were speedily supplied.

There was a good supply of water, but it appeared that some of the transmission pipes were not sufficiently large for such an unforeseen emergency ; a fact that gave rise to the apprehension that there was a deficiency. Some of the suffering business men were on the alert even while the conflagration was pursuing its fiery course, to secure new quarters, that their business might be as little interrupted as possible. And it was wonderful with what composure they met the disaster and with what energy they set about repairing their damaged fortunes. Some even claimed that the fire would prove of positive benefit, by sweeping away a number of dangerous old wooden structures whose places would soon be occupied by those of modern style, safer and more con-venient.

After the fire, from various causes, chiefly, perhaps because land was cheaper, some manufacturers began to plan for locating in sections more remote from Central square ; in East and West Lynn, especially, railroad facilities being far better than they were at the time when business began to centre about the square.

Lynn always contributed liberally to relieve the suffer-ings of others by fire or flood — the fire at Marblehead and the flood at Johnstown, for instance. And when the great calamity overtook her, she in her turn received the sympathy and contributions of others. The bread that she had cast upon the waters, when she had it to spare, floated back in her time of need.

Lynn Woods. By referring to date 1881 of the Annals something may be found regarding the incipient movements in the laudable enterprise of forming a Free Public Park, embracing as many acres as possible of the romantic and eminently appropriate territory that lies along our northern border. The shady glens, rocky heights, towering trees, wild shrubbery, vagrant streams and tranquil ponds, all con-spire by their varied charms and historic connections to ren-der it most fitting for such a purpose. By a legislative act of 1882, cities and towns are enabled to take lands for public parks : and under that act Lynn has proceeded to appoint Park Commissioners and do such other things as are neces-sary to carry out what is evidently the ardent desire of the citizens — to possess a public ground that shall be worthy of the opportunity now presented, and enduring evidence of the taste, liberality and discriminating forethought of the people of this our day. Four beautiful ponds add their charms to the grounds, already secured, namely, Breed's, Birch, Wal-den and Glen Lewis. These measure in the aggregate three hundred and twelve acres. It is easy to see of what inesti-mable value the Park will be to future generations by keeping the great water-shed from which our supply comes free from contaminations that necessarily appertain to dense settlements.

The names of the first Board of Park Commissioners are : Philip A. Chase, (Chairman) ; Aaron F. Smith, C. H. Pinkham, Frank W. Jones, Benjamin F. Spinney.

Many of our people, it is probable, do not fully realize the value of our ponds for sanitary purposes as well as for picturesque beauty. Nor is it probable that a just conception of their number and extent is usually entertained. The principal ones, covering five hundred and nine acres and a half, are as follows :

Birch pond,	84 acres.	Gold Fish pond, .	1 1-2 acres.
Breed's pond,	64 "	Holder's pond, .	7 "
Cedar pond,	43 "	Lily pond,	4 "
Flax pond,	75 "	Sluice pond, . . .	50 "
Floating Bridge pond,	17 "	Walden pond, . .	128 "
Glen Lewis pond, .	36 "		

There assuredly is a growing desire in the community for the preservation of natural scenery ; and already associations have been formed in various places with a laudable purpose of giving intelligent direction to that desire. Lynn may well feel that in her Woods she is not only protecting and preserving most superb natural scenery, but is at the same time adding to her sanitary safeguards, and preparing a delightful field for the healthful enjoyment of old and young, rich and poor.

1890.

The members of the Lynn bar gave a banquet to James R. Newhall, Jan. 2, he having completed, on the previous Christmas day, his four score years, and being the oldest member of the bar, by years.

Zachariah Graves died Jan. 15, aged 70. He had been a member of the Common Council, a County Commissioner for nine years, and twice a Representative in the State Legislature. He was always trustworthy and conscientious.

January 17, the Lynn printers, as usual, celebrated the anniversary of Franklin's birth by a banquet, gustatory and intellectual.

The new building of the Camera Club was dedicated Jan. 23.

On Jan. 27 an explosion and consequent fire took place in a cement factory, on Summer street, causing damage to the amount of $3,000.

The modest little Primitive Methodist chapel, on Flint street, was dedicated Feb. 2.

Died, Feb. 10, Oliver Ramsdell, aged 74. He was an

active and useful citizen residing in Glenmere, in which precinct he was born; was a prominent Methodist and did much
for the society in his neighborhood; was a good deal in public life especially in the early days of Lynn under the City
Charter, during which time his good judgment and efficient
action availed much. He was a member of the first two
Common Councils.

About the middle of February the tides ran very high, insomuch that parts of old Beach street were submerged.

The first meeting in view of the establishment of a home
for aged men was held, March 13.

A dead whale, about 60 feet in length, was cast upon the
shore near Sliding Rock, April 26. And the next day another,
somewhat larger, was cast upon the Swampscott shore. They
soon began to emit offensive odors, and were speedily removed
to a rendering establishment. Multitudes gathered for a look
at the huge denizens of the deep.

The value of new buildings erected in Lynn during the
year ending May 1 was $1,078,975.

A supposed Indian skeleton was exhumed at Atlantic Ter-
race, May 23.

May 30, Memorial Day. The weather was fine and the
military parade quite imposing. Other appropriate exercises
took place during the day and evening. Hon. Myron P.
Walker was orator.

While Myron Smith, of Lynn, was driving on the Peabody
road, June 11, during a heavy shower his horse was struck
by lightning and instantly killed.

The first complete circuit by a Belt Line car was made on
the evening of July 3. A number of city officials and business men were by invitation passengers.

Independence Day was celebrated with rather more than
usual "pomp and circumstance." There was a long procession, with city officials, various societies in regalia and a fine
military escort. But perhaps the most striking feature was
the tradesmen's display, so full was it of the insignia of the
various crafts.

The price of ice, which has now become a necessity rather
than a luxury, was this summer much higher than usual; attributable, no doubt to the fact that the mild weather of the
preceding winter produced a much smaller crop than usual.

A reception was given to the new rector of St. Stephen's
Church, Rev. James H. Van Buren, July 14.

About five o'clock on the afternoon of July 25, a short but

violent cyclone visited a limited tract in and near Robinson street. An unfinished dwelling house into which a number of school children had rushed for shelter was demolished and a girl, aged 13, killed.

A rattlesnake four and a half feet in length was killed on Lynnfield street, July 31, thus indicating that those reptiles, so much dreaded by our ancestors, are not yet exterminated.

Between nine and ten o'clock on the morning of Aug. 2, a fire commenced on the premises occupied by G. F. Bartol & Co., and others, on Munroe street, and destroyed property to the amount of some $11,000. An explosion of gas was supposed to have been the cause. James E. Tarbox, assistant engineer, lost his life by suffocation.

On the 12th of August there was a great parade in Boston of "Boys in Blue," G.A.R. veterans of the civil war. Some 40,000 marched in line. The veterans from Lynn were conspicuous by their number, and roundly applauded for their excellent discipline. After their return home they elicited much praise and many thanks for their hospitality to visiting troops. Post 5 kept " open house," entertaining visitors from Washington, D.C., Virginia, Philadelphia, Albany and Missouri.

A great strike of morocco workers in August.

Died, Aug. 20, Darius Barry aged 77. He was a native of Haverhill, but came to Lynn in 1837. He was a morocco manufacturer, and did considerable business. Several of the larger manufacturers in the line, of later years, began service under him. He was a man of great independence of thought and freedom of expression, read much and well digested what he read. He had a poetic vein and occasionally contributed verses that did not fail to attract attention. And he had an abundance of mother wit, which sometimes exhibited itself in stinging sarcasm. He had, too, a wholesome contempt for those whose selfishness infringed on the rights of others. And this trait was curiously illustrated in a relation that found its way into the newspapers some years since, though I believe another name was in some instances substituted for his. It was of this tenor, though not always given exactly in these words: He entered a railroad car in Boston to take passage for Lynn. The car was quite full. But on one seat sat a man with a valise by his side, which Mr. Barry proceeded to remove preparatory to sitting down in its place. " But," said the man, " that seat is already taken ; the valise was left there by a gentleman who just stepped out, but will be back before we start." "Very well," said Mr. B. whose suspicions were awake, "I will take the seat and give it up when the claimant comes; and I will take good care of the valise, too, in the mean time." The train moved from the station and the gentleman did not return. "What a pity," said Mr. B., when they were well on the way, "that the gentleman lost his passage; but he shall not lose his valise, for I will see that it is put into safe custody so that he can recover it." "You need take no trouble," said the other, "I know the man and will take charge of it." "My dear sir," replied Mr. B., "you ought not to expect that. We are strangers, and I do n't know what your purpose is." But the valise is *mine*, let me tell you," vociferated the other, growing a little excited; "there is no other man to claim it; and I want you to give it up without further parley." "But," says Mr. B., "do you expect me to believe that? You said it belonged to some one who had just stepped out of the car; and how do I know but you want to purloin it. I can 't consent to be a participator, if that is your game." The result was that the valise was given in charge of an employee to take back to Boston for deposit among the uncalled for luggage; and the poor man, who ·undoubtedly was the owner, had to go back to the city to recover it. Whether Mr. B.'s lesson had any good effect on his future conduct is not known. Mr. Eugene Barry, son of Darius, became a large and successful manufacturer in the line so long pursued by his father. And he, too, contributed to our local literature many choice poems, some of which had a circulation far beyond our own bounds.

The new Police Station, on Sutton street, was occupied for the first time, Aug. 26. The cost of the building was about $43,000.

A supposed Indian grave was discovered at Mt. Gilead, in Lynn Woods, Aug. 29.

Labor Day, Sept. 1, was appropriately celebrated. The weather being favorable, the procession was unusually large, numbering some 4,000, composed chiefly of various trade organizations. There was a meeting on the Common, at which stirring speeches were made in the interest of labor. And a mid-day entertainment was provided for the children.

The name of old Beach street was changed to Washington, Sept. 8.

Benjamin Sweetser, a native and life-long resident of Lynn, aged 82, was killed by a rail-road train at the Market street crossing, Sept. 18.

Rev. Samuel B. Stewart, minister of the Unitarian Society, was given an evening reception in the church parlor, Oct. 6, it being the conclusion of the 25th year of his pastorate. There was a large attendance, many from other religious bodies taking the opportunity to show their regard for one so much esteemed.

There was a large gathering in Music Hall on Sunday evening, Oct. 12, to hear a discourse on the position and claims of labor and laboring people, by National Master Workman Powderly.

The corner stone of the new High School building, Highland Square, was laid Oct. 22, Mayor Asa T. Newhall delivering an appropriate address.

Died, Oct. 22, Mrs. Lydia Rhodes, widow of Amos Rhodes, a lady of culture and estimable traits. Her benevolence was strikingly apparent in her liberal legacies to humane and educational institutions. Perhaps her most notable gift was that of $20,000 for the erection of a chapel in Pine Grove Cemetery, to be called the Rhodes Memorial Chapel, in memory of her husband.

On Sunday morning, Oct. 26, the fly wheel of the Lynn Gas and Electric Light power station, Pleasant street, exploded, alarming the neighborhood and doing considerable damage to the building and other property.

Very high tides prevailed during the latter part of October, overflowing the marshes and at times impeding railroad trains.

Died at the Home for Aged Couples, Brooklyn, N.Y., Rev. Joseph Blaney Breed, aged 83. He was a younger brother of Mayor Andrews Breed, of Henry A. Breed, for many years one of the most enterprising business men here, and of Daniel N. Breed, also long an active business man here, but an early emigrant to California. For a short time before he reached his majority Joseph Blaney acted as landlord of old Lynn Hotel, then a very popular house. He was in his early years a zealous Unitarian, and did a great deal for the support of the Lynn Society in its infancy. But he changed his sentiments, and while still a young man, joined the Baptist denomination, and in that connection passed the remainder of his life. When he became a Baptist he gave up all thought of a business life and zealously applied himself to study for the ministry. In due time he was ordained, and had settlements, during his many years of clerical service, in several places. Though he may not have been especially brilliant in the pulpit, he was greatly esteemed for his many virtues, his zeal in every good cause, for his genial manners, and for his benevolent acts which were only limited by his means.

The new Loretz steam pumping engine, at the Walnut street station, was ready for use, Dec. 19. Its cost, with the connecting apparatus, was $50,000.

The total loss by fires in Lynn, during 1890, was $48,987.35.

As this year, 1890, completes forty years since the adoption of our City Charter, it may not be inappropriate to make a few comparisons illustrative of our progress in different departments during that period.

```
Population in 1850 . .  . . . . . . . . . . . . . . 14,257
Population in 1890 . . . . . . . . . . . .  . . . . . . . 55,727
```

VALUATION.

```
1850 — Real Estate, . . . . . . . . . . . .  $3,160,515
       Personal Estate, . . . . . . . . . .  $1,674,328
                                             ———————— $4,834,843
1890 — Real Estate, . . . . . . . . . . . .  $29,390,332
       Personal Estate, . . . . . . . . . .  $11,340,046
                                             ———————— $40,730,378
```

RATE OF TAXATION.

```
1850 — On every $1,000 . . . . . . . . . . . . . . . . .  $9.00
1890 — On every $1,000 . . . . . . . . . . . . . . . . .  $15.00
```

VOTERS.

```
1850 — Number of polls, . . . . . . . . . . . . . . .  3,251
1890 — Number of polls, . . . . . . . . . . . . . . .  17,003
```

APPROPRIATIONS AND RECEIPTS.

```
1850 . . . . . . . . . . . . . . . . . . . . . . .  $45,000.00
1890 . . . . . . . . . . . . . . . . . . . . . . .  $1,745,299.59
```

EXPENDITURES.

```
1850 . . . . . . . . . . . . . . . . . . . . . . .  $36,704.19
1890 . . . . . . . . . . . . . . . . . . . . . . .  $1,508,947.92
```

BANKS.

```
1850 — Lynn Mechanics, capital, . . . . . . . . $150,000
       Laighton, capital . . . . . . . . . . . $100,000
                Total capital . . . . . . . . . . . .  ———— $250,000
```

Also Lynn Institution for Savings.

```
1890 — First National, capital . . . . . . . . . . $500,000
       Central National, capital  . . . . .  . . . $200,000
       National City, capital . . . . . . . . . $200,000
       National Security, capital . . . . . . . $100,000
       Lynn National, capital  . . . . . . . . $100,000
                Total capital . . . . . . . . . . .  ————$2,100,000
```

Also two Savings Banks: the Lynn Institution for Savings and Lynn Five Cents Savings Bank.

And besides these there were the Lynn Safe Deposit and Trust Company, with a capital of $100,000; and the Security Safe Deposit and Trust Company, with a capital of $200,000.

RELIGIOUS SOCIETIES.

The number of religious societies in Lynn, in 1850, was 17, including that at Swampscott. The houses of worship were all of wood, and most of them hardly above what would now be called shabby.

The number of religious societies is now (1890) 36. Within a few years, marked progress has been made in the architecture of our houses of worship, so that Lynn now has several edifices of stone and brick that will compare favorably with any in the Commonwealth out of Boston.

Whether the religious tone of our community has been elevated or depressed during these forty years, is a problem. But it is generally conceded that the comparative attendance on public worship is somewhat less, in these latter days. The very general closing of the churches on the afternoon of the Lord's day, has opened the way for meetings in the public halls and other places for the discussion of all sorts of secular topics, thus diverting minds from religious subjects, and perhaps loosening the faith of many. Others, who are averse to seeking edification within doors, are inclined to spend the vacant hours abroad, in the woods, the fields or on the beaches.

LAWYERS.

The number of lawyers in Lynn in 1850, was 5. In 1890, we have 40, which certainly indicates a great increase in business or in a love for litigation.

PHYSICIANS.

The number of physicians in Lynn, in 1850, was 17. In 1890 we have 80. This can hardly be taken as indicating a decline in the healthfulness of the place, for such sanitary improvements and appliances have been made during the forty years as would naturally tend to lessen febrile and pulmonary diseases, the two classes most to be feared hereabout.

The great progress made in the facilities for street travel; in the matters of drainage, street pavements, sidewalk construction, street lighting, and in many other like directions,

Sup. 3.

will at once occur to the mind. But above all, the water-
works stand pre-eminent in value and usefulness.

. A wonderful advance, too, has been made in the architectural style and costliness of our buildings, public and private,
business and residential, so that it may be said, the whole
aspect of the place has become changed.

Our schools and the various means for intellectual improvement and diversion have kept pace with the general onward
march.

For a simple simile let us illustrate by the progress of artificial lighting. In 1850 we were fast emerging from the tal-
low-dip and uncleanly whale-oil lamp, into the light of cam-
phene and other burning fluids, more or less endangering
from explosion. Then came kerosene, in a few years to be
to a large extent supplanted by coal gas. Then comes the
blazing light of electricity, which has already begun to illumine
our streets, many of our business places and homes. Yes,
and it is working its way with masterly rapidity, as a motive
power, that will give rest to many a weary heart, and before
which even our old and faithful servant, steam, seems already
drawing to a wheezy end. The extensive electric works here
in Lynn, which are spoken of somewhat at large elsewhere,
already indicate the development of unlimited capabilities in
the subtile agent, and presage effects hitherto unattained and
unimagined. What next it will accomplish, it would be daring to predict — perhaps the flashing forth of intelligence
from other worlds.

1891.

During the early part of this year, business generally, and
the shoe business in particular, was unusually dull. This
was attributable in a great degree to the labor troubles that
had long prevailed. Both employers and employed now became convinced that concession was needed on both sides;
and when the conviction was earnestly acted on affairs began
to mend.

The new City Government was organized Jan. 5 ; E. Knowlton Fogg, Mayor.

The 70th birthday of John W. Hutchinson, one of the
musical " band of brothers " known throughout the country,
and to some extent in Europe, as the Hutchinson family, was
celebrated at his High Rock home, Jan. 5. The day was not
very pleasant without, but within, the large gathering of
friends made everything cheerful and enjoyable. Some came

from distant homes, anxious to pay their respects to one who had so long added to the enjoyment of others, by his genial temperament, his sweet songs, and philanthropic acts. He was an early and zealous advocate for the abolition of slavery, as were his brothers; and likewise ardent as a temperance reformer. Their songs and persistent efforts, in divers ways, undoubtedly did much to advance the reforms alluded to.

The fine summer residence of Nathaniel Brewer, on Ocean street, was destroyed by fire, Jan. 7, the loss on house and contents reaching $31,000.

The Lynn Board of Trade held its first annual meeting in the Common Council room, Jan. 14, and completed the organization by the choice of Albert L. Rohrer, president, John B. Newhall, secretary, and James E. Jenkins, treasurer. It numbered among its active members some of our stanchest and most sagacious business men, and soon became a powerful aid to the business of the city, and its welfare in various departments.

Bog Meadow, so called, in the eastern section of the town, was formally taken possession of by the Park Commissioners, under a recent enabling legislative act, for park purposes, Jan. 16.

Died, Jan. 18, Edward K. Weston, aged 47, long a leading music teacher in various departments of the art. He was organist and choir master of St. Stephen's Church for a number of years, and acquitted himself in a manner most satisfactory, not only by his skill upon the instrument, but likewise by his facility in the control, as well as teaching, of the large boy choir of that church. He had previously served as organist in the First Universalist and one or two other Lynn churches. His manners were pleasing, and all his ways tended to inspire confidence in those with whom he became associated.

A fire occurred, Jan. 22, caused by an overheated boiler, in a wooden building on Bowler street, occupied by Charles E. Blake & Co. as a shoe factory. The loss on building and contents was $5,100.

The Manufacturers' National Bank, being the sixth bank of discount in Lynn, was organized Feb. 3, and opened for business June 22, with a capital of $200,000.

The First Methodist Society held a centennial celebration of the establishment of Methodism in Lynn, Feb. 20.

Died, March 22, Stephen H. Gardiner, aged 90. He was a well-known citizen, and during the many years of his residence here was universally known as " Captain " Gardiner.

He was a native of Sag Harbor, Long Island, and probably a descendant from one of the old Lynn emigrants to that vicinity, as his middle name was Halsey, and Thomas Halsey was one of the emigrants settling at Southampton. Captain Gardiner was a master mariner, came to Lynn in or about 1835, and sailed as commander of one of the Lynn Whalers mentioned under date 1832. He quit the vocation of mariner, however, many years ago, and engaged in other business. He invented one or two highly useful nautical appliances and obtained letters patent. He was a man of commanding figure, genial manners and friendly sympathies.

The great strike of morocco workers, which began in August, 1890, was declared " off," April 9.

A fire occurred, April 17, in the Pevear Block, Munroe street, caused by electric wires, and resulting in loss to the amount of about $7,000.

Monsignor Strain, so long a faithful minister in the Roman Catholic Church in Lynn, receives, April 30, at St. Mary's Church, the insignia of Domestic Prelate — a member of the household — of His Holiness Leo XIII. A solemn high mass with a select Boston choir added much to the solemnity. Monsignor Strain left Lynn soon after on a visit to Rome.

The recent introduction of military exercises in our common schools adds a new, interesting and perhaps useful feature to youthful accomplishments. There was quite a martial gathering here in Lynn, and a competitive drill, of what is known as the Second Massachusetts School Regiment, on May 9, Companies being present from Andover, Brookline, Chelsea, Gloucester, Lowell, Malden, Medford, Reading, Wakefield and Woburn. There was a great gathering of parents and friends, male and female, old and young, to greet the youthful soldier boys — " at least one girl visitor to each boy soldier," as a local paper said. The rivalry at the drill was quite spirited. Governor Russell and members of his staff were present. In the drill, Malden came in first of the winners.

A mass meeting was held at the First Universalist Church, May 20, to consider measures for the prevention of the rapidly increasing disregard of the Lord's Day.

A prize fight took place before the Lynn Athletic Club, May 25, at which one of the participants received such " punishment " as caused his death.

A choir festival was held in St. Stephen's Church, May 27,

in which fourteen surpliced choirs of young men and boys participated. The choristers numbered about four hundred. Memorial Day (May 30) observed as usual. The address was by Hon. F. T. Greenhalge of Lowell.

During the year ending June 1, there were erected in Lynn 465 buildings, of the aggregate value of $2,092,100. Some of them were superior brick, stone and iron structures.

The Lynn Boys' Club, an institution of a few years' standing, of great merit, intended for the training of youth, in all good ways, had June 1, according to the Superintendent's annual report, an enrolled membership of 631.

Hon. Harmon Hall, of Saugus, died June 30, aged 73. He was a native of Portland, Me., but came hither when quite young, and from a childhood of comparative penury worked his way to a manhood of competence and consideration, filling positions of usefulness and trust. Among the offices which he held were those of Town Clerk and Selectman of Saugus, Representative and Senator in the State Legislature, Governor's Counsellor, and Prison Commissioner. He was likewise for a number of years President of the Saugus Mutual Fire Insurance Company. He was a member of various organizations; a Freemason and an Odd Fellow. In person Mr. Hall was prepossessing, and in manners genial.

Independence Day was duly celebrated. The preparations were elaborate and successfully carried out, the procession especially being unusually fine.

The winter of 1890–'91 yielded a good crop of ice, insomuch that the price, which had greatly increased during the preceding summer, receded to about its usual figure.

A fire occurred, July 5, in a wooden dwelling on Tudor street, owned and occupied by Charles E. Peabody, caused by a defective flue, that resulted in a loss amounting to $6,700.

A destructive fire occurred, July 17, on Union street, near the Central railroad station, in the Blake, Strout and Currier brick blocks. Loss, $172,000. The cause of the fire was unknown.

The corner stone of the new West Lynn Odd Fellows' building, North Common street, was laid July 30.

Died, Aug. 15, at his residence on Green street, John B. Tolman, aged 84; a citizen widely known and worthily extolled for his benevolent and timely public gifts. He was born in Barre, Worcester county, but in boyhood went to Dedham, where he learned the printer's trade. In 1830 he came to Lynn, where his first employment was on the old *Lynn*

Record. And he continued in the printing business, by industry and frugality laying the foundation for the fortune which he finally secured and so judiciously disposed of. He was an ardent advocate for the reforms of the day ; and especially zealous in the temperance cause, in furtherance of which he gave a trust fund of some $30,000. To establish charitable institutions, by direct gift while living, and by will, he gave the further aggregate sum of $20,000. Mr. Tolman and his wife lived happily together far into old age. In 1881 they celebrated their " golden wedding." And death did not long part them, for she died at the age of 86, within ten days of his decease.

Died, Sept. 1, Timothy Lakeman, long known as the " Old Lamplighter," aged 79. He was a faithful official in the city lighting department for about thirty years, was intelligent and keenly observant of passing events ; was affable in manners, had a good common school education, and was full of reminiscences of old time events and people. Though not a political aspirant, he was quite remarkable for his knowledge of current political affairs and the characteristics of public men, and was a prompter, if not a guide, for many an active and ambitious partisan.

The weather on Labor Day, Sept. 7, was so unfavorable that the out-door proceedings were less satisfactory than usual. In Lasters' Hall, Andrew street, a meeting was held, at which Mayor Fogg made an address, and other brief speeches were made.

Mrs. Harrison, wife of President Harrison, and other members of the white house family made a short visit to Lynn, Sept. 23, and had a reception at the house of Mrs. C. A. Coffin, Nahant street. A drive about town and the vicinity, to Swampscott and Nahant, concluded their visit.

Died, very suddenly, Sept. 28, at his home, Linwood street, Cyrus M. Tracy, aged 67. He was a native of Norwich, Ct., came to Lynn while very young and began his education in our public schools. He possessed a literary turn, and while laboring day by day found means to gratify his taste and store his mind. He loved good books, and their teachings found congenial soil in his heart and mind, sinking deeply and bearing excellent fruit. He early acquired a felicitous use of the pen, and in almost every department of literature became conspicuous, in a local sense at least. His writings in poetry, history, and on the passing events of life, attracted marked attention. As the editor of a weekly paper he was

extensively and favorably known. Nothing like a full collection of his writings has yet appeared. He was a true
lover of nature and delighted to rove among her varied and
beautiful works; to him a day in the woods was worth many
days of what most of us call the pleasures of social life. It
is not overstraining even to call him the father of our late
splendid acquisition known as Lynn Woods. His little book
entitled " Essex Flora " will be studied long after the fragrant
beauties it classifies have been driven far away by the aggressive hand of " improvement." " Mr. Tracy," say the Park
Commissioners in their report for 1891, " was a versatile,
many-sided man. His call, his inner inspiration, was to teach
the people of Lynn that they had in the Woods ' an asylum
of inexhaustible pleasure.' Of all the work he accomplished
in his useful life he would undoubtedly desire to be remembered for this. . . . That to-day the whole magnificent
domain is the people's is due to the momentum which he gave.
The children of Lynn, in all generations, will cherish and
revere the memory of Cyrus M. Tracy for the marvelous
gift to which his seer's vision guided them." He delivered
the poem at the dedication of the City Hall, Nov. 30, 1867,
and the oration at the celebration of the 250th anniversary of
the settlement of the town, June 17, 1879. Notwithstanding
all his early disabilities, his physical imperfection and the
discouragement of stinted means, Mr. Tracy kept on his rising way with unwavering courage, till guiding purpose and
laudable ambition began to yield their ripening fruit. He
was one of the founders of the Houghton Horticultural Society, and never tired in his efforts to enhance the usefulness
of that and kindred organizations. The death of Mr. Tracy
was startlingly sudden. He was abroad as usual on the
evening of the 27th, and on the morning of the 28th was dead
and cold upon his bed.

John Wooldredge, whose death took place at the age of 68,
in San Francisco, Cal., on the 7th of October, was long a
conspicuous resident of Lynn, though Marblehead was his
native place. He came in 1847 and here passed most of his
business life. He was a prominent shoe manufacturer, and
amassed a large property ; was interested in municipal affairs,
and in the development of all promising resources. He
served in the City Government as an Alderman, and was for
some time President of the First National Bank. In railroad
affairs he became widely known, and was for a time President of the Eastern Railroad. His large and fine estate at

the corner of Ocean and Nahant streets, overlooking the
peninsula, the beaches and a large extent of the bay, must
have been the source of much enjoyment to him. But it has
now become the site of several less spacious but beautifully
appointed residential estates; thus affording pleasure to increased numbers of nature's votaries.

The neat Scandinavian Church, on Pleasant street, was
dedicated on the 11th of October. Its cost was $7,000.

On Sunday, Oct. 25, the weather was clear throughout the
United States. No signal station reported a drop of rain.
No other such occurrence reported for eighteen years.

Died, in Warnerville, Concord, Mass., Nov. 23, Gardiner
Tufts, aged 63. Death found him at his post of duty as Superintendent of the State Reformatory, which position he had
faithfully filled for some years. He was a son of Richard
Tufts, for a long time a deacon of the First Congregational
Church, well known as a rigid moralist and temperance advocate, and a grandson of David Tufts, spoken of elsewhere
as the first regular Lynn expressman. He was engaged in
mechanical employments during his earlier years, but before
middle life had conceived an ambition for a different and
wider field of action. Among his first public appointments
was that of Assistant Postmaster of the House of Representatives at Washington, a position which gave him an insight
into public affairs and an acquaintance with public men
that proved of great benefit in after years. Soon after the
breaking out of the Civil War he was appointed Military
Agent of Massachusetts at Washington, and in that capacity
received unstinted approbation from those in authority over
him, and the affectionate regard of the many to whom in the
exercise of his office he administered; long after the war
he continued to receive loving testimonials from the sufferers
and their dependents, whom he had done so much to relieve.
He was a friendly advocate for every worthy soldier, and a
faithful counsellor for the less deserving. His constant efforts
in behalf of the soldiers of our dear old Commonwealth are
still fresh in the memory of thousands. It need not be said
that he was universally esteemed in his native place, in
whose prosperity he ever retained an affectionate interest,
nor that he was called to fill various local offices of trust and
responsibility. He was a member of the Common Council,
an Alderman, and a Representative in the State Legislature.
Colonel Tufts — for he held that military title by brevet —
was a great lover of music, and an adept in its practice, at
least as a vocalist. He was also well skilled in the use of

the pen, often enriching our local papers with reminiscences and disquisitions. Many of his papers were much more deserving of preservation than some that we day by day see between handsome book covers. He was a steadfast friend of Cyrus M. Tracy, spoken of under this date, and who passed away but about two months before him. They were fellow-workers for a time, in early life, at the tool factory of Theophilus N. Breed, on Oak street. His death was sudden and peaceful; peaceful, for he who had so faithfully done his duty here could have no fear regarding his final acceptance.

A banquet was held in Lasters' Hall on Thanksgiving Day, Nov. 26, by our French citizens.

A fire occurred in the large wooden building, corner of Market and Andrew streets, belonging to T. E. Parker and heirs of James N. Buffum, Nov. 28. Loss on building and stocks, about $105,000.

Died, in Brookline, Mass., Dec. 25, Rev. Charles C. Shackford, aged 76. He was minister of the Unitarian Society in Lynn for nineteen years, commencing in 1846; was scholarly and vigorous, and took great interest in all enterprises for the promotion of intelligence among every class. For the efficiency and advancement of our public schools he was unwearied in his efforts. The Public Library received his fostering care, and he also did much by introducing lectures of the higher order. For some years he owned the chief part of the beautiful suburban precinct now know as Lynnhurst, and resided there, spending much time and money in improving the grounds and planting a great variety of choice fruit trees — trees which have already been largely uprooted through the demands for building sites. After leaving Lynn, Mr. Shackford became a professor in Cornell University, where he diligently labored for a number of years, the recipient of many encomiums for his capability and efficiency. He delivered the address at the consecration of Pine Grove Cemetery, July 24, 1850. It was at the ordination of Mr. Shackford, in South Boston, that Theodore Parker preached the sermon which for the first time brought into strong light his peculiar views, creating a sensation even before the congregation that listened to it dispersed, and long agitating the theological world — a sermon of which the Rev. Mr. Swett, then minister of the Unitarian Church here, said in his pulpit, "If that is Unitarianism I am not a Unitarian."

The total loss by fire, in Lynn, during 1891, was $352,119.06.

1892.

The new City Government was organized, Jan, 4, Elihu B. Hayes, Mayor.

Died, Jan. 14, Aza A. Breed, aged 72, a native and life-long resident of Lynn. He was a lineal descendant from Allen Breed, who came here among the first settlers, in 1630. Mr. Breed was an enterprising and esteemed citizen. He served in both branches of the City Council, and exercised much influence by his good judgment and prompt action. There was, however, one flighty episode in his life; and that was when, on the 4th of July, 1878, he made a balloon ascension from City Hall Square, in company with City Marshal, Charles C. Fry, C. Frederick Smith, a newspaper reporter, and the æronaut. But it was a depressing episode when, early in the afternoon of Oct. 5, 1878, he was attacked by two ruffians in Belcher Lane, Boston, and robbed of $8,000. The money belonged to the Central National Bank, of Lynn, and was in his custody as a public messenger. The robbers escaped with their plunder; but the bank, having full confidence in the honesty of Mr. Breed, and sympathy for his misfortune and personal injury, readily bore the larger part of the loss. He was a trustee of the Lynn Five Cents Savings Bank, a director of the Lynn and Boston Street Railroad, and held other offices, in which care and fidelity were prime requisites.

James Warren Newhall, an accomplished writer of prose and poetry, died, Jan. 22, aged 65. Mr. Newhall was long and favorably known, especially for his poetic contributions, which in a great measure had reference to passing events and local affairs. His lines furnished for festive and patriotic occasions were always greeted with applause, and now that he has gone from among us, it may surely be said that could his writings be gathered up, they would form a volume that would afford enjoyment to generations yet to come. He had a humorous vein that induced many a healthful smile, and one of tenderness that bore sympathy and consolation. He was for some years editor of one of our weekly newspapers, and in that capacity acquitted himself as one who well understood the duties and responsibilities of such a position. Physically, he was a cripple from his birth, and as years multiplied, found it more and more difficult to appear in the streets; but his spirits retained their buoyancy, insomuch that his presence was sought for on all sorts of festive occasions. He had no complaints to make about his hard fate, and had no moody or sulky hours. Possibly had it not been for his infirmities, we should never have had such estimable fruits of his genius, for it is often seen that the mind of the physical invalid, by its indisposition and inability to grapple with the cares and perplexities of active life, turns to higher and more ennobling pursuits. One of his longest poems was that delivered at the celebration of the 250th anniversary of the founding of the First Church of Lynn, June 8, 1882. It was happily conceived, well delivered, and much enjoyed by the refined congregation who listened to it.

On Wednesday evening, Feb. 3, the recently formed Board of Trade held their first regular banquet, about 175 partaking. It was a notable gathering and augured well for the future good of the business interests of Lynn. Earnest and well-considered addresses on various industrial topics were made, and it seemed as if the useful organization was fast getting into good working order, as it was full of promise for the stimulation of trade and aiding all healthful municipal interests.

The Thomson-Houston and Edison General Electric companies were consolidated, Feb. 5.

The double track on the Saugus Branch of the Boston and Maine Railroad, completed.

St. Luke's Methodist Church, Oakwood avenue, was dedicated Feb. 14.

A fire occurred in Riley's block, Market street, Feb. 20, occasioning a loss of some $8,500.

Died, Feb. 25, Henry L. Chase, aged 66. He was a native of Leominster, but came to Lynn in 1868 as principal of the Whiting Grammar School. He was a good teacher, and besides his service in that capacity did much to enkindle a taste for science and kindred pursuits. He loved to associate with ramblers in the hidden nooks of nature's domain, and to discuss with scholars topics of progressive education. He was a devoted member of the Unitarian Society, and a touching service was held over his remains in their house of worship.

A severe and long-continued storm commenced March 1, doing considerable damage along the Ocean street shore and in other exposed places. Lamper's tide mill, near the foot of Pleasant street, was wrecked.

Elijah D. Howard was found dead in his room, March 12. He was a machinist, having his place of business on Munroe street, and for twenty years had made his home in a room on Whittier street. He had the reputation of being in rather moderate circumstances, though not in absolute penury. Much to the surprise of his neighbors there was found in his room after his decease, in gold coin, mortgages, notes and other evidences of wealth, the amount of some $35,000.

Charles J. Van Depoele, an expert electrician holding a position at the Thomson-Houston works, died at his home on Essex street, March 18, aged 46. He was a native of Belgium. From early life he was fond of experimenting with electricity, and soon attained a wonderful insight into its power and capabilities. He came to this country in 1871, and was soon active in the establishment of electric plants in various places, largely at the West and in Canada. It is claimed that to him belongs the honor of being a pioneer in the electric street railway field. A solemn high mass was held over his remains at St. Mary's church, at which some 3,000 persons attended, 2,500 being from the Thomson-Houston works, which suspended labor on the occasion.

St. Patrick's Day, March 17, was duly celebrated by Irish-American citizens.

A fire in Sleeper's hardware store, Munroe street, March 20, did damage to the amount of $6,000.

The corner stone of the new Central Church edifice, Broad street, was laid March 21.

The new Club House of the Oxford Club, on Washington Square, was opened and a great fair for the benefit of the Club commenced, April 6, and continued four days. This fine building is furnished with every appliance necessary and convenient for those who take pleasure in such organizations, which, though of slow growth in this country, have now become a marked feature. Lynn at the present time numbers among her club members a considerable portion of our most prominent and representative citizens, and the associations without doubt as now conducted, are doing a good work in softening the asperities and frictions of common life, and aiding the development of resources most applicable to the needs of this our day. Time may even develop in some members the stalwart characteristics of old English club life.

The West Lynn Lodge of Odd Fellows dedicate their new quarters on North Common street, April 27.

Arbor Day, April 30, was noticed among other ways, by the assembling in the woods of representatives of the Houghton Horticultural Society, who planted, near Mt. Gilead, three trees, one to the memory of each of our three recently departed local lights: — Henry L. Chase, James Warren Newhall and Cyrus M. Tracy. There was a prayer, an address, and the reading of an original poem, all earnest and

sympathetic. The trees previously selected, were, for Mr.
Chase, a Norway maple, for Mr. Newhall, a cut-leaf birch,
and for Mr. Tracy, a purple-leafed English sycamore. It
was a touching and merited tribute.

On Saturday morning, April 30 — the next day, May 1,
being Sunday — the Associated Charities, an excellent organization whose purposes are indicated by its name, spread
a substantial May breakfast in the Armory building, Franklin
street. The number of partakers was between 1500 and
2000. Various other entertainments and diversions occupied
a considerable portion of the after part of the day. It was a
successful and enjoyable May-day celebration. The receipts
realized for carrying on this work by the Associated Charities
amounted to $678.27 for the day.

The first place for Jewish worship in Lynn, a hall in Clapp's
block, Market street, corner of Munroe, was dedicated on
Sunday, May 1. The exercises were in accordance with the
solemn Jewish ritual.

Quite a " mad dog scare " took place in Lynn and vicinity
about the middle of May. A small fox hound, belonging to
George Pranker of Saugus, rushed furiously about the streets,
manifesting every appearance of madness. He was finally
despatched by City Marshal Wells, but not before having
bitten, as was stated, not less than eleven persons and forty
dogs. That he was really mad, for sometime remained in
doubt. A professor of Harvard College, after critically ex-
amining the brain of the dog gave the opinion that he was not
mad. But the final death of two of the persons bitten, with
unmistakable marks of hydrophobia, led to the conclusion
that the examination of the dog's brain was not reliable.

A fire occurred, May 20, in J. Otis Marshall's wood-turning
establishment, Marshall's wharf. It was soon under control
but not extinguished till property to the amount of $17,464
was destroyed.

May 30, Memorial Day, was observed much as usual, 709
soldiers' graves being decorated. The address was delivered
in the evening, by Gen. John L. Swift.

Died, at Nantucket, June 16, William Foster Mitchell,
aged 67. He will long be favorably remembered as a City
Missionary in Lynn for a number of years. And a large
portion of his life both before and after his residence here
was spent in similarly benevolent work. Especially did he
labor during the Civil War, and subsequently, for the bettering of the condition of the emancipated slaves and other
colored people. He was born in Nantucket, and was a son

of William Mitchell, an accomplished scientist, well known
among scholars, especially those clustering around Harvard
College. Professor Maria Mitchell, the well-known proficient
in astronomical science, was a sister of his.

The new and stately High School building, on Highland
square, was dedicated on Friday evening, June 17, with appropriate ceremonies. Members of the School Committee,
the Mayor and other City officials made brief addresses, and
the musical renderings gave zest to the exercises. President Eliot of Harvard College, was the prominent orator.
There was a very large attendance of interested townspeople,
and every thing passed off with promptness and decorum.
The cost of land and building was $295,000.

July 2, Cora Beckwith succeeds in the extraordinary feat
of swimming from Egg Rock to Lynn Beach, landing nearly
opposite the foot of old Beach street.

Died, July 27, Abraham C. Moody, aged 65. He took
great interest in the fire department, was chief engineer for
seventeen years, during which time the most appalling conflagration with which he was destined to grapple was the
great fire of Nov. 26, 1889. He was a native of Newburyport but came to Lynn while a boy, and here worked at the
morocco business, which proved to be the chief occupation of
his whole life. He possessed much decision of character,
was trustworthy and reliable.

August 17 will be remembered in the history of Lynn
as the day on which the great gathering under the auspices
of the Boston Boot and Shoe Club, took place. It was an
occasion that called together leading men of the boot and
shoe trade from all parts of the country, the Lynn Board of
Trade acting the part of host. The day was pleasant, and
the early morning trains brought numbers of eager, expect-
ant and hopeful participants; for it was the first of a series
of annual trade gatherings which the club proposed to hold.
Governor Russell arrived at about ten o'clock, and held a
reception in the eligible rooms of the Board of Trade, on
Exchange street. An hour was spent by His Excellency in
shaking hands and exchanging brief greetings with the multitude of those eager to pay their respects. Then the members of the club and guests were driven to the grounds of
Francis W. Breed, on Ocean street, where a generous entertainment was spread. After freely partaking, the party
re-entered the carriages and were driven to various points,
chiefly those of historic interest or scenic grandeur, with
both of which, fortunately, Lynn abounds. Thus the hours

were occupied till the meridian was passed; and then the drive to "Lynn Woods," our newly-acquired sylvan domain, was commenced. An extended ride along the shady ways, with now and then a momentary pause to visit some wild glen, legendary shrine or commanding height, brought them to the vicinity of Mount Gilead. And there, on a spacious forest opening, carpeted by leaves and moss, they found ample preparations for a now highly appreciable banquet, for the ride had been long and the hour was late. The rustic seats along the tables were soon occupied by a hungry company of more than three hundred. In due time the appetites were appeased; and then began the intellectual exercises. The speeches were, of course, chiefly on topics connected with the shoe and leather interests, but not exclusively so, and elicited most hearty applause. The president of the club, F. G. Nazro, was the first speaker, then Mayor Hayes, of Lynn, expressed warm words of welcome to the visitors: next came our enterprising townsman, Francis W. Breed, a member of the World's Fair Commission and President of the New England Shoe and Leather Association; then spoke Gen. Augustus P. Martin, of Boston. Hon. Henry Cabot Lodge, of Nahant, a member of Congress, followed; then Isaac H. Bailey, of New York. Isaac B. Potter, of New York, read a paper on roadways and kindred topics. The last speaker was Charles Eliot, of Cambridge, son of the president of Harvard College; his speech, too, had reference to public grounds and reservations. Congressman J. II. Walker, of Worcester, not being able to be present, forwarded a letter of regret, which was read at the table. The day will be long remembered as the one especially on which good old Lynn was honored by unstinted encomiums on her thrift, her beautiful scenery, her hospitality; and as a day on which she, in her turn, honored her visitors by a rich display of her resources and her opportunities. It was an occasion that enhanced the reputation of Lynn wherever she was known; and which rendered her name familiar in many a place where it had not before been heard. Undoubtedly the main purpose of the gathering was to magnify and extend the fame of the shoe and leather trade of New England, and its success in that direction can hardly be questioned. Incidentally it did much other good work.

James E. Bessom, Aug. 30, performed the surprising feat of walking backwards from Lynn to Bass Point, Nahant, and returning in two hours and twenty-seven minutes.

Labor Day, Sept. 5, was celebrated by a parade and ad-

dresses. The weather proved favorable and the working
people had a gala time.

Died, Sept. 9, of Bright's disease, Abel Bates, aged 68.
He was a soldier in the Civil War, and at the battle of Spott-
sylvania lost his right arm. He returned to Lynn, on being
mustered out, and in 1865 was elected City Messenger, which
office he held till the time of his death — twenty-seven years.
He discharged his duties faithfully, and was unassuming and
courteous to all.

The Knights of Pythias, of Essex County, had a grand
parade in Lynn, Sept. 15.

A large number of members of Post 5, Grand Army, left
Lynn, Sept. 17, for Washington, to join in the great National
Encampment there.

The Board of Aldermen, Sept. 20, voted to accept the
bequest of $2500 made by William Shute for an electric
fountain.

Charles S. Ingalls conveyed the ownership of Mount
Spicket to the city, Sept. 20.

The North Shore Traction Company was incorporated at
Camden, N.J., with a capital of $6,000,000, Sept. 21. The
"Lynn and Boston" and "Belt Line" systems of street rail-
roads, together with other lines in neighboring places, soon
became the property of this absorbing company.

The Steamer Watertown, a packet plying between Lynn
and Boston, was burned, off Point Shirley, Sept. 28. She
was a wooden propeller, and had done a successful business
in the passenger and freight line during the season.

The Lynn Naval Company of fifty members was mustered
in at the Armory, Franklin street, Oct. 1, the oath of allegiance to Massachusetts and to the United States being taken.

"Gipsey" Smith, a celebrated English evangelist, commenced a series of revival meetings in Lynn, Oct. 16, chiefly
in the First Methodist Church. He claimed to be, and no
doubt was, a genuine gipsey. His discourses were fluent,
pointed, and attracted many hearers.

Died, at his residence on Mall street, Oct. 17, John T.
Moulton, aged 54. His death was very sudden, and sent a
thrill through the community not commonly experienced, for
he was a man extensively known and as extensively respected. He was one of our largest manufacturers in the
morocco line, his towering manufactory being on Marion
street, almost on the site where his ancestors had for two
centuries or more carried on business in one way or another
connected with the production of leather. His father had

for many years conducted a successful business on the same
spot. To his naturally intellectual quickness was added a
good education, for he graduated from our High School in
1855, well prepared to enter college. He was skilled in the
use of the pen and produced many pieces, both in prose and
poetry, well worthy of preservation. But his great, and as
may be said, chief inclination, was to historical and antiquarian studies. There he seemed to feel most at home, and
there his patience in research and reliability in statement
were conspicuous. He always took great pains to make no
statement that he did not feel assured was the exact truth —
a most commendable habit in any writer on historical topics,
but one far too uncommon. It was Mr. Moulton, who in
connection with Isaac O. Guild, in 1888, caused to be erected
in our Old Burying Ground a commemorative stone at the
grave of the celebrated fortune teller, Moll Pitcher, who
died in 1813; a simple stone, which has already become
a shrine at which many a young knee has bent, as is
shown by the depression of the sod. A strong love of literature, of one kind and another, seems to have run in the
family of Mr. Moulton, a love that cropped out now in prose
and then in poetry. His father took unbounded pleasure in
poring over old English tomes, as well as pursuing matters
of local history, though he wrote little or nothing for publication in endurable form. Dr. Joseph Mansfield, of the family on the maternal side, a graduate of Harvard College in
1801, and who the year before took the prize of eighty dollars for a poem delivered in the College Chapel, being the
best metrical production offered in the judgment of the
faculty, left poems enough to fill a volume, which it is yet
hoped may one day appear in a form where others than those
of the family may enjoy the perusal. Then there was Solomon Moulton, an uncle of John T., who early developed more
than ordinary poetic genius and aptness at versification.
Mr. Lewis spoke highly of his productions; but he died at
the age of 19, and what he would have accomplished had his
life been spared, can only be conjectured. Judging, however, from what he actually did, there was reason for great expectation. Mr. Moulton was not an aspirant for public office,
nor by any means what is called a politician, but he filled
several offices of trust with marked fidelity. During one or
two of the last years of his life he was subjected to sore trials
by the labor troubles that prevailed over most of the industrial world. There was a protracted " strike " at his factory,
and occasional threats of violence, but he exercised a

Sup. 4

manly forbearance while firmly maintaining his rights, and finally succeeded in re-establishing the harmony always so dear to him.

Oct. 21, it being Columbus Day — the four hundredth anniversary, according to new style, of the discovery of America by Christopher Columbus — business was generally suspended in accordance with the recommendation of the President of the United States and the Governor of the State. It was generally observed here as a holiday, though there was no very marked demonstration. At the schools patriotic addresses were made and patriotic songs sung. Veterans of the Grand Army were out in numbers, in some instances giving a military aspect to the proceedings, but on the whole, it being an anniversary of such a peculiar nature and so new in its apparent requirements, many seemed at a loss to determine what proceedings were most appropriate.

Egan & Bolger's shoe factory on Eastern avenue was burned, Oct. 25, involving a loss of $19,500.

A large convention of Associated Charities was held in Lynn, Oct. 25. Numbers from other places were present, and vigorous discussions were held touching the benefit, purpose and success of the organization.

The registration in Lynn closed Oct. 29. Of the 12,498 on the list, 10,790 voted at the election Nov. 8 — a remarkably large percentage.

Capt. William Phillips died Nov. 16, aged 93. He was born on the border district formerly known as the Marblehead farms, came to Lynn proper in early life and was long engaged in some branch of the shoe trade. His title of captain came from his having command of a company in the old Lynn militia regiment.

Nov. 21, there was presented to the City of Lynn, by John E. Hudson, a relic of singular interest. It was an iron pot of about the capacity of one quart, stated to have been the first piece of iron casting made in America. The presentation took place at the City Hall in presence of a number of leading citizens, and Mayor Hayes responded in a fitting speech. Two or three others made brief addresses, chiefly of an historical character. The inscription on the tablet provided for the relic embodies a succinct history, which is as follows: "*The first casting made in America. Saugus Iron Works, 1642. Presented to the City of Lynn by John E. Hudson, a descendant of Thomas Hudson, the owner of the site of the Iron Works, to whom the first casting was given. This case presented by citizens of Lynn,*

1892." The existence of this casting has long been known, and the question is sometimes asked how it is proved to have been the first casting. Probably nothing can be known beyond the statement of Mr. Lewis, in the History of Lynn, under date 1642.

The City Council vote, Nov. 29, $12,000 for a Marine Park ; $8,000 more to be raised by subscription.

St. Mary's Church was broken into on Monday evening, Dec. 26, by thieves who stole valuable gold and silver vessels.

The Lynn and Boston Street Railroad commence running their cars to Boston by electricity, Dec. 26.

The fine house of worship of the Central Congregational Society, on Broad street, was dedicated on the evening of Dec. 29. There was a large attendance and the exercises were impressive, the sermon being by Rev. Alexander McKenzie, D.D. This is the third edifice that the Society has reared since its organization in 1850. The first was entirely consumed by fire on the morning of Sept. 9, 1866 ; and the second, which was erected soon after, was destroyed in the great conflagration of Nov. 26, 1889. The first was of wood, the second of brick, and the present is of stone.

The total loss by fire in Lynn, during 1892, was $80,669.10.

INDUSTRIES OF LYNN.

The leading business of Lynn continues to be, as it has been for almost a hundred and fifty years, the *Manufacture of Ladies' Shoes*. And though the manufacturers lost largely by the great fire, it does not seem that there has been much diminution in the volume of trade, though it is carried on in some instances in different localities. But little need be said here in addition to what has been given elsewhere on these pages. There are 179 factories, with an aggregate capital of $4,550,000; average number of persons employed, 12,000; value of annual product, $21,300,000; gross profit, $4,000,-000; average yearly earnings of each employe, $465. Of course it is not claimed that these estimates are entirely unerring in every instance, but they are as reliable as diligent inquiries and care could make them.

Next in historical importance is the *Leather Manufacture* — chiefly that which comes under the general names of morocco and leather. It is probable that at no former period has this branch of industry been more active or profitable. The number of factories may be stated at 30; capital invested, $950,000; value of product, $2,450,000; stock used, $1,687,000; number employed, 800.

The recently established *Thomson-Houston Electric Works*, which are briefly spoken of under date 1883, bid fair to overshadow all the other industries of Lynn. They have attained huge proportions in a marvelously short time, the business having increased in five years from about $400,000 per annum to $12,000,000. At the present time, May, 1890, there are employed at the works here 2,500 persons; which number, by including those elsewhere engaged in the service of the Company, would be raised to more than 4,000. The amount of capital, including invested surplus, is about $9,000,000. The floor space now occupied by the Lynn factories is 281,586 square feet. The product of the Company is electrical machinery of all kinds, and is of course for the greater part disposed of in the United States; but there is a constant and increasing demand for their apparatus in all parts of the civilized world.

Of the various other industries of Lynn so much has been said elsewhere that nothing need be added in this connection.

So large a portion of the population of Lynn consists of working people, that it would be remarkable if there were not combinations of various orders formed in the hope of bettering the condition of those who are dependent for a livelihood upon the labor of their hands. We have had a large share of what are popularly known as labor troubles, but at the present time we seem measurably, though by no means entirely, free from difficulties of this kind. Such lessons however have been learned that the more considerate on both sides — employers and employed — see that forbearance and concession are very needful. It is said that the poor are always discontented. But are the rich ever contented? The whole civilized world is now agitated by labor throes : a condition that perhaps follows from the increasing intelligence of all classes, truer conceptions of individual capabilities, power, and natural rights. The result of this unrest will surely be the essential modification of some of the unnatural features of the present artificial condition of society. But these so called labor troubles are not the only elements that are working important changes in the texture of society. Among others is the marked change in the relative position of woman. We now find the fairer sex in about all the professions and relations that a few years ago were considered to appertain only to men. And it is a fact of rainbow promise. Especially is her healthful influence perceptible in the ever broadening field of literature. There, she is scattering seeds that will not fail to produce most wholesome fruit. But may we not indulge the hope that she will not soon be found on the turbulent borders of the political arena, panting to join in the feverish conflicts there? Permanent reforms must come, but need not be expected in whirlwind rush, such as characterized some of the vain attempts in years gone by, but by such peaceful gradations as nature herself exemplifies.

BENEVOLENT INSTITUTIONS, ETC.

Lynn has a full share of organizations, benevolent, social, literary and recreative. But few, however, can even be named here ; nor is it necessary that they should be, as our annual Directories give all the information that in most cases would be desired, their names usually indicating their fields of labor. But one or two merit special notice.

Lynn Hospital. Allusion to the history of this institution may be found on page 270. At the close of 1889, the finances appeared in a satisfactory condition. The receipts for the year from incomes, bequests, and donations, were $13,311.58, and the expenses $10,749.29. The average number of patients for the year was 21, and the expense for each patient for board, medicine, and attendance, was $511.87 per annum. The medical cases were in number 558, and the surgical, 703 ; diseases of the eye, ear, and skin, 136. The Hospital fund, June, 1890, has reached about $85,000. Of that, $26,000 have been invested in land and buildings, and $2,500 in furnishings ; leaving over $56,000 invested in securities, the income of which is devoted to running expenses. The annual expense of maintenance is now about $10,000. And the income from investments being about $3,000, some $7,000 have to be raised each year. The working men, in all departments of trade, have year by year liberally contributed. And indeed all classes have shown their appreciation of the value of the institution in the true way, by pecuniary aid. The Oxford Club, until its rooms were destroyed by the fire, raised each year, from $900, the amount of its first annual contribution, to $3,600, the result of its last entertainment. And there have been several opportune donations from sympathizing individuals, as well as bequests. The annual church collections have each year for several years amounted to $1,000. The late collections in response to the renewed appeals of the managers, when no single subscription above $10 was asked, resulted in nearly $6,000. The managers regard the Hospital as eminently an institution for the people, and the people, on

LYNN HOSPITAL. 1888.

THE above is a correct representation of one of the most excellent of our more recently established institutions — the hospital. The buildings are not costly, but are picturesquely situated on historic ground, on Boston street, between Franklin and Washington streets.

HOME FOR AGED WOMEN.

THIS is another of our praiseworthy institutions. The building is at the west end of the Common, on the north side, and was originally, in 1832, built for and occupied by the unfortunate Nahant Bank, which failed in 1836. An ancient dwelling gave place to the structure.

their part, cordially do what they can for its support. And all of us can give it our prayers, if we have nothing else to give. That its affairs have been skilfully and prudently managed, and with a single eye to the good of all concerned, there is no doubt; and by increased means its usefulness will be correspondingly increased. As will be observed, the means are still quite limited. The President is William F. Morgan, and the Treasurer, David H. Sweetser.

Lynn Associated Charities. This is another of Lynn's most commendable organizations, which has, in an unostentatious way, accomplished much good. Especially would its promptness and energy in supplying the immediate wants of sufferers at the trying time of the great fire, entitle it to grateful recognition. It was organized in 1885, as mentioned under that date, and has continued to increase in usefulness and public favor. Its President is William F. Morgan.

The *Home for Aged Women* is another institution that has had the careful attention of some of our best people, and the funds that have been secured have enabled the directors to conduct the affairs of that pleasant abode in the most satisfactory manner. The establishment of a home for aged men has for a long time been under consideration in many benevolent minds; and it is ardently hoped that the time is not far distant when so desirable an object will be accomplished. And then a home for aged couples would be a noble addition to our beneficent institutions. Who of our wealthy worthies will spare of their abundance the little that will at first be needed for such objects as these, and thus have assurance that their names will be pronounced with blessings by future generations?

The ancient institution of *Free-Masonry* has long had a foothold in Lynn. Mount Carmel Lodge was constituted in 1805, and with the exception of the singular Anti-Masonic episode that exerted its influence along from 1830 to 1840, has held a very respectable position. There are now four bodies here, with an aggregate membership of about 650.

The Independent Order of *Odd Fellows* have some twelve

lodges in Lynn, with a correspondingly large membership, and are a power among our provident organizations.

It is needless to add that Lynn, with its large proportion of working people, is well supplied with associations designed to provide for the contingencies of sickness or otherwise forced idleness; indeed for mutual aid in every approved way. And all such things show a prevalent good-will and fraternal feeling. May it ever continue!

Autographs of Mayors.

By turning to pages 292, 293, and 294 the reader will find fac-similes of the signatures of all the Mayors of Lynn, down to Mr. Lovering — 1882. And the following embraces all the succeeding ones down — 1893.

1883 and 1884, WILLIAM L. BAIRD.

1885, JOHN R. BALDWIN.

1886 and 1887, GEORGE D. HART.

[signature: Geo. C. Higgins]

1888, GEORGE C. HIGGINS.

[signature: Asa T. Newhall]

1889 and 1890, ASA T. NEWHALL.

[signature: E. Knowlton Fogg]

1891. E. KNOWLTON FOGG.

[signature: Elihu B. Hayes]

1892 and 1893. ELIHU B. HAYES.

CLOSING WORDS.

Considering that the writer has already passed the age of four-score years, it is hardly probable that he will again take up the thread of the history of Lynn, his native place : though it is not an inspiring belief that the pleasant employment that for so many years has occupied hours that, to say the least, might have been devoted to some worse purpose, is to be for-ever abandoned. In this whirligig world, however, there is a possibility that in accordance with the custom of our dramatic friends there may be other last appearances. He claims to have a pretty good knowledge of the goings-on in Lynn for

the last seventy years, and to have contributed something to
elucidate her history from its beginning.   With his own hands
he has set the types for these historical volumes even down
to the page now under the reader's eye.   But this is the place
for a few modest words of retirement rather than for amplifi-
cation.   If, however, any one is eccentric enough to desire a
glimpse at the chief landmarks in the life of one so little
known to fame, he may find in the History of Essex County,
published in 1888, by J. W. Lewis & Co., of Philadelphia,
an autobiographical sketch.   And for that history he prepared
the sketches of Lynn, Lynnfield, and Swampscott.   Were it
not doing violence to his native modesty he would also add
that the Centennial Memorial of Lynn and the account of the
proceedings on her 250th anniversary, both published by
order of the City Council, were prepared by him.

Since the writer undertook the recording of Lynn's general
history, several others have employed their pens in various
departments.   David N. Johnson, in 1880 published a volume
entitled " Sketches of Lynn, or the Changes of Fifty Years,"
a work of very good appearance, and containing many pleasant and graphic descriptions and faithful biographical deline-
ations.   It was deservedly received with favor.   Then there
came, also in 1880, " Lynn Pictures, by James Jeffrey, with
designs and engravings by the Author," an unpretentious but
companionable little volume.   " Lynn and Surroundings, by
Clarence W. Hobbs," profusely illustrated, appeared in 1888,
and was well received by a large circle of readers.   Many
other writers have appeared here from time to time, whose
valuable works do not come within the present line of notice.

As the main body of this work has been carried along from the beginning in the form of Annals, the Supplement is continued in the same style. It contains the events of eleven years — 1882 to 1893. The Annals from 1629 to 1865 are found in History of Lynn, Vol. 1. The present volume takes up the Annals on page 17, with the year 1865, and on page 96 closes with 1881. Pages 329 to 371 record the Annals of 1882 to 1893. By the Indexes, the contents of each page may be easily found. On page 295 the contents of all the pages preceding are noted. On page 310 is an Index to the Pictorial addenda following. On page 379 at the close of this Supplement is its Index. Of course, Vol. I has an Index of its own. . EDITORS.

INDEX — (to Supplement.)